KANT'S *CRITIQUE OF PRACTICAL REASON*

Background Source Materials

Kant did not initially intend to write the *Critique of Practical Reason*, let alone three Critiques. It was primarily the reactions to the *Critique of Pure Reason* and the *Groundwork of the Metaphysics of Morals* that encouraged Kant to develop his moral philosophy in the second *Critique*. This volume presents both new and first-time English translations of texts written by Kant's predecessors and contemporaries that he read and responded to in the *Critique of Practical Reason*. It also includes several subsequent reactions to the second *Critique*. Together, the translations in this volume present the *Critique of Practical Reason* in its full historical context, offering scholars and students new insight into Kant's moral philosophy. The detailed editorial material appended to each of the eleven chapters helps introduce readers to the life and works of the authors, outlines the texts translated, and points to relevant passages across Kant's works.

MICHAEL WALSCHOTS is Humboldt Postdoctoral Fellow in Philosophy at Martin Luther University Halle-Wittenberg, Germany. He has published widely on the historical context of Kant's moral philosophy.

KANT'S *CRITIQUE OF PRACTICAL REASON*

Background Source Materials

EDITED AND TRANSLATED BY

MICHAEL WALSCHOTS

Martin Luther University Halle-Wittenberg, Germany

Shaftesbury Road, Cambridge CB2 8EA, United Kingdom

One Liberty Plaza, 20th Floor, New York, NY 10006, USA

477 Williamstown Road, Port Melbourne, VIC 3207, Australia

314–321, 3rd Floor, Plot 3, Splendor Forum, Jasola District Centre, New Delhi – 110025, India

103 Penang Road, #05–06/07, Visioncrest Commercial, Singapore 238467

Cambridge University Press is part of Cambridge University Press & Assessment, a department of the University of Cambridge.

We share the University's mission to contribute to society through the pursuit of education, learning and research at the highest international levels of excellence.

www.cambridge.org
Information on this title: www.cambridge.org/9781108479981

DOI: 10.1017/9781108846899

© Cambridge University Press & Assessment 2024

This publication is in copyright. Subject to statutory exception and to the provisions of relevant collective licensing agreements, no reproduction of any part may take place without the written permission of Cambridge University Press & Assessment.

First published 2024

A catalogue record for this publication is available from the British Library.

A Cataloging-in-Publication data record for this book is available from the Library of Congress

ISBN 978-1-108-47998-1 Hardback
ISBN 978-1-108-81048-7 Paperback

Cambridge University Press & Assessment has no responsibility for the persistence or accuracy of URLs for external or third-party internet websites referred to in this publication and does not guarantee that any content on such websites is, or will remain, accurate or appropriate.

For Kacy

Contents

Preface	page ix
Acknowledgements	xi
General Note on Citations and Translations	xiii
General Introduction	1

I. PRE-KANTIAN MORAL PHILOSOPHY — 11

1. Christian Wolff: Introduction — 13
   German Ethics (1720) (selections) — 18
2. Christian August Crusius: Introduction — 40
   Guide to Living Rationally (1744) (selections) — 44

II. BETWEEN THE *CRITIQUES* — 83

3. Johann Friedrich Flatt: Introduction — 85
   Review of the *Groundwork* (1786) — 88
4. Gottlob August Tittel: Introduction — 93
   On Herr Kant's Reform of Moral Science (1786) (selections) — 96
5. Hermann Andreas Pistorius: Introduction — 118
   Review of Schultz's *Elucidations of Professor Kant's Critique of Pure Reason* (1786) — 122
6. Hermann Andreas Pistorius: Introduction — 149
   Review of the *Groundwork* (1786) — 151

7.	Thomas Wizenmann: Introduction	165
	'To Herr Professor Kant' (1787)	169

III. THE RECEPTION OF THE *CRITIQUE OF PRACTICAL REASON* — 197

8.	Johann Georg Heinrich Feder: Introduction	199
	Review of the *Critique of Practical Reason* (1788)	203
9.	August Wilhelm Rehberg: Introduction	225
	Review of the *Critique of Practical Reason* (1788)	229
10.	Christian Garve: Introduction	246
	'On Patience' (1792) (selections)	250
11.	Hermann Andreas Pistorius: Introduction	255
	Review of the *Critique of Practical Reason* (1794)	257

Bibliography	281
Index	293

Preface

This volume delivers both more and less than its title promises. It delivers less, because no single volume of this sort could ever provide *all* the background source materials that would be required to fully understand the *Critique of Practical Reason* in its historical context. My aim has been the rather more limited one of collecting only those materials that are: (1) the most essential for this purpose and (2) not already available in English. It delivers more, however, on three counts. First, the volume includes texts that help illuminate more than just the second *Critique*. The first part, for instance, contains substantial selections from texts by Wolff and Crusius that serve as background source materials for all of Kant's major texts on moral philosophy. Indeed, to the extent that any of the texts in this volume function as true *background* source materials, i.e., texts published prior to the second *Critique*, they also help illuminate many of the texts Kant subsequently published as well. Second, insofar as the volume's second part contains important reactions to both the *Groundwork* and the first *Critique*, the translations in that part offer an insight into the immediate reception of those texts as well. And finally, the third part includes several reactions to Kant's second *Critique*, which are included because they help situate the second *Critique* in its historical context by illustrating how the book was immediately received by some of Kant's most important contemporaries. Accordingly, the texts in Part III also serve as background source materials to some of Kant's later writings, especially when he explicitly responds to them, as I indicate in the introductions and editorial notes. To be sure, each of the volume's three parts could be expanded; indeed, they could each be an individual volume on their own. My hope, however, is that the selections I have made serve a variety of purposes and will help scholars and students better understand many of Kant's major writings on moral philosophy, especially but not limited to the second *Critique*.

In preparing the following volume it has been my practice to translate texts in full whenever possible. When this has not been possible, such as when selections are from book-length pieces, I have attempted to translate unified sections that stand alone and are not unduly harmed by extracting them from their larger whole. I have also attempted to strike a balance between being faithful to the original texts and making the translations readable for a present-day audience. I admit, however, that I have often favoured readability for particularly troublesome passages, or at least have tried to do so. I therefore apologize in advance to those whose sensibilities fall on the opposite side of the spectrum.

I hope that my efforts here make the texts I have translated better known, and that readers will be inspired to consult the original sources. Part of the reason for the obscurity of the texts in this volume, especially in the case of texts originally published in eighteenth-century journals, lies in the fact that the originals are often difficult to locate, and their bibliographic information is occasionally even listed incorrectly in the literature. But another reason why many of the texts translated in this volume are not especially well known outside of specialist circles has to do with certain biases: figures who were profoundly important at the time, such as Wolff and Crusius, are not presently major figures in the canon of Western philosophy. Furthermore, emphasis is often placed on studying monographs, when reviews and articles published in journals were extraordinarily important mediums for the exchange and testing of philosophical ideas, at least during the historical period that is my focus in this volume. The translations that follow therefore comprise my modest attempt to encourage readers to think beyond the canon, even if only to a small extent.

Acknowledgements

From its initial conception to its final version, this volume took approximately seven years to complete. During that time, I received an enormous amount of support from various individuals and institutions, without whom I would have never been able to finish the project. Thanks to the University of Western Ontario, the University of St. Andrews, Trent University, the University of Würzburg, and Martin Luther University Halle-Wittenberg for providing me with resources and office space, and to the Frederick M. Barnard Trust, the Social Science and Humanities Research Council of Canada, the German Research Foundation, and the Humboldt Foundation for generous financial support.

As far as individuals are concerned, special thanks are due to: Corey Dyck for his encouragement, support, and advice from the very beginning to very end; Jens Timmermann for his generous mentorship along the way; Heiner Klemme for his feedback and advice, and for hosting my stay as a Humboldt Fellow in Halle during the final stages of the project; John Walsh for reading nearly every word of the volume; Eric Watkins for his endorsement of the project and helpful advice; Daniel Fulda, Andrea Thiele, and the Interdisciplinary Centre for European Enlightenment Studies (IZEA) at the University of Halle for granting me a Wiedemann scholarship during a formative stage of the project; Hilary Gaskin for backing the project and for her understanding and patience; two anonymous referees for Cambridge University Press for their feedback; and Amanda Speake for creating the index.

For feedback, suggestions, and/or advice at various stages I further thank: Ruth Boeker, Alexander Douglas, Antonino Falduto, Christopher E. Fremaux, Michael Gregory, Paul Guyer, Knud Haakonssen, Stefan Heßbruggen-Walther, Andy Jones, Pauline Kleingeld, Dennis Klimchuk, Michael Kryluk, Michael Bennett McNulty, Jörg Noller, Gareth Paterson, Andreas Pecar, Anne Pollok, Fred Rauscher, Arthur Ripstein, Paula Rumore, Sonja Schierbaum, Friderike Spang, Emmanuel Stobbe, Achim

Vesper and the members of the online Crusius reading group, and Howard Williams and the Cardiff Kant Reading Group. As always, thanks to my parents Harry and Margaret for their unconditional support of everything I do, to my sister Natalie for being my role model, and to Michael Baumtrog for keeping me grounded. I would also like to thank my son Oscar for inspiring me to develop an altogether different set of translation skills as he learned to speak while I finished the book.

I dedicate this volume to my wife Kacy: pursuing an academic career in this day and age is difficult, to put it as kindly as possible, and her generosity, support, and patience have made doing so both possible and bearable. Her advice, including countless suggestions concerning the style and content of this volume, has continually helped me to succeed. If the next ten years of our marriage are anything like the first, then we have a lot to look forward to.

General Note on Citations and Translations

References to Kant's works cite the volume, page, and line number of his *Gesammelte Schriften* (see Kant 1900ff.), except for references to the *Critique of Pure Reason*, which follow the practice of referring merely to the page numbers of the first (A) and second (B) edition. Although I remain broadly consistent with the translations of Kant's texts available in the *Cambridge Edition of the Works of Immanuel Kant*, readers should assume that these translations are always modified. Translations from the *Groundwork*, however, are taken from the Gregor/Timmermann edition (Kant 2011), and again readers should assume they are modified. My primary reference for the German version of the second *Critique* has been a draft of Jens Timmermann's forthcoming edition that he is preparing under the auspices of the Berlin-Brandenburg Academy of Sciences.

Punctuation has been modernized in all the translations, and I often found it necessary to break up abnormally long passages into shorter sentences. New paragraphs have also been created at times, especially in texts that originally had no paragraph breaks whatsoever. Terms and passages that were emphasized in the original with slightly thicker type have been bolded, and Greek and Latin expressions have been italicized and translated in footnotes, unless the context makes their meaning clear. All footnotes in Arabic numerals are my own, and all footnotes marked with an asterisk are by the original author. Further translation notes that are specific to each individual text have been appended to the end of each chapter's introduction, where I have also mentioned the edition that formed the basis of my translation. The original page numbers from the translated text are given in square brackets throughout the translations. Original German terms are provided in square brackets throughout where I felt readers may wish to know how I have rendered a term. When my translation of a term is consistent

xiii

throughout a given text, the original German term is only provided once after the first instance so as to interrupt the flow of reading as little as possible. Finally, my translation choices often relied on the following dictionaries: Adelung (1811), Grimm and Grimm (2023), and Küttner and Williamson (1805–13).

General Introduction

Kant did not initially intend to write a *Critique of Practical Reason*, let alone three Critiques.[1] When the first edition of the *Critique of Pure Reason* was published in May of 1781, it was meant to be "a critique of the faculty of reason in general" (Axii), and thus a critique of *both* theoretical *and* practical reason, and which was thereby meant to function as a "propaedeutic" or preparation for both "the metaphysics of nature as well as of morals" (A850/B878, see also A841/B869). This is also how Kant conceived of the project carried out in the first *Critique* in the decade prior to its first publication,[2] and it is how he continued to see things during the first few years that followed. We learn from Kant's correspondence, for instance, that his next main focus after the first *Critique* was not any additional Critique, but the 'Metaphysics of Morals,' a project he had announced to have been working on for years already.[3] Kant's plans eventually changed, of course, and the *Critique of Practical Reason* was published in late 1787, with 1788 on the title page. What happened in the intervening years that caused Kant to decide to write a *Critique of Practical Reason*? In the following introduction, which has been kept brief intentionally so as to save as much space as possible for the translations that follow, I outline some of the major events in Kant's development during this period and highlight just one important factor that encouraged him to write the second *Critique*. As we will see, the story of the *Critique of*

---

[1] There is reason to believe that the origin of the *Critique of the Power of Judgement* is in fact connected to that of the second *Critique*. Although I mention this briefly below, addressing this topic in detail goes beyond the bounds of this brief introduction. For more information see Klemme (2010) and Guyer (2000).
[2] See, for instance, the letter to Marcus Herz from Feb. 21, 1772 (10:132.12–13) as well as Natorp's (1913) introduction to the Akademie Edition of the second *Critique* for a discussion of this point and an extensive list of sources.
[3] See e.g., the letter from Hamann to Hartknoch from Jan. 11, 1782 (Hamann 1959, p. 364) and Vorländer (1965) for more information. For an account of the long history of the 'deferred' publication of the *Metaphysics of Morals*, see Kuehn (2010).

I

Practical Reason's origin reveals that it is especially suited to being accompanied by certain background source materials that help illuminate its aims and contents.[4]

The initial reception of the *Critique of Pure Reason* was disappointing. Kant's ideal commentators, Johann Nicolaus Tetens and Moses Mendelssohn, had little or nothing to say about the book,[5] and the only reviews that appeared during the entirety of 1781 were just three short announcements and summaries.[6] So Kant somewhat quickly, namely by the fall of 1781 at the latest,[7] set to work on a popular version of the *Critique* that would make its contents more accessible, a work which eventually became the *Prolegomena*.[8] While he was working on this project, the first serious review of the *Critique of Pure Reason* came out on January 19, 1782, in the *Zugabe zu den Göttingischen Anzeigen von gelehrten Sachen*.[9] Originally published anonymously but later revealed to have been written by Christian Garve and edited by Johann Georg Heinrich Feder, the review claimed, among other things, that Kant's transcendental idealism was no different than Berkeley's idealism.[10] Kant was upset by the review and publicly responded to it in the *Prolegomena* (see 4:372–80 as well as 4:288–94). Unfortunately, the *Prolegomena* seems to have done little to make Kant's philosophy more intelligible; as Kant's future colleague Johann Schultz put it: "it almost appears as if one recoils before the *Prolegomena* only slightly less than one does before the *Critique*" (1784, p. 6). Indeed, the initial reception of the *Prolegomena* must have been disappointing too, for it gained only slightly more attention than the first *Critique*: after it appeared in the spring of 1783,[11] it received four

---

[4] Readers interested in more details surrounding the origin and aim of the second *Critique* should refer to the following sources, which were consulted when preparing this introduction: Beck (1960, pp. 3–18), Beck (1949), Bittner and Cramer (1975, pp. 9–29), Goy (2015), Gregor (1996), Klemme (2003, 2010, 2021), Kuehn (2001, pp. 311–14), Natorp (1913), Reath (2015), Sala (2004, pp. 53–56), Vorländer (1951, 1965), and Wood (2002).
[5] See e.g., the letter to Herz, whom Kant also identifies as one of his ideal critics, from May 11, 1781 (10:270.7–11) and Sassen (2000, p. 1) for a brief discussion.
[6] These are all reprinted in Landau (1991, pp. 3–6, 6, 6–9).
[7] See the letter from Hamann to Hartknoch from Aug. 11, 1781 (Hamann 1959, p. 323).
[8] See Hatfield (2002) for a detailed account of the origin of the *Prolegomena*.
[9] *Zugabe zu den Göttingischen Anzeigen von gelehrten Sachen*. 3. Stück, Jan. 19, 1782, pp. 40–48. See Sassen (2000) and Kant (2004) for English translations of the review.
[10] Garve later published the unedited version of his review in the *Allgemeine Deutsche Bibliothek*, Supplement to Volumes 37–52, Part II (1783, pp. 838–62). See Sassen (2000, pp. 59–77) for an English translation and Beiser (1987, Ch. 6.3) for a discussion of the Göttingen review.
[11] See e.g., the letter from Plessing to Kant from Apr. 15, 1783 (10:310.37–311.2) and Hatfield (2002, p. 33).

short announcements in 1783, only two longer reviews in 1784, and then one review each in 1785 and 1786.[12]

While all of this was taking place, Kant was still working on the Metaphysics of Morals.[13] In the fall of 1783, an important event happened that altered the subsequent development of that text, namely the publication of Garve's German translation of Cicero's *De officiis* (On Duties) as well as Garve's accompanying three-volume *Philosophische Anmerkungen und Abhandlungen zu Cicero's Büchern von den Pflichten* (Philosophical Remarks and Treatises on Cicero's Books on Duties). As we learn primarily from the correspondence of Kant's close friend Johann Georg Hamann, Kant considered writing an "anti-critique" to Garve and his characterization of Cicero in early 1784, and this might have even been meant as an indirect reply to Garve's review of the first *Critique*.[14] This eventually evolved into a "prodromus" or forerunner to the Metaphysics of Morals, however, which no longer contained any references to Garve or Cicero whatsoever,[15] and which Kant was still working on in August 1784.[16] The book Kant completed soon after was the *Groundwork of the Metaphysics of Morals*, which was sent to the printer in September of 1784 and published in April 1785.[17]

The *Groundwork* comprises an important stage in the development towards the second *Critique*, because in it we find Kant using the expression 'critique of pure practical reason' for the very first time in any of his writings, whether published or unpublished. Furthermore, Kant now contrasts a 'critique of pure speculative reason' with a 'critique of pure practical reason,' and claims that the latter serves as the foundation for the metaphysics of morals, just as the former serves as the foundation for the metaphysics of nature (4:391.18–20). This is a clear shift from his earlier view that one critique of the faculty of reason in general is sufficient preparation for both. Nevertheless, even at the time of the *Groundwork*'s

---

[12] All of these are reprinted in Landau (1991, see pp. 30–31, 32–34, 34, 55–63, 64–76, 85–108, 147–82, 324).
[13] See Hamann to Hartknoch, Jan. 11, 1782 (Hamann 1959, p. 364).
[14] See especially Hamann to Scheffner, Feb. 18, 1784 (Hamann 1965, pp. 129–30) as well as Vorländer (1965) and Kuehn (2001, pp. 277–83).
[15] See Hamann's letters to Müller from Apr. 30, 1784 (Hamann 1965, p. 141) and to Herder from May 2, 1784 (Hamann 1965, p. 147).
[16] See Hamann's letters to Herder from Aug. 4, 1784 (Hamann 1965, p. 174) and to Hartknoch from Aug. 10, 1784 (Hamann 1965, p. 182).
[17] See Hamann's letters to Scheffner from Sept. 19 and 20, 1784 (Hamann 1965, p. 222) and to Herder from Apr. 14, 1785 (Hamann 1965, p. 418). To be clear, it is a matter of debate just how much, if any, of Kant's engagement with Garve's Cicero can be detected in the *Groundwork*. For a discussion and sources, see the Introduction to Chapter 10 below.

publication, Kant did not intend to write a separate book entitled *Critique of Practical Reason*, nor did he intend to fully carry out a critique of this sort, whether as part of the *Groundwork* or otherwise. As Kant explains in the Preface to the *Groundwork*:

> there is actually no foundation for it [the Metaphysics of Morals] other than the Critique of a *pure practical reason*, just as for metaphysics there is the Critique of pure speculative reason already published. But in part the former is not of such utmost necessity as the latter, since human reason, even in the commonest understanding, can easily be brought to a high measure of correctness and accuracy in moral matters, whereas in its theoretical but pure use it is totally and entirely dialectical; in part I require that the critique of a pure practical reason, if it is to be complete, also be able to present its unity with [the Critique of] speculative reason in a common principle; because in the end there can be only one and the same reason, which must differ merely in its application. However, I could not yet bring it to such completeness here without introducing considerations of a wholly different kind and confusing the reader. On account of this I have availed myself of the label of a *Groundwork of the Metaphysics of Morals*, and not of a *Critique of Pure Practical Reason* instead. (4:391.17–33)

Indeed, later in the *Groundwork* Kant claims that, to the extent that such a critique of pure practical reason is necessary for his purposes, this is accomplished in Section III (see 4:445.11–15). Thus, once the *Groundwork* is finished, Kant does not turn his focus to a more complete version of the 'critique of pure practical reason,' but says that "I am proceeding immediately with the full composition of the Metaphysics of Morals."[18]

In the spring of 1786 Kant begins to work on the second edition of the *Critique of Pure Reason* at the request of his publisher.[19] It was while working on the B edition of the first *Critique* that Kant seems to have re-evaluated the need to undertake a more complete critique of pure practical reason, for in November of 1786 Kant published the following announcement in the *Allgemeine Literatur-Zeitung*, a somewhat recently founded pro-Kantian journal:

> ANNOUNCEMENT. Herr *Kant* in *Königsberg* is preparing a second edition of his *Critique of Pure Reason*, which should be published this coming Easter, and in which he has found nothing essential that needs to be changed, albeit after the most incisive examination and consultation of all the reproaches [Erinnerungen] he has encountered against that text. He has,

---

[18] See the letter to Christian Gottfried Schütz from Sept. 13, 1785 (10:406.32–33).
[19] See the letter to Jakob from May 26, 1786 (10:450.35–451.1).

however, changed its presentation here and there, and he hopes that these improvements, by means of removing misunderstanding, will remedy past difficulties and avoid future ones better and more permanently than any refutation (for which he has no time left anyway). To the *Critique of Pure Speculative Reason* contained in the first edition there will be added a *Critique of Pure Practical Reason* in the second, which can similarly serve to defend the principle of morality against the objections that have been made and are still to be made, as well as serve to complete the entirety of the critical investigations which must precede the system of a philosophy of pure reason.—Improvements to the *Groundwork of the Metaphysics of Morals* have already been given to the printer, and the new edition of the latter will therefore appear very soon.[20]

When the B edition was finally published in April of 1787, it did not contain the advertised 'critique of pure practical reason.' Already in June of 1787, however, Kant tells Christian Gottfried Schütz that he is "so far along with my *Critique of Practical Reason* that I intend to send it to Halle for printing next week" (10:490.12–14). This was ambitious, for it was not until September of 1787 that the book was actually in Halle for printing,[21] and it was not published until December of 1787 because J.F.A. Grunert, Kant's printer in Halle, wanted to print it with new, sharp letters.[22]

To summarize the story so far: Kant made significant changes to the plan of his Critical philosophy more than once over the span of just a few years. While in 1781 he conceived of the one Critique of pure reason as sufficient preparation for both the metaphysics of nature and of morals, as of the *Groundwork*'s completion in the fall of 1784 at the latest he came to think that the metaphysics of morals at least in principle required a critique of pure practical reason, even if he simultaneously thought that it was unnecessary to completely carry out such a critique at the time.[23] While he was working on the second edition of the first *Critique* in 1786, however, he changed his mind again and came to realize that carrying out a critique of pure practical reason in full was necessary after all, but he planned to include it in the second edition of the first *Critique*. Finally, sometime between November 1786 and April 1787[24] he decided to publish it as a

---

[20] *Allgemeine Literatur-Zeitung*. Number 278. Tuesday, Nov. 21, 1786, Column 359. See also Landau (1991, pp. 471–72) and 3:556. The second edition of the *Groundwork* was published soon after the announcement and before the end of 1786.
[21] See the letter to Jakob from Sept. 11, 1787 (esp. 10:494.13–14).
[22] See the letter from Grunert from Dec. 1787 (esp. 10:506.6–26).
[23] For some additional information on the transition from the first *Critique* to the *Groundwork*, see Timmermann (2019).
[24] When exactly Kant began writing the second *Critique* is a matter of debate. Beck (1960, p. 17) and Sala (2004, p. 53) claim that Kant did not start writing the text until *after* the second edition of the

separate book and, as we learn from the work itself, it is no longer a 'critique of pure practical reason,' but a critique of reason's entire practical faculty, whose aim is to show "*that there is pure practical reason*" (see 5:3.6–7). The questions that I want to briefly address in the remainder of what follows are: what was it that made Kant decide that a full critique of practical reason was necessary, that is, one that went beyond what was already accomplished in *Groundwork* III, and why did he decide to publish it as a separate book?

Kant likely decided to publish the *Critique of Practical Reason* as a separate book for pragmatic reasons: the first *Critique* was already quite long, for instance, and he probably wanted to avoid delaying the publication of the second edition any longer than was absolutely necessary.[25] That Kant 'discovered' the *a priori* principles of the faculty of feeling during this same timeframe[26] also might have motivated him to reserve a separate work for each of the three fundamental faculties. The more interesting question, however, is why he decided to carry out a more substantial critique of (pure) practical reason at all. This is a complicated question, and to fully answer it we would also need to consider Kant's allegedly different approaches to the deduction of freedom and morality in the *Groundwork* and the second *Critique*,[27] as well as his 'discovery' of the antinomy of pure practical reason,[28] to name just two of the most important advances made in the second *Critique*. The factor that I want to focus on for the purposes of this volume, however, is the role played by Kant's early critics and reviewers.

As has already been seen in the above 'Announcement,' the revisions Kant made to the second edition of the first *Critique* were at least in part intended to prevent any further misunderstanding of the text.[29] Kant's correspondence confirms that correcting misunderstandings and

---

first *Critique* was published in April 1787. I agree with Klemme (2003, p. xix) that it is much more likely that Kant was already writing it as of November 1786 at the latest when the 'Announcement' was published, even if it was considered part of the B edition of the first *Critique* at the time.

[25] See Wood (2002, p. 26), Beck (1960, p. 15), and Klemme (2010, p. 17). Another factor to consider is whether, and if so how, it would have been possible for Kant to incorporate a 'critique of pure practical reason' within the structure of the first *Critique*. I thank Jens Timmermann for bringing this point to my attention.

[26] See the letter to Reinhold, Dec. 28, 1787 (10:514.24–26), as well as Klemme (2010, pp. 19–22) and Guyer (2000).

[27] See Timmermann (2010) for a helpful introduction to this topic.

[28] See Klemme (2010) who argues that this 'discovery' was instrumental in the development of the second *Critique*.

[29] See also the letter to Bering from Apr. 7, 1786 (10:441.13–15), the letter to Jakob from May 26, 1786 (10:450.35–451.3), and the letter from Biester from June 11, 1786 (10:457.14–16).

responding to his critics were indeed major concerns of his both in revising the first *Critique* and when writing the second. In a letter to Johann Bering from April 7, 1786, for instance, Kant says that in the revised edition of the first *Critique* he will "attend to all the misinterpretations and misunderstandings that have come to my attention since the book began circulating."[30] Additionally, in a letter to Ludwig Heinrich Jakob from around September 11, 1787, Kant says that: "My *Critique of Practical Reason* is at Grunert's now. It contains many things that will serve to correct the misunderstandings of the [Critique of] theoretical [reason]" (10:494.13–15). Indeed, even after he decided to publish the *Critique of Practical Reason* as a separate book, Kant is clear in several places that the second *Critique* will serve to clarify views he presented in the first *Critique*.[31]

But it was not only the objections to and misunderstandings of the first *Critique*, and perhaps also the *Prolegomena*, that concerned Kant at this time. On the contrary, he must have been seriously concerned about the things that were being said about the *Groundwork* as well. In the above 'Announcement,' for instance, Kant claims that the 'critique of pure practical reason' that he intended to include in the B edition was in part meant to "defend" his principle of morality "against the objections that have been made and are still to be made." In fact, it was likely the reactions to the *Groundwork* in particular that played an instrumental role in bringing Kant to realize that he needed to carry out a more complete critique of (pure) practical reason beyond what he had already accomplished in the *Groundwork*, for in contrast to the disappointing initial reception of both the first *Critique* and the *Prolegomena*, the *Groundwork* was fervently reviewed immediately after it was first published. As can be seen from the following, roughly chronological list,[32] the *Groundwork* was reviewed no less than twelve times within the first eighteen months or so after it was available:

1. *Allgemeine Literatur-Zeitung.* Number 80. Thursday, April 7, 1785, pp. 21–23. (Landau 1991, pp. 135–39)

---

[30] 10:441.13–15 and see also the letter to Jakob from May 26, 1786 (10:451.1–3) for a similar statement.
[31] In addition to the letter to Jakob just cited, see the letter to C.G. Schütz from June 15, 1787 (10:490.12–23) as well as the letters to Reinhold from Dec. 28 and 31, 1787 (esp. 10:514.6–9).
[32] The list is 'roughly' chronological because some of the reviews only have generic dates, such as the fall of a given year. Even Landau (see 1991, pp. xi–xx and xlii) lists them in two different orders.

2. *Gothaische gelehrte Zeitungen.* 66. Stück, August 17, 1785, pp. 533–36; 67. Stück, August 20, 1785, pp. 537–44; Supplement to 67. Stück, August 20, 1785, pp. 545–50. (Landau 1991, pp. 183–97)
3. *Denkwürdigkeiten aus der philosophischen Welt.* Edited by Karl Adolph Cäsar. Erster Jahrgang. 3. Stück/Quartal, Summer/Fall 1785, pp. 433–67. (Landau 1991, pp. 203–18)
4. *Altonaischer Gelehrter Mercurius.* 37. Stück, September 15, 1785, pp. 291–95. (Landau 1991, pp. 219–22)
5. *Neueste Critische Nachrichten.* 11. Band, 40. Stück, October 1, 1785, pp. 314–16. (Landau 1991, pp. 223–25)
6. *Göttingische Anzeigen von gelehrten Sachen.* 172. Stück, October 29, 1785, pp. 1739–44. (Landau 1991, pp. 229–33)
7. *Tübingische gelehrte Anzeigen.* 14. Stück, February 16, 1786, pp. 105–12. (Landau 1991, pp. 277–83)
8. *Kritische Beyträge der neuesten Geschichte der Gelehrsamkeit.* 1. Band, 1. Stück, 1786, pp. 202–13. (Landau 1991, pp. 318–23)
9. *Russische Bilbiothek, zur Kenntniß des gegenwärtigen Zustandes der Literatur in Rußland.* 10. Band, 1–3. Stücke, 1786, pp. 165–66. (Landau 1991, p. 325)
10. *Allgemeine deutsche Bibliothek.* 66. Band, 2. Stück, May 1786, pp. 447–63. (Landau 1991, pp. 354–67)
11. *Altonaischer Gelehrter Mercurius.* 23. Stück, June 8, 1786, pp. 177–79. (Landau 1991, pp. 403–404)
12. *Allgemeine Literatur Zeitung.* Number 259, Monday, October 30, 1786, columns 193–98; Number 260a, Tuesday, October 31, 1786, columns 201–208; Number 267, Wednesday, November 8, 1786, columns 265–72. (Landau 1991, pp. 450–69)

Kant was aware of many of these reviews, including number 6, authored by J.G.H. Feder, the editor of the Göttingen review; number 7, authored by J.F. Flatt; and number 10, authored by H.A. Pistorius, as I explain in the Introductions to Chapters 8, 3, and 6 respectively. The majority of these reviews were critical, thus Daniel Jenisch's statement to Kant from May 14, 1787, can likely be generalized: "Your *Groundwork* [Grundlage] *of the Metaphysics of Morals*, my Herr Prof., has found incomparably more opposition among my scholarly acquaintances than your *Critique*" (10:486.24–26). Similarly, Jakob reports to Kant on July 17, 1786, that "the misunderstanding concerning your [*Groundwork of the*] *Metaphysics of Morals* seems to be far greater than that concerning your *Critique*" (10:462.6–7).

To be sure, the reviews of the first *Critique* and the *Groundwork* were certainly not the only things on Kant's mind at the time and which contributed to him deciding to write the *Critique of Practical Reason*. The first ever book-length commentary on the *Critique of Pure Reason*, namely Johann Schultz's *Erläuterungen über des Herrn Professor Kant Critik der reinen Vernunft* (Elucidations of Herr Professor Kant's Critique of Pure Reason), was published during this period, as was the first book-length commentary on the *Groundwork*, i.e., Gottlob August Tittel's *Über Herrn Kants Moralreform* (On Herr Kant's Reform of Moral Science). Kant knew of both these commentaries, as I explain in the Introductions to Chapters 4 and 5. The pantheism controversy was also raging at the time, and Kant finally decided to enter it in October of 1786 with his 'Orientation' essay, which itself received a critical response in early 1787 by Thomas Wizenmann. As I note in the Introduction to Chapter 7 below, Wizenmann is the only one of Kant's critics mentioned by name in the second *Critique*. This is all in addition, of course, to the 'misunderstandings' of the first *Critique* that the second *Critique* was meant to correct, as mentioned above.

Taking all of this together, it is hardly surprising that the *Critique of Practical Reason* is a somewhat unique work in Kant's corpus in that it addresses earlier reviews, reactions, and criticisms more so than any other, whether explicitly or implicitly.[33] In the Preface alone, for instance, Kant makes several explicit references to previous reviewers and objections.[34] It is therefore beyond question that the early reactions to Kant's philosophy were instrumental in his decision to write a full-blown *Critique of Practical Reason* that goes beyond that contained in the *Groundwork*. This is the case to such an extent that, as Heiner Klemme has claimed: "It is possible that there might not have been a second *Critique* in the form that we know it without the external criticisms that were levelled against his philosophy."[35] As such, the *Critique of Practical Reason* is especially well suited to being accompanied by certain background source materials that help illuminate its aims and contents, by way of illustrating the views and criticisms that he was reacting to. The chapters of this volume collect only

---

[33] See Klemme (2021, p. 641).
[34] See e.g., 5:6.12; 5:8.28–37n; and 5:8.26. In the Introductions to each of this volume's chapters I give further indications of passages in the second *Critique* where Kant might be responding to specific individuals and objections.
[35] Klemme (2021, p. 642). See also Klemme (2003, p. xi), Goy (2015, p. 1316), Sala (2004, p. 55), Beck (1960, p. 14), and Wood (2002, p. 26) for similar claims.

the most essential of these materials, and in most cases they make them available in English for the very first time.

The following eleven chapters, which have been organized chronologically by first publication date, are not limited to the period between the publication of the first and second *Critique* but are divided into three parts to indicate three distinct ways in which the selections serve to place the second *Critique* in historical context. In Part I, 'Pre-Kantian Moral Philosophy,' I have included selections from the ethics textbooks written by Christian Wolff and Christian August Crusius, arguably the two most important moral philosophers writing in German during the eighteenth century prior to Kant. These first two chapters represent two diverging approaches to moral philosophy, with which Kant was familiar and with which he engages in all his major ethical works, including the second *Critique*. In Part II, 'Between the *Critiques*,' which is the most substantial part of the volume, I offer five translations: reviews of the *Groundwork* written by Flatt and Pistorius, Pistorius's review of Schultz's *Elucidations*, selections from Tittel's first commentary on the *Groundwork*, and Wizenmann's reply to Kant's 'Orientation' essay. These are all profoundly important as background source materials because Kant was aware of and responds to them all at various points in the second *Critique*. In Part III, 'The Reception of the *Critique of Practical Reason*,' I have translated three reviews of the second *Critique*, namely those authored by Feder, August Wilhelm Rehberg, and Pistorius, as well as a selection from Garve's essay *Über die Geduld* ('On Patience'), which collectively offer a diverse insight into the early reception of the second *Critique*. In some cases, such as the selection by Garve, Kant was familiar with the text and responds to it in later works. I explain details such as these in the Introductions that precede each chapter, wherein I also briefly sketch the life and works of the author, indicate the relevance of the translated text for the second *Critique*, as well as provide an overview of the text's key points. To be noted is that the Introductions intentionally refrain from providing a full-scale analysis of each text, nor do they offer an exhaustive list of where Kant might have engaged with them. It is rather my hope that these translations speak for themselves and inspire readers to find connections that have not yet been discovered.

PART I

Pre-Kantian Moral Philosophy

I
Christian Wolff
Introduction

Christian Wolff (1679–1754) was born in Breslau, the then capital of the historical region of Silesia (now Wrocław, Poland).[1] After attending *Gymnasium* in Breslau, Wolff received a scholarship to go to Jena, where he began studying theology but quickly turned to mathematics and philosophy as well. Wolff eventually transferred to Leipzig where he received his *Magister* in philosophy in 1702 and defended his habilitation in 1703, the latter of which was entitled *Philosophia practica universalis mathematica methodo conscripta* (Universal Practical Philosophy Written According to the Mathematical Method). This was a highly original work establishing the new discipline of 'universal practical philosophy,' which was an abstract, general discipline that served as the foundation for all the other practical sciences (ethics, politics, and economics). After defending his habilitation Wolff spent a few years in Leipzig working as a lecturer (*Privatdozent*) as well as for the *Acta Eruditorum*, the first scientific journal of the German-speaking lands of Europe. During his time in Leipzig, Wolff formed a productive friendship with Leibniz that lasted until the latter's death in 1716.

Beginning in 1707, Wolff occupied the chair of mathematics in Halle, where he was a popular teacher. His success as a teacher was in part because, following in the footsteps of his new colleague Christian Thomasius, Wolff held his lectures in German rather than in Latin. Tension quickly built between Wolff and the theological faculty in Halle, however, especially with Joachim Lange, a leading Pietist who was not only jealous of Wolff's success as a teacher, but also disagreed with Wolff on fundamental issues surrounding the roles of reason and

---

[1] Details about Wolff's life and works are taken from Biller (2018), Kertscher (2018), and Schwaiger (2016). For an extended introduction to Wolff's life and works, as well as to his influence during the eighteenth century and beyond, see the 'Introduction' to Schierbaum, Walschots, and Walsh (2024).

revelation in philosophy and theology. The conflict came to a head on July 12, 1721, when, on the occasion of handing over the office of pro-rector to Lange, Wolff delivered a speech entitled *Oratio de Sinarum philosophia practica* (Oration on the Practical Philosophy of the Chinese). In this speech, Wolff argued that the ancient Chinese developed a perfectly plausible theory of morality based on reason alone, and thus without the help of divine revelation. The speech moved the theological faculty to petition officials in Berlin to investigate Wolff's writings for blasphemy with the goal of restricting his teaching to mathematics. The Berlin commission did more than this, however, and convinced the militarist King Friedrich Wilhelm I that the principles of Wolff's philosophy were deterministic, such that soldiers could not be held responsible for deserting the battlefield. On November 8, 1723, Friedrich Wilhelm I issued a decree, written in his own hand, stripping Wolff of his professorship and ordering him to leave Prussia within forty-eight hours.

After fleeing Halle, Wolff made his way to Marburg, where he became professor of mathematics. Wolff was in Marburg for seventeen years until King Friedrich Wilhelm I died and his son, Friedrich II (Frederick the Great), ascended the throne. One of Frederick the Great's first orders was to invite Wolff back to Prussia, and on September 10, 1740, Wolff was named vice-chancellor of the University of Halle and professor of both mathematics and natural and civil law. Wolff remained in Halle until he died in 1754, at the age of 76, having become not only a member of nearly every learned society of Europe, but also a Baron.

Wolff was an extremely prolific writer. In addition to dozens of papers and nearly 500 book reviews for the *Acta*, his most influential writings were a series of textbooks written in German that were based on his lecturing activity during his first period in Halle. This 'German' series of writings, as it has come to be known to distinguish it from his later Latin writings, was published between 1713 and 1726 and included: a successful textbook on logic, the *Vernünfftige Gedancken von den Kräfften des menschlichen Verstandes und ihrem richtigen Gebrauche in Erkänntnis der Wahrheit* (Rational Thoughts on the Powers of the Human Understanding and Its Correct Use in the Cognition of Truth), aka the *German Logic* (1713);[2] an incredibly influential work on metaphysics, the *Vernünfftige Gedancken von Gott, der Welt und der Seele des Menschen, auch allen Dingen überhaupt* (Rational Thoughts on God, the World, and the Soul of Human Beings, as well as All Things in General), aka the

---

[2] See Wolff (1770) for an early English translation.

German Metaphysics (1720);[3] a textbook on ethics, *Vernünfftige Gedancken von der Menschen Thun und Lassen, zu Beförderung ihrer Glückseeligkeit* (Rational Thoughts on the Action and Omission of Human Beings, for the Promotion of Their Happiness), aka the *German Ethics* (1720); as well as others on political philosophy, experimental physics, physics, teleology, and physiology.[4] The success of these works encouraged Wolff to rewrite his philosophical system in Latin, which he began doing in Marburg and continued to publish during his second stay in Halle, so as to reach a wider European audience. When Wolff died, he left this project unfinished, which is hardly surprising since he devoted thousands of pages, and in many cases multiple volumes, to each subdiscipline of philosophy.

Wolff's philosophy was profoundly influential during the eighteenth century. 'Wolffianism,' broadly defined as adherence to Wolff's teachings, was taught and promoted by faculty at all the major German universities for decades.[5] Ironically, and somewhat tragically, however, the influence of Wolff's own philosophy began to wane around the same time he started to rewrite his system in Latin, namely during the 1730s and 1740s. But even once the dominance of Wolffianism began to decline, it continued to shape the philosophical landscape because by then it had become so widespread that anyone hoping to move past Wolff's philosophy, such as the Pietists,[6] had no choice but to critically engage with it. Not only this, but the legacy of Wolffianism was extended by his many students, disciples, and interpreters, who developed modified versions of Wolff's system that went on to be influential up until the late eighteenth century. To mention just one important example, in the preface to the *Initia philosophiae practicae primae acroamatice* (Elements of First Practical Philosophy), the textbook that Kant lectured from in his ethics courses, Alexander Gottlieb Baumgarten states explicitly that his aim is that of "abridging" and "explaining" Wolff's universal practical philosophy (2020, p. 33).

Kant was therefore educated and began his career within an environment that was dominated by discussion between proponents of and opponents to Wolff's philosophy. At both the *Collegium Fridericianum*, Kant's early school, and the University of Königsberg, for instance, there were both Wolffians and Pietist critics of Wolffianism.[7] It is therefore no

---

[3] See Dyck (2019), Watkins (2009), and Beck (1966) for partial English translations.
[4] See Biller (2018) for a chronological list of Wolff's major publications.   [5] See Albrecht (2018).
[6] For an excellent introduction to Wolffianism and Pietism and the current state of scholarship concerning their place as movements within the history of German philosophy, see Grote (2023).
[7] See Albrecht (2018, p. 454).

surprise that in the *Critique of Pure Reason*, we find Kant calling the "famous" Wolff "the greatest among all dogmatic philosophers" (Bxxxvi). Thus, although we have no evidence that Kant owned or read the *German Ethics* firsthand,[8] it is without question that he was familiar with and profoundly influenced by Wolff's philosophy as a whole, including his ethics.

The *German Ethics* is divided into four parts: 1. 'On the Action and Omission of Human Beings in General,' 2. 'On the Duties of the Human Being to Itself,' 3. 'On the Duties of the Human Being to God,' and 4. 'On the Duties of the Human Being to Others.' As these titles indicate, the book has two main aims: to deal with general and foundational issues in moral philosophy and the philosophy of action (Part 1), and to present Wolff's doctrine of duties to self, God, and others (Parts 2–4). Accordingly, and although Wolff never says so explicitly in the book, the topics covered in Part 1 outline his 'universal practical philosophy.' What follows is a complete translation of Chapter 1 of Part 1 of the *German Ethics*. This chapter is arguably the most important of the entire book, for it is here that we find a general overview of almost all the core features of his universal practical philosophy, including his: theory of the good (§§2–5), theory of the will (§§6–7), definition of obligation (§8), principle of perfection (§12), conception of happiness (§52) and the highest good (§44), and account of virtue and vice (§64). The following translation therefore serves as a concise introduction to Wolff's ethics in general, and one that is especially helpful for better understanding Kant's own discussion of all the above concepts in the second *Critique*, including Kant's explicit reference to Wolff's principle of perfection (see 5:40).

Translation Notes

The following translation is based on the modern reprint of the fourth edition of the *German Ethics* (see Wolff 2006). First published in 1720, the second (1722) and third (1728) editions contained only minor changes, most of which were additions to points made in the first part of the text. From the fourth edition (1733) onwards (it went through eight editions in total), the text remained unaltered.

As is the case for all of Wolff's works, the *German Ethics* is divided into sections, and each section includes short descriptions of their contents in

---

[8] For some circumstantial evidence that suggests Kant had firsthand knowledge of the '*German Ethics*,' see Gawlick, Kreimendahl, and Stark (2019, pp. L and 170).

the margins. I have placed these marginal descriptions in italics and have inserted them where they occur in the text, which is either at the beginning of a section, where they serve as the section title, or partway through a section where Wolff seeks to clarify his topic. Also to be noted is that Wolff includes copious references to other sections of the *German Ethics* and to other works as well, and he uses his own abbreviations: Met. = 'German Metaphysics'; Polit. = 'German Politics'; Moral = 'German Ethics'; and Log. = 'German Logic.'

The *German Ethics* has been partially translated into English once in the past, by J.B. Schneewind (see 2003). My translation has learned much from Schneewind's, as well as from the other modern translations of Wolff's philosophy into English (see Dyck 2019, Watkins 2009, and Beck 1966). For an introduction to Wolff's ethical theory, see the chapter on Wolff in Schneewind (1998) as well as the contributions in Schierbaum, Walschots, and Walsh (2024).

German Ethics (1720)
Rational Thoughts on the Action and Omission of Human Beings, for the Promotion of Their Happiness

[1]

Part I
On the Action and Omission of Human Beings in General

Chapter I
On a Universal Rule of Human Actions and the Law of Nature

§1. *On what kind of human action and omission is treated here.* We find it grounded in experience that both some thoughts of the soul and some movements of the body stem from the will of the soul. Others, on the other hand, are not subject to the will (§325 Met.). For example: it is based on my [2] will that I now direct my thoughts to considering the good deeds of God, which he has shown me on previous occasions, but not that I see the person who encounters me or hear the shrieks of someone making noise (§219, 786 Met.), nor that I think of those things that occur to me in such circumstances (§238 Met.). No less does it stand under my will whether I now want to stand or sit, but not whether I digest the meal I have eaten or not (§519 Met.). *What ranks among the actions of human beings.* Since what stems from our will has its ground in the will (§29 Met.) and thus in us (§197 Met.), and similarly the movements of the body that are subject to the will have their ground in the state [Zustand][1] of the body (§878, 882 Met.), both the thoughts of the soul as well as the movements of the body that stem from the will rank among our actions (§104 Met.). *Which are free.* And since the will has a freedom to choose among possible things that which pleases us the

---

[1] Throughout my translation of Wolff I have rendered *Zustand* as 'state' rather than 'condition,' for example, in order to preserve some continuity with the meaning this term has in Wolff's metaphysics, according to which all things, even inanimate objects, have a 'state.' See *German Metaphysics* §121.

most (§510 Met.), so are such human actions free, and therefore receive the name of **free actions**. To be precise, the movements of the body, by means of which the desires of the soul are fulfilled, are free with respect to the soul (§884, 885 Met.). On the other hand, since we encounter no freedom independently of the will (§492, 519 Met.), so is there also [3] no freedom in human action, whether it consists in thoughts of the soul or movements of the body, if it is not subjected to the will. *Which are necessary*. The action in such cases is necessary and therefore receives the name of a **necessary action**. Here we are only concerned with the free actions of human beings and in no way with those that are necessary.

§2. *Difference between free actions*. The free actions of human beings bring about many changes, both in the internal state of the human being, with respect to the soul and the body, as well as in its external state, with respect to its honour, its assets, and what otherwise belongs to it, and not only under the general circumstances that occur every time with the same action, but also under the more particular circumstances that only arise in some cases and by means of which the particular cases are distinguished from one another. In this respect, the free actions of human beings are not all similar to one another. The internal state of the soul and the body, as well as the external state that is obtained by means of the assistance of our free actions, either agrees with the essence of the soul and the body and the previous state or is contrary to it. Since the proof of this point penetrates far too deeply into the most subtle of truths that I have in part presented in my *Rational Thoughts on God, the* [4] *World, and the Soul of Human Beings*,[2] and since what we should in general prove here will also be demonstrated of particular kinds of actions time and again throughout this entire book, I will merely refer to experience at this point and content myself with explaining the principle with some examples in advance. *Is explained by means of example*. The human being has a skill, by nature, to cognize the truth. The more it actually cognizes truth, the more skilful it becomes in cognizing it. Thus, the state of the soul that is brought about by its free actions, namely by varied efforts in cognizing truth, agrees with the natural state of the soul and is in no way contrary to it. Suppose that a human being is cheerful in its body and without pain. If this human being consumes a lot of food and drink, then it will feel dull and experience pain in the head and in other limbs as well. The present state of the body is therefore contrary to the previous one; indeed, it even conflicts with the

---

[2] Wolff is referring to his *Rational Thoughts on God, the World, and the Soul of Human Beings, as well as All Things in General*, otherwise known as the *German Metaphysics*. See the Introduction above.

previous state of the soul. For, in that the soul was previously in the state of gladly reflecting on something and of pondering what it wishes, it is now annoyed and cannot keep its thoughts together. Whereas it was calm and joyful before, it now becomes restless and distressed by pain and all kinds of [5] contrary affects. Whoever is in good standing and does something laudable thereby receives even higher standing, and therefore the subsequent external state agrees with the preceding one. On the other hand, if this person does something that is rightfully scolded by reasonable people, this is contrary to their good standing and therefore their preceding state. Whoever is rich and loses money thereby becomes poorer, and in this way the previous state is similarly contrary to the subsequent one. Poverty and wealth are two contrary things that cannot coexist simultaneously. *When the state of the human being is perfect.* Now, if the present state agrees with the preceding one and the subsequent one and all of these agree with the essence and nature of the human being, then this state of the human being is perfect (§152 Met.), and indeed that much more perfect the greater this agreement is (§150 Met.). *When it is imperfect.* On the other hand, if the past state conflicts with the present, or the present with the future, or if among coexisting things one thing conflicts with another, then the state of the human being is imperfect (§152 Met.). In such a way, the free actions of human beings promote either the perfection or the imperfection of their internal and external state. [6]

§3. *They are either good or evil.* What makes both our internal and our external state perfect is good (§422 Met.). On the other hand, what makes both more imperfect is evil (§426 Met.). Therefore, free human actions are either good or evil (§2).

§4. *How one judges actions.* If one therefore wants to judge whether actions are good or evil, one must investigate the changes they bring about both in our internal state of the body and the soul and in our external state, while paying attention to whether the modified state agrees with the essence and nature of the human being, that is, the essence and nature of the body and of the soul and the previous state or whether it is contrary to them (§2, 3). What has been briefly said about the excessive enjoyment of food and drink above, of its status as indecent behaviour and extravagance (§2), can serve as an example, and in the following where particular human actions are considered we have as many examples as there are kinds of actions.

§5. *They are in and of themselves good or evil.* Since the free actions of human beings become good and evil by means of their outcome [Erfolg], that is, by means of the changes that are thereby brought about in the internal and external state of human beings (§2, 3), and since what results from them must necessarily [7] come about and cannot fail to happen (§575 Met.), they are therefore in and of themselves good or evil and are not first made such by God's will. If it were therefore just as possible for there to be no God and the present relation of things could exist without him, then the free actions of human beings would nonetheless remain good or evil. For example: intoxication would still be harmful to a human being just as before and would bring about all kinds of disorderly things in its state, which do indeed vary in particular circumstances, but which nonetheless constantly remain the same in some general respects, as will be more extensively illuminated below in its appropriate place.[3]

§6. *Actions that are good in themselves can only be willed if one distinctly comprehends them.* The cognition of the good is a motive [Bewegungsgrund][4] of the will (§496 Met.). Whoever distinctly comprehends the free actions of human beings that are good in and of themselves (§5) cognizes that they are good (§206 Met.). And therefore, the good that we perceive in them is a motive for our willing them. Since it is not possible for something to simultaneously be a motive of volition and nolition[5] (§10 Met.), it also cannot be true that one should nill an action that is good in itself if one distinctly comprehends it. Such actions are therefore constituted in such a way that they can only be willed, but not simultaneously nilled, if one [8] distinctly comprehends them. Thus, if we nill them, there is no other reason than that we do not cognize them. If we were to even have an aversion to them, then we must conceive of them as other than they are.

§7. *Actions that are evil in themselves can only be nilled if one distinctly comprehends them.* In the same way, the cognition of evil is a motive of nolition (§496 Met.) or of aversion to a thing (§495 Met.). Whoever distinctly comprehends the free human actions that are evil in and of themselves (§5) cognizes that they are evil (§206 Met.). And therefore, the evil that we perceive in them is a motive for our nilling them. Now, since it is not possible for something to simultaneously be a motive for nolition

---

[3] See e.g., *German Ethics* §83, §86, and §97.
[4] In the first index to the *German Metaphysics* (unpaginated), Wolff states that '*Bewegungsgrund*' is his German term for the Latin concept '*motivum*'. I have therefore chosen to translate this term as 'motive.'
[5] I have rendered '*wollen/Wollen*' and '*nicht wollen/nicht Wollen*' as 'to will/volition' and 'to nill/nolition' respectively. To be noted here is that Wolff makes a sharp distinction between 'nolition,' i.e., positively 'not-willing' something, and 'omission' (*unterlassen*), i.e., the absence of volition. As he explains in the *German Metaphysics*: "when we will, our mind is inclined towards the thing. When we nill, it withdraws from it. When we omit willing, it remains, as it were, still and immobile, such that it is neither inclined towards the thing nor withdrawn from it" (§495). As such, Wolff understands 'nilling' to be "something more" (ibid.) than omitting. As Wolff goes on to clarify in §7 of the *German Ethics*, 'nilling' is therefore similar to having an aversion towards a thing.

and volition (§10 Met.), so is it also not the case that one should will an action evil in itself if one comprehends it distinctly. Therefore, these actions are constituted in such a way that they can only be nilled, or that one is averse to them, if one comprehends them distinctly. If we will them, then there is no other reason than that we do not know them and rather regard them as something other than they are.

§8. *What obligating is.* Obligating someone to do, or omit, something is nothing other than connecting a motive of volition or nolition to it. *Example.* For example: the sovereign [Obrigkeit] obligates subjects to refrain from stealing [9] by means of assigning the punishment of hanging to it. Since this punishment is connected to stealing by means of the sovereign's power and authority and follows necessarily such that the person who is placed on the gallows is the person who is convicted of stealing in such a way that this person cannot deny having done it, a person who gets the desire to steal realizes from all this that theft is evil because it results in the gallows and they thereby acquire an aversion to theft (§495 Met.). Accordingly, the sovereign obligates subjects to refrain from stealing by means of connecting a motive of nolition to this action. Therefore, whatever provides the motive for our willing or nilling of an action, this obligates us to perform it or omit it. *The fruitfulness of this concept.* How all obligation in all potential cases can be demonstrated on the basis of this concept and how fruitful it is for deriving other truths from it will be extensively shown both in this book as well as in the other on the societal life of human beings.[6]

§9. *Nature obligates us to perform actions that are good in themselves and omit those that are evil in themselves.* Since what results from human actions and makes them either good or evil (§2, 3) originates from the essence of things and nature (§614, 615, 754 Met.), and the good and bad that we encounter in actions are the motives [10] of volition and nolition (§496 Met.), so has nature connected motives to human actions that are good and evil in themselves (§5). And in this way the nature of things and our own nature obligate us to do what is good in itself and omit what is evil in itself (§8).

§10. *And also to prefer the better.* In a similar way it can be proven that nature obligates us to prefer the better to the worse. For, the better is more good than something else and is therefore a stronger motive (§521 Met.). However, its strength as well as its connection to human action stems from

---

[6] Wolff is referring to his *Rational Thoughts on the Societal Life of Human Beings and, in particular, the Body Politic*, otherwise known as the *German Politics*.

the nature of things, as has just been shown (§9). That more perfection in the state of a person results from one action rather than from another is in accordance with the nature of things (§630, 757 Met.).

§11. *Response to an objection.* Perhaps some of you will think that it follows from this that nature also obligates us to evil. Evil often has the appearance [Schein] of the good and this appearance is just as much a motive of the will as the truly good (§424, 502 Met.). In a similar way, only too often does the good have the appearance of evil and this appearance is just as much a motive of nolition as that which is truly evil (§ cit. Met.). However, [11] that the appearance of good or evil deceives us does not arise from the nature of things but from our ignorance and error. Thus, I cannot say that nature connects the motive to such things insofar as such actions, which have the mere appearance of either good or evil due to our imperfect knowledge, bring about no perfection in our state in the first case and no imperfection in the second. Nature, therefore, makes neither the first good (§422 Met.) nor the second evil (§426 Met.). As a result, I also cannot say that nature obligates us to such actions that have the mere appearance of good or evil (§8). We must judge on the basis of truth, not appearance.

§12. *Universal rule for free actions.* It is thereby established: nature obligates us to perform actions that are good in themselves and omit those that are evil in themselves (§9), and also to prefer the better to the worse or the greater good to the lesser (§10). As a result, since good actions make our internal and external state more perfect, but evil actions make it more imperfect (§3), so does nature obligate us to do that which makes us and our state, or, what is the same, our internal and external state, more perfect and on the other hand to omit [12] that which makes us and our state, or, what is the same, our internal and external state, more imperfect. Thus, we have a rule according to which we should direct the actions that are in our control, namely: **do that which makes you and your state or that of another more perfect, omit that which makes it more imperfect.**

§13. *How this rule is applied.* How one knows whether an action makes our state more perfect or more imperfect is clear from what has been previously said (§2). Namely, 1. one pays attention to the changes that an action brings about either in our soul and in our body, that is, in our internal state, or in our external state as well. Then, one investigates 2. whether the state that follows from the action agrees with the essence and nature of the human being and with the preceding state or runs counter to it, or similarly whether, after a change has occurred, something is encountered in the new state that runs counter to the rest, but which is encountered simultaneously with the rest. For, if a complete agreement is obtained by our actions, then they make us and our state more perfect. On the other hand, if this agreement is thereby disturbed, then they will make us and our [13] state more imperfect (§152 Met.). The previously given examples (§2) can explain this matter. Indeed, everything that will be proven about particular kinds of free actions in the following is to be regarded as examples that apply here.

§14. *The extent to which this rule applies.* It is to be noted that this rule applies to all free actions, and therefore no thought in the soul and no movement of the body that we have in our power is excluded (§1). However, we will show in the following how one applies it in particular cases and what kind of particular rules arise from it, for although this rule is universal, one must in no way think that one could immediately judge on its basis whether all free human actions are good or evil. It is known that one cannot conclude anything on the basis of a single proposition, rather only on the basis of two is a third inferred (§340 Met.). Therefore, in addition to the rule, another proposition concerning the constitution of the action is necessary before one can say whether it is good or evil. That is, our knowledge of free human action in the end depends on these two syllogisms:

1. We should do that which makes our state or that of others more perfect. [14]
   This action makes our state or that of another more perfect.
   Therefore, we should do it.
2. We should omit whatever action makes our state or that of another more imperfect.
   This action makes our state or that of another more imperfect.
   Therefore, we should omit it.

We will explain which actions are the ones that make us and our state either more perfect or more imperfect in the following. Here it is sufficient to say that if the internal and external state are to continually agree with the natural state, then free actions are to be determined by precisely those ends [Absichten], by means of which natural states are determined and which necessarily result from the essence of the body and the soul. And this is forgotten by those who deduce from the agreement of the preceding state with the present one and everything that is included in the present state that a vicious person must carry on in their vice.

§15. *It is grounded in the nature of the soul.* What can result from the power of the soul is grounded in its nature (§756 Met.). Since it can result from the soul that it wills action that is good in itself and nills those that are evil in themselves (§6, 7), so is this [15] volition and nolition grounded in its nature. Accordingly, since actions that are good in themselves make the state of the human being perfect, both internally as well as externally (§5), so is the rule that requires we do that which makes us and our state more perfect also grounded in the nature of the soul. And things are similar with the second part of the universal rule, namely that one should refrain from those actions by means of which our internal and external state become more imperfect.

§16. *It is a law*. A rule, according to which we are bound to regulate [einzurichten] our free actions, is called a **law**. Accordingly, since we are bound by the universal rule of free action to regulate these actions (§12), so is this rule also a law.

§17. *What the law of nature is, what a divine law is, what a human law is*. In particular, however, a rule is designated a **law of nature** when nature obligates us to regulate our free actions according to it, just as we call a **divine law** a rule, according to which God obligates us to regulate our free actions, and on the other hand we call a **human law** a rule, according to which human beings obligate us to regulate our free actions.

§18. *A law can simultaneously be natural, divine, and human*. Thus, the distinction between laws is essentially founded on obligation, [16] on the basis of it originating from here or there. Accordingly, if we have more than one obligation to direct our free actions according to a specific rule, e.g., if nature, God, and human beings simultaneously obligate us, then this one rule is simultaneously a natural, divine, and human law.

§19. *The content of the law of nature*. Because nature obligates us to do that which makes us and our state more perfect and to omit that which makes us and our state more imperfect (§12), so is the rule: **do that which makes you and your state more perfect and omit that which makes you and your state more imperfect** a law of nature (§17). Since this rule applies to all free human actions (§14), one needs no other law of nature, rather all particular laws must be demonstrated on the basis of it in the way and manner already mentioned (§14). This rule is therefore a complete ground of all natural laws.

§20. *The origin of this law*. However, because this rule becomes a law on account of obligation (§16), and obligation comes from nature (§12), the law of nature has thus been discovered by means of nature and would hold even if the human being [17] had no superior who could obligate it to the law. Indeed, it would hold even if there were no God.

§21. *The atheist is not permitted to violate it*. Those individuals are therefore mistaken who think that an atheist, however they might live their life, would commit numerous disgraceful actions and vices, if only they were free from civil punishments. For, this is only true if an atheist lacks understanding and does not properly have insight into the constitution of free actions. As such, atheism does not in fact introduce the atheist to the evil life, rather their ignorance and misunderstanding of good and evil does, which is the source of a disorderly life and an incorrect lifestyle even for others who are not atheists.

§22. *An objection and its reply*. It is nonetheless true that an atheist can utilize atheism to corroborate their ignorance and misunderstanding of good and evil, and for this reason persist therein. But because of this, a dissolute life is not necessarily connected with it, that is, an atheist does not make a correct inference when they reason as follows: there is no God, thus there is no difference between good and evil, rather the human being can live as it wants (§5). We know that even the teachings of Christian truths lead those people to sin who are wrapped up in ignorance and misunderstanding of good and evil. [18] It is far from true that I want to defend the atheist! I cannot, however, be opposed to truth. One always comes further with the truth than with baseless stipulations. And it is precisely this truth that disgraces those who convince themselves to live as if there were no God out of a wicked desire for personal pleasures and delights.

§23. *Reason teaches the law of nature*. Since our free actions are good and evil by means of what necessarily results from them either absolutely or under certain circumstances (§4, 5), an insight into the connection of things is required in order to judge this. Since the insight into the connection of things is reason (§368 Met.), so is good and evil known through reason. Thus, reason teaches us what we should do and omit, that is, reason is the teacher of the law of nature (§19).

§24. *A rational person is a law unto themselves*. Whoever regulates their actions and omissions according to reason, that is, acts rationally, lives according to the law of nature and one cannot act contrary to the law of nature insofar as one is rational. Indeed, because we know what the law of nature dictates [haben will] by means of reason (§23), a rational human being needs no further law, but rather [19] is a law unto itself by means of its reason.

§25. *The law of nature is immutable* [unveränderlich]. Since actions that are good in themselves are necessarily good and those that are evil in themselves are necessarily evil (§5), both are immutable (§41 Met.). The law of nature bids us [will] to commit the former and refrain from the latter (§9) and is therefore immutable.

§26. *eternal.* However, what is necessary is eternal (§39 Met.). Since the law of nature is necessary (§25), so is it also an eternal law.

§27. *complete.* This eternal law applies to all human actions in all instances. For, it is determined by the nature of things that whatever follows from each particular occurring case under the present circumstances must so happen (§575 Met.). Since human actions are good and evil by means of what necessarily results from them (§4), all human actions are determined by nature to be either good or evil. The law of nature therefore commands in each particular occurring case what a human being should do or omit under the present circumstances. *A common misunderstanding is rejected.* As a result, it is also the most complete law, and those individuals are seriously mistaken who claim that the law of nature leaves many human actions [20] undetermined, actions which first become determined afterwards by means of human laws. The law of nature has determined everything and is in itself fully complete, regardless of it not yet having been completely known.

§28. *is based on the agreement of actions with our nature.* What makes us and our state more imperfect is contrary to our nature, and thus does not agree with it (§152, 628, 756 Met.). On the other hand, what makes us and our state more perfect is not contrary to our nature, but rather agrees with it (§ cit. Met.). For this reason, because the law of nature dictates [will gethan wissen] that we do that which makes us and our state more perfect and, on the other hand, omit that which makes it more imperfect (§19), those individuals who have said that the law of nature is based on the agreement of our actions with our nature have not spoken incorrectly. And after I have shown on what basis this agreement can be known, it will no longer be an indeterminate standard, which some have considered it to be, and not without good reason.

§29. *is simultaneously the divine law.* Since the divine understanding makes everything possible (§975 Met.), and the possible achieves actuality through his will (§988 Met.), so has it also become possible through God's understanding that either the perfection or imperfection of a human being's state results from their free actions, [21] and on the basis of his resolution [Ratschlusse] (§997 Met.) it does in fact take place. Therefore, since the representation of this perfection is the motive for our completing some actions and, by contrast, the representation of imperfection the motive for omitting others (§422, 436, 496 Met.), so has God connected motives with actions and therefore also obligates human beings to do what the law of nature bids us [haben will], and to omit what it does not bid us [nicht haben will] (§8). In such a way, natural obligation is simultaneously divine obligation, and the law of nature is simultaneously a divine law (§17). Indeed, from this it is evident that God can give the human being no other law than the law of nature and in no way a law that is contrary to the law of nature.

§30. *is confirmed further.* Aside from natural obligation we find yet another very particular divine obligation, whereby the law of nature becomes the law of God. We experience that good fortune often follows upon good actions and misfortune upon evil actions (§1002 Met.), and God has confirmed through his resolution that they should so happen (§1003 Met.). Therefore, [22] the good fortune that results from good actions and the misfortune from evil actions should be regarded as motives to perform the former and omit the latter (§496 Met.). Consequently, since God voluntarily connects these motives to human actions (§980 Met.), he thereby obligates human beings to do good and refrain from evil (§8). And in this way the law of nature is simultaneously the divine law.

§31. *An objection and its reply.* Some might say that misfortune also tends to happen to those who do no evil and who rather do good to the best of their ability, and in turn the worst human beings most often have the best fortune. Accordingly, it cannot be said that God intends to obligate us to refrain from doing evil by means of misfortune and conversely to do good by means of good fortune. Much can be said in response to this. *First answer.* First, it is certain that many human beings appear good from the outside but not only commit evil in secrecy, rather they also wreak much disaster and great harm through their external actions and omissions in such a way that not everyone knows this, in part because not everyone knows how to correctly distinguish between good and evil and in part because not everyone knows the source from which the evil [23] flows. Therefore, we regard many to be unworthy of the misfortune that befalls them when they have in fact deserved it. *Second answer.* Accordingly, it is to be noted, 2., that the good fortune of those who do evil is also a motive to renounce evil and perform the good. For, in that it does not necessarily result from the action and omission of human beings (§1002 Met.), one sees quite well that one possesses no skill that would explain why one deserves the fortune earned by others or is free from the misfortune that befalls others. One realizes from this that such things are attributable not to oneself, but entirely and only to divine goodness, which he proves by means of his providence for the world (§1062, 1063 Met.), which is a motive to love and admire God, which are virtues that bring about everything good, as I will show below in its proper place (§673). *Third answer.* Beyond this, 3., fortune [Glück] can be the way to a greater misfortune, as one has long noticed from experience: the human being is raised up high so that it may fall even harder. Good fortune [Glücks-Fälle] is therefore a motive to not be arrogant about fortune, but rather to be careful in one's entire way of life. [*Fourth answer.*] Indeed, 4., misfortune is also a means to greater fortune (§1060 Met.) and thus a motive to [24] hope and trust in God, as will be further illustrated in its proper place (§720). [*Fifth answer.*] Precisely the same misfortune, 5., is a means, whereby the human being is deterred from much evil, into which it would otherwise fall if misfortune did not greet it, and it is thus a reason to renounce evil or to refrain from it and consequently to perform the good that opposes it. *General answer.* On this basis one realizes that God does not use good fortune and misfortune for one and the same application in the world, but nonetheless always connects them to human actions in such a way that they can serve as motives in all cases, sometimes to do good and sometimes to omit evil, that is, to regulate one's free actions according to the law of nature. *A prejudice is removed.* Accordingly, what we have said about divine obligation (§8) is confirmed. Namely, if one is to prove that, by means of good- and misfortune, God obligates human beings to do good and omit evil, it is not necessary that those who do good are always happy and alternatively that those who do evil are always unhappy. Rather, it is enough that good- and misfortune are made use of in every single case as a motive to do good and omit evil (§ cit.).

§32. *Doubt is raised, whether the law of nature applies to all cases.* It might strike some as strange [25] that I extend the law of nature to all free human actions. For, they might think that the law of nature only applies to those cases where the human being must do or omit something, but not to where it can do so in a variety of ways. I will provide an example in order to be better understood. When a human being dies, it must leave behind its assets [Vermögen], and is thus permitted to arrange who should get them after its death before its end. This arrangement can take place in more than one way, however, and is therefore regulated differently in various places within human laws. One might think to have found here a free human action, concerning which the law of nature decrees [verordnet] nothing. It is certainly true that this arrangement can happen in a variety of ways, but it is also certain that one of them is better than the others. *What the law of nature obligates us to do in this case.* Since we now know that the law of nature simultaneously obligates us to prefer the better to the worse (§10), we can say nothing other than that the best arrangement is that which the law of nature requires, for we would choose this arrangement and prefer it to the rest if we were to know it. *The cause of the human being's imperfect obedience.*

Regardless of the fact that it tends to happen that human beings do not know which arrangement is best, and therefore prefer the worse to the [26] best, a human being losing their way invalidates neither the law of nature nor their obligation to live by it. On the contrary, the human being's inability to know must be entirely subordinate to the law of nature.

§33. *Why one does not also consider civil laws here.* I easily predict that uncertainty concerning civil laws could arise for some at this juncture, but since I speak about the origin and the true constitution of civil laws in a different place (§401 & seqq. Polit.) and show there the extent to which they must agree with the law of nature, that they are permitted to deviate from it on account of human imperfection, I leave to the side here what I could otherwise additionally say about this until then.

§34. *How one lives according to God's will.* Because God obligates human beings to precisely that to which nature obligates them (§29, 30), so is the will of God in agreement with the regulation of free actions according to the law of nature. And whoever regulates their life according to the law of nature also regulates it according to God's will and lives according to his will. And in turn, whoever regulates their life according to the will of God regulates it according to the law of nature.

§35. *The will of God can establish no other law of nature than that which we have indicated.* Accordingly, even if someone were to establish the will of God as the source of the natural [27] law, they could produce no other law of nature than that which we have offered above (§19). For, the greatest perfection is the motive of the divine will (§981 Met.) and it can therefore demand no actions other than those that increase the perfection of human beings and their state and it must prefer the actions that bring about the greatest perfection to all others. And in this way it is clear that God does not require the law of nature to be altered, indeed by virtue of his nature it cannot happen that he alters it. *Why one cannot pass him off as the ground of the same.* Furthermore, it is clear from what has been proven above that the law of nature does not originate from the divine will, rather human actions were good or evil, or better or worse, before one could say that God willed or nilled them. Indeed, this is also clear from the general principle that the will of God creates no truths (§976 Met.) and has already been proven above (§5).

§36. *What a punishment and reward is.* The ill [Ubel] that the lawgiver connects to an action as a motive to omit it is called a **punishment**. On the other hand, the good that the lawgiver binds to it as a motive to do it is called a **reward**. [28]

§37. *The natural outcome of actions, good fortune and misfortune, are divine punishments and rewards.* Since the ill that results from the human actions that are evil in themselves is to be regarded as a motive that God has connected to them in order to omit them, and the good that results from actions that are good in themselves is to be regarded as a motive that God has connected to them in order to perform them (§30), so is the ill, even if it results from evil actions in a natural way (§630 Met.), nonetheless to be regarded as a divine punishment and the good that arises from good actions as a divine reward (§36). And because things are the same with good fortune and misfortune (§31), so are these also to be regarded as divine rewards and punishments. But how there can be a mere paternal penalty for one, but punishment for others, is clear from what has previously been said about divine obligation (§31).

§38. *A rational human being does not do good and omit evil with a view to reward and out of fear of punishment.* Since a rational human being is a law unto themselves, and apart from natural obligation needs no other (§24), so are neither rewards nor punishments motives for such a being to do good actions and avoid evil ones (§36). Thus, a rational person performs the good because it is good and omits the evil because it is evil, in which case such a person becomes similar to God as one who has [29] no superior who could obligate them to do the good and omit the evil (§947 Met.). Rather, the rational person merely does the former and omits the latter by means of the perfection of its nature (§981 Met.).

§39. *But an irrational person would.* On the other hand, since an irrational person needs another obligation in addition to natural obligation if they are to live according to the law of nature (§24), so are rewards and punishments motives for them to perform good actions and omit evil ones (§36). And therefore, an irrational person performs the good and omits evil out of fear of punishment and with a view to reward. As such, they are similar to children who are driven to good and deterred from evil by means of punishments and rewards because they assign no importance to natural obligation from a lack of reason. Indeed, both they and children are together similar to irrational animals that are brought to do that which they otherwise would not do by being beaten.

§40. *The final end* [letzte Absicht] *of all free actions.* Since we strive to obtain the perfection of ourselves and our state and to avoid imperfection by means of our actions (§12), so is the perfection of ourselves and our state, and similarly the avoidance of imperfection, [30] the end [Absicht] of our actions (§910 Met.). Alternatively, actions are the means whereby we obtain these ends (§912 Met.). Accordingly, since all free actions are directed towards this end (§14), so is it the final end of all our free actions and the main end [Haupt-Absicht] in our entire life.

§41. *Objection.* I know quite well that it will strike some as strange that I have made the perfection of our nature and our state the final and main end of all our free actions. They would believe that this should be the glory of God, just as God himself has made this his final and main end (§1045 Met.). Indeed, they would believe that the common good [das gemeine Beste] must be preferred to the particular advantage of an individual. And therefore, one cannot possibly prefer their own advantage to the glory of God and the common good. In this way, the law of nature would create selfish people, who are the most dangerous in human societies, as is, unfortunately, all too clear from present experience.

§42. *Reply.* At this time I do not wish to explain that the perfection of our nature and our state is very different from self-interest, rather I only wish to remind the reader, [31] which will be proven as clear as daylight in the following, that both the glory of God as well as the promotion of the common good are included in the perfection of our nature, and later we will infer the former two from the latter.[7] The understanding and will of the person who does not promote the glory of God and the common good with all of their powers will have only achieved a very low degree of perfection.

§43. *Self-interest is not the foundation of the law of nature.* Accordingly, we do not approve of the opinion of those who make self-interest the foundation of the law of nature. Whoever is selfish only considers themselves and seeks their own advantage even to the disadvantage of others, provided that such a person only obtains their own advantage without greatly harming themselves. On the other hand, whoever seeks to make themselves as perfect as possible also seeks something for others and strives for nothing that brings harm to others. This truth will first be demonstrated later on[8] and is only touched upon here so that we remove all malicious suspicion of our rule, which will be of significant advantage in the following.

§44. *The bliss* [Seeligkeit][9] *of human beings.* Since the greatest perfection is a characteristic of God and cannot be imparted to any creature (§1088

---

[7] See e.g., §654 and §768. [8] See e.g., §767.
[9] Wolff's equivalent Latin concept for '*Seeligkeit*' is '*beatitudo*' (see Wolff 1739, §374). An alternative English translation could therefore be 'beatitude,' but I have chosen 'bliss' to convey its sense as a feeling similar but superior to happiness, i.e., '*Glückseeligkeit.*'

Met.), so is it also not possible that a human being can ever achieve this even if they apply all of their powers daily. One can obtain no more than progressing from one particular [32] perfection to another and continually avoiding imperfections more and more. This is the highest good that one can achieve (§422 Met.), thus the **highest good of the human being** or its **bliss** is rightly defined as an unhindered progress towards greater perfections (§36 Ch. I Log.).

§45. *It is obtained by fulfilling the natural law.* Since the human being always progresses towards greater perfections if they regulate their action and omission according to the law of nature (§19), the highest good or the bliss that one is capable of is obtained by observing the law of nature, and its fulfillment is therefore the means whereby we attain the highest good or our bliss that we are capable of on earth (§912 Met.).

§46. *But it is lost by violating the natural law.* Thus, the more the human being deviates from the law of nature, the more it strays from the highest good or from its bliss. And therefore, by violating the law of nature one forfeits it and lapses into a miserable state. Indeed, if one does not continue to regulate one's action and omission according to the law of nature, the bliss already acquired is lost, just as, on the other hand, we can be extricated from a miserable state in no other way than by beginning to uphold the law of nature. [33]

§47. *Necessary reminder.* I am speaking here as a philosopher merely about that bliss that the human being can attain by means of natural powers, and therefore in no way do I attribute to nature what our theologians tend to ascribe to grace. *Correspondence of philosophy with theology.* At the same time, since grace does not inhibit nature but rather buttresses it, and similarly, since grace is not contrary to nature but rather agrees with it (for how could things be contrary to one another that come from a God who is perfectly wise?), so will rational individuals who consider, without prejudice and bitterness, what I have said about the earthly bliss of human beings see all too well just how far philosophy agrees with the doctrines of theology, and that the difference between nature and grace and the priority of grace over nature, and whatever else belongs here, can be most distinctly and thoroughly shown by means of my teachings. Perhaps there will be an opportunity for me to thoroughly discuss this point according to the insight that God himself has given me. For now, I must keep myself within the bounds of philosophy that are in front of me.

§48. *What the highest ill or human misery* [Unseeligkeit] *is.* From what has been said about the highest good of human beings or their bliss (§44), it is simultaneously clear [34] that **the highest ill** or **the misery** of human beings consists in the constant progress towards greater imperfections, and thus the violation of the natural law is the means of falling into this (§45).

§49. *Human bliss is connected to a constant satisfaction* [Vergnügen]. Whoever progresses from one perfection to another, unhindered, and avoids but also thereby pays attention to imperfection, has an intuitive cognition of perfection (§268, 316 Met.). But since the intuitive cognition of perfection begets pleasure [Lust] or satisfaction (§404 Met.), so does a person have constant satisfaction. The highest good or the bliss of human beings is therefore connected to a constant satisfaction (§44).

§50. *The constancy of this satisfaction is explained further.* One should not fear that the satisfaction once had will turn into sorrows [Trauren] in the future and that one will have to pay for their pleasure with a greater displeasure [Unlust]. For, displeasure is born from an intuitive cognition of imperfection (§417 Met.). If pleasure were thus to turn into displeasure, one would have to regard that which one considered to be a perfection as an imperfection. But whoever knows how to properly distinguish between perfection and imperfection cannot possibly mistake one for the other (§17 Met.), and therefore their satisfaction remains constant (§407 Met.).

§51. *Bliss is connected with constant joy* [Freude]. Where one progresses without hindrance from one perfection to another and avoids all imperfections, there arises a constant satisfaction (§49), and one need not be afraid that it will turn into dissatisfaction [Mißvergnügen] (§50). In such a way, the satisfaction or pleasure constantly maintains the upper hand and is therefore here a lasting joy (§446 Met.). Bliss is[10] thus connected to a continuous joy (§44).

§52. *What happiness* [Glückseeligkeit] *is and where it is to be found.* The state of a constant joy is what **happiness** consists in. Since the highest good or bliss is connected to a constant joy (§51), so is the human being who possesses it in the state of constant joy. The highest good is therefore connected to happiness.

§53. *How it is obtained.* Since the highest good is obtained by fulfilling the natural law (§45), so is the observance of this law also the means whereby one obtains happiness.

§54. *What an apparent happiness is.* From this it is clear what an apparent happiness is, namely a state of joy that either turns into sadness

---

[10] Reading '*ist*' for '*in*,' the former of which is correctly printed in the fifth, 1736 edition of the *German Ethics*.

[Traurigkeit] or begets sadness. For example: to live in indulgence brings [36] many people joy, and they regard this life as a happy one. But if one person deprives themselves of health, and another deprives themselves of their assets, such that the former is tormented by great pain or must even end their life before its time, and the latter, on the other hand, begins to suffer want and go hungry, and yet another falls into all sorts of disgrace and serious punishable crimes on account of drunkenness, all three of them have more unhappy and displeasurable hours than joyful and pleasurable ones, and each one must pay for the enjoyed pleasure with discontent dearly enough. All sorts of peculiar, uneasy affects belong here, such as revenge, shame, fear, timidity, and those that are similar (§464, 465, 476, 482 Met.). Accordingly, the state of joy that arises from indulgence is only an apparent happiness because it does not persist constantly (§52.), but rather eventually turns into sheer discontent [Verdruß].

§55. *Apparent goods do not make human beings happy, only true ones do.* Since apparent goods are those that bring about only an inconstant pleasure that often turns into a greater displeasure (§424 Met.), so are they only able to offer human beings an apparent happiness and not a true one (§52, 54). On the other hand, since true goods bring about a constant pleasure that never turns into displeasure (§424 Met.), so can they never make human beings [37] unhappy, but only happy (§52, 54).

§56. *Objection and its reply.* It is certainly true that the human being can be displeased about a true good, just as one can be pleased about an apparent good, namely because one knows nothing of them or otherwise misunderstands them, such as when a person thinks they have learned a foundational science in order to become respected by others, even by the ignorant who are not skilled in judging such things, and to be assigned to a profitable post. But since both displeasure as well as pleasure are produced by our misunderstanding, I cannot say that the true good displeases me but the apparent good pleases me, and thus that the former makes one happy and the latter unhappy (§52, 54). For, what is produced by my ignorance and my misunderstanding can in no way be ascribed to the thing that I do not know and which I misunderstand. It is the same with displeasure, which arises for some on the basis of the deficiency of an apparent good.

§57. *The law of nature is the means to happiness.* Since true goods are grounded in a true perfection within human beings or in their external state, but apparent goods absolutely are not (§425 Met.), only that which [38] is grounded in a true perfection within human beings or in their external state can make human beings happy, but in no way can that which is not in the least so grounded (§55). Accordingly, since one achieves the perfection of one's nature and one's external state by observing the law of nature (§19), so is the law of nature the means of obtaining one's happiness (§921 Met.).

§58. *It is due to the goodness of God that he obligates us to the law of nature.* Since God obligates human beings to live according to the law of nature (§30) in a particular way in addition to natural obligation, he thereby proves how he is ready to promote the happiness of human beings (§57), and thus bring about good things for them (§52 Moral & 424 Met.). He thereby offers an example of his goodness (§1063 Met.).

§59. *In this he acts like a father.* Those who think that God places a burden on them through the law therefore deceive themselves, and I do not know what kind of glorification of power would be sought by restricting their freedom by the law. If we regard God as a legislator, we do not see him in the image of a power-hungry master who would be pleased by this, and this he seems to be if he makes it difficult for others with commands. Rather, we see him in the image [39] of a kind and loving father who warns us against what will bring harm, and admonishes us towards that which makes us happy, and applies all his powers to deter us from the former and persist with the latter, of which the privy councillor Thomasius has long reminded us according to his insight into this kind of truth.[11] Whoever finds that the law of nature thereby loses its bindingness [Verbindlichkeit] and becomes a mere counsel [Rath], which one can obey at one's own discretion, such a person maintains what they cannot prove.

§60. *How much hinges on this observation.* It is desirable that this truth penetrate deeply into the minds of human beings and put down firm roots therein. I am confident it would bring them to reflect on their actions and omissions with great care and, as a singular act of God's good will, would drive them to have a fervent love towards him, in that he, in addition to nature, obligates them to the law of nature and from this makes fatherly admonitions and warnings. Nothing need be proven at great length. One can sufficiently see from daily experience that most human beings regard the law as a burden.

§61. *What unhappiness* [Unglückseeligkeit] *is.* Human happiness is a state of lasting joy (§52). [40] Accordingly, unhappiness is, as that which is opposed to it, a state of lasting sorrow and, consequently, since sorrow is a noticeable degree of displeasure (§448 Met.), unhappiness is a state of constant displeasure or of constant dissatisfaction.

---

[11] See for instance §41 of Thomasius' *Foundations of the Law of Nature and Nations* (Thomasius 2011, p. 614).

§62. *Violating the law of nature makes one unhappy.* Dissatisfaction or displeasure arises from an intuitive cognition of imperfection (§417 Met.). Accordingly, since the violation of the law of nature makes us and our state more imperfect (§12), so does dissatisfaction thereby arise, and thus it makes human beings unhappy (§61). For, if one disregards it for a time, appearances can be deceiving, as has already been proven (§55), such that apparent goods are not able to make one happy.

§63. *The teachings up to this point do no harm to the Christian religion.* To what extent the human being can fulfill the law of nature and thereby find its happiness must be judged on the basis of what will be said in the following concerning its observance in specific cases. For, if we know what is required for its observance, so does each individual's own experience reveal how far one can bring oneself by applying all of one's powers, and it is not necessary that one sets boundaries that should not be overstepped. Whoever [41] cannot go any further, going further is absolutely prohibited for them. *When self-deception of the good does not take place.* However, if one possesses distinct cognition of what is to be done, there is no need to discuss whether one could have done more than what actually took place (§206 Met.); this kind of self-deception only takes place where one is confused by indistinct concepts (§214 Met.). And therefore, one need not be concerned that nature is elevated to the disadvantage of grace by means of the truths that I have proven. *How philosophy awakens admiration for the Christian religion.* On the contrary, if we understand how the human being is to attain their happiness by means of the law of nature and then see how we are unable to entirely achieve this through our natural powers, so does one thereby recognize all the better the necessity and excellence of grace, which is offered to us in the Christian religion, and which replaces that which is lacking in nature. I consider this remark to be necessary so that one does not oppose truth on the basis of a misunderstanding and so that those without understanding do not take the ill-affected opportunity to blaspheme against the truth. Despite this, there have been people who have persuaded themselves to do this to their advantage.

§64. *What virtue, vice, human weakness, and natural inability are.* The habit of regulating one's actions according to the law of nature is what we tend to call **virtue**. [42] On the other hand, **vice** is a habit of acting contrary to the law of nature. **Human weakness**, however, is the natural inability to regulate one's actions according to the law of nature. I say: natural inability. For, whoever is themselves responsible for their inability cannot pass off their deviation from the law of nature as a natural inability. For example: if someone misses the opportunity to be rational in doing the good and after the fact makes a hasty decision when judging the good, in no way can they attribute their mistake to natural weakness. Such a person could be stronger if they wanted to be. Whoever wants to blame nature must not participate in it. Rather, **natural inability** is here called that which we are not capable of doing through our powers according to the circumstances in which nature has placed us.

§65. *The true constitution of virtue.* Since the law of nature requires the perfection of ourselves and that of other human beings, and concerns both our internal as well as our external state (§19), so is virtue a habit of making oneself and other human beings, as well as both our own and the external state of others, as perfect as possible.

§66. *It makes human beings happy.* The observance of the law of [43] nature is that which makes human beings happy (§57). Since the habit of living in accordance with the law of nature is virtue (§64), so does virtue make human beings happy. Accordingly, one can call no person happy without virtue.

§67. *Objection and reply.* It is not to be denied that some will call this truth into doubt in that they believe that experience testifies to the contrary, to the extent that it has become a saying that the worst rascal has the best happiness in the world. But there is a distinction to be made between fortune [Glück] and happiness [Glückseeligkeit] (§1002 Met. & 52 Moral), and between a true and an apparent happiness (§52, 54). Many become unhappy by means of good fortune (§1002 Met. & 61 Moral) and on the other hand many become happy by means of misfortune (§1002 Met. & 52 Moral). The misunderstanding, upon which this objection is founded, will be shown more clearly below once we more thoroughly expand upon the kinds of goods.[12] What has been said above for another purpose (§31) can also serve as clarification.

§68. *Virtue promotes the bliss of human beings.* Additionally, since the bliss of human beings consists in an unhindered progression of ever greater perfections (§44), but a virtuous person has a habit of performing that which makes them and their state more perfect [44] (§65), so does virtue promote the bliss of human beings and nobody can be in a blissful state without virtue. I am speaking here as a philosopher of no other bliss than that which can be obtained by means of natural powers in this life (§47).

§69. *The true constitution of vice.* It is precisely because the law of nature requires the perfection of ourselves and other human beings, as well as of

---

[12] See e.g., §242 and §§244–48.

our own external state and that of others (§19), that vice is a habit of acting contrary to the law of nature (§64). Thus, vice is a habit of making oneself and other human beings, as well as the external state of ourselves and other human beings, more imperfect.

§70. *It makes human beings miserable* [unseelig] *and unhappy.* Accordingly, vice plunges human beings into the greatest evil (§48) and makes them unhappy (§62). Therefore, no vicious person can be in a blissful state, nor take part in true happiness. In order for one to accept these truths, one must have the distinctions between good fortune, bliss, and happiness, and between misfortune, misery, and unhappiness before one's eyes at all times (§67).

§71. *Necessary reminder.* It should also be noted here that some vices can arise for a person with some virtues, [45] of whose miserable and unhappy state it is to be judged much differently than if they were to be entirely embedded in vices. *Why no human being can be completely happy.* In the following[13] we will be able to better comprehend that no human being is capable of complete bliss and happiness (at the very least by means of natural powers), precisely because they never fully achieve virtue, rather, even if one has rid oneself of vice entirely, one is nonetheless subject to human weakness.

§72. *Human weaknesses make human beings unhappy.* Since human weaknesses are natural inabilities to regulate one's actions according to the law of nature (§64), so does the human being unintentionally deviate from the law of nature on account of human weakness and occasionally along with one's greatest disinclination (§507 Met.). What is more, since the deviations from the law of nature make human beings miserable and unhappy, no matter where they come from (§62), so do human weaknesses result in nothing different. *They often cause serious harm.* Indeed, experience confirms that human weaknesses can often cause serious harm and misfortune, occasionally more than the greatest vices. Vicious human beings are not always the most dangerous. This will become clear at the appropriate place once we comprehend the connection between [46] human actions and the common happiness and unhappiness influenced by them, and also the fortune and misfortune that arises thereby in human societies and in the body politic.[14] It is therefore necessary that one fights against both human weaknesses and vices and pays attention to them with complete diligence.

---

[13] See §72 below.   [14] See e.g., *German Politics* §§215–18.

2

Christian August Crusius
Introduction

Christian August Crusius (1715–1775) was born in Leuna, a small town in Saxony near Merseburg, and he was the son of a pastor.[1] Starting in 1729, Crusius attended a prestigious grammar school (*Domschule*) in Merseburg until he moved to Leipzig in 1734, where he studied theology, philosophy, mathematics, and history. In Leipzig, Crusius obtained a *Magister* degree in philosophy in 1737 and completed his habilitation in 1740. He also obtained a baccalaureate in theology in 1742, followed later by a licentiate and a doctorate, both in 1751. After completing his habilitation in philosophy, Crusius held two disputations to qualify as a university professor, the second of which was entitled *De usu et limitibus principii rationia determinantis vulgo sufficientis* (On the Use and Limits of the Principle of Determining Reason, Commonly Called Sufficient Reason).[2] This dissertation criticized Wolff's understanding of the principle of sufficient reason and attracted considerable attention to Crusius; afterwards, more than 150 students began attending his lectures, and the dissertation itself was translated into German twice (in 1744 and 1766). Crusius became junior professor (*außerordentlicher Professor*) of philosophy in Leipzig in 1744 and, after receiving attractive offers from many other institutions of higher education, he accepted the chair (*ordentlicher Professor*) of theology in Leipzig in 1750. He remained in Leipzig for the rest of his life, dying there in 1775, unmarried, at the age of 60.

Although Crusius continued to lecture on philosophy after having become the chair of theology, aside from a single Latin work in 1752, his publications from 1750 onwards were confined to theology. Crusius' philosophical output is therefore almost exclusively confined to his Latin

---

[1] Information about Crusius' life and works are taken from Dyck (2019); Grunert, Hahmann, and Stiening (2021); Hogan (2016); Saring (1957); Watkins (2009); and the anonymous obituary published after his death (1776), which is still the only comprehensive account of Crusius' life ever printed.
[2] See Dyck (2019, pp. 197–225) for an English translation.

dissertations and a series of four German textbooks that he published between 1744 and 1749. The first of these textbooks is his ethics, the *Anweisung vernünftig zu leben* (Guide to Living Rationally) (1744); followed by his metaphysics, *Entwurf der nothwendigen Vernunft-Wahrheiten* (Sketch of the Necessary Truths of Reason) (1745); his logic, *Weg zur Gewißheit und Zuverläßigkeit der menschlichen Erkenntniß* (Path to Certainty and Reliability of Human Cognition) (1747); and his physics, *Anleitung über natürliche Begebenheiten ordentlich und vorsichtig nachzudenken* (Guide to Properly and Carefully Reflecting on Natural Events) (1749, 2 vols.). When these works were published, Wolff's philosophy dominated university education and, taken together, they offered a systematic and sophisticated alternative to Wolffianism, especially when compared to the sometimes-crude polemics offered by some of Wolff's Pietist critics. They also expanded upon the ideas Crusius started to develop in his Latin dissertations, and which had already made him famous, so his German textbooks solidified his reputation as one of the most important German philosophers in the middle of the eighteenth century.[3]

Kant was at the beginning of his academic career when Crusius' philosophical works were first published, so it is not surprising that Kant would come to be influenced by Crusius' philosophy. Kant speaks about "the penetrating Crusius" (1:405.16–17, see also 1:397.5–6) in the *New Elucidation*, for instance, as well as praises Crusius' approach to the supreme principles of reason in the early *Prize Essay* (2:295.13–15). Kant is also critical of Crusius, such as in the *Prolegomena* when he ridicules Crusius' system for containing false principles (see 4:319.31–37n). But most generally speaking, Crusius was an important figure in Kant's development because Crusius offered sharp criticisms of Wolff's philosophy and presents promising alternatives on issues such as: the difference between mathematical and philosophical method, the nature and significance of the principle of sufficient reason, and freedom of the will, among other things.[4]

The *Guide* is divided into five main parts or books: 1. 'Thelematology' or his doctrine of the will as it exists by nature; 2. 'Ethics' or his theory of how the will *should* act; 3. 'Natural Moral Theology' or our duties to God;

---

[3] For information on Crusius' subsequent influence on thinkers other than, but also including, Kant, see Tonelli (1969).
[4] For a brief account of Crusius' importance in the development of Kant's philosophy, as well as additional sources discussing each of these points, see the introduction in Rumore (2018).

4. 'The Law of Nature' or our duties to others; and 5. 'The Doctrine of Prudence' or our duties to self. The following selections are taken from books 1 and 2 of the *Guide* and are meant to offer an insight into four aspects of Crusius' moral philosophy: (1) his theory of the will and desire (§§1–26 and §§89–137); (2) his theory of freedom (§§37–52); (3) his voluntarist theory of ethics (§§155–206); and (4) his theory of the end of human life and moral proof of the immortality of the soul (§§207–23). I have chosen these aspects for the following reasons: aspects 1 and 2 shed light on Crusius' incompatibilist conception of freedom and choice, which has been widely recognized as an important precursor to Kant's own theory of freedom;[5] aspect 3 is meant to help readers gain an insight into Kant's reference to Crusius' moral philosophy as one based on the "will of God" (5:40);[6] and aspect 4 offers an interesting comparison to Kant's moral argument for the existence of God, his doctrine of the highest good, as well as the immortality of the soul as a postulate of practical reason.[7] While these aspects do not exhaust the ways in which Crusius' moral philosophy can shed light on Kant's own, they are nonetheless the most important aspects presented in the *Guide* that Kant has been thought to engage with in the second *Critique*, whether implicitly or explicitly.[8]

Translation Notes

In preparing this translation I have primarily used the first edition (1744) of Crusius' *Guide*. I have done so because, as Giorgio Tonelli, the editor of the most modern edition of Crusius' works (see Crusius 1964ff.), notes, the first editions of all Crusius' German textbooks "were the editions, by means of which Crusius first and most meaningfully had an impact (in the polemic against Wolff)" (see Tonelli 1969, p. LIII). Kant himself, however, owned the second edition (1751) of the *Guide* (see Warda 1922, p. 47), so I have included the minor additions that Crusius made in that edition to the sections I have translated in footnotes. As was the case for Wolff's *German Ethics*, marginal descriptions of the contents of each section have been italicized and inserted where they occur in the text.

---

[5] To name just a few examples, see Allison (2006) and Hogan (2013), as well as Walschots (2021b) for a discussion of Crusius' theory of freedom itself.
[6] See Schneewind (1998, pp. 445–56) for an introduction to Crusius' voluntarist theory of ethics.
[7] See Rumore (2018) for a discussion of Kant's debt to Crusius on this latter point.
[8] For more details on Crusius' influence on Kant's moral philosophy, as well as further sources, see Rivero (2021).

The *Guide* has been partially translated into English once in the past, by J.B. Schneewind (see 2003). The following translation has learned from Schneewind's, as well as from Eric Watkins' (2009) translation of selections from the *Sketch*.

Guide to Living Rationally (1744)

[1]

Thelematology

or

the Doctrine of the Powers
and
Properties of the Human Will

[2]
[blank]

[3]

Chapter I
On the End [Endzweck][1] of Thelematology and the Human Will in General

§1. *What thelematology is.* Before I turn to the guide to living rationally itself, it is necessary that I issue the doctrine of the human will as preparation in advance, without which one cannot possibly succeed in the following. For, since the guide to a rational life includes solely those rules that are prescribed to the will, and which must therefore be derived, for the most part, from the constitution of the will, it is easy to see that one must first know how the will is constituted and works by nature before one can sufficiently explain how it ought to be. One can justifiably call this doctrine **thelematology** or **the doctrine of the will**, a name by which I mean nothing other than a theoretical science of the properties, powers,

---

[1] Crusius uses the term '*Endzweck*' in a very broad sense to mean simply 'end' in general and not something like final or ultimate end more specifically. This is confirmed in the Index to the *Guide*, where the entry for '*Zweck*' simply refers back to the more extensive entry for '*Endzweck*.' Additionally, Crusius also occasionally refers to a '*letzter Endzweck*,' i.e., final or ultimate end, such as the final end of the world. (See e.g., *Sketch* §335.)

44

and effects of the human will. The idea is therefore that we here seek out, as far as possible, the causes [4] of that which we perceive in the will through experience with the intention of learning to both better recognize and judge good and evil as well as promote the former and eradicate and hinder the latter. *Why it is treated here.* I believe that this is the correct place to treat this important subject. It is indeed known that many tend to include it in metaphysics. It seems to me, however, that this is not done correctly, in that metaphysics must without a doubt lose all determinate boundaries if one is also permitted to treat contingent truths in it, concerning which one has no assurance that they cannot be otherwise in a different world, and which one cannot know *a priori* on the basis of the necessary essence of a thing or of a world in general. Nonetheless, one can simply grant each scholar their own freedom on this matter.

§2. *What the will is.* I understand the **will** to be the power of a spirit [Geist][2] to act according to its representations. That is, the will is the efficient cause, but representations are the model or *causa exemplaris*. One acts according to representations when one makes a represented thing actual or strives to do so. By means of this action a thing is either brought about for the very first time, or it is only [5] placed in a certain relation to us, or both happen simultaneously. In this way, my definition captures everything that is attributed to the will by virtue of the use of language, for one attributes desire and aversion, as well as all the actions and omissions flowing from them, to the will. In all of these cases it is clear, however, that a spirit's action takes place according to its ideas. *What a spirit is in the broad sense.* I here call a spirit in the broad sense any kind of substance that has ideas or, which is the same to me, that thinks.

§3. *Why the concept of spirit has been broadened.* In this way I make the concept of both spirit as well as that of the will and of thinking broader than is commonly done. Others conceive of thinking as the representation of abstract concepts only. The will for them is similarly only the power of acting according to abstract concepts, which they oppose to sensible desires.

---

[2] As we will soon see in §3 below, Crusius makes a subtle distinction between a spirit (*Geist*) and the soul (*Seele*). In his *Sketch of the Necessary Truths of Reason*, Crusius explains that matter and spirit are the two highest classes of substance (§362). Matter has no other power than that of motion, but spirit (in the broad sense) is the kind of substance that has a power other than motion, whether motion is also present or not. A soul, on the other hand, is a spirit that has been connected to a body (§372). Thus, these two concepts are not identical, and a soul is a specific kind of spirit. Furthermore, Crusius' view has the somewhat odd consequence that a substance that can think and will, but which does not have a body, is not a soul, properly speaking (see §374).

And they call spirits only those substances that cognize truth with consciousness and distinct discrimination. I have the following reason for broadening these concepts: very much depends on the fact that one carefully considers and independently studies the universal essence jointly possessed by all substances that have the capacity to both represent something and act according to their representations. [6] This is because animal souls and properly so-called spirits are only particular species, in which this universal essence is encountered but always found to be determined differently, and these determinations cannot be thoroughly explained without knowing the common essence befitting them all and by means of which they are differentiated from matter. Since I can find no better-fitting designation, and the designations that I have distinguished above seem to have arisen because one has not paid sufficient attention to their common essence, I consider it the most helpful option to broaden the concepts connected to them for the sake of cognizing the truth. The present remark will suffice to avoid all misunderstanding. I nonetheless leave it to each individual's discretion whether one wants to follow my determination of the mentioned concepts, so long as one acknowledges that, in the opposing case, it would lead to a mere nominal dispute. *There are more noble and less noble spirits.* One will easily see that, according to my concepts, I divide spirits into the more noble and less noble, the rational and the irrational, and that I similarly place many very different levels [Stuffen] of perfection in the species of the will. [7]

§4. *All spirits must have a will.* All spirits must have a will. For, if they were to not have one, they would not at all be able to act according to their representations, and therefore their representations would be of use neither to themselves nor to other things but would be entirely in vain.[*] Yet, it is completely against the perfection of God to create something entirely useless and vain.

§5. *Volition presupposes the representation of the thing.* Any given volition[3] presupposes the representation of the thing that we will in the understanding, and as such the possibility of willing something always depends on the understanding, which must think the corresponding representation in advance. For, one would otherwise contradict oneself (§2). This is the true meaning of the well-known principle that the will is,

---

[*] This is precisely why the will must also be the ruling power in a spirit, which must nonetheless be properly understood. See *Metaphysics*, §454. [Footnote added in the second edition. Crusius' references to his *Metaphysics* are to the *Sketch of the Necessary Truths of Reason*.]

[3] As is the case in my translation of Wolff, in my translation of the *Guide* I have rendered '*Wollen/wollen*' and '*Nichtwollen/nicht wollen*' as 'volition/to will' and 'nolition/to nill' respectively.

in itself, a blind power whose existence and effect would be completely impossible and contradictory without an understanding and without the representation of the thing willed.

§6. *The will is a special foundational power distinct from the understanding*. This notwithstanding, in all finite spirits the will is a special foundational power distinct from the understanding or, if one wants to speak precisely, it is an overarching concept [Inbegriff][4] of particular foundational powers that one brings together under one name due to their common essence, just as [8] one similarly calls the foundational powers that make the cognition of truth possible by one name, namely the understanding. I claim this only in relation to finite spirits, and for good reason. For, in God I grant no more than one single true foundational power, namely the infinite power, which already contains the capacity for all merely possible actions by virtue of its concept, thus the divine understanding and will are nothing but different actions, or activities, and capacities of the infinite power. *How the foundational powers must be determined*. In finite things, however, we can have no other concept of a foundational power than as the possibility of a certain immediate effect, on the basis of which the rest must be understood.[5] For, if one were to accept the possibility of a distant or composite effect independently of a foundational power, the greatest inconsistencies would arise in the doctrine of nature, and one would not in fact be pointing to a foundational power but only to the effect itself and will have grouped the latter together with the universal concept of a power under a common word. [. . .]
[12]
[. . .]

§9. *What desire and aversion are*. That volition,[6] by means of which we try to make something actual that does not yet exist or try to unify ourselves with this thing, insofar as one [13] regards it as an action within the willing spirit, is called a **desire**. On the other hand, an **aversion** is

---

[4] '*Inbegriff*' is a notoriously difficult term to translate. I have adopted 'overarching concept' as opposed to 'sum total,' as is used in the Cambridge Edition of the Works of Immanuel Kant, to better convey its sense of a general concept that encompasses other more subordinate concepts.
[5] Inserted in the second edition: ", and which is not in turn an effect itself, and neither a part nor an aspect of a different power of the same thing, *Metaphysics* §73f. And since I say that the remaining effects that must be attributed to a foundational power aside from the immediate effect must be understood on the basis of the latter, it should be stressed that the remaining effects do not follow from the immediate effect as if subsumed by a general concept, but rather they are actually derived from it as effects flowing from and thereby *caused* by the immediate effect."
[6] Inserted in the second edition: "which is directed towards something which agrees with it, and"

when[7] we try to prevent the actuality of a thing or, more particularly, when we try to avoid unifying with it. A separate striving is distinguished from both of these, where one also seeks to bring about the willed object outside of the soul. Desire or aversion is the ground and efficient cause of this. However, since one calls both of these activities of the will the volition or nolition of a thing, they are sometimes confused with one another.
[...]
[15]
[...]

§13. *What an intention* [Absicht] *or end is and how many kinds there are.* That which a spirit wills can be called an **intention** or **end** in the broad sense. In the narrower sense, however, one understands by an end only something that one wills with consciousness and distinct cognition. Whenever a spirit strives towards an end, three things present themselves as to be distinguished in relation to this striving. *What the subjective end is.* First, there must be a potent volition present that is the efficient power to strive towards something. I want to call this **the subjective end**. It will be shown in the following that one continually becomes tangled up in not insignificant difficulties if one does not notice this concept distinctly enough and does not separate it from the others when analyzing the circumstances that must present themselves when striving towards an end.[8] *What the objective end is.* Additionally, a certain object must be thought, towards which one strives, and which is called the **objective end**. *What the formal end is.* Finally, a certain relation of this same object to the willing spirit must be thought, which the spirit seeks to bring about, and for the sake of which it undertook the action, which is called the **formal end**. For example, when Alexander carried out the campaign against the Persians, the Persian empire was the objective end, the formal end was that he wanted to bring this under his dominion and control it, and Alexander's thirst for power was the subjective end. [...]
[29]

§26. *What a good or evil is.* One calls something **good** insofar as it is in accordance with the volition of a spirit, just as one calls something **evil** insofar as it is contrary to it. Accordingly, the goodness of things consists in

---

[7] Inserted in the second edition: "volition is directed towards something that does not agree with it, and thus when"

[8] Inserted in the second edition: "For, what is distinctly formal about human actions depends on what is distinct about the subjective end, and without properly acknowledging the concept of a subjective end, circles arise in the elucidation and proof of moral things."

their relation to a will, with which they are compared, just as truth is based on the relation to the understanding. Alternatively, if we were to call that which is in accordance with perfection 'good,' it is undeniable that we would do so because all rational spirits desire perfection both in itself and for other things, and we would call such things good to the extent that such spirits desire these things. For, otherwise, there would be no reason available to explain why one would not also call that which is imperfect good, since many things first promote the perfection of spirits because they are good for them, that is, because they serve to fulfill their wishes. The perfection of a thing consists in the relation of its state to the sum of the effects it should be proficient at, and the more things it is proficient at, and the more proficient it is at such things, the more perfect it is. Goodness and perfection are therefore not the same thing. The concept of the good that I have offered can be applied to the kinds of goods offered below and which are known to philosophers with little effort. *What metaphysical, physical, and moral good is.* For, [30] something is **metaphysically** good to the extent that it is found to agree with the natural intentions of God, that is, to the extent that it is found to be capable of the effects that God wanted to make possible by means of the essence conferred upon the thing. Something is called **physically** good to the extent that it agrees with the will of creatures. Now, if the creature itself has a will, then what serves to fulfill its will is called good for that thing. On the other hand, if the creature itself does not have a will, that which serves the perfection of such a thing is nonetheless called good for that thing because perfection is that which we decently wish for such a thing, and for this reason it is clear that the thing is compared to a will of a creature and is called good with respect to its agreement with such a will. **Moral good**, however, is that which is in accordance with the moral intentions of God, that is, those intentions which he demands be promoted by means of the reason and free wills of created spirits or, what is the same, that which agrees with his laws. In all these examples it is clear that the object is always compared to a will and is called good or evil on account of this relation to it. *How true and apparent goods are distinguished.* We can easily derive the distinction between [31] **true** and **apparent physical goods** from precisely this point. That is, if something is presently in accordance with our volition but subsequently brings about certain consequences, whereby our volition is contradicted either just as much as or even more so than the agreement that the thing previously had with our will, then the thing really has no true agreement with our volition even if we thought it did. This is so, because one must pay attention to the whole sum of agreement with and adversity to the will,

if one wants to judge the truth of the agreement, and for this reason the thing is therefore an **apparent good**. On the other hand, if one finds, after one has assessed the sum of all the thing's effects that agree and conflict with the will, that the agreement, on the one side, is greater than the conflict, on the other side, then the thing is a **true**, **physical good**, even if it were to cause us trouble and pain for a period of time.
[...]
[43]

Chapter III
On the Freedom of the Human Will

§37. *In what sense freedom must be treated here.* We are not considering the word freedom here in those political senses of the term, where it occasionally indicates only a right of being able to do something without fear of punishment or where it only expresses the state of affairs [Stand] where one is permitted to follow one's own judgement when tending to one's ends. According to this sense freedom, the state of subjection and rule are opposed to one another. Rather, we here wish to investigate freedom insofar as it is a natural power of the will. At this juncture we are thus not yet discussing its correct or incorrect use, but only its natural properties or essential constitution. I am making this preparatory remark for good reason, namely because it will be seen in various ways that one confuses these meanings with one another and subsequently fails to notice the correct point in the definition of the power of freedom.

§38. *The foundational concept of freedom and its proof.* I first want to seek out the correct concept which one must connect to the word freedom [44] in accordance with the general use of language, where it is taken to be a natural power of rational spirits, and then show that there is in fact this freedom of the will. A free volition, according to the common concept, is said to be neither an externally forced [erzwungenes] nor an internally necessary volition. It is said to make the human being capable of the imputation of its acts in such a way that one is able to not only attribute these actions to the human being as the efficient cause, but is also able to praise or reproach them, recognize them as capable of blame, and on this account consider them worthy of punishment or reward, namely because they proceeded in one way rather than another. Freedom is said to be that which makes it possible for us to be subjected to a law and obligation and makes us accountable for the arrangement [Einrichtung] of our actions. If one considers these presupposed properties together, a **free being** can be nothing other than one that can do or omit something at a single time and in the same circumstances, or can do one thing instead of another, and the power, by means of which one is capable of this, must be called **freedom**. Precisely for this reason one distinguishes between two capacities in freedom, namely, first, the capacity of being able to do or omit something in the same circumstances, [45] which is called *libertas contradictionis*,[9] and the capacity to undertake a different action instead of the present one in the same circumstances, which is called *libertas contrarietatis*.[10]

§39. *An additional definition of freedom that can be inferred from the previous one*. One can therefore express the essence of freedom through the following concept: that it is a power to determine oneself to an action without being determined by something else, whether within us or outside of us. For, determination is the actual establishment of one of the possible ways of existing that can be attributed to a thing. Thus, if something besides the free act is present which makes it such that the act now has this and no other determination, the effecting substance is thereby determined. But if such a thing is not present, and the substance nonetheless has the power to undertake something, then it determines itself.

§40. *Further elucidation of the proof of the foundational concept*. If one does not grant the concept I have provided, then no act would ever come about that is without necessity. For, if one were to allow those acts to be free, to which the acting substance is determined by its own representations [46] and desires, and which one calls **spontaneity** or **spiritual self-activity**, then the act would not thereby cease being necessary, because everything that is determined is necessary insofar as it is determined. It would also make no difference to this topic to specify by means of what kind of representation an acting spirit is determined, nor, similarly, whether the determining motives [die determinirenden Bewegungsgründe][11] in one's understanding are distinctly represented or not. All our virtue would thereby be transformed into mere fortune [Glück], in that it would arise if a person were to have a good disposition [Naturell] or were to be placed in connection with other things in such a way that they would thereby be determined to actions that are in accordance with perfection. Vice, on the other hand, would be mere misfortune [Unglück], hence nobody could ever truly be held responsible

---

[9] *freedom of contradiction*   [10] *freedom of contrariety*
[11] In §59 of the *Guide*, Crusius explains that everything that stimulates (*reißet*) the will is a motive (*Bewegungsgrund*), and that the will is stimulated by means of certain ideas being made lively (*lebhaft*). Thus, as Crusius stresses again here, all motives are ideas and thus cognitive grounds of action, whether distinctly represented or not, so long as they are lively enough to stimulate the will.

because it would not be possible for one to avoid vice, rather, everything would depend on the disposition that the creator gave to a person and on the connections with other things, in which the creator placed them. I nonetheless know quite well that it is considered to be praiseworthy not only when one does nothing evil but also when one is incapable of it, just as, on the other hand, one takes a person to be a disgraceful human being [47] when they not only do not have virtue but are incapable of it. But a rational person must not allow this tendency to confuse them in the determination of the concept of freedom. For, praising and blaming are nothing more than judging whether certain properties of a thing agree with perfection or not. In this way, there are two kinds of praise and blame, first the non-moral kind, which is nothing other than a judgement of the perfection or imperfection of a thing, and the moral kind, where we take a person to be the free author of a property that we cognize to be worthy of praise or blame. In the following I will also show that many things that happen without complete freedom, or with no freedom at all, can nonetheless be attributed to us with true moral praise or blame, because we at one time brought about their causes.[12] One can therefore quite appropriately praise a natural property of a person. But, for this reason, one must not deny that a person can be praised for wilfully brought about acts or properties, and one must not confuse these two types of praise and praiseworthy properties with each other. It should also be noted that it is often a [48] mere flattering remark based on ignorance when, for example, clients say so much about hereditary virtue to their patrons. However, the following reason is to be applied here: since, in human life, we cannot rely on what a person does wilfully, in that we can have no guarantee that they will do something similar far in the future, we therefore esteem it especially highly when people, whom we need for certain services, are inclined by nature to do that which we require of them, or that which we depend on the most. Regardless of whether it is therefore a rule of prudence to seek out the people who have a good mind by nature in human life, and regardless of whether this is itself a natural perfection, one is nevertheless not permitted to think that the other kind of perfection, namely the moral kind, consists in a good disposition, or that one performs an action freely on account of the fact that it is praiseworthy, as opposed to thinking that a praiseworthy action is a free action only once one has decided it for themselves, without being determined to do it.

---

[12] See below §52.

§41. *Additional definition of the essence of freedom.* If we further consider the matter of how a power [49] such as freedom, according to our concepts, is possible, then we find that it must consist in a perfect, internal activity. It is a matter that belongs to metaphysics to prove that one must eventually arrive at first actions or foundational activities, before which no other activity of an efficient cause can in turn precede, but which rather immediately spring from the essence of an active foundational power itself, because between the effect and the efficient cause there must be the action or activity.[13] Different kinds of such things are possible. Some are continually effective according to their nature, such as the foundational powers of the elements. Others are connected to certain conditions and are therefore unable to be effective if such conditions are absent, but as soon as the required conditions are present, their efficacy inevitably takes place according to their nature. Of this kind are, for example, the powers of the human understanding. Still others are such that their efficacy is only made possible by the conditions that are thereto required. Thus, as soon as the conditions are present, they can initiate effects, although they need not do so, they can [50] continue the initiated activity in proportion to the degree of their power for a period of time and to a certain extent, and they can in turn also stop acting. This is precisely how such a power becomes suited to both action and omission in the same circumstances, as well as to more than one undertaking. The freedom of the human will must be of this sort, and one can therefore further define the concept of it as follows: freedom is the highest degree of activity in a will, by means of which it can itself initiate, direct, and also stop being effective, notwithstanding the fact that this is no more than made possible by all the required conditions. It would be entirely too hasty if one were to think that I infer the actuality of an action from its mere possibility. For, we are not talking about premises and conclusions here, but about powers and activities. The question is not whether one could infer actuality from possibility, but only whether an active power can progress from the possibility of its action to actuality. Nobody doubts here that it does not follow for a thing to actually take place because it is possible. But nobody is saying this, rather I am only claiming that there are efficient causes [51] which can initiate one of their possible activities and which are sufficiently capable of initiating more than one activity at one time, namely this one or that one, and nobody can illustrate to me that this is impossible. Only this much follows from the above: by means of a finite understanding, one cannot

---

[13] Crusius discusses this topic in detail in §§81–83 of the *Sketch*.

demonstratively determine *a priori* whether such a power will be efficacious at a certain time and what it will do, only that this is either known without inference by an infinite understanding, which needs no inferences, or the result is to be expected *a posteriori*.

[...]
[54]
[...]

§43. *The most complete definition of the essence of freedom.* Every time we freely will something we always resolve to do something, for which one or many desires are present in us, and the formal end (§13) therefore consists in the relation that a thing has to one or more of our drives. I am referring here to experience, and it will become even more clear once I have explained desires.[14] One will see, for example, that we act according to the drive for perfection when we do something merely in order to reassure ourselves or others that we are capable of doing it. Freedom is therefore a power that can only choose one among our many desires, according to which it acts or with which it wants to connect its activity. And with this we discover the most complete concept of freedom. That is, freedom consists in an internal, perfect activity of the will, which is capable of connecting its efficacy [55] with one of the currently aroused drives of the will, or of omitting this connection and remaining inactive, or of connecting it with another drive instead of the previous one.[15]

§44. *That we ascribe a goodness to everything that we will.* Since a thing is called good or evil in the physical sense (§26) because it is in accordance with or contrary to our volition, one can truly say of such a volition, whether it is freedom or a mere drive that is effective, that one always ascribes a goodness to that which one wills, and by contrast one holds something to be evil insofar as one is averse to it. On the other hand, it has already been noted above (§27) that it is not yet sufficient to conceive of the will as a power to desire the good and be averse to evil, without distinguishing between the differences that have been explained up until this point.

[...]
[60]
[...]

---

[14] Crusius discusses the nature of desire in Chapter IV of the Thelematology, §§58ff.
[15] Inserted in the second edition: "It can be easily seen that freedom can also connect its activity with those efficacious desires to a higher or lesser degree."

§49. *What perfect and imperfect freedom are.* Freedom is either **perfect** or **imperfect** (*Libertas* [61] *plena vel minus plena*). **Perfect freedom** obtains where the omission of something or the performance of another, with which it is presently compared, would be just as easy for us. **Imperfect freedom** obtains where it would not be just as easy for us to choose the alternative. Indeed, certain things can be completely impossible for freedom to do because the opposition that must be overcome entirely exceeds its capacity.

§50. *When perfect freedom takes place.* Perfect freedom is also called *libertas indifferentiae* or *aequilibrii*.[16] It does not always take place, but only in those cases where two objects are indifferent towards an end, at least as far as we know, or when we determine ourselves to one of two ends that we desire with an equal degree of strength. Given, as experience teaches us, we deceive ourselves in many ways when judging the indifference of both the ends and the means, when it comes to important matters, namely those cases where we have honestly intended to try our absolute best, we will be hesitant to recognize as indifferent the means that currently appear to us to be indifferent and to choose one among them (§45). This brings about hesitation and [62] in many cases true timidness. It might then come to pass that a certain kind of superstition arises in a soul or the opinion, based on confused representations, that in this way one would not be held responsible for taking a different point of departure when doing something. In such a case the free will would be determined by its own preconceived intention (§45) of preferring to leave the decision of something to lottery or blind luck as opposed to determining itself to something, by which means the sought-after end might possibly be harmed.

§51. *Kinds of imperfect freedom and how one assists it.* Imperfect freedom is when one must overcome an opposition when resolving to do the alternative (§49). Since the opposition can be greater or smaller, imperfect freedom varies greatly in degree. Even if the alternative were to sometimes come across as objectionable to us, we could still both undertake and achieve it. If we want to do the alternative, however, it is often necessary that we first think of motives for doing it and that we take control of and utilize all sorts of auxiliary causes, by means of which we can put the otherwise all too weak power of freedom in the position of being equal to the opposition. This is [63] similar to the case of a driver who wants to raise his carriage but finds himself too weak to do so himself, and so makes use of his winch or employs suspension, and in such a way advances a thing

---

[16] *freedom of indifference* or *equilibrium*

through clever means for which he was otherwise too weak. When one assists, in this way, one's all-too impotent resolution to accomplish that which one is not immediately capable of doing through contemplation, the representation of motives, and other means of assistance, then sometimes more and sometimes less time, effort, and prudence are required before one is in a position to actually put the resolution we have made into practice. This is why the mere intention to improve oneself, for example, does not generally succeed if one does not make the necessary preparations of strengthening the weak capacity for good against the overpowering strength of evil and thereby make the actual performance of good possible.

§52. *Imperfect freedom is not, on that account, always an imperfection.* Nonetheless, one should not be tempted to believe that every such imperfect freedom is in general and in every instance a defect and imperfection in the substance in which it is found. It is such only when [64] the end of freedom is contradicted, namely when one does not find oneself in a position to be able to choose the good or the better (§46). However, we should not abandon good ends. In fact, we should make them so firm through the correct use of freedom and habituate the mind to them in such a way that we are either not at all, or not very easily, capable of diverging from them. This kind of conditioned necessity can even subsequently be imputed to us in a true, moral way, just as that which we immediately perform freely. This remark must hold with respect to becoming accustomed to good as well as evil. *Three kinds of freedom: freedom to good, freedom to evil, and freedom to good and evil.* There are therefore three kinds of freedom: (1) a **freedom only to good**, which can only freely choose one among possible good deeds, (2) a **freedom only to evil**, which can only freely choose one among possible evil deeds, and (3) a **freedom to good and evil**, which can determine itself to good as well as evil deeds because both are possible for it. A finite spirit must be placed in the position of the latter at least once if it is to be capable of true moral virtue. The second kind is a disgraceful corruption of a free spirit. But the first is, in finite spirits, the aim [Endzweck] of conferring freedom upon them [65] and which they should attain by means of the correct use of the third kind of freedom (§46). Accordingly, freedom is not necessarily a power to act according to the best representations of the understanding. Rather, when one among the represented actions really is the best, in this case freedom **should** only be a power to be able to choose the best, and from God's point of view it **should** be employed in order to actually seize hold of this.
[...]
[109]

Chapter V
On Foundational Desires in General

§89. *There are first desires.* A desire has its ground in one or many other desires (§§74–77). But since this series cannot continue into infinity, we must eventually come upon **first desires** [110] that have not arisen through the impetus of others, and which are the ground of all the rest.

§90. *They are either essential or contingent.* We can conceive of two kinds of first desires. First and foremost, there must be those that belong to the human being itself as God has arranged it, because without these, all other contingent desires would be impossible. I wish to call these **foundational desires** in the broad sense. But there can also be **contingent first desires**, which count as first desires only because they are passed down from parents to children and which therefore do not belong to the first desires of human nature in general, but only to the first desires of human nature in the present state of the world or to this or that person in particular. Even if we do not sufficiently understand the way in which they are passed on, one can still infer from what experience teaches us that they do in fact exist. Many people have, for example, a natural aversion to certain animals because their mother was scared of them during pregnancy. One will be further convinced of this if one remembers from the holy Bible that there are [111] innate, evil inclinations, which will also be demonstrated from reason at the appropriate time.[17]

§91. *It is necessary that there are foundational desires.* Each and every rational spirit must have foundational desires. For, if such a spirit did not, it would not be capable of enjoying pleasure, nor of experiencing displeasure, and thus neither would it be capable of happiness (§24). Alternatively, if such a spirit were able to make any given thing pleasurable by means of its free volition, not only would all regularity in the consequences of its actions be abolished, because one would not be able to control such a spirit by means of motives, but it would also be an independent master of its own happiness, in that it could achieve happiness from all things, but thereby make all punishment of evil impossible.

§92. *For this reason, there are also innate ideas.* Each and every volition is an action according to ideas (§2). A desire, however, is a persistent striving to act in a certain way according to certain ideas (§23). Thus, if there are foundational desires, there also innate ideas belonging to them, and which

---

[17] Crusius discusses this topic in Chapter 4 of the Ethics section of the *Guide*. See especially §§250ff.

must be simultaneously accepted as a presupposed and inseparable fact along with them. *Of which, however, we cannot become conscious.* However, it does not therefore follow that we must be capable [112] of becoming conscious of such ideas, since experience teaches that we cognize them by means of nothing other than inferences. For, consciousness has its special causes and conditions, which is undeniable on the basis of the fact that, among the large number of ideas that are currently in our memory, we are conscious of only very few of them at once. Thus, the constitution of the soul may be such that the necessary conditions of consciousness cannot be connected to the innate ideas belonging to foundational desires. Immediate consciousness of them must therefore be excluded. Experience teaches that things really are this way. The laws, according to which our soul has been connected to the world and made a resident of it, include one that says we can become conscious of no other ideas than those to which external perception gives rise, or those which can be extracted from external perception through analysis and inference. Now, since the stated innate ideas are aspects of efficient causes, namely foundational desires, they are already efficacious before we cognize them distinctly, and it is on the basis of this efficacy that we must prove their existence.

[...]
[115]
[...]

§95. *Foundational desires are either animal or human.* Foundational desires are either **animal**, which we have in common with other animals and which concern the ends of animal nature, or **human**, which we have over and above animals, [116] and which concern an object that must be thought in an abstract idea.
[...]
[133]

Chapter VII
On Human Foundational Desires

§111. *The first foundational drive: for our own perfection.* I understand human foundational desires to be those whose object is something that must be thought in an abstract idea and which human nature therefore has over and above other animals. I oppose these to merely animal drives (§95). The first among human foundational drives is the **drive for our own perfection** or the striving to see our condition in its appropriate perfection and to perpetually make it more perfect. The idea belonging to this drive in the understanding, and which offers the model of its actions (§92), is a continual *plus ultra*, that is, **the idea of the continual increase** of our powers and perfections.

[...]
[136]
[...]

§114. *How many kinds of perfection there are.* In order to understand the diverse effects of the drive of perfection, one must consider that, in general, a thing always becomes more perfect when it becomes capable of more activities and effects, and thus the sum of the things that are possible by means of it increases. For, perfection in general consists in nothing other than the comparison of the state of a thing with the sum of those activities and effects that are possible by means of it, and as these increase, so does perfection, which is a topic that belongs to ontology.[18] More specifically, however, one must assess the perfection of a thing on the basis of the idea that one has of the essence of that thing. For, one could not really say that this or that thing has become more perfect if it has not become more perfect with respect to the essence, by means of which we conceive of it. There are therefore **two kinds of perfection**: **essential** perfection, by means of which the essence that we consider in relation to a thing becomes more perfect, and **contingent** perfection, by means of which the thing in general becomes capable of more effects, [137] even if such things do not concern the currently considered essence. For example, it is an essential perfection of an astronomical globe that the poles are placed in the correct location but, on the other hand, it is a contingent perfection that it has an expensive stand.

[...]
[145]
[...]

§122. *The second foundational drive: the striving for unification with that in which we perceive perfection.* The second among the human foundational drives is the **striving for unification with those objects, in which we perceive perfection**, or in which we think we perceive perfection. It is distinguished from the former in that by means of the first we desire our own perfection, but by means of the second we wish for and take pleasure

---

[18] Crusius discusses perfection in Chapter XI of the Ontology section of his metaphysics. See *Sketch*, §§180ff.

in the unification with that which is perfect even **without relation to ourselves and to the advantage** that we can expect from it.
[...]
[157]
[...]

§132. *The third foundational drive: the drive of conscience.* Finally, the third among the human foundational drives is the natural drive to cognize a divine moral law, that is, to believe in a rule of human action wherein it is determined what God demands be done or omitted out of obedience and for the sake of our dependence on him and which he would otherwise punish. Since it is one of the natural, foundational laws of the human soul, according to which the effects of the soul follow upon one another, to compare the concepts of the understanding to our desires in order to become conscious of what in the objects of desire are in accordance with or are opposed to the understanding (§60), an inclination arises to judge the morality, that is, the correctness [Gerechtigkeit] or incorrectness [Ungerechtigkeit] of one's acts and to fear God's wrath and punishment insofar as they are not in accordance with the law. [158] *What conscience is.* Now, one calls the judgement about the morality of one's acts **conscience**. *First concept of the drive of conscience.* We therefore wish to call the foundational drive to cognize a divine, moral law, which is the ground of this law, the **drive of conscience**. *That conscience has its ground in a drive of the will.* That conscience is no mere theoretical judgement of the understanding but must have its ground in a drive of the will can already be judged from the fact that conscience pleases and frightens (§24). *Caution against confusion.* One should not, however, confuse conscience with consciousness in general, or with consciousness of the perfection or imperfection of one's acts in general.[19] For it is one thing to have a conscience about something and another to be conscious[20] generally of an imperfection in one's action and omission and to experience remorse for one's acts because one is conscious that they are of no use, or contrary to their end, or harmful, or that one thereby acted contrary to love. For, even if other kinds of remorse can be connected to the consciousness of a violated divine law at the same time, this does not also mean that the state of saying

---

[19] Inserted in the second edition: ", nor with the mere consciousness of dissimulation [Verstellung] or of one's own prompting a thing, even if one tends to say in common conversation that, in these two latter cases, someone has a good or evil conscience, or that such a person is punished by their conscience."

[20] Inserted in the second edition: "of the absence of truth, or"

that we have a conscience about something is connected to the latter. For example, one can be conscious that [159] one has improperly cut a quill due to rashness, and the rashness can therefore cause us to feel remorse without our having a conscience about it. The German word conscience [Gewissen] does not express that which is called *conscientia* by the good Latinists, but that which is called *religio*.

§133. *What obligations of indebtedness* [Schuldigkeiten][21] *are*. The drive of conscience is therefore merely a drive to cognize certain **obligations of indebtedness**, that is, those universal obligations [Verbindlichkeiten] that one must observe even if one does not wish to take into consideration the advantage or harm resulting from them, and whose violation God will nonetheless punish and also must punish if his law is not to be in vain. The proof that there are such obligations of indebtedness, and thus that there are true, moral laws of God, does not yet belong here but will be thoroughly carried out at its appropriate place.[22] Presently, and for the sake of explaining things further, I only wish to include the proof that we connect the concept I have provided to the word 'indebtedness' in line with the guidance of nature. *Proof of the provided definition*. This is clear in the following way: we differentiate that which lays an obligation of indebtedness upon us from motives in general, and if we have been made to be inclined towards something by means of motives [160] or even thereby completely determined, it does not therefore follow that we had an obligation of indebtedness to do it. For, there are also motives to evil as well as to indifferent things. Furthermore, indebtedness is distinct from all internal and external constraint [Zwange]. For, if one is constrained to something, then one does not yet for that reason have an obligation of indebtedness to do it. We distinguish indebtedness even further from that which one does out of fear or hope. For, how much does one do out of fear, but to which one is not obligated, and how often do we say that such things are advantageous but that we also have an obligation of indebtedness to do them? Finally, indebtedness is also not the same as that which one does merely from love. For, all human beings agree that an obligation of indebtedness cannot be the kind of thing that depends on our own discretion when it comes to whether or not we do it. That is, the essence of indebtedness is not the kind of thing

---

[21] The most obvious translation for this term is simply 'obligation,' but since 'obligation' is reserved for '*Verbindlichkeit*' and, as Crusius goes on to explain in this section, a *Schuldigkeit* is a specific kind of obligation, namely one that we should perform out of the obedience that we owe (*schuldig*) to God, I have rendered '*Schuldigkeit*' as either 'obligation of indebtedness' or simply 'indebtedness,' depending on the context.
[22] See below §§168ff.

that can cease to exist through the alteration of our will. Accordingly, nothing else remains than for an obligation of indebtedness to be the kind of action or omission that we should observe solely from obedience to God as our highest sovereign, creator, and keeper and for the sake of his command. [161] *What statutory[23] obligation and dependence are.* The true, basic essence of statutory obligation therefore resides in the drive of conscience. For, the obligation of the law should be that which drives subjects to obey the commands of their sovereign. But this can be nothing other than the representation of their dependence on such an authority. With respect to spirits, dependence should be understood as nothing other than the kind of relation of one to another where the one receives certain goods from the will of the other, in such a way that if this will were absent, so would be the goods. It is therefore obvious that we depend on God in every respect. *The necessity of a foundational drive to this.* But how could the representation of dependence in and of itself drive us to satisfy the commands of our sovereign, if there were no natural, foundational drive in us to act in accordance with our dependence on God?

§134. *That the drive of conscience is a distinct and good drive.* It will not therefore be necessary to separately prove that the drive of conscience is a foundational drive that is distinct from the others, since its object is so very different from the objects of all the other drives. It would be just as unnecessary to prove its goodness, since [162] it is clear from itself that nothing can be good without agreeing with divine law. For, not only would there be no moral goodness, but, because God must punish the violation of the law, there would also be no physical good (§26).
[...]
[166]
[...]

§137. *That we have an innate idea of divine law.* Now, if there is a drive in us to cognize a divine law and act in accordance with it, then there must be an innate idea of the natural law in us, which is the model, according to which the drive of conscience dictates [wissen will] human acts be arranged. But one need not accept this in a way that would imply that the idea of all individual duties must be implanted in us. It is sufficient if God has impressed upon us a universal rule of our acts, on the basis of which individual cases can be judged. *What this is.* If we now consider, *a posteriori,*

---

[23] The German word here is '*gesetzlich.*' The obvious translations for this term, namely 'legal' or 'lawful,' have undesirable connotations in English, so I have chosen 'statutory' in line with the archaic sense of 'statute,' namely a law or decree made by a sovereign or by God, which, as we will see, is precisely the sense in which Crusius uses this term.

the material duties that conscience teaches, it becomes clear that the majority of them can be captured [167] by this rule: **do that which is in accordance with the perfection of God and your relation to him, and furthermore what is in accordance with the essential perfection of human nature, and omit the opposite.** However, the acts of a spirit are only said to be in accordance with a perfection if one can understand on the basis of their arrangement that the spirit cognized perfection and had it before its eyes. *Complete definition of the essence of the drive of conscience.* Accordingly, we can justifiably establish the full concept of the drive of conscience in the following way: **the drive of conscience** is a natural, foundational drive, which urges us to observe that which is essentially in accordance with divine and human perfection, from obedience to God's will and for the sake of our dependence on him, and to otherwise fear his wrath and punishment. *That there is an innate idea of God.* We simultaneously note here that, for this reason, there is also an innate idea of God. [...]

Ethics
or
the Doctrine of the Virtuous Arrangement of the Mind

[195]

Chapter I
On Virtue in General
and the Concepts Belonging therein,
as well as the Moral Sciences in General

§155. *What the guide to living rationally is.* After having treated the powers and properties of the human will in the thelematology and thereby explained the way in which the will exists and operates by nature (§2), I can now turn to the guide to living rationally itself or the doctrine of how the human will **should** be and act, the doctrine one also calls **moral science** [Moral] or **practical philosophy**. Accordingly, I understand the **guide to living rationally** to be the science containing the rules of how the human will should be constituted and how it should act according to the prescription of reason.

§156. *How many kinds of rules there are to live rationally.* If one asks how the will should be constituted, and wants to determine this solely according to the [196] prescription of reason, then one compares the will either to the universal laws of God that are to be known through reason, that is, through the observation of created things, and seeks to know what these are and how one should conduct oneself in conformity to them, or one compares the will to human happiness and perfection only and seeks to clarify the rules of how the will must arrange its action and omission in order to promote, as best as possible, the perfection and happiness of both each individual human being in particular and everyone as a whole. To summarize, one asks either how the human will should be constituted **in relation to divine natural laws**, which one regards as the ends of the creator, or how it should be constituted **in relation to the ends** that all human beings desire, namely in relation to the promotion of their perfection and happiness.

§157. *That the state of human perfection and happiness are the same thing.* I have combined the state of one's own perfection and that of human happiness for good reason. For, these two concepts refer to the exact same thing. For, human perfection obtains when one's condition agrees with all of one's ends [197] (§115). Consequently, all of a human being's wishes must thereby be fulfilled as best as possible and as many good things as possible must be achieved for them (§26). Happiness, however, is a state, in which all our wishes are fulfilled with pleasure and with complete assurance (§106). Happiness therefore arises from the state [Stande] of perfection, and in both cases, one refers to the same thing.

§158. *The striving for happiness first leads human beings to the necessity of moral science.* Now, that which tends to lead human beings to the necessity of moral science or of a guide to living rationally is nothing other than the striving for their happiness. The necessity of finding rules for how one can obtain this important end as best and as securely as possible is incontrovertibly clear from the fact that human beings universally [allerseits] desire and pursue happiness, as well as from the fact that experience teaches us not only that there is more than just one path leading to it, but also that many human beings deceive themselves terribly when it comes to choosing the means to it. Accordingly, it is incontrovertible that the means to happiness must be investigated and presented in the guide to living rationally. [198]

§159. *Human beings are thereby led to investigate both divine laws and their actuality.* But if one determines the concept of moral science from the beginning in such a way that it is to signify the science of the rules that show the path to human happiness, this is how we will be led to the necessity of investigating whether there are divine laws, on the one hand, and to their actuality, on the other hand.[24] Thus, assuming that

---

[24] Inserted in the second edition: "For, if there are divine laws, then God intends the moral obedience of his rational creatures; he asks of them that they make it their highest end to seek God and do his will, and he has resolved that they will attain happiness on these conditions. These two aspects are, at all times, inseparable. If divine laws are possible, then it must be granted that it is possible that God's main intention is that we morally choose him and obey him. And if divine laws do actually

there are divine laws, we would forfeit our happiness if we were to not concern ourselves with them and not live according to them. Consequently, we must concern ourselves with them. Additionally, however, if we ourselves consider the means to our happiness and on this account investigate the essence and perfection of human nature, we would thereby simultaneously discover incontrovertible grounds of proof that there are divine laws and why they exist, as will become clear further below.[25] Indeed, it will be shown that divine laws prescribe to us nothing other than the true means to our happiness and perfection, that concern for our perfection and happiness itself is included in them, and that they, for the most part, must be proven from the arrangement of the world, by virtue of which God has inexorably [199] connected certain means to the end of our well-being. From this it is clear that the guide to living rationally is both a doctrine of the natural laws of God as well as of the means to our perfection and happiness, and that it must simultaneously be the one if it is to also be the other. Nevertheless, it will be shown in the following[26] that there are also rules for the attainment of our own good ends which are, for that reason, not yet laws and must not be confused with them, but which, this notwithstanding, are to be examined in moral science so long as they are universal. *More detailed description of the guide to living rationally.* I can therefore describe the **guide to living rationally** in more detail in the following way: it is a science which illustrates, from reason, both divine laws as well as other universal rules for the attainment of good ends, and thereby shows, as best as possible, the way to attain human perfection and happiness.

§160. *What duties and obligations are.* A **duty in the broad sense** is an action or omission, to which there exists a moral necessity. A **moral necessity** is the kind of relation of an action or omission to certain ends, on the basis of which a rational spirit can understand that [200] it should be done or omitted. The state in which a moral necessity to something exists is called **obligation** in the broad sense. Accordingly, moral science deals with duties and obligations.

---

exist, then it is certain that God intends to be freely chosen as our highest good and demands that he be obeyed."

[25] See §170 of the *Guide*, where Crusius presents his second proof that there are natural laws, which is derived from the nature of happiness.

[26] See §161 and §162 below on prudence and §165 on the nature of laws.

§161. *What prudence and virtue are and, similarly, what 'moral' means.* By **prudence** we understand the proficiency in choosing and applying good means to one's ends. **Virtue**, on the other hand, is the agreement of a spirit's moral state with the divine law. One therefore calls each individual part of such a state a virtue. I am not oblivious to the fact that the word 'virtue' is sometimes used in the broader sense of each and every praiseworthy property. This meaning does not currently serve my purpose because I want to distinguish things that are essentially different from each other. I call **moral** everything that produces its effect by means of a free will. For example, a speech is a moral means of moving someone. Accordingly, when I say that virtue is an agreement of a spirit's moral state with the divine law, I mean that everything that depends on our free will in any way and is either immediately produced by it, [201] or is a consequence of its activities, or could have been subordinated to it, should agree with divine law.

§162. *What a duty or obligation of prudence is and, similarly, what a statutory duty or obligation is.* I am now able to illustrate the two kinds of duties and obligations, concepts which were discussed in §160. That upon which the moral necessity of an action or omission is based, I mean, that on the basis of which moral necessity is to be understood, is to be sought, first, in certain ends already desired by us in advance. Since we only need to consider the ends that are essential to thelematology in accordance with human nature, which one would not be able to encounter in any other form, I call the duty that is grounded thereupon, and to the extent that it is so grounded, a **duty of prudence** (§161), just as the obligation that emerges from it can be called the **obligation of prudence**. Or, second, the ground of moral necessity lies in a law and in our indebtedness to fulfill it. I call such a duty a **duty of virtue**. The obligation that emerges from this can be called **statutory obligation** or the **obligation of virtue** or also **true obligation** in the narrow sense. Accordingly, the **obligation of prudence** in [202] moral science is the relation of an action or omission to certain ends that we desire on account of our nature and to the extent that we desire them, which makes it such that if we do not proceed in this or that way, these ends cannot be obtained. The **obligation of virtue** is the relation of an action or omission to a divine law, which makes it such that if we do not proceed in this or that way, the law will be infringed upon. A **duty of prudence** is that to which an obligation of prudence exists. A **duty of virtue**, on the other hand, is that to which an obligation of virtue exists. That to which a statutory obligation exists one also tends to call an obligation of indebtedness.

[...]
[206]
[...]

§165. *What a law and a sovereign are.* It is necessary that I here further explain the concept of divine law, even though the definition of it has already been given (§132, 133). A **law** is a general will of an authority who does not in turn have another authority above it, by means of which those [207] who are subjected to the authority are issued an obligation of indebtedness to do or omit something, which originates from the authority's will. The same authority that gives the law is called a **sovereign**. I therefore always require there to be a kind of generality in the law so that it is distinguished from individual commands. This is done only to determine the concept very precisely. For, with respect to the obligation to the will of God it does not matter whether this is a general will or a particular command, only that we know nothing of the latter in philosophy. *What obedience is.* When one observes the will of one's sovereign out of indebtedness, this is called **obedience**. Now, all indebtedness is grounded on dependence. For, since this is supposed to be, according to its primary concept, the kind of relation that carries along with it a moral necessity to fulfill a law, insofar as the law is a law, even if we do not therein include consideration of our own advantage and disadvantage, nothing else remains than for it to be the representation of dependence, which is made efficacious in us precisely by means of it being able to drive us to obedience, because there is a foundational drive in us to act in accordance with it (§133). *Further definition of law.* Accordingly, a **law** is a general will [208] of an independent sovereign, wherein it is determined what the people who depend on the sovereign should do or omit out of obedience to the sovereign's command, with the intention of acting in accordance with their dependence on the sovereign.

§166. *What dependence is.* Two things depend on each other insofar as the one must receive something from the other. Accordingly, the **dependence** of spirits on each other is the relation, by means of which the one receives certain goods from the will of the other in such a way that, if this will were absent, the goods would also be absent (§133). On this basis, one sees how true moral dependence is distinct from the mere overpowering authority of one individual over another, as well as what kind of difference there is between a sovereign, whose will has an obligating power, and an authority who only constrains another to carry out their will. For example, a street robber can compel us to give them our cash, but no obligation to

do so issues from the will of such a person, which would take place with a true lawgiver. That is, we owe thanks to a lawgiver for certain goods that are to be ascribed solely to its will [209] because it has no other superior above it. Thus, not only does our advantage require that we obey the lawgiver so that we do not lose these goods, but our perfection requires this as well because resistance would be to no avail, and both together comprise the obligation of prudence. Additionally, we experience an obligation of indebtedness to obedience and we naturally approve it by means of the drive of conscience (§133), and on this basis a statutory obligation comes into being. [...]
[210]
[...]

§168. *What is involved in proving the actuality of natural laws.* I must now, first and foremost, demonstrate the actuality of divine laws according to the precise sense in which I have adopted and proven on the basis of the use of language in §133 and §165. Three things are involved in this: (1) that one cognizes that there is an independent God, (2) that human beings depend on him, and (3) that he demands [211] of them that something be done or omitted in relation to, and for the sake of, this dependence, and has revealed this will in nature. For, if it is true that the lawgiver exists, if the previously stated dependence is a true one such that the law, if there is one, is able to obligate, and if he also demands that something be observed for the sake of dependence and has revealed this will in nature, then no justified possibility remains of calling the actuality of divine natural laws into doubt. Now, I here presuppose the actuality and properties of God from natural theology. Precisely for this reason, I also presuppose that the human being absolutely, singularly and alone, and necessarily, and thus completely, depends on God with respect to its existence, essence, and entire well-being. Accordingly, in this instance I only need to prove that God demands of human beings that certain things be done or omitted and that they thereby make it their end to be obedient so that they act in accordance with their essential dependence on God. Since I will prove this from reason, it is clear of itself that God's will is revealed to human beings through nature [212] and can be cognized by them if they only use their understanding. *Complete definition of a natural law.* The complete concept of a **divine, natural law**, if we concisely summarize everything, is therefore this: it is a general, obligating will of God's, which is revealed to human beings through the nature of created things themselves and the use of their reason, wherein what they should do or omit is

specified so that they thereby may act in accordance with their dependence on God.
[...]
[213]
[...]

§171. *Third proof of the actuality and necessity of natural laws a priori.*[27] Furthermore, the necessity of divine laws, [214] as well as their content, can be proven *a priori* in the following way.[*] I presuppose that God necessarily wills the essential perfection of things and what is essentially connected to this because, without this will, he himself would not possess all possible perfections and thus would not be the most perfect being. I am only speaking about essential perfections (§114, 115) on purpose, for I have no reason to make this claim in relation to those that are contingent, precisely because they are contingent and therefore have no connection to the ends that God has put in place, and towards which a wise being orients itself singularly and alone; this is how he is able to concern himself with such things, his wisdom notwithstanding. From this it follows that, as soon as we assume that there are free creatures, God must also necessarily will that their free actions and what depends on them should be in accordance with the essential perfection of things. Now, two things should be considered in relation to such matters: first, the essence of any given thing in particular and, second, the relations and connections that hold among things. Accordingly, God necessarily wills that free actions and what depends on them should be in accordance with that which is in agreement with the rules of [215] essential perfection with respect to: the essence of God, the essence of free creatures themselves, the essence of other creatures, and finally also with respect to the relations in which they stand to both God and each other. We will now set aside the first part of the

---

[27] Crusius presents three proofs for the actuality of natural laws, the first two of which are *a posteriori* proofs. According to the first, there must be natural laws because the drive of conscience must have an object; otherwise, God would have created this drive for no reason (which would be contrary to divine perfection). According to the second, there must be natural laws because living according to them is the only way we can satisfy the drive of conscience and thereby achieve happiness. The idea of the second proof is that, if there were no natural laws but we were to nonetheless possess the drive of conscience, then we could never satisfy all of our drives and become truly happy (but, again, God's perfection prevents this from being the case). I have only translated the third proof because it is the only *a priori* proof that Crusius offers, and thus the one most worth comparing to Kant's deduction of the moral law.

[*] Compare *Metaphysics* §§282–85. [Footnote added in the second edition.]

conclusion we have illustrated and consider, more particularly, what is in accordance with the relation that a creature has to God.

§172. *Continuation.* An action of a rational spirit is in accordance with perfection when one can understand from its arrangement that the spirit cognizes perfection and has it before its eyes (§137). Thus, the action is in accordance with the relation to God when one can infer from its arrangement that the rational spirit cognizes that same relation and has it before its eyes. Now, the natural relation in which we and all creatures stand to God is this: that we in every respect necessarily depend on him entirely and alone (§166, 168). This is the only state that is absolutely essential to us. All other states are contingent to us. Thus, a being who loves essential perfection must focus more on that state [216] than on all others. God therefore necessarily wills that all the free actions of rational creatures, and what depends on them, are arranged in such a way that one can understand from their arrangement that such creatures cognize their complete and necessary dependence on God and have this before their eyes. Alternatively, but which is the same, God wills that rational creatures arrange their free actions in accordance with dependence on God.

§173. *Continuation.* Now, our acts are not yet in accordance with dependence on God if we will precisely that which he wills, even though this is also required for another reason with certain qualifications (§171). For, on the basis of two wills being similar, it cannot yet be seen that the one cognizes a dependence on the other. Furthermore, it is not yet sufficient if we do everything that God wills because he wills it and out of love (§125), even though this is also required for other reasons. For, that a spirit seeks to make itself agreeable to another out of love does not yet let one see that a spirit cognizes a dependence on another and has this before its eyes. Consequently, besides the former, the following must also be added: that we do everything God demands, [217] namely that which is in accordance with the essential perfection of things, out of obedience to him as our creator, keeper, and our sovereign and lawgiver who bindingly commands us. For, it is on the basis of such an arrangement of our acts that it can be seen that we cognize dependence on God and have this before our eyes. Since God necessarily wills that we should act for the sake of our dependence on him, a divine natural law is necessary as well, whose content hereby simultaneously becomes clear. *Whether something can be morally good without relating to the divine will.* Precisely this necessary will of God's is the ground of moral goodness (§26), from which one sees that moral goodness has its ground in a will, as do all the other goods. Regardless of whether one can likewise say that something is in accordance with or contrary to perfection without relating to the will of God, it is nonetheless not possible for one to grant that something is morally good or evil without relating to the will of God, because, if one were to do this, one would either contradict oneself or unnecessarily alter the customary concepts of good and evil (§26). However, moral goodness is not for this reason arbitrary, because the will of God, in which the natural, highest laws have their ground, is not a free but a necessary volition. [218]

§174. *What the highest natural, foundational law is.* Thus, I have hereby derived the highest, natural foundational law *a priori*, which I only accepted on the basis of experience in §137, and which is this: **do everything that is in accordance with the perfection of God, the essential perfection of your own nature and that of all other creatures, and finally also the relations of things to each other that he has established, and omit the opposite, out of obedience to the command of your creator, as your natural and necessary sovereign.**

§175. *Complete definition of virtue.* Since **virtue** is an agreement of a spirit's moral state with divine law (§161), according to its complete concept it is also a proficiency in observing everything that is in accordance with the essential perfection of God, ourselves, and all other things, from obedience to the divine will as our sovereign.

§176. *Elucidation of what the resulting end of virtue is.* The view is that obedience to God (§165) should be our absolute highest (§18) subjective end, God himself the [219] highest objective end, and the fulfillment of his will and command the highest formal end (§13), to which all other ends and desires should be subordinated (§17), even the desire for our advantage and the aversion to our harm. Our happiness therefore results from virtue and occurs in the state [Stand] of virtue itself, which we can and thus also should desire, seek, and accept with gratitude. However, we are not permitted to make happiness the end of obedience, because the latter would thereby lose its essence (§133). *By what means the exercise of virtue becomes possible.* In order for it to be possible for us to make the desire to act in accordance with our dependence into a main end, the drive of conscience has been implanted in us, by means of which the sensation of dependence urges us to obedience and we are able to be obedient with pleasure, if only we grant the drive of conscience authority in our soul, which we will soon treat in more detail.[28] If the drive of conscience were not in us, neither obedience nor virtue would be possible, because we would only ever make our advantage or pleasure into an end by means of

---

[28] See for example §178.

our other essential drives, or at the very least act merely from love (§43), but which would not [220] yet be obedience (§165, 173). *That one can prove a sufficient obligation to virtue in no other way.* Quite a lot depends on the fact that one correctly comprehends this ground of the obligation of virtue, because not only can no true statutory obligation be proven otherwise, but neither can a sufficient obligation of prudence (§162). For, should the obligation to virtue be based on nothing other than the fact that virtue promotes our own advantage in the world, one would be able to shirk such an obligation if one were to say that they do not want to follow virtue in certain situations and voluntarily renounced the advantage to be expected from it. One could also object that virtue would be the best means to happiness if it were practiced by everyone. But since this is not the case, the guarantee of this means disappears and so does the obligation to it as well. Indeed, if one does not accept true statutory obligation but only takes the obligation of prudence to be the basis of natural duties, then it might follow from this that the more a human being allows themselves to be driven by God's command and one's indebtedness to virtue, the more imperfect his virtue becomes, which is frightening to say.[29]

[...]
[247]
[...]

§203. *What the law of nature is in the broad sense.* The overarching concept of all duties of virtue taken together, which reason illustrates, is called **the law of nature in the broad sense**. Now, since all duties of virtue have their obligation from God and [248] must be performed out of obedience to divine command (§173), the law of nature is, according to its essence, nothing other than the practical part of natural theology.

§204. *Division of it into natural moral theology, the law of nature in the narrow sense, and ethics.* So that the extent of a single science does not become too great, custom has established setting that which is similar apart from the rest, and the law of nature can be quite comfortably divided into three sciences, according to the three main species of duties that occur in

---

[29] Inserted in the second edition: "This implication follows because, according to the opinion of those who do not base virtue on true, divine obligation, the people who obey God's command replace the internal and either the one true or at least the most honourable ground of obligation with an external and merely contingent, and thus dishonourable, one. In this way, the essence of virtue must necessarily become worse, just as a mass of matter becomes less valuable if instead of a precious material one inserts a non-precious one instead or if, for example, one pours water into wine or mixes silver into a mass of gold."

it, which division I will follow here. That is, **natural moral theology** treats immediate duties to God, **the law of nature in the narrow sense** the duties and rights of human beings to other human beings, and **ethics** the duties that immediately concern the virtuous arrangement of our own mind and state, which one commonly calls duties to oneself. Even though a considerable number of things can, in my opinion, justifiably be objected to the correctness of this designation, I do not wish to pursue this matter further because it concerns a semantic dispute [Wortstreit]. There are indeed other duties that reason cognizes, namely duties with regard to non-rational and [249] lifeless creatures.[30] But since they can be easily understood on the basis of the universal, foundational laws of virtue (§174) and can justifiably be included in the other sciences, it is not necessary to create a special part of natural law for it. *Why ethics is treated first*. Since, however, the duties to be explained in ethics are not only natural duties but are simultaneously preparation of the mind for the remaining virtues, by means of which the fulfillment of such duties is first made possible, it is in accordance with the natural order of things that they are treated first.

§205. *What the doctrine of prudence is and how one arrives at the concept of it.* One of the ethical duties is the obligation to prudence (§161), as will be shown in the following. But there are also certain universal and useful rules of prudence that one can subsequently employ in relation to all other ends, even those to which one has no obligation. These must also be treated in moral science. But they do not belong to the law of nature itself, just as there is little reason to include the doctrine of reason, for example, in the law of nature on account of the fact that we have the duty to strive for the cognition of truth. On this basis, [250] a special science emerges, namely the **doctrine of prudence**, which treats the universal rules of how one should acquire a proficiency in prudence. *What the two essentially distinct parts of moral science are.* Moral science therefore includes two essentially different parts, namely, first, the **doctrine of the duties of virtue**, or the **law of nature** in the broad sense (§204) with its three sciences, and second, the **doctrine of prudence**.

§206. *How universal practical philosophy will be treated.* One could also create an additional moral science [moralische Wissenschaft], namely **universal practical philosophy**, wherein one would define and prove

---

[30] *Pflichten in Ansehung der unvernünftigen und leblosen Geschöpfe.* This calls to mind Kant's distinction in the *Metaphysics of Morals* between duties to (*gegen*) other beings and duties with regard to (*in Ansehung*) other beings (6:442.24–25). Crusius uses the same language here.

the concepts and principles of moral things that are already presupposed when defining determinate duties. Included here are the doctrine of virtue in general and the concepts that arise in it, e.g., those of laws, punishments, imputation, and so forth, as well as the actuality of divine laws, the division of duties and rights, the settling of conflicting duties, and similar things. But because this science, if it is to be foundational, is very abstract, and therefore dry, and because one does not need everything that arises in universal practical philosophy in ethics and natural moral theology, I have [251] preferred to distribute the material and, in the presently treated chapter, supply only as much as has been necessary. I have saved the rest, without harming truth and order, for the law of nature in the narrow sense, where we will need it for the first time.[31]

Chapter II
On the End of Human Life

§207. *Why the end of our life is treated first.* In the ethics (§204) we should now show how we should arrange the state of our soul virtuously (§174), that is, in accordance with the rules of essential perfection. But because this can be judged on the basis of nothing other than the nature of perfection in general and the specific intentions of God, according to which we were created (§181), we must first treat the end of human life.

§208. *What the end of human life is.* The **end** of the world, as far as human beings are concerned, is this: **that they** [252] **cultivate, practice, and strengthen virtue in their souls through their free, collective efforts** (§175), **and thus that they should be permitted to enjoy the goods of the world, without damaging virtue** (§186), **for their contentment and pleasure, after which they will be placed in a different, eternal life, in which the virtuous will be made completely happy and the disobedient will be punished, and in which both rewards and punishments are distributed according to the proportion of virtue or vice**. I will now go through this principle and prove it piece by piece.

§209. *A posteriori proof that the world was created for the sake of an end.* That **the world was created by God for the sake of an end** is clear, first, *a posteriori* from the regularity shining forth from both the individual parts of the world as well as from contemplating the whole. One might of course

---

[31] Crusius treats the law of nature in the narrow sense, i.e., duties and rights to others, in part four of the *Guide*.

object that much in the world seems to be entirely disorganized and irregular. But I answer that this only appears to be the case because we do not assess the whole in its context. An order [253] can indeed be gleaned from a part of the whole, namely the kind which is to be found in that part. On the other hand, if one wants to reliably judge disorder, one must sufficiently assess the whole and know its purposes, because it can very well be that something appears to be a disorder in the parts but serves the end of the whole or can at the very least coexist with the latter. True disorder only takes place in that state of the world that is subordinated to the free actions of created beings, and which therefore could have caused destruction in it without God being to blame. *A priori proof.* But it is clear *a priori* that the world must have been created by God for the sake of an end because he is the most perfect and most wise being. *How the end of the world must be constituted.* Since striving for perfection and goodness are the only two final subjective ends in God (§13, 15), as is to be proven in natural theology, it is also immediately clear that the end of the world must be constituted in a way that is in accordance with these divine properties.

§210. *That human beings are the final, objective end of God*. We now further inquire into the **final, objective ends of God** (§13). These must be constituted [254] in such a way that they can cognize and enjoy the world, because otherwise many goods that are capable of being enjoyed would have been created for nothing. Now, only rational enjoyment (§13)[32] is to be considered a real enjoyment. Accordingly, the world must have been created for rational spirits, among which human beings are included. If God is good, then he must have wanted to reveal his goodness in the world (§209). But since this is not possible if rational spirits do not enjoy certain goods in a way that is in conformity with the perfections of God, it is obvious that the world must have been intended for rational spirits. *A posteriori* we find no other rational spirits on earth's surface than human beings. For, other animals do not have reason (§25, 147). Beasts and plants are of no further use to human beings than to the extent that they are further cultivated, that is, become suitable to our ends. Thus, we are not here for their sake, but they are here for our sake. Accordingly, human beings are God's final, objective end, and the earth's surface, at least, was created for their sake.

---

[32] In §13 of the *Guide* Crusius defines enjoyment (*Genuss*) in the broad sense as "that state of a spirit where the desired object is unified with this spirit in the way that it wishes." In the narrow sense, however, he says that 'rational enjoyment' is this same desired unification with the object, but of which the spirit is distinctly conscious, and thus which only noble spirits are capable of experiencing.

§211. *God's end with respect to human beings must be something that can be fostered through free acts.* It is now to be further inquired, what kinds of acts and what kind of human state [255] are God's formal end with respect to human beings (§13). Concerning this, it can first be proven that God's **formal end** with respect to human beings must be something that should be fostered through their **free acts** (§38, 39, 41, 43). One can understand this *a posteriori*, in that God made human beings free.[33] *A priori*, however, the necessity[34] is to be gleaned from the fact that, were this not the case, the world would have been created in vain from God's point of view. For, it would be as if God did everything himself. Things would therefore receive, through their existence, no other relation to God than that which they had previously in the state [Stande] of their possibility, namely that their possibility and actuality depended on God. But the idea that God has of his power to create a world does not thereby become more distinct if he creates one. Thus, if he brings about only those things that are, in every aspect, determined by himself, from his point of view it does not matter whether they exist or not, thus creation is, from God's point of view, pointless. But on account of his perfection God can do nothing that is pointless. Thus, when he creates a world, things must come about in it that are not [256] determined by him in every aspect, that is, which happen freely (§47), and the freedom of such things must be a necessary aspect of his final, formal end.[*] *Reply to an objection.* I know quite well that some think that the creation of the world would not be pointless even if no free acts at all were intended, because creatures would thereby still be blessed with an enjoyment of the good. But this is not the question. If a rational being does something according to the rules of wisdom, then, with respect to the acting being itself, a certain relationship must be made possible which the thing, to which it relates, did not have previously. For, otherwise it would act without an end, namely without a formal end, which must indeed accompany every end (§13), and this would be contrary to wisdom.

§212. *The end of human beings should be obtained communally.* Furthermore, we learn *a posteriori* that God's end with respect to human

---

[33] Inserted in the second edition: ", and at the same time because freedom is, according to its nature, and insofar as it does not help achieve God's main end, the kind of power that necessarily conflicts with the intentions of a wise God in the world. For, freedom makes all the aims of natural things, insofar as they are subordinated to the capacity of freedom, insecure, in such a way that these aims can be prevented. Accordingly, free acts must necessarily be among the relevant conditions of either the end itself, or no freedom at all can be bestowed upon creatures."

[34] Inserted in the second edition: "of such an end of God's, which is to be promoted by means of the free acts of rational creatures,"

[*] Compare *Metaphysics* §281. [Footnote added in the second edition.]

beings is something that should be obtained **through their communal efforts**. For, God created human beings communally, such that one always needs the help of another. *A priori* I see no necessary reason why God [257] has to create communal spirits in every single world.

§213. *The main end of this life is virtue.* **God's main end in this life is virtue.**[35] First, one can show *a priori* that in any world God must first prescribe to certain rational spirits the kind of life in which the achievement and expression of virtue is its main end.[*] For, in any world free actions must take place (§211). Furthermore, God wills that these are necessarily arranged in accordance with virtue (§171, 172, 173), on the basis of which a reward or punishment subsequently follows (§189, 190). But on account of his goodness, he wants to make rational spirits happy. These principles cannot coexist with each other unless God, in a world, first puts rational spirits in the position of being able to perform a free virtue, and happiness is only subsequently conferred upon them in proportion to virtue. In this way, both the perfection and goodness of God are revealed to such spirits. But if he simultaneously creates rational spirits in this world who subsequently become unhappy on account of their vice, this only happens in order to reveal divine perfection, namely [258] his just punishment (§193).[36] His goodness is not hereby infringed upon, because it does not extend to those cases that necessarily conflict with divine perfection.[37] On the other hand, divine perfection would be infringed upon if absolutely no free virtue were rewarded in the world. Indeed, nothing is possible for God except that which can coexist with the presupposition of all of his properties.

---

[35] Inserted in the second edition: "I mean, it consists in the fact that moral acts should happen, namely that, on the one hand, the internal state of human souls are morally and freely cultivated by human beings themselves and that, on the other hand, moral actions happen externally by means of the use of all the powers that are subject to their choice. In both cases, however, human beings follow a guiding principle [Richtschnur] and, more specifically, they observe that which is in accordance with the rules of the essential perfection of things when they arrange their entire state. This should also happen for the right reason, namely for the sake of dependence on the creator who wills and commands this."

[*] Compare *Metaphysics* §§282–85. [Footnote added in the second edition.]

[36] Inserted in the second edition: ", which is amply cognized in many ways, not only via abstraction and inference, but also via specimens and examples that actually lay before one's eyes."

[37] Inserted in the second edition: "On the contrary, an additional, incidental advantage arises from this for happy creatures, which is in accordance with the goodness of God towards such creatures. For, comparing their own state with the state of those who are punished improves the sensation of their own happiness, and therefore presents it to them all the more excellently. And supposing a sufficient degree of perfection and wisdom in such creatures, neither does a sympathy with the misery of the person punished arise here, nor does there arise in us a displeasurable representation of the danger of falling into the same evil in the present life, and nor do such things tend to weave themselves into our judgements without our noticing."

[...]
[260]
[...]

§215. *Virtue should be cultivated and practiced in this life.* If virtue is the main end of human life in this world, then it is necessary for it to either be **cultivated** in minds from the very beginning entirely and completely, or, if nature has already provided a noticeable basis for it, it is necessary for it to be **further developed, and brought to completion**. But in both cases, it is necessary for it to be subsequently **practiced**, **strengthened**, and increased in degree for a period of time up until a certain point that God must arbitrarily set. It is therefore also necessary that certain objects be made available to rational spirits, with which they are to practice virtue.

§216. *How experience agrees with this.* Experience also agrees with this *a posteriori*, by means of which we perceive the present world to be arranged in such a way that we would fall into insoluble difficulties, indeed into contradictions, if we were to accept an end of human life intended by God that is different from the cultivation, strengthening, and practice of virtue. For, should virtue [261] not be the end, then perhaps it must be the cognition of truth or happiness. But cognition cannot be the main end. For, according to its nature, the understanding can exist in no other way except for the sake of the will, because this is how an acting being is able to be assisted in achieving certain ends (§4). Neither can happiness in this life be God's main end. For, the arrangement of the world is not at all suited to achieve this end. We are born with mere potentialities. Nature supplies us with almost all of the materials we would want to make use of, but raw and unrefined; indeed, it conceals its treasures and secrets from us. We can achieve nothing without bitter effort and labour. What else can one conclude from this but that the intention of the creator is that we ourselves should make the effort, and that the human race should possess only as much proficiency of the understanding and of other powers, and only so much enjoyment of the goods to be found in the world, as it can acquire through its own efforts? Since God must demand that these efforts be arranged in conformity with the rules of perfection (§171), [262] precisely in this way it is proven that virtue is the main end of human life (§174). And anyone can set this end for themselves and actually advance it from one's position [Stande], no matter what kind of work one does. Since all the powers of human beings are first strengthened by means of frequent effort and repeatedly overcoming obstacles, it should no longer be considered a problem that God in part supplies human beings with numerous obstacles to be overcome in nature itself, and in part allows them to be supplied. On the other hand, those hindrances that are placed in the way of virtue, which is the main end of God, by the destruction caused by human beings themselves, are not included here. Rather, what can be concluded from them will be dealt with in its proper place.[38] At present, it has been my intention to ascertain the end of human beings in the world that can be investigated through the constitution of the world that God himself has made, and which can be proven on this basis.

§217. *Comfort and enjoyment are the secondary ends of human life.* **Human beings should above all have the right to make use of the goods of the world for their contentment and enjoyment**. We are not here speaking [263] of the consumption of goods of the world that is unavoidable when it comes to the necessities of life and which is therefore commanded on account of its connection to the essential perfection of human nature, but rather of that which only serves the delight and comfort of human beings. And herein consists the secondary end of human life. That one is only permitted but not obligated to seek comfort and pleasure, insofar as it does not damage virtue, is instructed by the drive of conscience *a posteriori*, because one experiences no pangs of conscience when one forgoes an enjoyment. However, one can also prove it in the following way: what merely serves to be enjoyed leaves no further effect behind with any regularity when it is over. It is therefore coincidental to human perfection that God did not see it necessary to provide a law in relation to this. Furthermore, it is indeed a real possibility that God created so much good in the world in order for it to be enjoyed. But it is also possible that we are to practice obedience by abstaining from this enjoyment, in which case the creation of enjoyment would also not be in vain. But since no obligation to either of the two can be proven, [264] because the alternative possibility always remains just as well, the law prescribes nothing at all in relation to mere comfort and enjoyment. It is nonetheless permitted (§185), and we have a right to it (§200), and it must have been God's secondary aim to grant us this right (§16).

§218. *First proof that the human soul is immortal.* The divine end with respect to human beings extends further, however, than to this present life, and **the soul of human beings is immortal**. Immortality is that property of a living being by virtue of which it never stops living. That this belongs to the human soul can be proven in the following way: human beings are God's final, objective ends (§210), that is, they were created not merely as a means for other creatures but for a determinate end in themselves.

---

[38] Crusius discusses this topic in Chapter V of the Ethics. See especially §§284–91.

Accordingly, a reason can be found in no other end for why God should in turn destroy or ruin them. As a result, if he were to destroy or ruin them, he would have to do so either without any end at all, which would be contrary to wisdom, or he must have created them from the very beginning for an end that only lasts for some time. But this is not how final, objective [265] ends are constituted. For, as soon as this time passes, it would be as if the creatures had never existed. Therefore, a time would come to pass when it would not matter whether the world had been created or not, that is, when its creation would be pointless. Since, again, it is contrary to divine perfection to do pointless things, God cannot allow such things and must eternally maintain his final, objective end. On the other hand, one sees quite well that this proof does not apply to matter and other base creatures, because these were created as the means to other ends and would still have an influence on the determination of the condition of everlasting creatures even if the latter no longer existed. Thus, a time never comes to pass when, with respect to all things that still exist, it does not matter whether they had been there or not.

§219. *Second proof of the immortality of the human soul.* Another proof of the immortality of the soul can be gleaned from the fact that God has made human beings, according to their nature, fit for the cognition, desire, and enjoyment of an eternal end by bestowing reason and human desires upon them. From both of these [266] there emerges a drive for happiness of the sort that continually strives for more without end (§106). For, if God were not to preserve the soul eternally, he would have given human beings this essence for no reason. Since God can do nothing for no reason, he thus wills to preserve the soul forever. On the other hand, this proof does not apply to the souls of beasts. For, even though these too always strive to act in new ways, as is involved in the nature of each and every living activity, they are nonetheless capable of neither cognizing (§147), nor desiring (§107), nor enjoying (§25) an infinite object.

§220. *Third proof.* Additionally, we have proven that God rewards all goodness in proportion to its magnitude, and all evil must similarly be punished in proportion to its degree (§189, 190). Since, as experience teaches us, this happens in the present life either not at all or very seldomly, another life must still be to come, which he must have established in order to reveal his rewarding and punishing justice. Since the rewards and punishments must be everlasting (§191), that other life must be a state of actual immortality. Anything else that could be required to prove the principle (§208) [267] is either clear from itself or has already been proven in the previous chapter.

§221. *Why the immortality of the soul cannot be proven from its essence.* I still have a few remarks to add in relation to the proofs of the immortality of the soul. One should not wonder that I have derived this from purely moral grounds. For, these are the only kind that are suitable for proving this. The immortality of the soul cannot be derived from its essence. For, since our soul was not previously alive, one sees that life is contingent to it. Since all of the living activities of our soul are connected to a particular state of our body and would, as experience shows, cease if this state were to oppose the soul too greatly or were to otherwise bring it into great disorder, which is why these activities are quite imperfect in childhood and in old age, no other likely conclusion can be drawn, if one judges on the basis of the mere physical constitution of things, than that the death of our soul must take place simultaneously with the downfall of the body. For this reason alone, the soul can and must be immortal, if one can prove that God wants to preserve the soul's life, that is, in the position of living activities. One should not confuse immortality [268] and incorruptibility with one another. If the incorruptibility of the soul, which is opposed only to deconstruction, can be proven on the basis of its simple essence, immortality is not yet hereby demonstrated, which is opposed to the cessation of living activities in the soul, and must be a state in which the soul remains conscious of itself and retains distinct concepts. Elements are simple as well but are neither mortal nor immortal. The souls of beasts are just as incorruptible as the souls of human beings, but they nonetheless die with their body. Whoever completely accepts pre-established harmony must, if they do not want to draw false conclusions, incontrovertibly grant that the souls of human beings die with their body, and at the very least that they remain dead until they at some point receive a different body. For, according to them, distinct concepts are limited in their power to represent the world by their body. They must therefore pass away with the body just as they came to be with it and were always guided by it. All our distinct thoughts that are not themselves sensations are generated by us from sensations. Thus, as soon as the possibility of sensation vanishes, so must, [269] in a natural way, all remaining distinct thoughts vanish as well, and therefore the entire moral condition of the soul. It becomes clear from all of this how necessary it is to obtain proof of the immortality of the soul from moral grounds. Indeed, on this basis one immediately understands that God cannot leave separated souls in this world after they part from the body because they would die or, if this sounds too harsh, they would fall asleep. Rather, he must place them in a different nexus of things, which at the very least does not hinder the state of distinct thoughts, as much as it might be more believable that the virtuous are, in being rewarded, simultaneously made more advanced and perfect.

[…]
[271]
[…]

§223. *Why some imagine that reason knows little about the immortality of the soul.* It is often lamented that reason cognizes little that is certain about the immortality of the soul. If one means subjective reason, namely the state of the understanding that is to be found in this or that human being, then I grant that it is rarely able to defend the immortality of the soul by means of distinct inferences, even though the drive of conscience compels people to believe this, if they are impartial. But with respect to reason *in abstracto*, that is, the capacity to bring about truth through correct inferences, I cannot concede this. For, the proofs that I have advanced for the immortality of the soul from moral grounds are as concise as one can ask [272] for. But that many do not allow such things proper entry into their mind, the following can be offered as causes. First, moral proofs, if they are to be completely carried out, are commonly more elaborate and more difficult than in other sciences, and they also find fewer followers because one cannot satisfy the hunger of the deniers by means of experience, as one can in mathematics. Rather, one must grasp the proofs solely through the understanding. The present proofs in particular presuppose the entire thelematology, natural theology, and the previous chapter on virtue. It is therefore no wonder if they cannot exert their power on people who are not sufficiently trained in these disciplines. Furthermore, they all face the obstacles that are opposed to the drive of conscience and virtue (§§56, 100). With respect to those who have an evil conscience, it is a lesser evil to simply pass away than to be preserved in a miserable life (§142). They therefore believe either that this will happen, or they are more inclined to believe that it is easily possible and thus are more inclined to manufacture unnecessary doubt and put conscience to sleep (§140). To this is added, finally, the negligence [273] or ineptitude of many authors themselves, who do not present these proofs in their appropriate clarity or leave out the proof entirely because they are stuck in the prejudice that everything that belongs to a thing must be derived from its essence.

PART II
Between the *Critiques*

3
Johann Friedrich Flatt
Introduction

Johann Friedrich Flatt (1759–1821) was born in Tübingen and began studying theology, as well as philosophy and mathematics, at both the local monastery (*Stift*) and the university when he was sixteen.[1] After studying for five years (1775–1780) he became a librarian at the monastery before going on an academic study tour to Göttingen, where he met Christoph Meiners, who was a student of Johann Georg Heinrich Feder, and both of whom were staunch critics of Kant. In 1785, Flatt was offered a position as junior professor (*außerordentlicher Professor*) in philosophy at the University of Tübingen to take over the teaching of Gottfried Ploucquet, the professor of logic and metaphysics who had suffered a stroke in 1782. Flatt taught theoretical philosophy in Tübingen for six years until Ploucquet died and Jakob Friedrich von Abel replaced him in 1791. In 1792 Flatt began lecturing in the theology faculty in Tübingen before he was named chair (*ordentlicher Professor*) there in 1798. Flatt taught in Tübingen for over twenty years, covering a variety of subjects including: Christian ethics, New Testament exegesis, and practical theology, in addition to philosophy. He did not write much but he trained an entire generation of students, including Hegel and Hölderlin, the former of whom is thought to have attended Flatt's lectures on empirical psychology.[2] Flatt died in 1821, having become a nobleman of his home state of Württemberg.

While Flatt was a lecturer in theoretical philosophy in Tübingen (from 1785–1791), he not only lectured on Kant's philosophy, but as the resident Kant expert he was also responsible for reviewing both pro- and anti-Kantian works in the local academic journal, the *Tübingische gelehrte Anzeigen*. Although his contributions were in the first instance anonymous (as was the norm at the time), Flatt's authorship of his contributions is

---
[1] Biographical information about Flatt is taken from Raupp (2016), Pältz (1961), and Franz (2005).
[2] See Franz (2005, pp. 540–41).

given away by his style of engaging with authors argumentatively and qualitatively rather than superficially, as well as by the fact that only in rare cases were reviewers for the journal not based in Tübingen.[3] Thus, again as the Kant expert, Flatt almost certainly authored the reviews of Kant's works themselves, including the following review of the *Groundwork*. His authorship of this review in particular is confirmed by the fact that some of the points raised in the review are repeated in two later books Flatt published, both of which deal with Kant's philosophy: the *Fragmentarische Beyträge zur Bestimmung und Deduktion des Begriffs und Grundsatzes der Caussalität, und zur Grundlegung der natürlichen Theologie, in Beziehung auf die Kantische Philosophie* (Fragmentary Contributions to the Determination and Deduction of the Concept and Principle of Causality, and to the Groundwork of Natural Theology, in relation to the Kantian Philosophy) (1788) and *Briefe über den moralischen Erkenntnisgrund der Religion überhaupt, und besonders in Beziehung auf die Kantische Philosophie* (Letters on the Moral Ground of Cognizing Religion in General, and Especially in Relation to the Kantian Philosophy) (1789).[4]

We have good reason to believe that Kant read Flatt's review of the *Groundwork*. Johann Georg Hamann, a close friend of Kant, reports the following in a letter to Friedrich Heinrich Jacobi dated May 13, 1786, after having recently met with Kant: "An authorial matter is going through his [Kant's] mind, which he immediately confided in me. It is the Tübingen review of his moral science [Moral]."[5] The main theme of the review is Kant's inconsistency. Flatt claims, for instance, that Kant cannot prove that there are beings other than rational beings without violating the principles of the first *Critique* (see p. 106, original pagination). As we will see in later chapters, Flatt also makes a claim that is repeated by other early critics, such as Tittel and Pistorius, namely that Kant's own examples reveal that the categorical imperative cannot determine concrete duties without referring to experience, despite what Kant says (see p. 110). Flatt ends the review by pointing out that Kant seems to have changed his mind about moral motivation since the first *Critique*: whereas in the earlier text Kant says we need the ideas of God and an afterlife for morality to motivate us, Kant now claims that the representation of pure duty on its

---

[3] See Franz and Bürzele (2005, p. 138).
[4] See Mbuyi (2001) for an extensive discussion of Flatt's critique of Kant in these works. Flatt repeats points made in the *Groundwork* review in letters 2, 3, and 4 of his *Letters*, and the eighth letter engages with §8 of the Analytic in the second *Critique*.
[5] See Hamann (1975, p. 389).

own is sufficient.[6] Kant likely has Flatt, and perhaps others, in mind at 5:4.28–37n and 5:5.24–6.11 when discussing various alleged inconsistencies in his writings.[7]

Translation Notes

Flatt's review of the *Groundwork* has never been translated into English before. In preparing it I have used the original 1786 review, which contained no paragraph breaks. Readers should keep in mind that even when Flatt places a passage in quotation marks, he is paraphrasing and not directly quoting.[8]

---

[6] See p. 112 of the original review below as well as Walschots (2022, p. 247) and Allison (1990, p. 67) for details about the theory of moral motivation Kant offers in the first *Critique*.
[7] To be noted here is that Flatt also wrote to Kant directly on Oct. 27, 1793 (11:461–4) about how it is possible to consistently apply the concept of causality to God.
[8] The publication information of Flatt's review is often listed incorrectly; the date of the journal issue in which the review appeared is occasionally listed as May 13, which is the date of Hamann's letter to Jacobi mentioning the review. The correct citation information is listed below at the top of the review.

Review of the *Groundwork* (1786)

Tübingische gelehrte Anzeigen. 14. Stück, February 16, 1786, pp. 105–12.

[105]

Riga.
Groundwork of the Metaphysics of Morals by Immanuel Kant. 1785. 128 pages.

This text, as with all the other works by the Königsberg philosopher, unmistakably bears the mark of an original, deep-thinking mind and contains many characteristic ideas and excellent observations that are often mentioned only in passing and which cannot easily be condensed in a short summary. As undeniable as this is, we regret that Herr Kant cannot be absolved of the charge that, in the present text as in other previous ones, he often substitutes a **dialectical illusion** for a proof or (to use his own expression) a cloud for Juno. [see 4:426.17–18] We consider it to be that much more of a duty to illustrate this with some examples, given Herr Kant looks down upon the most famous philosophers from his dialectical peak, just as a giant looks down upon the race of pygmies, and does not seem to be very far [106] from mistaking his subjective reason for objective reason or for an ideal of human reason.

The main purpose of the entire present text is this: to destroy all previously proposed empirical principles of moral science and establish a new principle in their place, which, just like Kantian intuitions and categories, is to be deduced entirely *a priori* and independently of everything empirical. We cannot concern ourselves with thoroughly judging the Kantian execution of this idea. We therefore wish to limit ourselves to testing some of the primary and secondary propositions [Säzen] that occur in this treatise according to the same principles that Herr Kant himself often brings to bear on other philosophers.

On the basis of the fact that no moral principle valid for **all rational beings** without exception can be derived from experience, the author infers (pp. 28, 90) [4:408.12–19, 4:442.6–11] that **empirical principles of moral science are, on the whole, of no use**. But how can Herr Kant prove, according to **the principles of his own *Critique***, that there are **any rational beings other than the human being**? And if we ever wanted to be lenient and exempt Kant from this proof, the burden of which he must necessarily bear, then with what right does he assume that the principles of **human moral science** are established only if it can be shown that they are valid for **all rational beings in general**? Admittedly, human moral science must in certain respects always coincide with the **universal moral science of spirits** [mit der allgemeinen Geister-Moral] because humanity has certain internal determinations and aspects in common with all higher, finite spirits. But how far this similarity, [107] how far the identity of human moral science and the general moral science of spirits goes, whether the established principle of the one belongs only to it or also to the other, this, it seems to us, is a question that can be bracketed if we are talking about the grounding [Gründung] of a moral science valid **for human beings** only.

Herr Kant objects (p. 90) [4:442.13–22] to the principle of **one's own happiness** that: **(1) experience contradicts the claim that well-being always follows from behaving well; (2) making a human being happy is something entirely different from making it good; (3) the specific difference between virtue and vice is completely and entirely dissolved by that principle**. This latter claim is nothing but an empty decree [Machtspruch] that we would be forced to believe on the basis of Kant's reputation, but only if he were to convince us of his infallibility. For, we absolutely do not see how one can prove what Herr Kant prefers not to prove, namely that there is no specific difference between that which makes us **happy** and that which makes us **unhappy**. The first two objections, however, are based on the false attribution of a concept of happiness that the author has only presumed on sufferance, and that even the best of the empirical moral philosophers (such as Eberhard[1]) have not taken as their foundation.

We are not shrewd enough to see how the following claim is compatible with another passage (p. 50) [4:420.4–8]: "**that the imperative of prudence** (as the author calls the prescription that relates to the end of our happiness) **cannot be called a law because what is necessary merely to attain a discretionary purpose can be regarded as in itself contingent**

---

[1] See e.g., Eberhard's *Sittenlehre der Vernunft* (1781).

[108] **and we can be free of the prescription at any time, if we give up the purpose**." In the second passage it is said that (p. 42) [4:415.28–33]: "**There is one end that can be presupposed as actual in all rational beings (in so far as imperatives suit them, namely as dependent beings), and thus one purpose that they not merely can have, but that one can safely presuppose they one and all actually do have according to a *natural necessity*, and that is the purpose of *happiness*.**" But if this is correct, then on our understanding it necessarily follows that no rational being can ever give up the purpose of happiness like other discretionary purposes, and thus that no rational being can ever be free from the prescription that relates to that purpose. The former proposition (p. 50) [4:420.7–8]: **we can be free from the prescription at any point if we give up the purpose**, therefore contains an impossible requirement when applied to the principle of happiness, and contingency can only be attributed to this principle in so far as it is based on the contingently existing nature of rational beings. Indeed, Herr Kant cannot deny the property of universality to this principle according to the passage cited above (p. 42) [4:415.28–33], if we are already not in a position of understanding how the claim put forward above, that no empirical principle whatsoever has this property, is compatible with it. If the text that we have before us were a few centuries older, we would hardly be able to [109] resist the temptation of doubting the authenticity of one of the cited passages. But since this doubt is entirely absent in the present case, nothing remains but for us to take the inconsistencies and paralogisms that we come across for **antinomies of Kantian reason**. We include among these the following falsities which seem to us to be so blatant that we cannot leave them uncriticized. In order to prove that **happiness** is not the actual natural end for a rational being, Kant says (pp. 4f.) [4:395.13–21]: "**that end would have been obtained much more reliably by instinct than can ever be done by reason; and if in addition reason should have been bestowed on the favoured creature, it would have had to serve it only to contemplate the fortunate predisposition of its nature…; but not to subject its faculty of desire to that weak and deceptive guidance etc.**" One alternative is that the first claim can be reduced to the following argument [Schluß], which we know cannot be proven on the basis of Lambert's *Organon*:[2] if we can attribute the predicate B to a species of the genus A, then this predicate can also be attributed to other species that belong to that genus. If therefore a specific kind of happiness (the kind of happiness

---

[2] See Lambert's *Neues Organon* (1764), Volume I, Book I, Chapter 2 'On Classification', §§79–117.

that does **not presuppose reason**) can be obtained by mere instinct, then this is true of another kind of happiness as well (of the kind that **presupposes reason**). Or, if this argument does not underlie Kant's first claim, then nothing at all is proven other than that the kind of happiness that does **not presuppose** [110] **reason** cannot be the actual end of nature for a rational being. The second claim is partly based on the false assumption that the influence of reason on the faculty of desire contributes more to the misfortune than to the happiness of a rational being, and partly on the idea, grasped out of thin air, of the possibility of a reason that has no influence on the faculty of desire—an idea, the reality of which can least of all be proven according to the principles that Herr Kant himself employed to judge **possibility** in his *Critique of Pure Reason*.

We consider the main principle that the author makes the foundation of moral science (pp. 17, 52) [4:402.8–9, 4:421.7–8], **act in such a way that you can will that your maxim should become a universal law**, to be demonstrable if the universality of lawfulness is restricted to the rational beings that we know, i.e., to humanity. But how one can derive the most noble kinds of duties out of that principle **without any reference to experience**—how one can judge what is universally in accordance with law in the most important cases, *a priori* and without reference to the consequences that we know only from experience, this we cannot understand at all. Even the examples that Herr Kant offers on pp. 18, 19, 54–56 [4:402–3, 4:421–23] illustrate that at least some of the most important applications of that principle are not at all possible without reference to the empirical. For precisely this reason we also believe that the objection Herr Kant makes to the principle of happiness (p. 47) [4:418–19] applies to his own principle just as well.

The author [111] seeks to show (pp. 64ff.) [4:428–9] that **every rational being exists as an end in itself** and derives from this a new formula of the supreme principle of morality. But the argument by means of which he proves this principle (p. 65) [4:428.30–31]: **if the existence of every rational being were not an end in itself, then nothing whatsoever of absolute worth could be found anywhere**, possesses absolutely no evidence (for what would Herr Kant then answer to the person who accepts that only one species of rational being has an absolute worth, and exists as an end in itself?). And the first application that he makes of that principle (p. 67) [4:429.15–28] to the impermissibility of suicide, contains a paralogism, to which we would give pride of place if we had to write a critique of **subjective Kantian reason**. "**Rational nature** (this is the argument that is made on pp. 66–67 [4:429.2–3 and 4:429.23–25]), and therefore also the human being regarded as a rational being, exists as an end in itself. ... Thus the human being in my own person is not at my disposal, so as to kill him**." But this argument either presupposes what Herr Kant himself does not accept, namely that along with the animal body of human beings their rational nature would also be destroyed, or he very clearly violates a main law of inferences, for in the premises we are talking about the **rational nature** of human beings, and in the conclusion of their **animal** body.

The space of these pages does not permit us to discuss Herr Kant's idea of freedom, which also seems problematic to us. But we cannot very well omit a remark which relates to the connection of Kant's *Metaphysics of Morals* [i.e., the *Groundwork*] to natural theology. [112] Herr Kant wants to make moral science [Moral] the foundation of natural theology (as is known from his *Critique of Pure Reason*), and in the [*Groundwork of the*] *Metaphysics of Morals* (pp. 4, 7, etc.) [4:395.4–11, 4:396.14–37, etc.], he even mentions ends and the **wisdom of nature**, just as if one could accept these entirely independently of theism. Similarly, we do not know how to explain how he can attribute **such a powerful influence on the human heart to the pure representation of duty** (p. 33) [4:410.35–411.1], since he utilizes the following as a main premise in the derivation of natural theology from moral science (p. 813 of the *Critique of Pure Reason*) [A813/B841]: that **without a God and a world that is not now visible to us but is hoped for, the marvellous ideas of morality are, to be sure, objects of approbation and admiration but not incentives of resolve and execution.**

4

Gottlob August Tittel
Introduction

Gottlob August Tittel (1739–1816) was born in Pirna, Saxony, a town on the outskirts of Dresden.[1] He completed his studies in Jena in 1760 and then lectured on philosophy there for four years (as a *Privatdozent*) before accepting a professorship at a *Gymnasium* in Karlsruhe in 1764. In Karlsruhe Tittel lectured on philosophy as well as physics and mathematics, disciplines which required extensive knowledge of Latin. In early 1767 Tittel founded the Karlsruhe Latin Society (*Lateinische Societät*), whose aim was the promotion of literature, understood in the sense of '*belles lettres*' or '*die schönen Wissenschaften*.' Tittel remained in Karlsruhe for the rest of his life, where he became rector of the *Gymnasium* in 1797.

Tittel was an empiricist and an admirer of Johann Georg Heinrich Feder (1740–1821), the latter of whom was professor of philosophy in Göttingen, one of the most well-known 'popular philosophers' of the period, and the editor of the infamous Garve/Feder review of Kant's first *Critique*.[2] One of Tittel's major publications was a six-volume series of textbooks published between 1783 and 1786 entitled *Erläuterungen der theoretischen und praktischen Philosophie nach Herrn Feders Ordnung* (Elucidations of Theoretical and Practical Philosophy, According to Herr Feder's Arrangement), whose aim was, as the title suggests, to provide an overview of Tittel's philosophy modelled on Feder's own. Like Feder, Tittel was highly influenced by Locke's philosophy, and in 1791 Tittel published a book of excerpts from Locke's *Essay* wherein he offered both German translations of key sections and the occasional commentary, sometimes polemically directed against Kant. Tittel argues, for instance, that the distinction between analytic and synthetic propositions that Kant

---

[1] Information about Tittel's life and works is taken from Thomas (2016), Liebmann (1894), Kühlmann (2009), and Beiser (1987).
[2] On Feder see the Introduction to his review of the second *Critique* in Chapter 8 of this volume.

"flatters himself to have discovered for the very first time" can already be found in Locke (see 1791, pp. 479–80 and 4:270.15–16).

Tittel is best known for his criticisms of Kant's philosophy. He wrote two short books against Kant's practical and theoretical philosophy: *Über Herrn Kants Moralreform* (On Herr Kant's Reform of Moral Science) (1786) and *Kantische Denkformen oder Kategorien* (Kantian Forms of Thought or Categories) (1787). In the latter, Tittel discusses topics such as the artificiality of Kant's table of the categories and their inapplicability to experience.[3] In the *Reform*, selections from which are translated below, Tittel makes several important objections to the *Groundwork*, many of which have since become classic, such as: that the categorical imperative is empty (p. 33, original pagination), that the motive of duty for duty's sake is impotent in human nature (pp. 92–93), that Kant is a covert consequentialist (pp. 33–36), and that Kant is a mystic (see pp. 6 and 23). Tittel's most well-known objection, however, is that the categorical imperative is not a new principle of morality, but merely a new formula of a previously established and more plausible principle.[4] Kant famously responds to this objection in a footnote in the Preface to the second *Critique* (see 5:8.28–37n).

If Kant did not initially discover Tittel's commentary on his own, Kant's contemporaries made him aware of it. In a letter to Kant from Johann Erich Biester on June 11, 1786, for example, we learn that Kant was planning to defend himself against the objections of both Tittel and Feder (Kant's previous letter to Biester has been lost): "You write to me of a defence that you want to make against the attacks of Herren Feder and Tittel. Like everything you have penned, it will be instructive and useful to the public" (10:457.14–16). Similarly, in a letter from July 17, 1786, Ludwig Heinrich Jakob writes to Kant that "I do not know if the brochure of a certain Tittel is known to you, who wagers to judge your [Groundwork of the] Metaphysics [of Morals], but without understanding that which your investigation hopes to accomplish" (10:462.7–10). As these letters from Kant's fans indicate, in one way or another Kant was aware of Tittel's commentary soon after it was published (which was in the spring of 1786), and he even went so far as to ask Christian Gottfried Schütz to send him a copy.[5] More generally, the *Reform* itself was quite

---

[3] See Beiser (1987, p. 186) for a brief discussion of the objections contained in this text and Sassen (2000) for a partial translation and brief introduction.
[4] See below p. 35 of Tittel's text and Walschots (2020) for an in-depth discussion of this objection.
[5] Kant's original letter is lost, but see Schütz's response from Nov. 3, 1786 (10:468–70).

popular and was reviewed no less than seven times in the first six months or so after its initial publication.[6]

Translation Notes

The *Reform* is made up of thirty-eight sections where Tittel first paraphrases a passage or passages from the *Groundwork* and then offers critical commentary. Tittel did not number these sections, but I have done so for ease of reference by inserting numbers in square brackets at the beginning of each section. Tittel paraphrases from the first edition of the *Groundwork*, but only when he supplies page numbers do his quotations even roughly approximate the original text. I have also included the Akademie page number for the passages that Tittel is paraphrasing in case readers wish to reference the original themselves. In agreement with Timmermann (see Kant 2011, p. 161), I have translated '*Moral*', as in the title of Tittel's text, as 'moral science' throughout this volume. As the entry in Grimm and Grimm (2023) indicates, '*Moral*' was sometimes used interchangeably with '*Sittenlehre*' (doctrine of morals), which confirms that 'moral science' is a fitting translation for this term. What follows is the first English translation of selections from the *Reform*.

---

[6] All of these reviews have been reprinted in Landau (1991). See pp. 378–80, 398–99, 403, 405–406, 407–409, 450–69, and 472–73.

On Herr Kant's Reform of Moral Science (1786)

[3]

To the Reader

Philosophers need no courtesies when they make their remarks publicly known to each other, even where they diverge. Truth—their only goal—vindicates them. Whoever seeks and assesses truth with sincerity, in whatever corner of the earth they may live, is a friend of the philosopher.

I admire the author of the **Metaphysics of Morals** on account of his talent for thinking deeply, without considering it a duty to applaud every application of that talent or to agree with his views on that basis.

One might suppose three situations to be possible in relation to this Kantian text. Either the author seeks to place the doctrine of morals [4] in a precarious position, in that he supports it on principles—and declares these to be the **only ones possible** and the **only ones necessary**—concerning which he himself in the end comprehends nothing more than that they are incomprehensible. But how dishonourable would it not be to think something dishonourable of the honourable man! Or does he only, in jest, intend to test the extent to which otherwise healthy and honest human reason can be mistaken about a multitude of high-handedly devised phrases and ideas on account of an artificially devised wisdom (if one can call it wisdom) that is shrouded in darkness and has itself been replaced by a different, purely self-affirming reason? This too, when it comes to such a topic, tone, and procedure, is surely not to be imagined. Or, if Herr Kant is truly sincere with all of this (this is the third case), then I can explain it to myself by means of nothing other than the author's much too frequent use of abstract terminology, with which even the best thinker eventually encounters danger and completely loses themselves in the blind alleyways of a fantasy that appears purely rational, by means of allowing himself to be led too far away from the real world.

On Herr Kant's Reform of Moral Science (1786)

Be that as it may, I have followed the author step by step in this serious and arduous text [5] and have made it my duty to summarize the Kantian principles in a comprehensible brevity where it seemed necessary to me, in order to make insight into such things easier for the reader as far as possible and to make the course of the Kantian inquiry more apparent.

I hope to have done a welcome service to the public, who have been eagerly awaiting the **Kantian reforms**, in that I have taken it upon myself to precisely but modestly assess this newly published Kantian work, which, due to the particular obscurity and difficulty of Kantian texts, may have frightened so many away. And even Herr Kant himself, as a philosopher, will find this undertaking to be innocent, if not of benefit.

Where the expression may perhaps seem too strong and enthusiastic, I request that those passages always be considered in conjunction with the author's already harsh statements and objections to that innocent and admirable system, and to the many worthy men who have accepted it, which connects happiness and morality [Sittlichkeit] in their innermost aspects [6] (as has already been sharply denounced by others in, for example, the *Tübingische gelehrte Anzeigen* of 1786, pp. 106f.; and has not gone unnoticed in Herr Prof. Cäsar's philosophical journal of 1785, Part 3, p. 467[1]). Those passages are thus to be regarded in no way other than is necessary to defend the good cause. The cause of which I speak is the cause of happiness as the principle of morality, which, if not ruined, is placed in the most unfortunate position by **Kantian mysticism**, since it is obvious that, within its boundaries, pure duty (pure virtue) for Herr Kant is nothing other than a surrogate for that which (in the mystical sense) is the pure love of God.

On the basis of the arguments presented here, judge for yourselves, my readers! Judge—without prejudice and any esteem for the person—for the truth itself. Written in Karlsruhe in March of 1786.

Tittel.

[...]
[8]
[...]

[§3.] "Reason was given to human beings merely to establish a good will in them, not, as if the good will should be a means to happiness, rather as **in itself** the highest good. If happiness were the true end [Zweck] of a rational being, nature would have obtained this much better by instinct than through the

---

[1] Tittel is referring to two early reviews of the *Groundwork*: J.F. Flatt's initially anonymous review, published in the *Tübingische gelehrte Anzeigen*, 14. Stück, Feb. 16, 1786, pp. 105–12, translated in the previous chapter of this volume, and another anonymous review published in *Denkwürdigkeiten aus der philosophischen Welt* (edited by Karl Adolph Cäsar) Drittes Quartal, 1785, pp. 433–67 (reprinted in Landau 1991, pp. 203–19).

deceptive guidance of reason. Enjoyment of life and contentment is only too often lost during the cultivation of reason. However, if the good will is taken to be the first, unconditional, and happiness the second and conditional purpose [Absicht] of reason, then it can be seen how happiness, as the second purpose, can itself be limited by reason for the sake of the first purpose, i.e., the good will." [4:396.14–32]

> However! If the good will—soundness and harmony of dispositions—is not merely a condition but an essential part of happiness, does reason not then also simultaneously contribute to happiness in that it establishes the good will? What is the good will to a human being if it does not promote its happiness? [9] Goodness of the heart cannot and may not make me less happy than I would have been without it. Of course I must denounce many momentary, apparent, and sensible advantages in order to maintain a good character! But **on the whole** it is impossible for me to thereby lose any of my happiness. I must gain much more. Either one must assume a very one-sided concept of happiness—such as one abstracted from certain present, bodily advantages and enjoyments—or the following is a harsh principal incompatible with common human understanding: that the **good will** (a good character) is the absolute and highest good of human beings and yet hinders and limits their happiness. The philosophy that hears the voice of nature enticing and calling the human being to happiness at first only obscurely and through feeling but then learns how to understand this voice more clearly, completely, and distinctly through the additional teachings of reasons—that can never be a philosophy for human beings. I do not know whether good willing—instructing that one must be good and will good only because it is good—without asking or knowing **what for?** and **why?**, without any view to happiness—effect and end—can be called anything other than destroying human happiness. Speculating up until an absolute good that is unfruitful for human happiness [10] is overstretched and dangerous speculation. **Dangerous**, because the human being cannot love such a good! I should be good in order to be less **happy**. Who would dare make such a demand of human beings? I want to be a good-willing, good-minded human being precisely because the good human being (on the whole and taken in its true sense) is always happier than the evil one. Even if the most common human being ever had cause and impulse to some sort of evil action but did not commit it from an unwaveringly good disposition, if one were to ask them after that struggle has been overcome why they did not do it, they would seldom answer: "I did not do it because good willing is good in itself." But "how great!," they will say, "how easy it now is on my heart that I did not do it! What sort of reproaches and torments

I would now meet! How much I would have to suffer for it!" Our nature is attuned to happiness (well-being) in its foundation. Reason should evaluate and direct, and recommend what is more important and what is better to human beings. Good willing—willing the good only because it is good—provides the understanding and the heart with no meaning and no power. With all respect for higher, speculative knowledge, [11] I would never bend my knee to such a vain idol of abstraction. Did the Stoics themselves (good will "*bona mens*" is certainly a Stoic concept) not connect the ideas of cheerfulness, contentment, and happiness to their concept of the highest good in the most intimate way? And what person can think of their highest good as anything other than under the concept of the happiness achievable and possible for them? I must be able to enjoy my highest good and to promote my happiness to the degree that I enjoy it. Furthermore! If reason is so deceptive, as it is here accused of being, in showing human beings the way to happiness, will it be any less deceptive in establishing a good will? It is a false principle, and a charge that is offensive to reason, that the cultivation of reason diminishes human happiness. That is exactly how the human being is given access to the highest and most dignified joy, whereby much sensible enjoyment, which on that account it admittedly must refuse, is by and large replaced and compensated. This is exactly when the human being experiences the execution of its more honourable capacities and the distinctive privilege of its nature. [12]

[§4.] "The human being with a good will always meticulously acts **from duty**. Thus, not at all for the sake of utility. Neither does such a being act merely in accordance with duty but from inclination; [4:397.11–17] they even act against inclination and only because something is duty, just as, for example, an unfortunate person preserves their life without loving it. [4:398.3–6] An action can even be amiable but nonetheless be without moral worth, namely when it takes place from inclination and not **from duty**. [4:398.12–14] The command to love our neighbour and even our enemy does not say that we should do it from inclination (for inclination cannot be commanded), but that we should do it with all disinclination—**from duty**. [4:399.27–31] Only the **law** (as objective principle of the will) and pure respect for the law (**maxim**), separated from the purpose and effect to be thereby attained, e.g., any kind of pleasurable condition or the promotion of one's own or another's happiness, provides the pure concept of duty." [4:400.31–33; 4:401.3–16]

> It seems to me that much ambiguity lies in these sentences. The moral worth of the human being consists in the fact that duty itself becomes one's overriding inclination. The strength of this inclination increases one's worth. The more repellants or attractors that stand in the way, which this inclination overcomes, the stronger it must be. Its worth is

now that much higher as well. One therefore distinguishes between only inclination for duty (as main inclination) and the [13] **particular** inclinations of another kind that oppose the inclination that is in conformity with duty. To act from duty without inclination is a yoke and a moral form of slavery. Pure respect for the law cannot take place without inclination. I must love the law itself. And in order to love it I must first cognize and sense its beneficial effects and salutary influence. I should also love my enemy, but this does not mean that I should do them good with reluctance. Rather, it is from the rational consideration of the salutary consequences, such as my own contentment and the common best, that I should allow benevolent, friendly, and favourable dispositions, even towards my enemies, to become inclination in me, that is, allow my mind to become accustomed to the kind of mindset that is even disposed towards one's enemies (although not specifically **because** they are enemies) with kindness and affection.[2]

[§5.] "The universal law, which must be the final determining ground of a will good in itself and without limitation, is contained in the principle: **act in such a way that you can also will that your maxim** (your practical principle) **can become universal**. [4:402.1–9] Therefore—may I, for example, save myself from a predicament by means of a false promise? [4:402.16–17] Ask yourself: can I will that this maxim become universal? Now! If you cannot will this, [14] then your maxim must be rejected. Thus, let only this principle always be your compass." [4:403.21–22]

But does this law not immediately refer to the consequences that such a maxim would have, according to its universality, on myself and others? Only from the consequences can I first determine whether I can wish and will that it become universal or not. I cannot even conceive of a law without action, to which the law has a necessary relationship, as if to its object, and I cannot conceive of an action without consequences that are thereby brought about for us or others, and which then make the actions—or a maxim related to such actions—to be recommended or reprehended. The law is just the general expression, or that which is abstract, wherein what is common to certain actions and their consequences is summarized and described out of a multitude of singular cases. The general expression, as a formula, both in the theoretical and practical sense (**axiom** or **law**), always breaks down into the singular concepts and cases, from which they were abstracted, and the former reaches not a hair further than the latter. Just as I come not a step further [15] once I have learned the

---

[2] Compare the above paragraph to 5:84.13–14 and 5:85.2. Thanks to Jens Timmermann for pointing out this connection.

formula that something cannot simultaneously both exist and not exist (as the wise **Locke** has already noted[3]), so am I not brought any further when one says to me: "act in such a way that you can also will that your maxim may become universal." When it comes to application, in one sense we are indeed always concerned with the relations of individual concepts, and in another we are concerned with the characterization of particular cases, i.e., with the effects and consequences of each and every action. Everyone is permitted to choose formulas for themselves that they find to be most suitable. "Act in such a way that you can also will that your maxim may become universal." This formula in essence says only so much: act in such a way that you can rationally wish that others might so act in every such case (especially towards you, and one towards another). In addition to the fact that this latter expression is already better known and clearer, it seems to have yet another advantage in that common reason much more preferably and easily decides on the individual and present case, as opposed to **generalities**. And this generality itself must be understood in terms of every such completely determined case. I say to the common person: in order to save yourself from the most extreme necessity, you want to seize [16] foreign property. Do you also will that such a course of action (maxim) becomes universal? In every such case they would have to say that under the specified circumstances and conditions, everyone else may also so act.

[...]
[17]
[...]

[§7.] "Duty and morality are not experiential concepts and cannot be, rather they are entirely independent of all experience and grounded only in **pure reason**. [4:406.5–8] Experience shows not a single example, neither in a conspicuous nor in an inconspicuous way, neither in a familiar nor in an unfamiliar relation, where a drive of self-love could not have contributed to a good and honourable action. For, in that case, it did not actually proceed from **duty**. [4:407.1–11] The ideas of duty and morality would be lost if one were to derive them from experience, and the enemy of virtue would have then won. [4:407.17–23] In order thus to not lose these great concepts, one must reinforce the internal conviction that they are pure concepts of reason and that the question is not whether they can also be proven by experience. [4:407.34–408.3] Moreover, in that the law of morality must be a necessarily universal law for all rational beings, with whom we are not at all familiar from experience (except for the human being), it is therefore impossible to allege that experience is the epistemological principle of moral laws. [4:408.12–19] [18]

---

[3] See e.g., *Essay* IV.vii.14.

And with such an allegation it would turn out very badly for morality. For, examples (to the extent that experience is able provide them) must be examined and assessed by antecedent principles of morality [Moralität]. The original of these lies entirely in reason alone. [4:408.28–33] Raise oneself up to these pure rational sources first, and then lower the doctrine of morals to popularity after it has been sufficiently supported by such principles in order to furnish it with access and approval." [4:409.20–24]

> So, we are talking about **pure reason** here. But is human reason always pure reason? And if it is not, what do we want to decide on the basis of pure reason? The various capacities of the soul have been described with particular names in order to make the various further developments of its operations more recognizable. In the system of nature all of these capacities are fundamentally cobbled together. One proceeds to the next: from the first raw impression that the soul receives up until the degree of cultivation it can achieve. By means of the senses the soul first gathers singular images and impressions. The imagination [Phantasei] turns them into various shapes and forms by means of a number of combinations. The understanding extracts the more important ones and elucidates and orders. The power of judgement investigates [19] relations, compares, separates what does not fit, and combines what is fitting. Reason connects entire series of concepts to one another. Only gradual elevation of the soul! Progressive, continual operation! But where does it begin? From the senses. Without having received the initial material from the senses, the entire operation of thought would suddenly stand still. The soul must climb from this most foundational level up to the highest, by means of the path that nature has set for it. The highest and most dignified concepts are built out of the material of experience by means of processing and development. This developmental and processing power is reason. The experiences that are processed, cultivated, compared, and connected to one another make up the entire extent and collection of rational cognition. Even the concept of God could only be furnished from this source and through this process of the soul. By means of intuiting the sensible world and comparing human achievements and human qualities, the soul was gradually raised up to the highest concept of the divine—an all-powerful and all-perfect spirit. Whoever still has doubts about this should inquire into human history. **Pure** reason—not extrapolated from experience, entirely independent of all [20] experience—is not human reason. All abstractions must eventually dissolve into elementary concepts that are based on experience—no matter how far back this pursuit may extend. And every abstraction that is not built on this foundation is a chimera. **Reason** is not an isolated province cut off from the rest of human nature in such a way

that one can set its concepts apart from all connection to the others. Continuity reigns in human beings, as it does in all the rest of nature. Sensation proceeds to thought, experience proceeds to reason.
A rational concept is only an enhanced concept of sensation. Rational concepts always indirectly take their origin from experience (internal or external experience; actual sensation or reflection). The concepts of duty and morality (with or without a relation to happiness) must also eventually lead back to experience. And why shouldn't they? "Because it is not possible to put forward a single example of an action performed strictly and actually from duty with complete certainty." [4:407.1–2] For the time being, are we not merely talking about the concept and how it comes to be? Not yet of reality and actuality? Through the wilful combination [21] of singular concepts drawn from experience we can form a composite that cannot be found anywhere in reality. But through decomposition into its composite parts such a concept turns into experience. And if a human being cannot know with certainty what kind of motives [Bewegungsgründen] another person acted from—whether they truly and strictly were moved to such an action by the representation of right [Recht] and the love of the law—they can surely determine this by persistent self-reflection. The human being can thus obtain the concept of duty from **its own** experience. "They cannot do this" Herr **Kant** says. And why not? "Because the human being cannot say with certainty of a single one of their own actions that they did it from pure duty, i.e., that no other drive of self-love, or a view to one's own well-being and benefit, was involved, at least covertly." [4:407.8–11] Very well said! Without a view to well-being and benefit the human being cannot act at all. But should something cease to be duty and no longer take place from duty because it was done in order to bring about and promote well-being? This would be nothing [22] less than to ruin the entire natural economy of the human being. **Herr Kant** will never be able to justify his arbitrarily created concepts of duty and morality which (by his own admission) conflict with all of the actual appearances in the human being. Why must the concept of duty be placed at such lofty and superhuman heights, separated from all connection to benefit and happiness, enjoyment and pleasure, and be so sternly separated and removed that one cannot find it anywhere in reality? That which is recommended to human beings, that which they should love, this must be attainable for them. Indeed! The duty-loving human being is not permitted to be **selfish**, is not permitted to have one's eye on biased, often inferior rewards in relation to every good action. But the human being is permitted to love itself, and in the entire system of its actions and its duties, it is permitted to keep its attention on the establishment of its highest well-being from natural urge and longing.

It will often sacrifice insignificant, vain, or apparent advantage, which self-interest seeks, for a higher and more noble contentment, and for this reason it will express itself generously, benevolently, tolerantly, etc. But one would not want to deny or rob the reward of contentment from a human being for that reason. Was [23] it not noble enough to achieve its contentment through fine actions? If one wishes to impel the concept of duty even higher, this would be to lose it entirely. It would no longer remain an object of human striving. Fighting against nature is futile. A doctrine of morals that one wants to erect on concepts that transition and emanate into the superhuman and the unnatural must be thoroughly infertile and dangerous.

Indeed, it seems that what the Stoics have long taught: "one must love virtue, **as virtue**, for its own sake" is what Herr Kant now teaches under this different expression: "one must love duty, **as duty**, in and of itself." Only the Stoics included in their concept of virtue superior contentment, peace, and joy, and the entire essence of human happiness (one only has to read Seneca on the happiness of life). But Herr Kant wants all of this to be entirely separate from his concept of duty. What could make this barren and infertile concept of duty—wholly stripped of all attractive stimuli, of all expectations of blessings and any sort of advantageous effect—worthy of love for the human being? Be on guard against **philosophical mysticism**! The mystic says precisely this: I am supposed to love God for his own sake, without [24] considering that he is kind to me. But without the goodness of God, I cannot conceive of or love God. Just the same! I am supposed to love duty **as duty**, because it is duty, without a view to contentment and happiness. But without a relationship to human happiness, I know nothing of duty. Duty is to receive its entire dignity and its entire strength from the law alone. But to what is the law accountable? How do I test whether the law is good? To what does the law allude? From where do all laws originate? And to what do they all trace back? What is the internal and essential character and the ultimate source of all duties and all laws? These questions must be answered, otherwise any blind will could pass itself off as a law. It must be the agreement with human nature and its internal determination [Stimmung] towards happiness, on which all rules of correct action and all laws eventually converge.

[...]
[29]
[...]

[§11.] "For the most perfect will, that is, the one that is in conformity with the objective good according to its nature, **no ought** is necessary.

Only for the will that is not in itself necessarily in conformity with reason is the '**ought**' necessary. [4:414.5–11] (What might the **objective good** be, since Herr Kant wishes to know absolutely nothing of objects?) **Good** is (in contrast to the **agreeable**, i.e., what is valid as a sensation only for the individual from **subjective grounds**) what must be valid for everyone as rational beings from **objective grounds**, as reason. [4:413.18–25] **The ought** (the imperative) always signifies a necessitation or a practical necessity. [4:413.12–15] But is called either [30]

1. a **hypothetical** (conditional) imperative in relation to a certain end, to which the action is only a means. [4:414.13–15] And according to which this end
   a. is merely taken to be **possible** (still uncertain): a **problematic** imperative (imperative of skill in relation to **art**)
   b. or as **actual** (already decided and determined): an **assertoric** imperative (imperative of prudence in relation to **well-being**). [4:414.32–415.2]
2. or a **categorical** imperative or **apodictic** imperative (the imperative of morality, in relation to duty), without all relation to an end whatsoever, where the action is commanded **in itself**, as an action." [4:414.15–17; 4:415.2–5]

With this classification one immediately encounters a number of difficulties.

1. Herr Kant says of the **imperative of skill** (p. 41 [4:415.14]): "The question here is not whether the end is **rational** and **good**" and he elucidates it with the example of the **physician** and the **poisoner**. "The prescription has the same value for the purpose [Absicht] of the one—to reliably heal their person—as for the other—to reliably kill their person." [4:415.15–18] And Herr Kant even says just before this that "**all** imperatives (thus also the imperative of skill) [31] are expressed by an **ought**, and by this indicate the relation of an **objective law of reason** to a will that, according to its subjective constitution is not necessarily determined by it (is not entirely perfect in its nature). They say that to do or to omit something **would be good**, but they say it to a will that does not always do something just because it is represented to it that it would be **good** to do it." (p. 37) [4:413.12–18] Is this not a contradiction?
2. To elucidate the **imperative of prudence** Herr Kant adds the following: "There is one end that can be presupposed as actual in all rational beings, and thus one purpose that they not only merely **can** have, but that one can safely presuppose they one and all actually do have according to a natural necessity, and that is the purpose of happiness." (p. 42) [4:415.28–33] And indeed the principle of happiness ought not be a law, "because one can always be rid of this prescription of aiming towards happiness (the imperative of prudence) as soon as one gives up the purpose (to be

happy)." (p. 50) [4:420.7–8] Consider this: "**from natural necessity it is an end** for me to be happy"; and yet "**if I want to, I can also renounce this end.**" One almost does not believe one's eyes when encountering such passages in the text of a man whom one wishes to consider the model of precision. [32]

3. The following passages seem just as incompatible: "that the categorical imperative alone can be called a law, the others can indeed be called principles of the will but not laws" (p. 50) [4:420.3–5] and the passage already previously cited: "that all imperatives indicate the relation of an objective law of reason to a will." (p. 37) [4:413.12–14]

4. The definition of the **moral (categorical) imperative** is, first, completely arbitrary and against all use of speech. Herr **Kant** only wants to call that prescription **moral** that commands something merely for its own sake. Therefore: look after your health in order to preserve your life; be temperate in order to be healthy, etc. are indeed rules of prudence according to him, but not moral rules. Of course! Everyone may use names as they wish and explain themselves how they want. But one must not forget that what one finds in such an arbitrary definition, or believes to find in it, is precisely as arbitrary as the definition, i.e., one must not take it to be proven. Just look! The categorical or moral imperative, says Herr **Kant**, is (according to precisely that arbitrary explanation) limited by no condition whatsoever, and is therefore universally valid. This **universality** therefore provides the character of the **moral good**, as well as the formula, by means of which the supreme principle of morality can be expressed: **act in such a way that you can will that your maxim becomes universal** (a universal law of nature). [33] I will accept that this rule is valid (but only as a consequence of an arbitrary concept). But this law itself, which Herr Kant believes to have found in pure reason, if it is not an entirely empty and sterile expression but is to be capable of some application, is entirely empirical with respect to its **content**, i.e., it immediately refers to the **consequences** and **effects** that we know from experience. One might very well think that Herr Kant chose applications and examples that seem to fit his formula the best. And indeed, the empirical everywhere comes to the fore in the applications he himself chose (pp. 53–56) [4:421–23]. Accordingly: "one is tempted to take their own life out of despair. But he asks himself: but is this also right? That is, can I will that this maxim (namely to help oneself by means of death in such a desperate state) become universal? The result is: no! For it would be a contradiction in nature to drive human beings towards the advancement of life, and to destroy life, by means of the same sensation (self-love)."
[4:421.24–4:422.11] See! We have already been introduced to self-love, and thus to the empirical. It would not therefore be a contradiction to promote life (make the human being happy) and death (as the only

possible means against suffering) at the same time. One must make use of entirely different reasons against suicide. "Another must borrow out of necessity, but promises to pay the money back at a determinate time and [34] knows that he cannot do this. Is it right, he thinks to himself, to still promise to do so? That is, can I will that such a maxim (to promise something that one cannot do in order to save oneself from necessity) becomes universal? The result is: no! For if everyone were to do this, nobody would ever lend their money on the basis of such a commitment." [4:422.15–36] Is it not true that in the end everything is indeed decided on the basis of the **consequences** (empirically)? In this case too we might not be able to completely decide, but nothing depends on this here. "A third finds talents in themselves, but would prefer to entirely devote themselves to pleasure, because they find themselves in good circumstances. But they ask themselves: **is this right**? That is, can I will that this maxim (not to make one's talents fertile in good circumstances, but only to seek amusement) becomes universal? The result is: no! For they see that they should develop their capacities as a rational being, **because they can serve them for all kinds of possible purposes**." [4:422.37–423.16] Purposes! All kinds of possible purposes! How could Herr Kant write this without having entirely forgotten his categorical imperative, his pure, rational law, his absolute command, which is independent of all purposes? "The command which—**without presupposing as its condition any other purpose to be obtained by a certain course of action**—commands this action immediately." (p. 43) [4:416.7–9] A fourth is rich and happy but is apathetic and indifferent [35] whether it goes well or badly for others. Can this person will that such a disposition becomes universal? They cannot, "for such a will would conflict with itself, for many cases can yet come to pass, in which one **needs** the love and compassion of others, and in which, by such a law of nature sprung from one's own will, one would rob oneself of all hope of the assistance one wishes for oneself." [4:423.31–35] Herr **Kant** himself thus lowers himself to human **needs**, by means of which the will must receive direction towards the moral good. Thus, if Herr Kant wishes to give his supreme principle of morality only the least applicability, he himself must consider purposes and consequences, as well as needs of human beings, and take all of this from the world of experience. How might the astute man, with his pure principle of reason, with which no human being—not even himself—could make any progress without the help of experience, nevertheless raise himself so far above all empirical philosophers, and dare to make so many bitter objections against them? Should then the entire Kantian reform of moral science thus confine itself to a new **formula**? How can an empty formula help, to which one wishes to give the appearance of pure rationality, but which is entirely unsuitable for use to the extent that one does not bolster it with the material of experience? It does not help if Herr Kant then says: "all duties are dependent on that single principle of morality [36], but only as far as the kind of obligation is concerned, not the object of action." [4:424.12–14] For one can see in these examples distinctly enough that it is precisely on the basis of the constitution of the object and its relation to human nature, on the basis of its consequences, that the point of obligation or lawfulness itself must first be determined. The categorical imperative (so that I say it once and for all), with all of the telltale signs of pure reason, seems to me to be a true work of fancy. "Act in such a way that you can will that your maxim becomes universal" does indeed sound nice and new. However! If one wants meaning and not words, then it can mean nothing other than: **act** in such a way that you would consider it **good** and **beneficial** if all other beings (who could also so act) were to actually so act. An antecedent concept of **goodness** and **benefit**, determined from somewhere else, is thereby necessarily presupposed, or the entire formula has no meaning. I do not therefore learn what is good on the basis of the formula, rather the formula only tells me in general: "Do that which is good (generally useful)." I am not brought a step further by that altered, new-seeming formula: "act in such a way that you can also will that your maxim becomes universal," than by one of the most well-known principles: "act in such a way that through your action and your maxim of action perfection is promoted (considered on the whole and in general)."[4] I must first abstract the concept of the good and perfection from the material of experience [37] (empirically) by means of the collection and comparison of singular cases.

[§12.] "It seems to be a contradiction in the human will if it violates a law. For, in that the will recognizes the law, it must will that it be universal, and in that the will makes an exception for itself, it wishes to in turn limit it in its universality. But this apparent contradiction is only a conflict of inclination with reason." [4:424.22–29]

> Do not place reason and inclination (interest) in contradiction! The supreme interest of human beings must be to act according to reason and the rational law. The human being just does not always know its true interest. In the moment of action, for instance, something appears to it to be more important and more interesting than the opposite. Only afterwards, from the consequences, does the human being see that it acted against its true interest. The most important business of moral science is to instruct the human being on the correct calculation of its core interests! And this is done in order to obtain the greatest possible sum of delights and enjoyments for itself, but which it can only achieve in connection with the common best, in accord with the wisest order of nature. It calculates incorrectly as

---

[4] This is the Wolffian principle of morality. See *German Ethics* §12.

soon as it imagines [38] achieving such things in a different way and apart from this connection.

[§13.] "If there actually are duties, then there must be categorical imperatives, i.e., there must be something commanded in and for itself, without any other incentives, for no other purpose or relation. [4:414.15–17] And these categorical imperatives must contain precisely that which was previously indicated, namely the suitability of the maxim for a universal law. [4:420.26–28; 4:421.3–5] But the reality of neither the one nor the other is thereby proved—neither that there is such an absolute command, nor that there are actually duties." [4:425.1–11]

> It is true that something must be good and worthy of desiring for its own sake, as a final end and **final purpose**, on which all duties converge; something, in which all of moral science terminates. But if this absolute something—this **highest** and most **supreme** thing—were nothing other than the common world best—human happiness and the greatest possible sum of the perfections for sensing and thinking beings (as far as they are accessible to human cognition)—would this not provide moral science with a very useful and clear principle, an absolutely foundational command, or (if it should be called such) a categorical imperative: "**act in such a way that through your action** [39] **and disposition the common world best**, the well-being of sensing and thinking natures—and thus also **your own happiness—is preserved and promoted**"? Indeed! One should not quarrel over formulas. Still, if one were to adopt that other formula: "act in such a way that your maxim is suitable as a universal law," I now say: this formula, if it is to have meaning and truth, contains nothing other and reduces to nothing other than precisely that which is contained in the other formula. Why do philosophers wish to make distinctions only on the basis of stubborn attachment to names? Just consolidate whatever can be consolidated! For, when Herr Kant completely separates his absolute command from happiness, the reality of the categorical imperative might admittedly be difficult or completely impossible to prove, and then the entire edifice of the doctrine of morals simultaneously stands or falls with the categorical imperative, if the former depends and rests on the latter.

[…]
[44]
[…]

[§17.] "But suppose there were something whose existence **in itself** had an absolute worth, which, as an end, in itself could be a ground of determinate laws. Then in it and in it alone the ground of a [45] possible categorical imperative, i.e., of a practical law, would lie. Now I say: the human being and generally every rational being exists as an end in itself, not merely as a means for this or that will, but must always be considered simultaneously as an **end** in all of its actions, directed both towards itself as well as towards all rational beings." [4:428.3–11]

> Now with all of this I am once again only better off in terms of a name or a different expression. In the past it has been said to me: reason must command **on its own**. This of course meant only having **oneself** and no other kind of object or end under consideration. The question was: how is this possible? And the answer is: "because rational nature regards itself **as an end**." In essence, no more and no less is thereby said than what was said previously. Nonetheless, by means of this expression the absolute command (the categorical imperative) is brought closer to human beings and the formula is as follows: "**act in such a way that you regard humanity (in yourself and every other person) always as an end.**" [4:429.10–12] Just analyze this formula! So, I should regard **humanity** as an end. But I have to ask here: humanity, according to its entire and complete concept, i.e., the complete human being, the entire overarching concept [Inbegriff] and [46] complete sum of its powers, predispositions, and capacities (body and sensibility included)? Or only according to a part, such as only insofar as humanity belongs to **rational** nature? If the latter, then concrete humanity would not be helped much by this. For I would not have the human being but only a piece of the human being under consideration. Thus, I should regard whole and complete, not divided, humanity as an end; I am also simultaneously empirical. For natural predispositions, natural drives, and natural inclinations certainly also belong to the complete essence of human beings. Where then is **pure** reason? To put it briefly: I cannot survive with pure reason in the actual human world! I am actually very happy to let the principle of always regarding humanity as an end stand. I say only: if it is to contain meaning and truth, it means and indeed can mean nothing other than: "make it the end of your action to preserve and perfect the humanity in your own person and that of everyone else." But is this not the long known (and according to Herr Kant the so notorious and depraved) principle of **happiness**, i.e., of self-love and benevolence? Both of these, **self-love** and **benevolence**, reduce to [47] respect for the humanity that we find in ourselves and beings similar to us. I also wish to admit that, on account of this internal agreement of the principle, whether under the one or

> the other formula, the more determinate kinds of duties can be reduced to the Kantian principle: "regard the humanity in your actions always as an end" just as well as to this other similar principle: "make it the end of your action to preserve and perfect humanity, i.e., love yourself and other human beings." But in the applications made by Herr Kant I really do find much that is unnatural and compatible with evil. [. . .]

[49]
[. . .]

[§22.] "To the first principle (act in such a way that you can will that your maxim become universal) and the second one (always regard humanity as an end) the following third is added: the idea of a universally legislating will, or the formula: (as it will be put later) to **always simultaneously regard your will as a universally legislating will**." [4:431.12–18]

> We will have to wait for the explanation of this last formula. They are just formulas, and Herr Kant passes them off as nothing more. Because of this one expects no mysteries. The same thing, with one meaning, is said in three different ways. Pure reason, says Herr Kant, demands of me that which is good in itself and unconditionally (**universal validity**), i.e., that which is an end in itself (**precedence of an end** [Zwecksvorzug]) [see 4:431.27] and is commanded through itself (**autonomy**). In this property of a supreme, self-legislating will, Herr Kant believes [50] to have found the solution to the difficulties, and the cause of all alleged aberrations of all the philosophers before him who wanted to connect the concept of duty with some kind of human interest. Nobody considered, says Herr Kant, that the rational will is not merely subject to the law, but is also **supremely self-legislating**. It seems that I should imagine the wills of all rational beings as a collection or a group, in which every member themselves takes part in legislation, but is also themselves subject to the law. "This **supremely self-legislating** will cannot depend on any kind of interest. For, such a dependent will would itself require a new law, which would require that the interest first qualify as a universal maxim." (p. 72) [4:432.7–11] But if I conceive of something as the highest and absolute interest, as the final and necessary condition of a rational will, e.g., happiness, this can indeed coexist with supreme legislation quite well. I want to know: can duty be commanded without any interest? "A will that commands duty is a supremely legislating will," it is said to me. But could the supremely legislating will itself, I might then ask, ever be legislating [51] without an interest? That is the point. Prove that such a will stops being

supremely legislating when connected to a highest and absolute interest, e.g., happiness.—With the flashy idea of a universally legislating will Herr Kant transitions into a **kingdom of ends**. And in this kingdom of ends the categorical imperative is once again the focal point, i.e., every rational being honours themselves and also every other rational being as an end, and is honoured as an end by every other being, who in turn honour themselves as an end. "In this way a systematic union of several rational beings through common laws comes into being." [4:433.17–18]

[§23.] "In this kingdom of ends it becomes a principle to: **act in such a way that your will can regard itself through its maxims as a universally legislating will**. [4:434.12–14] The rational will must always apply to every other rational being. And the rational will obeys no other law than the one it gives itself. [4:434.25–30] And its dignity consists merely in the fact that it is itself an end. Other things can have a price (market price or fancy price), in accord with need or inclination. Only morality has **dignity** in itself. For morality alone is the condition [52] under which the human being can regard itself as an end. [4:434.35–4:435.6] And virtue receives its lofty and incomparable worth solely by means of the **share** it obtains for the human being, as a rational being, **in universal legislation**, in that virtue, by means of its maxims, makes the human being fit to be a legislating member in the kingdom of ends. [4:435.29–33] Autonomy is the ground of the dignity of human and rational nature, etc." [4:436.6–7]

> Something of the truth is contained in these sentences. Only wrapped up in too much fiction on the whole, encased in too much obscurity, mixed with too many inanities, expressed through too many digressions and circumductions (do not take the sentences in the brevity with which I have arranged them here, examine them rather by the author of the [*Groundwork of the*] *Metaphysics of Morals* himself (pp. 74f. [see above references])). Why must I first imagine myself into an intelligible world, into an ideal kingdom, into a collection of legislating spirits, in order to learn that morality and virtue gives human beings their highest dignity? And (if I have then imagined myself into it) what are these collected spirits supposed to then decide both with and for one another? What does this universal legislation have as an **object** and for an end? "Everyone regards themselves and everyone else as an end." Indeed! If this means only so much as: everyone seeks their [53] own happiness and that of others. But according to Herr Kant it should and may not mean this. His universal legislation intends only willing, **as willing**; not the object of willing. It wills and commands, because it wills and commands. But no soul understands any of this. And that legislator most certainly also understands nothing about it. Is that the deep workings of reason?

Is that the lofty power of research? Is that the purely philosophical spirit? None of this! It is rather the true luxury of reason, or how else should one call it?—And another thing! If Herr Kant places the high value of virtue and morality in the share of universal legislation that virtue obtains for human beings, then I would like to ask if this share in universal legislation is virtue itself or the interest of virtue? It cannot be the first. The tautology would be too strong: "Virtue receives its high privilege precisely by means of obtaining a share in universal legislation for human beings." It must therefore be the interest of virtue. But in this way Herr Kant, whose entire improvement of moral science aims at establishing the absolute will of reason solely by means of reason, secretly connects to virtue the proud thought of "being the universal legislator": [54] and replaces the real interest of happiness with the merely ideal interest of a **universal legislation**. Why does one make the cognition of truth and virtue so difficult, which nature wishes to teach it so easily? Even for the most capable earthling the flight over and above the entire world of humanity and into the clouds is too bold, as is preaching a law for **all spirits** as if an oracle. Where would this universal teacher of law get the data? "From pure reason." Right indeed! If only this pure reason, which must indeed reside within the human being (insofar as it is to actually use reason), and which is ripped from the rest of human nature, if only this were not an absurdity. Other spirits do not need to get their moral science from our **earthly word**. Let us teach ourselves and our earthly brothers to bring about our common happiness by means of clear and distinct instructions. That is human moral science. The surest way to bring philosophy and reason into poor standing and disrespect, where the human being is to be given a distinct and certain norm in order to organize its conduct, is to place the human being on such a height that it is thereby made dizzy and no longer recognizes itself. [55]

[§24.] After **Herr Kant** believes to have elaborated and bolstered his allegedly new principle of morality in this way, he sequentially scrutinizes the principles believed and accepted by other human moralists until now. First, these principles are arranged in such a way that, as might be imagined, they can be rejected collectively and without exception, because Herr Kant now believes to have found the one true one. In general, those principles are:

1. either of the empirical kind, such as **happiness** and **moral feeling** (self-love and benevolence) or
2. of a rational nature, such as **perfection**: whether this is
   a. **ontological** (abstract) perfection, i.e., the rational concept of perfection in general, or
   b. **theological** (independent) perfection—God's perfection (**God's will**). [4:441–43]

And what is so reprehensible about all of these principles? Just listen!

[§25.] "Empirical principles are not at all suitable to ground moral laws. For, the universality, with which they are supposed to be valid for all rational beings, the unconditional practical necessity with which they are imposed upon these beings, falls away if the ground thereof is taken from the particular arrangement of [56] human nature or the contingent circumstances in which it is placed." (p. 90) [4:442.6–11]

> However! How can I venture to decide, without impudence and recklessness, what must be valid for **all other** rational beings **as such**, who are completely unknown to me, other than at most and only insofar as I allow myself to be guided by analogy? Even the thought of one other rational being aside from myself refers back to our self-feeling, as its first source. All of our pneumatological cognition springs from this source alone. Herr Kant and I, and nobody else would know anything about what reason and a rational being would be if we did not have the initial facts about this from ourselves. Only as far as this analogy and abstraction can bring me am I permitted to accept similar sentiments and similar laws for every other rational nature, as for my own. And to this extent **self-love** and **benevolence**, i.e., the determination to promote one's own happiness and that of other similar beings, also in fact hold as a **universal law** for all rational natures. And this law can indeed consist in its unconditional practical necessity. And Herr Kant lectures against both with much intensity—the principle of one's own **happiness** (self-love) and of **moral feeling** (benevolence).

[...]
[66]
[...]

[§29.] One can wager whatever they want, (and by means of the foregoing remarks [67] it has, I think, been made clear) that Herr Kant, as soon as he gives his supreme principle of morality any kind of sufficient clarification, and illustrates any kind of fecundity or applicability of it, either thereby comes to a standstill or immediately has to fall back on what he so contemptuously rejected. Take the Kantian principle under any formula you like (for countless formulas can be made)! "**Universal validity** of the maxim" is what it is supposed to mean. But why else is a maxim suitable as a universal law than because it promotes universal welfare? It is supposedly called the "**precedence of the end**." But what does humanity point towards, as an end, if not human happiness? Supposedly the **supremely self-legislating will**. But by what other means can it raise itself to this dignity than by terminating in the universal world best—the supreme and sole destination of all laws? If the Kantian principle says anything, it must say this. And with that I now stand in the exact position that I stood in before I had become aware of and learned the Kantian formula—which is admittedly mounted quite high but (as tends to happen with all cases of excess) is quick to descend once again. And once we have become completely wrapped up in subtleties and speculations, in the end we must [68] uncontestably be left with this single, lofty interest: **true human happiness**, to which the creator himself has incontrovertibly attached the entire system of human activity within the initial predisposition of our nature; or one is blindly up in arms against the unconquerable fortress of nature.

[...]
[88]

[§37.] "Legislation in this world of the understanding limits itself entirely to the **formal** condition of the universality of the maxim, as law. All laws that are already determined by a particular object lie entirely outside of autonomy and come up against the sensible world." [4:458.25–31]

> If I understand it correctly, this can only mean the following: pure reason only provides the general character that all particular laws must bear, namely that one must be able to wish their **universality**. But in application to particular objects and cases, i.e., in order to be able to judge whether this or that is suitable as a universal maxim, e.g., whether one can accept it as a universal rule that one is permitted to tell a lie in order to save oneself from an urgent necessity, one immediately refers back to the sensible world, i.e., this must be decided based on experience (empirical interests), the relation to happiness, needs, inclinations, etc. In fact, Herr Kant himself has judged in this way when applying the supreme principle of morality that he himself chose (p. 69) [4:430]. Thus, only the form is purely rational, and the contents are empirical. However! I cannot conceive of anything under an empty form without contents. Indeed, what is an indicative [89] character supposed to be, if it does not indicate particular objects? I cannot conceive of **universality** except as taken from experience and particular, compared cases. The universality of the maxim (insofar as I can will it) is supposed to be the character of the **moral good**, and indeed independent of all experience. I am only supposed to ask myself, in order to judge the morality of my action, whether the maxim, according to which I act, can also become **universal**. This only means so much as: whether this maxim, if it is accepted by all as a maxim and placed in practice, would remain good and beneficial. But good for whom? For what purpose? "Without a purpose! Good

in itself. Good for rational beings." But what is the determination of these rational beings? Is it not their happiness and well-being? "Away with happiness! Happiness is an empirical, very weak, and indeterminate concept. Morality must not be grounded on happiness." Put it and turn it as I may: I don't know what any of this is. And with the greatest effort to be clear and the most careful attention, I almost need to take care, amidst so many obscurities, to not be obscure myself in the end. [90]

[§38.] "It is thoroughly impossible to explain how **pure reason can be practical** (i.e., proceed to action without any other incentive, without any further end, and independently of all view to happiness) or to explain how **freedom is possible** (i.e., how the rational will can be legislating for itself). [4:458.36–459.2] There is no elucidation and no explanation for this entirely unique kind of causality on the basis of experience and example. [4:459.3–9] Freedom is merely **an idea** that one must presuppose insofar as the human being believes itself to be aware of an independent will. [4:459.9–14] It is just as impossible to explain **how?** and **why?** the human being can take such a big interest in duty and in that supreme principle of morality, namely the universal validity of a maxim, in order to determine its causality in accordance with this principle. [4:459.32–460.1] Duty is also merely an **idea** and something entirely non-sensible. And it is therefore **completely incomprehensible** for us how a sensation of pleasure can thereby be brought about in the human being. [4:460.12–18] The moral law (the categorical imperative) therefore receives its possibility merely from the presupposition of freedom. [4:461.7–9] But one is permitted to presuppose this freedom in a rational being (because it contains nothing contradictory) and one must do so, at least **in idea** (without considering its objective reality), insofar as the rational being is conscious of a will independent of sensibility, as its condition. [4:461.17–25] But how pure [91] reason, without other incentives, is practical **in itself**, without any object of the will, in which one first takes any interest, can bring about a **purely moral** interest on its own, human reason is entirely incapable of explaining this, and all effort and labour to do so is lost." (pp. 120–25) [4:461.25–35]

> Nothing else was to be expected from the entire construction and course of the investigation than that, in the end, the whole doctrine of morals would have to be placed in this unfortunate position. Indeed, the moral system could not be more unfortunate than as follows: "that the supreme principle of morality is something, of which nothing more can be **comprehended** than that it is **incomprehensible**." (p. 128) [4:463.29–33] (With which the entire **Metaphysics of Morals** is concluded.) One must eventually arrive at this result quite naturally, seeing as everything was designed and prepared for this. Under the brilliant title of **pure reason**, from whose

characteristic source the first principles of the doctrine of morals are supposed to be forged, one creates a completely abstract capacity that falls to human beings—who knows from where—not constructed from experience, nor supported by experience, but is self-efficacious entirely from itself and is conceived above human nature and human happiness. With [92] this pure reason—extracted from all connection to the economy of the senses and the entire system of its essential drives and sentiments—one places the human being into an **intelligible world**, as if in a completely separate kingdom. In this world of the understanding this pure reason also becomes efficacious (practical), i.e., becomes a **will**. One connects to this will, just as pure as reason, a completely sovereign causality, i.e., **freedom**. By virtue of this pure, free will reason issues a **universal law of spirits** that is valid for all rational beings, as a law, entirely unconditionally, without an object and without an end, merely on its own. Absolutely all duty and morality rests on this **self-legislation** and the concept of freedom that underlies it. The entire honour and dignity of duty and morality is supposed to consist in the fact that every view to happiness and contentment is entirely excluded.—At the conclusion of this deduction it must obviously be found that, in this way, the most supreme concept of the whole **doctrine of morals**—connected to absolutely nothing and supported by nothing—must thoroughly lack support, and that for the person who wishes to know **why?** something is duty and **what for?**, only this single and final answer remains: **because** [93] **it is duty**—**that is why it is duty**. It must of course be entirely incomprehensible how this barren, withered down, skeletal concept of duty—separated from all influence on happiness and from everything that could give it appeal, interest, and something deserving of being loved—how something so completely stripped could ever become an effective determining ground for human beings. Nothing more is needed to turn **morality** and **duty** into an idle shadow. They become all the more shadowlike in that they are supported by freedom as a foundation—not in reality and actuality, but merely **in idea** (as if it were also in itself an empty concept and illusion). And this is supposed to be the fruit of ideas worked out purely, the entire harvest of an investigation that is so highly acclaimed and so eagerly awaited, and which goes so far beyond what the most capable minds have thought until now—the obscure course of which and whose frequent abstractions and terminology one can only attain with effort and strain? And this is supposed to be the **Groundwork of Morals**?

5
Hermann Andreas Pistorius
Introduction

Hermann Andreas Pistorius (1730–98) was born in the city of Bergen on the island of Rügen, where his father was a deacon.[1] After attending *Gymnasium* in Stralsund and then the *Collegium Carolinum* in Braunschweig, Pistorius studied at both the University of Greifswald and the University of Göttingen. Once he finished his studies, Pistorius worked as a private tutor and translator, and among his early accomplishments are the first German translations of David Hume's *Political Discourses* and *Enquiry Concerning the Principles of Morals*, which were parts one and three, respectively, of the four-volume *Vermischte Schriften* (1754–56), all four volumes of which Kant owned.[2] Pistorius eventually returned to Rügen and received his *Magister* degree in philosophy from the University of Greifswald in 1756. A year later, in 1757, he was appointed pastor on the island of Rügen. In 1764, while visiting his brother-in-law, J.J. Spalding, in Berlin, he made the acquaintance of Friedrich Nicolai, the founding editor of the *Allgemeine deutsche Bibliothek*, an important journal of the German enlightenment.[3] From then on Pistorius began working for the journal and over the span of thirty-three years he wrote more than one thousand reviews of various philosophical and theological texts, including nearly every one of Kant's major works as well as many texts by both Kant's defenders and critics. Among Pistorius' other noteworthy accomplishments is a German translation of David Hartley's *Observations on Man* (see Hartley 1772–73). The annotations Pistorius attached to this translation were apparently so important that they were translated into

---

[1] Information about Pistorius' life and works is taken from Häckermann (1888), Gesang (2007 and 2016), Sassen (2000), and the anonymous (1799) obituary published soon after his death.

[2] See Warda (1922, p. 50). It is possible that Pistorius translated the second volume as well, which was the *Enquiry Concerning Human Understanding*, but this volume might have been translated by its editor, Johann Georg Sulzer. See Klemme (2000) and Nowitzki (2011, pp. 150–51) for a discussion.

[3] For information on this journal and its role in the early reception of Kant's philosophy, see the introduction to Sassen (2000).

English and appended to a later edition (see Hartley 1791). Although Pistorius never wrote a philosophical treatise of his own, his contributions to the scientific community via translations and reviews were substantial, so much so that the University of Greifswald awarded him a doctorate in theology in 1790. Pistorius died of pneumonia on November 10, 1798.

This volume includes three of Pistorius' reviews, each of which helps to contextualize the second *Critique* in its own unique way. Chapters 6 and 11 contain Pistorius' reviews of the *Groundwork* and the second *Critique*, respectively. The present chapter contains his review of Johann Schultz's 1784 book: *Erläuterungen über des Herrn Professor Kant Critik der reinen Vernunft* (Elucidations of Herr Professor Kant's Critique of Pure Reason).[4] Schultz (sometimes spelled 'Schulz' or 'Schulze,' as Pistorius does) was a second court chaplain (*Hofprediger*) and eventually became Kant's colleague as a professor of mathematics at the University of Königsberg. Early in his career, while he was still a pastor, Schultz wrote a positive review of Kant's *Inaugural Dissertation*,[5] which resulted in Kant praising Schultz as "the best philosophical mind I know" who "has grasped the points of the system very well" (10:133.25–27). Thus, once the first *Critique* was published and Kant was not only disappointed by the lack of attention it received (see e.g., 10:270.7–9), but was also surprised by how poorly some had understood it (such as in the infamous Göttingen review, see Kant's response in the Appendix to the *Prolegomena* at 4:372–80), Kant turned to Schultz. Kant wrote to Schultz on August 3, 1781, to send him a copy of the first *Critique* and ask if he would evaluate it.[6] Schultz took more than two years to respond, but once he did (on August 21, 1783), he offered to review the first *Critique* and even sent Kant some extracts from the planned review. In the correspondence that ensued, Kant expressed his approval and convinced Schultz to publish it as a book rather than a review. The result was the *Elucidations*, the first commentary written on the first *Critique*, and which consists of two parts: a first part in which Schultz outlines the major arguments of the book, and a second in which he presents some suggestions or 'hints' (*Winke*) for better understanding it. A third part, in which Schultz planned to evaluate Kant's system, was not included in the 1784 *Elucidations* but was later published as the

---

[4] An English translation of Schultz's *Elucidations*, under the title *Exposition of Kant's Critique of Pure Reason*, was done by James C. Morrison (1995) and includes both a helpful introduction and a number of appendices.
[5] See Schultz (1771) and Morrison (1995, pp. 163–70) for an English translation.
[6] See 10:274. An English translation of the correspondence between Schultz and Kant is included as Appendix A of Morrison (1995).

two-volume *Prüfung der Kantischen Critik der reinen Vernunft* (Examination of the Kantian Critique of Pure Reason) (see Schultz 1789/1792). The *Elucidations* is an important book not only because it is the first commentary on the first *Critique*, but above all because even years later, in 1797, Kant publicly declared Schultz to be his most accurate interpreter (see 12:376).

The *Elucidations* was reviewed four times,[7] but Pistorius' is by far the most extensive review and is certainly the most important when it comes to understanding the second *Critique*. In the review, Pistorius essentially uses Schultz's *Elucidations* as the occasion for examining some of Kant's own doctrines directly, namely those that Pistorius still finds to be obscure after having read the *Elucidations*. Pistorius focuses primarily on Kant's theory of space and time as well as on what he calls Kant's "theory of appearance [Schein] and truth," namely the distinction between appearances and things in themselves. Discussing these topics leads Pistorius to make several important points over the course of the review, some of which have become classic objections. For instance, Pistorius articulates what is now known as the 'neglected alternative' objection, i.e., the idea that space and time might be *both* subjective *and* objective.[8] Indeed, a main aim of the review is to show that this neglected alternative is not only plausible but also consistent with Kant's broader system and has a number of advantages over the theory Kant proposes, namely that space and time are merely subjective forms of intuition. Pistorius was also the first to formulate what has come to be called the 'problem of affection,' i.e., the problem of how objects, which are allegedly mere appearances, can affect or influence the sensibility of a subject that is also mere appearance.[9] In fact, a main theme of the review is Pistorius' attempt to show that both the subject and the object of knowledge cannot be mere appearances but must be assumed to really exist.

Especially relevant as background to the second *Critique* in this review are: (1) Pistorius' criticism of Kant's conception of freedom and the solution to the third antinomy (see pp. 109–13, original pagination); (2) the claim that certain doctrines in the first *Critique* are inconsistent with what Kant says in *Groundwork* (see pp. 117f. as well as p. 98); and (3) the claim that Kant is illegitimately biased towards moral ideas (pp. 108 and

---

[7] All of these are reprinted in Landau (1991, see pp. 140–42, 147–82, 223–25, and 326–52).
[8] For a recent discussion of this objection, which takes Pistorius into account, see Specht (2014).
[9] For an introduction to the problem see Stang (2022), and for Pistorius' version of the problem see Gesang (2007, pp. XIII–XXII) and Sassen (2000, pp. 14–16).

122). When Kant mentions "the most considerable objections to the *Critique* that have so far come to my attention" (5:6) in the Preface to the second *Critique*, he almost certainly has in mind many of the points raised in this review (see e.g., Beck 1960, p. 16).

Translation Notes

Pistorius' review of Schultz's *Elucidations* has received partial English translations twice in the past: by Sassen (2000, pp. 93–105) and Noller and Walsh (2022, pp. 3–8). What follows is the first complete English translation of the review. In preparing it, I have referenced both the modern edition included in Gesang (2007) as well as the original review (1786). Throughout the review, Pistorius uses '*Schein*' and '*Erscheinung*,' and their variants, interchangeably, thus I have translated both of these terms as 'appearance' throughout. '*Schein*' is his preferred term, however, so I have only indicated when '*Erscheinung*' or its variants have been used.

Review of Schultz's *Elucidations of Professor Kant's Critique of Pure Reason* (1786)

Allgemeine deutsche Bibliothek. 66. Band, 1. Stück, 1786, pp. 92–123.

[92]

Elucidations of Herr Professor Kant's Critique of Pure Reason by Joh. Schulze, Royal Prussian Second Court Chaplain. Königsberg, Dengel, 1784. 8. 254 pages.

That it is neither unnecessary nor superfluous to elucidate Herr Prof. Kant's *Critique of Pure Reason*, by means of which the content of this important but difficult to comprehend work is disclosed to those readers who lack the leisure time and patience, even if they are not entirely lacking in ability, to delve into the system of the deep-thinking philosopher, and disclose it in such a way that such readers are now able to understand its content with little effort and are able to busy their philosophical reflection with it, this, it seems to me, has been admitted by all experts and half-experts who have to some degree expressed themselves about it by complaining about the obscurity of the work. Herr second court chaplain Schulze has therefore done an agreeable and important service to philosophy and her devotees with these *Elucidations*, in that he has provided us with this clear commentary, approved by Herr Prof. Kant himself,[1] on the most important book on metaphysics that has been written since Aristotle's times, and he certainly deserves the gratitude of all speculative thinkers. [93]

These *Elucidations* consist of a concisely composed summary of the contents of the Kantian work, wherein the system is presented in generally intelligible language, but also wherein Kant's terminology has been presented and defined, and then of several suggestions for a closer

---

[1] As mentioned in the Introduction to this translation, Kant read parts of Schultz's initial review and encouraged him to publish it as a book. For a more detailed account of Kant's involvement in the publication of the *Elucidations*, see the introduction in Morrison (1995).

examination of this system. I think that there will be few readers of Herr Kant's *Critique* and the *Prolegomena*, for whom many obscurities will not have been clarified and many difficulties not overcome by these *Elucidations*, insofar as these concern Herr Kant's actual meaning. At the very least, the reviewer acknowledges that he can think of many things in the *Prolegomena*, with which he could not come to terms, but which have now become clearer such that, at the very least, he now believes to understand Herr **Kant**. And yet I find the most considerable difficulty caused to me by Herr **Kant's** principles concerning time and space, and the theory of appearance and truth that is based upon them, to be unsolved. I have already mentioned this difficulty in the review of the *Prolegomena* (A. D. Bibl. Band LIX. p. 345),[2] and I picked up these *Elucidations* with interest in order to perhaps find a solution to my doubts in them. As mentioned, however, I encountered nothing whereby it has been explained to me how appearance is even possible according to the author's system, if that by means of which all appearance [alles Scheinen] is possible (which, therefore, must always be presumed prior to all appearance and thus cannot itself be appearance), in a word, if representation and thought are themselves supposed to be appearance. And yet they must be, because all our thought takes place in succession and in accordance with determinations of time, if space and time are **merely** subjective forms of our sensibility and everything that we intuit in space and perceive and think according to temporal determination is nothing but appearance [Erscheinung].

Instead of providing even further information about Herr **Kant's** principles and system by providing excerpts from these *Elucidations*, which, it seems to me, is quite unnecessary in light of them, I wish to try following Herr Schulze's suggestion of more closely examining the *Critique*, as far as my powers allow and, first, attempting to further develop the above-mentioned doubt concerning appearance and reality, and thus to turn my attention to the considerations, towards which this doubt has led me, without [94] restricting myself to a strict order. When doing so, I will refer to both Herr **Kant's** larger work and to the *Prolegomena* in particular.

Only by presupposing that representation and thought are appearance [Erscheinung] could the author claim that we know absolutely nothing of our thinking subject, for if representations and thoughts were true effects

---

[2] *Allgemeine deutsche Bibliothek*. 59. Band, 2. Stück (1784), pp. 322–56. Reprinted in Landau (1991, pp. 85–108).

of the subject, i.e., effects similar in kind to the subject itself, then on this basis we would know that there is a power of representation or a source of thought. But now, since representations are said to be only apparent effects, that is, according to how one usually understands 'apparent', things that are, in themselves, not that which they appear to be to a third subject or how this third subject represents them, we lose ourselves from one appearance to the next and, as far as our individual existence is concerned, we get into such an unfortunate and uncertain situation that we have nothing to hold on to and cannot find our footing. It is now just as uncertain and problematic whether an independently existing subject, the modifications of which are our representations and thoughts, even exists as it is uncertain and problematic whether objects actually correspond to our external sensations. According to this system it can therefore very well be that there is nothing but appearance into infinity, that we only appear to exist, and that, by means of reflection, we can just as little assure ourselves of our real existence as of a firm and secure foundation of everything that apparently exists [alles dieses Scheinwesens]. What we call the soul in line with the common use of language is, according to this system, only a logical, i.e., apparent subject, not a true, independently existing substance. In fact, the soul is merely a series of fleeting representations, which are connected to thoughts by means of self-consciousness (which is also a species of fleeting representation), which are brought into orderly connections by means of other apparent representations (which are called the concepts of the understanding or categories), and which are again expanded into an infinitely connected series through other representations (the ideas of reason), but which are also merely subjective and deceptive. One does not know from where this stream of representations springs; one does not know for whom and where it continues to flow; and one does not know where it ends. According to this system there are intuitions without a **reliable** subject who intuits and without a **certain** object that is [95] intuited. According to this system, there is no **true** unity of the thinking subject, rather, all unity is only logical and subjective connection, only a collection of the manifold; and indeed there ought not be a simple, collecting subject if one infers a simple, connecting, and collecting subject from the sensation of simple self-consciousness, or infers a true unity from an apparent one, and it is not a fallacy to do so. According to this system, then, even the representation of the **self** [Ich] must be completely empty and issue absolutely no valid conclusions. It is nothing but this consciousness itself, a representation, that must accompany certain other representations if they are to be brought together into a thought, but which refers to nothing real and is said to contain nothing that could inform us about the nature of our thinking being. And yet, it seems to me that this representation of the **self** contains, first, a difference from all other objects and, second, a collection of all the representations grasped by this **self**, and, finally, an adherence [Zueignung] of these to the thinking subject referred to by this **self**. Accordingly, this representation contains the sensation and the concept of individuality and that which one calls egoism. If we do not wish to become lost in an infinity of appearances [Schein und Erscheinung] here, then we must accept that this thinking, individual being, which is conscious of its difference from other thinking beings and can never become a property or a predicate of something else, actually exists, is actually a thing in itself, and that representation and thought are actual and true effects of this subject, i.e., effects similar in kind to it. For, by what means could they become appearance? Surely by means of nothing other than a new power of representation. And if this were then in turn to require an additional power of representation to be appearance [Erscheinung], then we would have to accept a true *regressum in infinitum*.[3]—If what has been said thus far is only an implication of the author's principles, and no true refutation of them, then it seems to me to be a real problem that must first be eliminated before one can come to terms with this system. I might therefore be permitted to carry on with these implications even further, [96] or rather to apply them to other parts of the Kantian system.

According to this system, reason demands the completion of the series of natural events and causes, it seeks a boundary external to this series, proceeds from the conditioned to the unconditioned, and must accept a boundary, an unknown something as the unconditioned, because it can find the sought-after completion and satisfaction nowhere else.—If I am not mistaken, then reason, instructed and guided by this theory of the apparent and the true, can and must find the completion of all experiences and their causes in nothing other than the series itself. Supposing that a world of the understanding underlies and corresponds to the world of the senses, and something real underlies and corresponds to appearances [Erscheinungen]; supposing that all successive representations or those that relate to determinations of time are merely apparent and subjective, to which there is nothing similar or commensurate in reality or the objective world of the understanding, then this world is indeed an independently existing thing, is self-sufficient, and bounds itself; then it

---

[3] *infinite regress*

has just as little a beginning as an end; then the entire manifold, which is simultaneously represented as existing in space and as successive in time, the same manifold and sequence that reason compels to search for a boundary and an unconditioned, is merely a deception [Täuschung], similar to that of the human being who, without knowing they are travelling through a river made up of a crooked line that turns back upon itself, imagines that they will continually travel downstream and never back upstream and that the river has a beginning, a source, and an end or break off point, on account of the fact that all of this is just appearance. Admittedly, as long as we consider time to be something objective, to be a representation that at the very least is partially grounded in things **in themselves**, as philosophers and lay people have believed up until now, then we must presuppose a beginning and an end of the series of nature, and our reason must seek the completion of this series external to it, and demand something unconditioned for everything conditioned. However, if, better instructed, we were to recognize all succession in time and all manifold in space as only subjective and apparent, then we would also have to instruct reason [97] to not transfer this succession and manifold over into the objective world of the understanding. We would have to say to it: this circumstance, that we will never come to an end in the search for natural causes but will proceed from conditioned to conditioned into infinity, is based on the fact that neither succession nor manifold, as little as beginning and end or any kind of boundary, neither infinite divisibility nor indivisible parts, take place in the actual objective world. All of this only takes place in the world of the senses, not in the world of the understanding, is only appearance and deception, as is the fantasy of taking ourselves to be real substances. Insofar as anything exists at all, there is, rather, only one single substance and this is the one and only **thing in itself**, the one and only noumenon, namely the intelligible or objective world. This world bounds itself; this is the domain that has neither beginning nor end. This is the only ideal of pure reason. Thus, according to this theory of the apparent [vom Schein] and the real, the ideas of pure reason would and must be determined in the way that Spinoza determined them. For him, as is known, the world is the one and only substance, the self-completing series, or the domain with no boundaries; for him it occupies the place of the deity. His pantheism would rescue the author's theory from the important objection that an infinite, thinking substance cannot be composed of innumerable finite, thinking substances, for if, according to the author's theory, our substantiality is merely logical and apparent, if our **self** is nothing other than self-consciousness, and this is only a subjective condition of the connection of representations, a modification of other modifications, then what prevents all of these representations from being modifications of the single substance? If determinations of time and all the representations relating to them are merely apparent and subjective, then reason would find all its demands satisfied in Spinoza's system, and after this satisfaction reason would be in the wrong if it were to still look for a particular deity. At the very least, the interest of truth requires no other deity than the world of the understanding.

Again, these are just implications, one will say, and on top of that implications that paint Herr Kant's theory in an unfriendly [98] light, but they do nothing to refute the theory, even if Spinozism can be deduced from it, which, as far as we know, he has thus far not claimed. It is true that they are only implications, and that they appear unfriendly. I am sorry about that, and to that extent they should not prove anything against the Kantian theory. But they must be worked out if it is to be shown that precisely this theory is inconsistent with other parts of the system and seems to contradict the profound philosopher's other principles and claims. Among these is the statement made in the *Prolegomena*: "That, to Hume's principle, not to drive the use of reason dogmatically beyond the field of experience, we must conjoin another principle that Hume completely overlooked, namely this: not to look upon the field of possible experience as something which, in the eyes of our reason, bounds itself."[4] Let us see where this new principle will take us. The meaning can be nothing other than this: reason must presuppose not only appearances [Erscheinungen], but also **things in themselves**, to which appearances [Erscheinungen] relate, and which underlie appearances [Erscheinungen], because, as the author explains at this juncture, if I am not mistaken: "appearances [Erscheinungen] always presuppose a thing in itself, and so provide notice of such a thing, whether one can become more closely acquainted with it or not." [4:355.3–4] According to this, the existence of an objective world would also no longer be problematic. Appearances [Erscheinungen] in the world of the senses would refer to realities in the world of the understanding, but there would not only be real objects that appear, but one would also have to assume a subject, to whom these objects appear, or which represents these objects differently than they are in themselves, and which must originally and essentially be a thinking or representing subject, because thinking and representing is the necessary

---

[4] This is a paraphrase of a claim made at 4:360.4–9.

condition, under which appearance [Erscheinung] is even possible. Indeed, the actual existence of a thinking subject is (no matter what the author might say against this; the author who, according to his critical idealism, places the **actual** existence of the object that appears and the subject to whom it appears on a completely identical level of certainty or uncertainty) an even more necessary condition for [99] the possibility of appearances [Erscheinungen], as that which is objectively real, for at the very least we can imagine (as Berkeley's idealism shows) that, without being grounded in something real, all representations of an external world would be empty deceptions or mere modifications of the subjective power of thinking. But we cannot conceive that there are modifications without there being a subject whose modifications they are, or that expressions of a power exist without subjective power. Now, supposing that appearances [Erscheinungen] relate to real objects, and that the latter underlie the former, then a certain relation between the two must be assumed. And there the question is whether this relation is merely subjective (or apparent) or is subjective and objective (or real) at the same time. If it is merely subjective, i.e., involves only the nature of my faculty of thinking in such a way that, if I think of an appearance [Erscheinung], then I must also think of something distinct from the appearance outside of me that appears to me, and also another thing inside of me to whom it appears, without anything following from this subjective law of my power of thinking with respect to the actual reality and existence of that which appears and that to which it appears—in this way we have appearances [Erscheinungen] into infinity, in this way our Pyrrhonism has no limits, and we must say that it **appears** to us to **appear**, and Descartes's *cogito, ergo sum* is an unreliable principle, for then we would even have to doubt our individual existence, even whether we are a thinking subject. If we want to escape from this labyrinth of endless doubt, then we must contend that the relation between appearances [Erscheinungen] and **things in themselves** is not only subjective and apparent, but objective and real as well, or assume that the concepts that our understanding makes of a true substance, of a world of the understanding, and of an ideal of reason, in a word, of a noumenon, are grounded not only in the nature of our power of thinking, as the subjective form of its activity and its thought, but also in objects, noumena; we must contend that our soul could not have these concepts and would not have them if there were no true, real objects that correspond to these concepts. If this is the case, then we must further assume that the noumena, which reason must assume to actually exist, also contribute something to the way [100] in which reason conceives of our faculty of thinking, whether this faculty of thinking expresses itself as sensibility, as understanding, or as reason. Each of these sources of cognition will therefore have to comply with the laws laid down to it in particular or with its subjective form, but also with the nature of the **things in themselves** underlying its intuitions, concepts, and ideas when it comes to the way in which it represents **things in themselves**.

Assuming this, one would have to regard and determine the concepts of space and time, which are so important to the author and serve to support his entire critical system, somewhat differently. To be precise, one would have to define them as relational concepts that are not merely grounded in the nature of our sensibility and do not amount to the mere subjective form of it, as Herr **Kant** intends, rather, they would also have to be regarded as being grounded in the nature of **things in themselves**, which appear in space and time, and in this way an approximation of the Leibnizian conception of the two would emerge. However, can this conception be saved from the author's objections? We shall see. I must first explain my understanding of these two objects, so singular in kind. According to my understanding, the concepts of space and time are not strictly empirical but can also be counted among *a priori* concepts. They constitute the boundaries between the intelligible and sensible world, and connect the two with each other, or make it possible for **things in themselves** to become appearances [Erscheinungen]. This mixed nature of the concepts of space and time can, to a certain extent, explain to us why they are so unusual, so singular in kind, and why it is impossible for our understanding to view them as things, and for our imagination to regard them as relations. Because they lie in the middle between our activity and the objects of our activity as the uniting and unifying middle ground (between the subjective and the objective), and come into contact with both, they possess, as it were, something of them both, and this, their intermediate nature, enables one to count them to a certain extent among both, depending on whether one regards them from this or that side. Insofar as they are grounded in what is subjective, that is, as [101] I understand it, in the limitation [Einschränkung] of the human power of thought, they have the nature of *a priori* concepts, but insofar as they are grounded in **things in themselves** or in what is objective, that is, space in **actual** plurality [Mehrheit] and time simultaneously in plurality and the **actual** variability of represented **things in themselves**[*], they must be

---

[*] In general, one could say: the plurality that is distinct from ourselves (intuited or felt in space) provides the concept of extension [Ausdehnung], of constant magnitude [stetigen Größe] (*quantitatis*

similar to empirical representations or concepts of experience. It is grounded in our limitation that we must place the objects of the outer senses, particularly those of sight, outside of us, or that we must perceive them in space insofar as we distinguish them from ourselves. In this way it can and must seem as if the concept of space is an innate idea, that it must precede all sensations and must underlie all intuitions. But how are we to determine that absolutely nothing empirical mixes into it, or on what basis are we to prove that this does not happen? Our first perceptions by means of sight and touch take place at an age when we cannot be conscious of whether it is the concept of space or the concept of the object that is in the soul first, or whether, as it seems to me, both are not in the soul simultaneously. At the very least, the latter must be the case if space is a relational concept, for in that case it must be in the soul immediately along with the things that stand in a relation, namely the object and our self (which must distinguish itself from the object by means of this representation). It would offer us some insight into this obscure matter [102] if we were to know precisely how those who are born blind conceive of space, and more particularly if we were to know what kind of concepts of space were had by Saunderson, a profound mathematician who was born blind and who wrote about light and colours in his blindness. That something empirical is mixed into the representation of space is also clear to me on the basis of what is said about a person born blind and operated on by the famous Cheselden, namely that it seemed to this person as if all visible objects lay directly upon and touched his eye as soon as their vision was activated. This person therefore knew nothing of distance and even less of its measure, and similarly had no innate geometry. And do we not all judge of distance and the size of distant objects gradually and through experience?

But how can the author's so-called **pure intuition** be reconciled with the concepts of space that have been explained up until this point? How does the certainty and evidence of pure geometry, independent of all experience, accord with it? I think a reconciliation can be found. If we consider that everything that is intuited must be perceived in space, then space is indeed a universal, relational concept for us that recurs with every

continuae), insofar and so long as it is not different within itself. But the plurality that is not only different from our self, but also within itself, provides the concept of number [Zahl] (*quantitatis discretae*). Since, in general, no further division of plurality can be made, one sees from this that the general science of plurality (pure mathematics) can have no other and also no more parts than pure arithmetic or the general science of the magnitude of numbers [Zahlgröße] (*quantitatis discretae*), and pure geometry, or the universal science of constant magnitude (*quantitatis continuae*).

intuition and external perception, no matter how different they may otherwise be. But what then prevents us from separating this concept from the objects themselves, which are given to us in space, on the one hand, and from the specific limits set by the shapes and positions of objects in space, on the other? What prevents us from conceiving of it as a uniform, independent, and composite whole, and in this way creating or rather fabricating the concept of a universal space as a receptacle, wherein bodies or objects can exist? Once we reach this point, we can then divide this universal receptacle into compartments, so to speak, and give them all kinds of shapes or assign various limits and modifications to space. These compartments indicate the locations we allocate to objects; the limits and modifications of universal space indicate the various shapes and positions, pure creations of the imagination, that we arbitrarily construct. What we confer to these constructions must indeed be valid; they [103] must be that which we make them out to be. Should it happen that an object has precisely the shape and location that we have constructed, such that it fits into our compartments, then what is valid and true of the creations of our power of imagination must also be valid and true of the object's shape and position, precisely to the degree that is constructed by our power of imagination.

Let us now consider what the author's remaining reasons for the exclusive truth of his conception of space and time prove against the validity of the one I have offered. "Space and time," it is said, "are completely necessary representations, they cling to us with complete necessity. Although we can think of all objects without space and time, we cannot think without space and time themselves."[5] We cannot think without the concept of time because all our thought is successive and thus happens in time, and precisely this successive thinking leads us to the concept of time. But if the concept of time as well as space is subjective and grounded in the nature of our mind, more specifically in our limitation, then this limitation is something essential and constant, and as such the concept of space and that of time must be necessary as well, either as a consequence or as an inseparable accompanying aspect [Mitumstand]. The essential limitation of our power of thought renders the concepts of space and time necessary conditions of our sensibility, and the inescapable feeling of this limitation means we always expect that objects must relate to our sensibility in terms of space and time. We can distinguish objects

---

[5] This is a paraphrase of Schultz (1784, p. 22). For the corresponding passages in the first *Critique*, see A24/B38–39 and A31/B46–47.

from neither ourselves nor from each other unless we in part place them outside of us, i.e., see them in space, and in part perceive them in succession, i.e., in time. But none of this prevents the concepts of space and time from also having an objective foundation.—"All axioms of space and time entail apodictic certainty, and consequently cannot be derived from experience; in that case we would only be able to say that this is what common perception teaches, but not that it must be so. They therefore precede all experience and are *a priori* propositions, e.g., the principles that various spaces cannot follow upon one another, [104] and various times cannot exist simultaneously, that only one straight line is possible between two points, etc."[6] I think that the exact same must be the case according to my conception of space and time, for if these concepts express the relation of **things in themselves** to our sensibility that is made necessary by the essential limitation of our mind and, more specifically, the concept of space expresses plurality without considering variability, and the concept of time expresses this same plurality but considering the variability of either objects themselves or their modifications, then it is obvious that these different relations are not to be confused with one another, and thus axioms that convey this difference are not to be transmitted from one relation to another, and we cannot say that different spaces follow upon each other, or that different times are simultaneous. As far as the third axiom is concerned, it expresses a necessary relation between two objects that does not depend on the constitution of those objects, but on their actual or assumed existence, and in essence conveys nothing other than that two objects actually have the position we take them to have. Their position determines their distance, and there can only be one of these.

The reasons the author uses to prove that space and time are not discursive and universal concepts, but intuitions, do not affect my conception either, for I derive these concepts not from reasoning by means of an abstraction, but from the necessary relation of **things in themselves** to our sensibility. Space and time are always perceived and intuited along with objects, and the concept of space in particular is a necessary appendix or auxiliary aspect of every external appearance [Erscheinung]. The proposition: 'what is and ought to be an object of our external senses must be somewhere or occupy a place,' is not a proposition that we owe to reasoning, but to the inescapable feeling of our limitation. But the proposition: 'there is a universal, empty space, of which all spaces or places are

---

[6] This is again a paraphrase of Schultz (1784, p. 22). For the corresponding passages in the first *Critique*, see A24/B38–39, and A31/B47.

not composing parts but limitations,' is partially the product of fantasy and partially a product of reasoning. But it is not an innate proposition that would be operative in someone's thought without the use of sight, without instruction from others, and without one's own practice. [105] In any case, space and time are, on my view, partially grounded in objects, and thus are to this extent empirical, and are intuitions and not abstractions. I can therefore happily accept the author's reasoning, that, because all principles of time and space are synthetic propositions, they must be intuitions and not universal concepts. That is, they are intuitions insofar as they are grounded in what is objective or are relations that are perceived simultaneously along with the things that stand in a relation. But if one separates them from these things, then they are creations of the power of the imagination, namely universal empty space and infinite empty time, which are constituted in the way we have already illustrated, and which will be illustrated further.—I can also happily concede the author's following reasoning, which concerns the final inference he draws from the above: "because we conceive of both space and time as an infinite magnitude, all determinate magnitudes of their parts are possible only by means of the limitations of infinite space and infinite time, but in no way on the basis of a universal conception of space and time. If space and time were not intuitions but universal concepts, absolutely no concept of magnitude and of relations in space and in time would be possible."[7] I only have something to say about that which concerns the genesis of the concept of magnitude and relations in space and time provided here. The author claims that a somewhat innate concept of an immeasurable, empty space and of an infinite, empty time must underlie all concepts of determinate spaces and times, and in such a way that one can only obtain the latter by means of limiting the former, or that they are actually nothing other than certain incisions that one makes into immeasurable space and infinite time. In my opinion, things are the other way around, and the concept of limited spaces or places, and of a determinate time, is in the soul first and is intuited along with every intuition and sensed along with every sensation. It is from this that an immeasurable space and an infinite time are first fabricated by the imagination [Phantasie]. But once one has a concept of such things, then a philosopher can in turn take this concept as a foundation and, as the author does, regard all [106] limited spaces and times as so many limitations of it. The philosophical layperson at the very

---

[7] This is a paraphrase of Schultz (1784, pp. 23–24). See A25/B39–40 and A32/ B47–48 for the corresponding passages in the first *Critique*.

least seems to be able to do nothing other than progress by means of the faculty of invention[8] up to the concept of the immeasurability of space and the infinity of time. They would have to proceed more or less like the Psalmist who wants to imagine the omnipresence of God: **if I ascend into Heaven, you are there; if I make my bed in hell, you are also there; if I were to take flight at dawn and remain at the outermost ocean**[*], etc., or like the poet who seeks to help themselves to an approximate concept of eternity:

> I heap up giant numbers,
> Pile millions on millions;
> Eon upon eon and world upon world,
> And when I am on that endless march
> And dizzy on that terrifying height
> I seek you again,
> The power of numbers, though multiplied a thousand-fold,
> Is still not even a fraction of you.
> I blot them out and there you are, complete, before me.[9]

Since it is therefore far from true that the concepts of immeasurability and eternity underlie all limited concepts of magnitude in space and time *a priori*, we first encounter the former once we extend and assemble the latter into infinity, i.e., without stopping. How many human beings could there possibly be who are capable of conceiving of the concepts of immeasurability and eternity with complete precision and correctness without admixture of limits?

And what is the point of all this? It is not, in fact, to prove that the conception of space and time offered by me must be the only true one, but only to prove that it is possible, that it can withstand Herr **Kant's** objections, that the phenomena and appropriate principles that he presents in relation to space and time can just as well be reconciled with the supposition that these concepts are not merely subjective but also objective and, as a result, that we are not absolutely forced to accept, along with

---

[8] The word Pistorius uses here, '*Dichtungsvermögen*' (*facultas fingendi* in Latin), is a technical term for the faculty that composes a new thing out of many individual things. It is therefore a creative faculty closely related to the productive imagination. See Wolff, *German Metaphysics* §§241–42, *Psychologia Empirica* §144, Baumgarten *Metaphysics* §§589–94, and 7:174–82.

[*] See also Klopstock's ode on *The Omnipresence of God*.

[9] Pistorius quotes, without naming his source, from Albrecht von Haller's 'Uncompleted Poem on Eternity.' I have here reproduced the relevant part of the poem from Arnulf Zweig's (2002) translation.

Herr **Kant**, [107] that space and time are nothing other than subjective forms of our sensibility and contain nothing objective. For, we could only adopt the author's conception out of absolute necessity, or because of the impossibility and inadmissibility of every other conception of space and time being apodictically proven. Just as the author's system can only be built on the ruins of all the others, so, it seems to me, is this conception like an oriental despot who, after murdering all his brothers, places himself on the throne and defends himself from there. On the other hand, if any other view can only be shown to be possible, such as the one offered here, which takes space and time to be in part grounded in objects as well, then it would, it seems to me, be entitled to preferable approval on account of the following advantages.

First, by means of it we would be removed from the above-mentioned extremely unpleasant and precarious situation, into which the author's theory of appearance and reality, which is built on his concepts of space and time, places us, a situation which itself concerns our individual existence. The actual existence of an objective, intelligible world would no longer be so problematic, but would be reliable and certain. And what is even more important and interesting for us, we would be able to trust our inner sensation that we are not merely logical and apparent, but *actual* individual thinking subjects or substances, if we could convince ourselves that representations and thoughts are the true effects of a power similar in kind, i.e., of a thinking power. In a word, we would no longer be permitted to doubt whether there are **things in themselves**, which make up the substratum of our intuitions and which appear to us, and even less, it seems to me, would we be permitted to doubt whether there is in fact a thinking subject, to which **things in themselves** appear, and whether the subject that we call our **self** is this thinking subject. In general, the theory of the apparent [vom Schein] and the true would be capable of attaining more correctness and the self-consistency [Selbstbestand] which, it seems to me, the author's theory is lacking. For, it goes without saying that, according to his theory, the existence of **things in themselves** is sometimes given as merely problematic and sometimes as certain, the former because we [108] cannot know and cognize anything about them and the latter because all appearances [Erscheinungen] must be grounded in **things in themselves**, to which the former refer, whether we know anything about this or not. In this way, the author's concepts of space and time make it, if not impossible, then extremely difficult to conceive of **things in themselves** as the possible foundation or substratum of appearances [Erscheinungen], as I will soon show in more detail.

Additionally, the author's known fondness for moral ideas, the advantage of reliability and truth that he grants to these over all the speculative claims of the power of thinking, which are aimed merely at cognition, seems biased and unfounded. The greater and more important interest that these moral ideas might have (although, what can be of more importance to us than being convinced of our actual individual existence or of our substantiality, and what else do we have to lose if we have lost our **I** [Ich] and have to regard our **self** [Selbst] as a drop that has been swallowed up and devoured by the ocean?) cannot establish this advantage. Nonetheless, they are nothing other than effects or modifications of the power of thinking, and if speculative effects as a whole, from sensible intuitions up to the ideas of reason, are apparent and deceiving and have only the logical use of giving our representations order and coherence, what advantage, then, do moral concepts have? If representations in general are capable of being deceptive and apparent, where is the reliable characteristic, with which we are able to identify that some of them are not deceptive and apparent, and cannot be? Again, this characteristic cannot be their greater interest, for, if we were to admit that we must have concepts of the understanding and ideas of reason in order for us to be able to think systematically and in an orderly fashion, as empty of all content and as deceptive as they may be, and that they are only necessary for a logical purpose, then what prevents us from granting that we must also have moral concepts, with all their ostensibility [Scheinbarkeit] and emptiness, in order to be able to act systematically and in an orderly fashion, and that they are necessary for a practical purpose?

Indeed, nothing in the author's theory [109] of the apparent [vom Schein] and the true brings about more confusion and inconsistency than his solution to the so-called third antinomy, which is entirely built upon that theory, or the removal of the contradiction between the two propositions: **the human being is bound by natural necessity in its actions**, and **the human being acts with freedom**, both of which are, as the author claims, simultaneously demonstrable. The author seeks to show that both propositions are simultaneously true, or at least can be true, from a different point of view. These different points of view are, on the one hand, the human being as phenomenon with its actions as appearances [Erscheinungen] and, on the other hand, the same human being as a member of the intelligible world and its very same actions regarded as **things in themselves**. From the first point of view, its actions are (according to appearance) subjected to natural necessity and happen, just as all other effects in experience, according to the principle of sufficient reason. From the second point of view, on the other hand, they are, as **things in themselves**, free, i.e., they presuppose no other actions as necessary conditions, from which they must follow according to a law.* I have already confessed my inability to follow the author here in my review of the *Prolegomena*,[10] and even now, although I see that what has just been said does indeed express his opinion, this solution strikes me as perhaps the most obscure thing in his entire system. What seems so inconsistent and absurd about it to me may rest upon some sort of misunderstanding, but I still wish for this obscurity to be clarified, and for the apparent contradictions to be cleared away. Above all, my doubts concern the concept of freedom itself: its origin, content, and objective validity. Freedom is said to be the capacity of a being to begin a state in such a way that its action is not [110] subject to another cause, which determines it temporally, according to the law of nature [see A445/B473]. I ask: where do we get this concept? We did not extract it from experience, this singular source, from which **non-empty** concepts are said to flow. It is therefore a pure concept of reason or is essential and, as it were, innate to reason. But as such it has no advantage over the so-called ideas of pure reason; the psychological, cosmological, and theological. Thus, by what means does it acquire the advantage of being not merely subjective and deceptive, as these have? Where does it get this objective validity, such that it can be applied to the world of the understanding, and such that what it indicates, namely transcendental freedom, can be predicated as a property of **things in themselves** or of the members of the world that is entirely unknown to us? Is it consistent to claim, on the one hand, that we can know absolutely nothing of this world of the understanding (which for us is = x) and, on the other hand, to not only assume that it is composed of parts and members and appoint reason to be one of those members, but also to confer upon this reason a property corresponding to a concept that might be a mere phantom of the brain, or perhaps a deception that is necessary in and for the sake of the world of the senses? Supposing that one does this only hypothetically, this is already a violation of the first critical rule to not go beyond the field of experience when using the understanding and reason. This is the case, above all, because this rule is also violated when one similarly transfers a concept of reason, such as that of cause and effect, into the

---

* It is peculiar that other philosophers maintain the exact opposite, namely that the belief in natural necessity is not based on both feeling and reasoning, but that, by contrast, the idea that we possess freedom is based more on a somewhat enlightened feeling that we cannot entirely deny, and they therefore make an effort to discover its origin and the reason why it deceives us.

[10] See *Allgemeine deutsche Bibliothek*. 59. Band, 2. Stück (1784), p. 346.

intelligible world and must apply it to **things in themselves**, if one alleges that reason, a **thing in itself**, causes and determines actions that are free in themselves but appear to be necessary. Is the content of this concept consistent with itself? As belonging to the world of the understanding, it is supposed to exclude all time and determinations of time, and freedom is indeed said to be a capacity to begin a state. How can we conceive of a beginning without the admixture of the concept of time, and how can we conceive of the end that opposes the beginning, similarly with 'starting,' 'stopping,' and 'passing'? A state beginning presupposes that this state **was** not yet, and thus also presupposes a time when it was merely possible and another time when it [111] became actual. Consequently, this concept seems to simultaneously presuppose the determinations of time that it is supposed to exclude. How can this be reconciled?* I ask further, if the entire human soul [Seelenwesen], its entire power of representation with all its effects, must be taken to be appearance [Erscheinung] (which, in my view, must take place according to the author's principles and his conception of space and time), how can one then define one part of this soul [Seelenwesens]—and reason is nothing other than this—as a noumenon or a **thing in itself**? Presupposing complete unfamiliarity with the intelligible world and **things in themselves**, on what basis can we know that something belonging to the human being's subjective and apparent power of thinking, namely its reason, and consequently **it** itself insofar as it is equipped with reason, is a part of the world of the understanding and a **thing in itself**? Even to presuppose this we must already be familiar with this world insofar as we know it contains manifold things or actual parts, and how are we to experience this here in the world of the senses given the insurmountable [112] chasm that the author has placed between the two worlds? But supposing we were to know that the human being is a **thing in**

---

* The reasoning that the author uses in the first antinomy to demonstrate the proposition that the world can have no beginning in time can also be used to demonstrate that no state can begin anywhere but in time, because a beginning always presupposes the concept of time. Herr Kant reasons as follows: "Suppose the world has a beginning, then there must be a preceding time, in which it was not, namely an empty time. But no origination of any kind of thing" (and consequently no origination of a state) "is possible in empty time, because no part of an empty time prior to another contains, in itself, any kind of condition of existence prior to that of non-existence, whether one assumes that it originates from itself or by means of another cause, thus the world can have no beginning" [A428/B456], that is, none other than a beginning in time, and because it cannot have a beginning in time, it can therefore have no beginning whatsoever. One is now just as entitled to infer: if a state should have a beginning, then it must have it in time, and should it not have a beginning in time, then it can have no beginning at all. Thus, according to this style of reasoning the concept of freedom cancels itself out, insofar as it is said to exclude the concept of time.

itself insofar as it possesses reason, then we would also simultaneously know with the same certainty that the rational being is a thinking, independently existing subject, or is a thinking substance, not merely according to appearance [dem Scheine nach] but **actually in itself**; thinking, because reason necessarily entails thinking and we cannot conceive of an **unthinking** reason; a substance, because it is impossible for this **thing in itself** to be conceived in any other way than under the presupposition that it is an independently existing subject, as a true cause of true effects or **things in themselves** (free actions). In this way we would, without noticing, come back to the common concepts of not only cause and effect, but also of substance and accident, which the author continually seeks to present as merely logical and applicable only to appearances [Erscheinungen], especially in his paralogism of reason, but which he here, it seems to me, must accept as objective or valid for the world of the understanding.—If human actions are free **in themselves** and only appear to be necessary, then I ask: to whom does the human being and its actions appear as mere phenomena and appearances [Erscheinungen]? It is beyond dispute that some subject must be assumed for this purpose, for it would be extremely absurd to speak about appearances [Erscheinungen] as things which, to a certain extent, exist on their own and without relation to a representing subject, and elsewhere as being able to exist in a representation, more specifically in a mistaken, limited, and incorrectly perceived representation.—Thus, the human being, along with its actions, is an appearance [Erscheinung] to the human being itself.—I ask further: to the human being insofar as it is an appearance [Erscheinung], or insofar as it is a thing in itself? To assume or state the first, or to say that an appearance [Erscheinung] appears [erscheint] to another appearance [Erscheinung], seems so extremely absurd to me that one must indeed assume the second, and as a result also assume this: that the human being's actions, which are free in actuality (and which are things in themselves), appear to be necessary to the human being, which is a thing **in itself** as well, i.e., they present themselves as other than they are in themselves. Consequently, it is things in themselves, things that belong to the objective world of the understanding, that the human being sees, but [113] which are obviously obscured and obstructed by the fog of sensibility. In this way we would in essence return to Leibnizian idealism, which the author so strongly rejects, and the only difference between this and the author's critical idealism would solely consist in the fact that Leibniz applies his own merely to the objects of outer sense in space, but the author extends critical idealism to the objects of inner sense in time as well. According to this assumption, however, both philosophers would have to agree that all appearance and all deception [Täuschung] stem from the senses only, or from the limited capacity of representation, especially insofar as it manifests itself in sensibility. According to this solution, the author would distance himself from his own system and approximate the Leibnizian one in the sense that both place worlds that are otherwise so entirely separate in a precise connection, such that the world of the understanding not only comprises the actual object and that which is material of the world of the senses, but the one also intervenes in and has an effect on the other. For, reason, a thing **in itself** and part of the objective world of the understanding, causes and determines actions that appear in the world of the senses, which, admittedly, are free actions in the world of the understanding only in the first instance, but which become apparent once again and become parts of the world of the senses insofar as human beings take them to be not only that which they are in themselves, namely free, but necessary as well. These doubts and problems concerning the author's theory of appearance and its application to his conception of freedom should suffice. I repeat again that they may entirely or in part stem from misunderstanding. Nonetheless, it is necessary for them to be cleared away if this system is to be recognized as lucid and consistent with itself, since they could also arise for other investigators of the Kantian system.

I now return to my conception of space and time and note that, in relation to the seemingly necessary correction to the theory of the apparent and the true, the following aspect (insofar as it is found to be justified) should not be ignored, namely that the concept of time (and consequently everything that relates to it) contains more [114] of what is objective than space, and also less of what is apparent and deceptive, and by comparison must possess more of what is true, objective, and real, because the concept of time is based not merely on the plurality of objects, as the concept of space is, but also at the same time on the variability of objects.

Second, according to our concepts of space and time, appearances [Erscheinungen] and things in themselves, the subjective world of the senses and the objective intelligible world, would be brought into an actual and true connection, and in this way the most important and, in my opinion, fundamental error that pervades the author's entire system can be avoided. The error is this: that, according to his system, an objective, intelligible world is assumed for no reason, and things in themselves are, as we say in our provincial dialect, assumed for naught and naught again [für nichts und wieder nichts angenommen werden]. Were it not but for the sake of giving the fluctuating whole a kind of stability and foundation, there would be absolutely no need for any objects except those that are apparent, and for no subjects except those that are merely logical.* But this stability and foundation are indeed only apparent. There is no true connection between the world of the senses and the intelligible world, for, if there were, **things in themselves** would actually have to be the objects of our sensibility, and how would we see them except as in space? How would we perceive them, except as in time and according to determinations of time? Space and time are therefore the only middle path between **things in themselves** and our faculty of representation, through which the avenue of communication between both worlds leads. But now, since space and time are merely subjective forms of our sensibility, contain nothing objective in themselves, are based on nothing objective, and thus do not relate to **things in themselves**, [115] all communication is therefore cut off and a gulf between both worlds is established in such a way that **things in themselves** can just as little reach our cognition as our faculty of representation can reach over to them. The author makes the admittedly not unfounded objection to the Leibnizian philosophy that it assigns to the senses the wretched task of presenting an obscured and distorted image of the objective, intelligible world to the soul. But I think that this task is not as horrible as when one has the senses present an entirely false image, and this is what the author actually does. According to Leibniz, our senses are a cloudy, crudely cut lens, through which our soul actually views **things in themselves**, even if at a dark and dim distance, and time and again contorts, distorts, and displaces things. But according to our author, they are as though they were a lens, onto the outer surface of which a completely foreign painting is affixed, and which does not at all present the objective world, not even a feature of it, but a landscape that is completely isolated from it that is nonetheless nicely illuminated, well-ordered in all its parts by means of the understanding and its concepts, and superbly harmonizes with our instruments of sight, with which it alone fits and for which it is determined. By and large, it does not at all occur to the majority of those who see through the telescope of the senses that what they see is not the actual, true, external word, and that it is not in itself actually constituted as

---

* The author's entire reasoning, by means of which he wishes to illustrate the so-called paralogism of reason in its bareness, boils down to the fact that he attempts to show that the unity of consciousness leads us no further than to the presupposition of an apparent and logical subject, i.e., one assumed for the sake of thought, but in no way entitles us to infer the actual existence of a single thinking substance. We must therefore assume that we can manage with a merely apparent, logical subject and that this will suffice. If this were not so, then one could rightly infer the former from the latter.

they view it. On the basis of the distorted features of the painting which, in their opinion, do not correctly fit with one another and do not completely harmonize with one's trained or meticulous power of judgement, only just a few will become suspicious that they are not entirely viewing things in their actual and true form, and that those unharmonious features are indeed due to the imperfect instrument and their limited power of sight. Yet another wishes to reverse their telescope, as it were, and not look outside themselves with it but look into themselves because they believe there are absolutely no external things to be seen, no objective world, nor could there be. Everything that is thereby presented to such a person would only be images of thought that appear to and alternate in front of their soul, but some of which are imagined with such admirable skill that one must believe that [116] they are not merely images in us but actual objects outside of us. Eventually, our author arrived and explained that, after he had closely examined our telescope, although there actually is and must be an objective world and real things outside of us, we nonetheless do not perceive the slightest of such things with our instrument and through it due to its particular form, nor are we capable of discovering anything about them. What we believe ourselves to see would be nothing but appearances [Erscheinungen] that have been produced and formed onto the instrument itself by means of its artificial cut and construction. Nevertheless, these appearances [Erscheinungen] could function for us as if there were actual realities, if we only knew how to properly order, separate, and connect them in a regulated whole. But setting aside all analogies, we can always say that, according to the author's system, the intelligible world is all but eradicated for us, for, if **things in themselves** do exist, then they exist entirely severed from the world of the senses, in which everything remains as it is and everything happens in its proper, regular manner, whether there is also an objective world or not. Indeed, we cannot even suppose that the one is there for the sake of the other, nor that the one is organized harmoniously in accordance with the other, nor that there is a previously determined harmony between the world of the senses and the intelligible world. For, if both worlds hang together only by means of this most subtle thread, then our sensibility and its form, the concepts of space and time, must also have a relation to the world of the understanding that is to be represented and must be organized in accordance with it or, put differently, in this case this form of our sensibility could no longer be merely subjective, but must also be objective and grounded in what is objective.

Third, supposing the above, if we are now permitted to assume that, just as the concepts of space and time are not merely subjective but are also objective at the same time, the same is the case for the concepts of the understanding and the ideas of reason, then this would require some qualification and correction regarding the overall outcome of the *Critique of Pure Reason*, namely that the concepts of the understanding, which are in themselves empty, are to be granted absolutely no other application than to appearances [Erscheinungen] and that they are to be dogmatically extended beyond the field of experience just as little [117] as the ideas of reason. If the concepts of time and space are not merely subjective, then the concepts of the understanding cannot be either, and for the following reason: because they are designed to process, order, and make intelligible the appearances [Erscheinungen] that are given in space and time. For, if these appearances [Erscheinungen] themselves contain something objective, if their substratum and their real foundational material [Grundstoff] are **things in themselves**, or if, as Herr **Kant** explains himself on this matter in plain language in another text, namely his *Groundwork of the Metaphysics of Morals* (admittedly, in my opinion, quite divergent from the principles of the *Critique*): "**The world of the understanding contains the ground of the world of the senses, and hence also of its laws**" [4:453.31–32], then the nature of the understanding and the constitution of its concepts must be presumed to be attuned to and arranged in harmony with this world of the understanding and its laws in order to fit this objectivity, in order to be able to properly process it, and in order to bring into it no laws that contradict the laws of the world of the understanding, or that would not be appropriate to it. If there is nonetheless an **actual** plurality of objects in the intelligible world, which are **actually** variable and do change, then analogical relations must be assumed to be between them, specifically those of inherence, causality, and reciprocal influence; relations which very likely underlie and correspond to the relations in the world of the senses. For example, the relational concepts of cause and effect and of reciprocal influence might be grounded in this relation of **things in themselves**, by virtue of which they all belong to and comprise one system of being, and by virtue of which one exists for the sake of the other. In a word, they might be grounded in the universal harmony of all the parts of the intelligible world. The universal laws of nature: **nothings happens by chance; nothing happens by means of a leap; there are no gaps; there is no fate;**[11] the laws, which Herr Kant derives from the nature of our faculty of thinking *a priori*, and puts

---

[11] These are the so-called cosmological laws, see A226–30/B279–82 and Watkins (2001) for a discussion.

forward as necessary laws of thought, have either been regarded by all other philosophers (if one excludes those idealists who completely eliminate the external world) as if they were constructed from the observation of nature and abstracted from constant experience, [118] or have been presupposed as axioms that require no proof. Against the first idea, Herr Kant objects that they could not then have the mark or the character of necessity that so typically describes them. Against this objection it can of course be noted that the ever-present constancy of these laws of nature, which can be found in all experience and which does indeed underlie all experience to a certain extent, forms an indissoluble association of concepts, by means of which we must take them to be necessary even if we do not know how to strictly prove or legitimately deduce their necessity. But in a different way, both opinions can be reconciled if we assume that the connection, the effects, and countereffects of the parts of the objective intelligible world are also established according to precisely those laws that are prescribed to the human understanding for its operations. Thus if, e.g., the nature of our mind requires completely connected representations, then the things that occupy its representation would also be placed in connection in conformity with this law.* I think that we must conceive of things in this way, for, in general, only the following three options are possible, namely: either the world of the understanding has no laws whatsoever, or it has completely different laws that diverge from the laws of the world of the senses, or the laws of both worlds agree with each other and are at bottom one and the same. With respect to the first case, I do not at all wish to avail myself of the peculiar definition of the world of the understanding and its laws from the author's *Groundwork of the Metaphysics of Morals*, referenced above, rather I only wish to remark that everything that exists, be it what it may, must have a form of existence or must exist in a **certain determinate** [119] way, and precisely this form of existence, this manner and way in which the world of the understanding exists, comprises its laws. Should it be a complete unity and that which necessarily exists, then this complete unity, this unconditional necessity is its law. But should it consist of parts, then these parts must coexist in a **certain determinate** way, and this manner of coexistence comprises its law. If we were to assume the second case, then

---

* The commentator of Hartley's *Observations of Man* has already attempted to give a psychological proof of the universal validity of the principle of sufficient reason in this fashion, on the basis of the nature of the human mind, which can think of nothing other than connected representations, and, in this respect, on the basis of the harmony existing between the objective nature of things and the nature of our power of thought. Hartley's *Observations of Man*, Part I, p. 62. [This 'commentator' is Pistorius himself. See the Introduction to this chapter.]

we must maintain that our understanding processes things **in themselves** completely contrary to their nature and according to laws that conflict with those of things in themselves, and thus entirely falsely and incorrectly, and the result of this would be nothing other than a thoroughgoing deception, and the above accusations against the author's system, that according to it the world of the understanding would be as good as eliminated, would thereby be entirely confirmed and justified. Only the third case therefore remains to us, to which we must all the more adhere, because it is on the basis of this supposed harmony of the laws of both worlds, this agreement of both sides in the universality of all experience, that we can explain to ourselves why these laws of nature, which are simultaneously the laws of human thought insofar as they are both simultaneously, must appear to us to be necessary, and how and why it is possible that the mind constructs them from its nature *a priori* or can determine in advance that they must appear in every experience by means of a synthesis. But it also allows us to understand how philosophers who have observed the nature and process of their mind in its operations and made this an object of reflection less so than they have the external world of experience could have regarded precisely these laws as residing and given within the latter. In this way the author's exceptionally shrewd deduction of the concepts of reason preserves its complete value, as does the clear account of how the logical need and interest of systematic thought can be satisfied by this deduction and by the ideas of pure reason. But if one were to assume that the laws that are presented in it as given to the human mind are laws of the objective world of the understanding as well, only then would a true connection between the world of the senses and that of the understanding be furnished and an awe-inspiring harmony be established. Only then would our representing and thinking acquire [120] a reliable and secure foundation, which, because it is lacking delusions, reverie, and hallucinations, makes up the actual and only feature, by means of which real sensations can be distinguished from phantasms, and true, natural thinking from false philosophy and fanaticisms [Schwärmeryen] of all kinds.

I must hasten to the end, otherwise I will continue to talk about the difference between sensation and prevailing phantasy, which, as the reviewer of the *Critique of Pure Reason* correctly notes (A.D. Bibl., Pt. II of the Suppl. to Volumes XXXVII–LII, p. 860),[12] the author has not

---

[12] *Allgemeine deutsche Bibliothek*, Supplement to Volumes 37–52, Part II (1783), p. 860. This is Garve's original, unedited review of the first *Critique*. See Sassen (2000, pp. 59–77) for an English translation.

considered. I must only note this, that insufficient provisions are made for an appropriate and secure distinction of both states of the soul according to the author's system, in my opinion. If absolutely nothing real underlies our sensations, they contain absolutely nothing objective and our concepts of the understanding, principles, and operations apply to and operate on nothing but appearances [Erscheinungen] and everything is therefore only subjective, then it is difficult for there to be a reliable feature to distinguish between real sensations and fantasies. For, since both are subjective and have nothing to do with and nothing in common with what is objective, it cannot easily be explained how it comes to be that some of these merely subjective representations not only generally agree with the representations of other human beings, whom we take to be clever and rational and who regard their representations as true and real, but also, and above all, why some of them agree with the actual requirements, needs, and transactions of life and human society and others do not. If both are subjective it cannot easily be seen why, when I act according to one, I achieve my wish and purpose and, when I allow myself to be led by my fantasies, as convinced of their actuality as I might be, I everywhere come up against resistance and am found to be a fool. One could perhaps say that this distinction can be explained in that a clever and rational human being organizes its sensations and thoughts according to **all** the laws of the faculty of representing and thinking without exception, but the fantast and madman, on the other hand, organizes their fantasies and visions only according to **some**, or that these fantasies and visions can be distinguished [121] from real sensations and true, natural thoughts in that they do not agree with all the principles and rules of rational thought, as the former do, but only with some of them. On the one hand, however, this would not exclude what is objective nor make it superfluous. And on the other hand it could be objected to this, first, that there are actually fantasts and dreamers who wish to bring their visions into an orderly system of reason, such that one can counter them with no concept of reason, no axiom that they are not capable of uniting with and adapting to their delusion and, second, that, if one could bring some of the concepts and principles of the understanding into harmony with these fantasies (as experience teaches in relation to the madmen whose madness consists in some kind of fixation), it would not at all be impossible to bring this about in relation to those that remain as well. It therefore seems to me to be overwhelmingly probable that one must accept something objective as underlying sensations and thoughts if one wants to find a secure mark to distinguish between real and false sensation, true, natural thoughts and fanaticism.* Insofar as this is now possible according to the way of conceiving of space and time presented thus far, this would be a new advantage connected to it.

Finally, the connection between **things in themselves** and our understanding, between their laws and the laws of the human power of thought, and the harmony between the objective and the subjective [122] world, would only be thoroughly and entirely complete if we were also permitted to assume that true objects likewise underlie and correspond to the ideas of pure reason. This would be true of both the psychological and the cosmological, as well as of the theological ideas in particular, or of the so-called ideal of pure reason. And what would this be but a highest and most perfect reason, if by reason we understand that which, among noumena, is analogous and corresponds to our human, discursive reason, so that we avoid all, even the most subtle anthropomorphism. Sufficiently, the ideal of pure reason would therefore function for us as a true, actual object, by means of which all that perfect, awe-inspiring harmony between our understanding and objects, between the world of the senses and that of the understanding has been conceived and formed. And in this way truth would reign not only in the kingdom of grace (of morals), but also in the kingdom of nature, the precise kind of justice would be done to the interest of truth that the author does only to the interest of morals, and in this way no additional biased preference for moral ideas and principles and no undeserved discrimination of merely epistemological ideas and principles would take place.

I hereby conclude these already too longwinded reflections on the Kantian system, without getting involved in a closer discussion of those qualifications, modifications, or corrections that its main principle, regarding the use, or rather non-use, of the understanding beyond the field of experience, might require. I will also say nothing in defence of Leibniz's familiar principles against the author's objections, even if I believe that they can be vindicated and some material and some suggestions have already been given in their defence in the above remarks, insofar as they have not been entirely unfounded.

---

* If one were to assume that the same laws and a harmonious course exist in what is objective and in what is subjective, in the universal nature of things and in the nature of human mind, on this basis one could comprehend that the study and observation of the first would correct and promote the cognition and orderly course of the latter, and the precise cognition and compliance with the laws of the mind would in general both correct and make the cognition and observation of nature easier, in a word, one could comprehend that both must be of such important and reciprocal help to each other as experience seems to attest.

It might seem bold that the reviewer, a mere admirer of speculative investigations, wishes to point out errors to the foremost of our speculative thinkers in his system, the fruit of many years of reflection. But if it only has the benefit of prompting Herr **Kant** to a more detailed explanation and removal of the true or imagined difficulties and offences in his system, or [123] of inspiring more clever and shrewd examiners of it, or to in general only provide the opportunity of pulling the objects that are of such extreme importance for thinkers, which Herr **Kant** has treated in such an original way, out from the dead silence in which they lie buried and offer them up for investigation, then it will not have been for nothing to have dared this attempt at an examination. And even if nothing of what I have brought against the *Critique* and its system were to survive cross-examination, I would still have no reason to regret my efforts as long as they instructed me on important and interesting points. The saying *in magnis voluisse sat est*[13] always remains to excuse me. And to those who love truth just as much as they are deep-thinking philosophers, and from whom I expect advice about my concerns, every similarly imperfect attempt to judge his masterwork must always be more agreeable and welcome than the calm indifference (as well as idolizing and thorough-going but uncritical approval), with which so many who should and could have examined it have thus far adopted.

---

[13] *it is sufficient to wish for great things*

6

Hermann Andreas Pistorius
Introduction

Although Pistorius' review of the *Groundwork* was by no means the first,[1] it was without a doubt the most important early review, at least with respect to its influence on the second *Critique*. Kant not only knew the review, but he also knew that Pistorius was the author: in a letter to Kant dated May 14, 1787, Daniel Jenisch reports that, "Your reviewer in the [*Allgemeine*] *deutsche Bibliothek* is allegedly Provost Pistorius [...] the translator of Hartley. His review of your *Groundwork* [Grundlage] etc., even though it does not go deep enough with all its apparent rigour, has found many adherents, because in moral science minds happen to be distorted by popularity" (10:486.35–487.2). Given the objections Pistorius raises in the review, which I briefly outline below, he is without a doubt the "certain reviewer" that Kant mentions in the Preface to the second *Critique*, and whom Kant praises there as "devoted to truth and astute and therefore always worthy of respect" (5:8.25–27).

Pistorius raises several important objections in his review of the *Groundwork*, many of which are now regarded as classic responses to Kant's moral theory in the literature. Pistorius raises the 'empty formalism' objection, for instance, namely that a purely formal principle is not sufficient to judge whether a maxim or a will is good.[2] On the contrary, Pistorius argues that we need to define the nature of the good first before we can determine if a law or a will is good.[3] As Kant states in the Preface to the second *Critique*, he deals with this objection in the second chapter of the Analytic in direct response to the "certain reviewer," i.e., Pistorius, who claimed against the *Groundwork* that "*the concept of the good was not established before the moral principle*" (5:8.27–9.2). Other notable remarks

---

[1] See the General Introduction to this volume for a (roughly) chronological list of the first reviews of the *Groundwork*.
[2] See below pp. 455–57 of the original review, as well as Guyer (2021) for a discussion.
[3] See e.g., p. 449 of the original review. We might call this, with Gesang (2007, p. xxvi), the 'priority of the good' objection. See Timmermann (2022, ch. 3) for a discussion.

in the review include: (1) Pistorius' claim that, in order to make sense of Kant's principle, we need to take the consequences of universalizing a maxim into account;[4] (2) that a categorical imperative is impossible because human beings can only be bound by a law that appeals to an interest (pp. 455–56), thus there are only hypothetical imperatives (pp. 457 and 462); and (3) that there is a difference between the happiness produced by instinct and that produced by reason (see p. 450). This latter point is a response to Kant's claim in the *Groundwork* (see 4:395.8–12) that reason's purpose is not to produce happiness, and Kant likely responds to it in the second *Critique* (see 5:61.32–62.7). The review ends with the claim that if Kant's moral theory appears better than others in theory, it is certainly not better in practice (see p. 463). Kant offers some remarks in the second *Critique* on this point as well (see 5:35.11–18), which might be a response to this claim of Pistorius'.

Translation Notes

In preparing this translation I have referenced both the original review (1786) and the edition printed in Gesang (2007). In this review, Pistorius both paraphrases and directly quotes extensively from the *Groundwork*, but he only occasionally uses quotation marks to indicate that he is doing so. In this translation, double quotations marks are used when they were present in the original review, but I have also inserted quotation marks in square brackets around blocks of text that paraphrase Kant heavily, if not quote him directly, even though they were absent in the original review. I provide references in square brackets to the one or more passages that Pistorius paraphrases or quotes from throughout.

---

[4] See p. 455, original pagination, and Walschots (2020) for the claim that Kant responds to this charge in the 'Typic' chapter of the second *Critique*.

Review of the *Groundwork* (1786)

Allgemeine deutsche Bibliothek. 66. Band, 2. Stück, 1786, pp. 447–63.

[447]

Groundwork of the Metaphysics of Morals by Immanuel Kant. Riga, Hartknoch, 1785. 8. 128 pages.

[448]

Intending to someday publish a Metaphysics of Morals, which is a pure moral philosophy completely cleansed of everything that might be empirical, Herr Professor Kant issues this *Groundwork* in advance, wherein he presents the subtleties that the Metaphysics of Morals unavoidably contains, in order to not mix them up with more accessible doctrines in the future, and wherein he wishes to seek out and establish the most supreme principle of morality, which he considers a business that is separate from every other moral investigation in its purpose.[1] He is of the opinion that ["]it is of the utmost necessity to at some point work out a pure moral philosophy, for that there must be one is of itself clear from the common idea of duty and of moral laws["] [4:389.7–11]—and indeed ["]not merely on the basis of a ground [Beweggrunde] of speculation, in order to investigate the source of the practical principles that lie *a priori* in our reason, but because morals themselves remain subject to all sorts of corruption as long as we lack that guideline and supreme norm by which to judge them correctly.["] [4:389.36–390.3] The author has hereby taken the path that is, in his opinion, the most fitting ["]if one wants to take one's route analytically from common cognition to the determination of its supreme principle and in turn synthetically from the examination of this principle and its source back to common cognition, in which we find it used.["] [4:392.18–22] This remarkable text

---

[1] This long sentence is a paraphrase of a number of different claims made at 4:391.16–17; 4:388.35–37; 4:391.36–392.2; and 4:392.1–6.

has therefore been given the following three sections: I. Transition from common to philosophical moral rational cognition; II. Transition from popular moral philosophy to the metaphysics of morals; III. Final step from the metaphysics of morals to the critique of pure practical reason. [see 4:392.23–28] I will extract the author's main propositions and append some explanatory and critical remarks.

The author remarks, first, that ["]nothing can be taken to be good without limitation except a good will,["] [4:393.6–7] that this will is good ["]not because of what it effects or accomplishes, not because of its fitness to attain some intended end, but good just by its willing, i.e., in itself and, considered by itself, it is to be esteemed beyond compare much higher than anything that could ever be brought about by it in favour of some inclination, and indeed, [449] if you will, the sum of all inclinations.["] [4:394.13–18] The author admits that ["]there is something strange in this principle for the estimation of the worth of the will, even if it should have the approval of common reason.["] [4:394.32–35] He therefore considers it necessary to examine it more closely. [see 4:395.2–3] Here I wish the author would have found it preferable above all to discuss the general concept of that which is **good**, and to determine more closely what he means by this, for we clearly must come to an agreement on this before we can establish anything about the absolute worth of a good will. I am therefore justified in asking, first: what is **good** in general, and what is a good will in particular? Can we even conceive of a will that is good in and of itself, regarded as having no relation to an object of any kind? If one says: 'good is that which is universally approved and esteemed,' then I may ask further: why is it approved and esteemed, and does this happens rightly and for a reason or not? A universally agreed upon approval, if it were to ever take place and be possible, would never be able to function as the final ground of judgement for a philosophical researcher. Here I do not see how one could admit of anything at all as entirely and absolutely good, or could call something good, which in fact comes to nothing good, and just as little do I see how one could admit of a will that is good absolutely, considered merely on its own. But the will is said to be absolutely good **not** in relation to some object of the will, but **only** in relation to its principle or to a law, for the sake of which it acts.[2] Let this be so. Then I ask further: does it

---

[2] The emphasis in this sentence is added because I have reversed the positions of 'not' and 'only.' Based on the surrounding context, Pistorius seems to be paraphrasing Kant's view in order to criticize it, but if that is the case then the original position of 'not' and 'only' gets Kant's view backwards. If the original positions of 'not' and only' are to be retained, then Pistorius is describing his own view, but this does not easily fit with the surrounding context.

suffice to make a will good that it acts according to any principle or from respect for any law, be it what it may, good or evil?—Impossible! Thus, it must be a good principle, a good law, the following of which makes a will good. And the question 'what is good?' turns back around, and if we have pushed it back from the will to the law, then we must now answer it here in a satisfactory way, i.e., we must eventually come to some kind of object or to an ultimate end of the law, and we must avail ourselves of what is material, because we cannot get by with what is formal in relation to either the will or the law. What consequence this has for the entire moral system we will see later on. For now, I continue and relay a remark of the author's, [450] by means of which he intends to prove his above principle of the worth of an absolutely good will. It is this: 'in the case of a being that has reason and a will, if the actual end of nature were this being's preservation, its prosperity, in a word its happiness, then she has made very bad arrangements for this' (entirely against the principle that ["]in the natural predispositions of an organized being, no organ will be found in it for any end than that which is also the most fitting for it and the most suitable["] [4:395.4–7]) ["]in appointing this creature's reason as the accomplisher of this purpose. For, all the actions it has to perform with a view to this purpose would be marked out for it far more accurately by instinct, and that end would thereby have been obtained much more reliably than can ever be done by reason, which at the most would have been able to serve it only to contemplate the fortunate predisposition of its nature, to admire it, to rejoice in it and to be grateful to the beneficent cause for it, but not to subject its faculty of desire to that weak and deceptive instruction and meddle with nature's purpose. In a word, nature would have prevented reason from striking out into practical use etc.["] [4:395.8–23] In this reasoning, it seems to me that proper attention is paid neither to the question of whether a completely unpractical reason might also be possible, nor to the nature of reason as developing only gradually and to the similarly progressive development of human happiness. Nature, the author says, if happiness were its end, would have led us to it by means of instinct far more accurately and without error. Yes, I answer, if happiness by means of reason and happiness by means of instincts are the same thing, and there is no difference between the two other than that the former is weaker, inferior, and less pleasant than the latter; if we were not at all permitted to consider the fact that we are indebted to our own efforts for it; and [if we were not permitted] to be aware of the pleasant fact that it is in large part the work of our own self-activity—only then would it be more accurate and expedient to drive human beings to happiness by means of instinct or, what is the same, to give them an animal or instinctual happiness. But what, then, is reason, the insight and knowledge of that which makes the human being happy, supposed to achieve for the human being? If it should entirely agree with the instincts that drive us to happiness, [451] and this must surely be the case if it is to do the job identified by the author, then its maxims could not be distinguished from the instruction of our drives, and we would never be able to determine how much of a share the force of instinct or the choice of reason has in making us happy. If reason should disagree with instinct, then it should disapprove of the compulsive laws of instinct and reject the enslavement of sensibility. As such, it would not only be a useless but also a dangerous addition to our self-contradictory nature, and all the pleasures of the drives would be disturbed and spoiled by this indeed rational but completely useless critic. It therefore seems that if we are to have reason, then it must be a practical reason. Our reason, not immediately perfect but only gradually cultivated, only leads to a progressive happiness, which, similarly, is not perfect all at once nor at any particular moment of our existence, but progresses along with our perfecting reason seemingly in parallel (which shall be understood as true inner happiness). On this basis we are entitled to conclude neither that our happiness is not an end of nature, nor that reason was not given to us to make us happy. That it achieves this end so seldomly and incompletely gives us no reason to deny that it is meant to make us take part in happiness. Its inadequacy and incapacity to in some way make human beings virtuous or worthy of happiness just as little proves something against the assumption that reason has been given to us to lead us to virtue.

With this first proposition the following one is connected: "an action from duty has its moral worth not in the purpose that is to be attained by it, and it does not depend on the actuality of the object of the action, but merely on the principle of willing according to which, regardless of any object of the faculty of desire, the action is done." [4:399.35–400.3] "In what, then," the author adds, "can the moral worth of the action lie, if it should not lie in the will with reference to the action's hoped-for effect? It can lie nowhere else than in the principle [452] of the will, for the will stands halfway between its *a priori* principle, which is formal, and its incentive, which is material, at a crossroads, as it were. And since it must after all be determined by something, it will have to be determined by the formal principle of willing in general when an action is done from duty, since every material principle has been taken away from it." [4:400.6–16] The third proposition expresses this formal principle in the following way: "duty is the necessity of the action from respect for the law,"

[4:400.18–19] which is to say: ["]nothing remains for the will that can determine it or make it a good will than **objectively** the law and **subjectively** pure respect for this practical law, and hence the maxim of complying with such a law, even if it infringes on all my inclinations.["] [4:400.31–401.2] The following serves as further elucidation: ["]All effects, e.g., agreeableness of one's condition, advancement of the happiness of others, could also have been brought about by other causes (but indeed not in the same way and to the same degree) and thus there was, for this, no need of the will of a rational being, even though in it alone the highest and unconditional good can be found. Nothing other than the representation of the law in itself, which of course can take place only in rational beings, in so far as it, not the hoped-for effect, is the determining ground of the will, can therefore constitute the pre-eminent good that we call moral, which is already present in the person themself who acts according to it, and is not first to be expected from the effect." [4:401.6–16] The author continues: "but what kind of law can that be, the representation of which must determine the will even without regard for the effect expected from it, so that this can be called good without limitation? The mere conformity with law is all that remains, which alone serves the will as its distinguishing feature, i.e., **I ought never to proceed except in such a way that I could also will that my maxim should become a universal law.** Here, then, the mere conformity with law as such, (not founded on any law determined with a view to certain actions) is what serves the will as its principle, and also must serve it, if duty is not to be at all times an empty delusion and chimerical concept, but common human reason in its practical [453] judgement is also in perfect agreement with this, and has the envisaged principle before its eyes." [see 4:402.1–4, 4:402.6–9, 4:402.10–15] All of this the author makes clear through the following example, which I wish to present in abbreviated fashion: ["]There is the question of whether I, when I am in trouble, may not make a promise with the intention not to keep it. Here I readily discern the different meanings the question can have: whether it is prudent or whether it conforms with duty to make a false promise. I see very well that it is not enough to extricate myself from the present predicament by means of this subterfuge, but that it requires careful deliberation whether this lie may not later give rise to much greater inconvenience for me, and since with all my supposed cleverness the consequences cannot be so easily foreseen that trust once lost might not be far more disadvantageous to me than any ill that I now mean to avoid, whether one might not act more prudently in this matter by proceeding according to a universal maxim, and by making it one's habit to promise nothing except with the intention of keeping it. But here it very soon becomes clear to me that such a maxim will still only be founded on the apprehended consequences. Now, to be truthful from duty is something quite different from being truthful from the apprehension of adverse consequences, since in the first case the concept of the action in itself already contains a law for me, whereas in the second I must first look around elsewhere to see what effects on me this might involve. For, if I deviate from the principle of duty, this is quite certainly evil, but if I only defect from my maxim of prudence, this can sometimes be very advantageous to me, though it is of course safer to adhere to it. However, to instruct myself in the quickest and yet most infallible way when responding to the problem of whether a lying promise conforms with duty, I ask myself: would I actually be content that my maxim (to extricate myself from a predicament by means of an untruthful promise) should hold as a universal law, for myself as well as for others? And would I be able to say to myself that everyone may make an untruthful promise when one finds oneself in a predicament from which one can extricate oneself in no other way? I soon become aware that I could indeed will the lie, but by no means a universal law to lie. [454] For, according to such a law there would actually be no promise at all, since it would be futile to profess my will to others with regard to my future actions, who would not believe this pretence, or if they rashly did so, would pay me back in like coin. And hence my maxim, as soon as it were made a universal law, would have to destroy itself.["] [4:402.16–403.17] From this the author draws the following conclusion: "I do not, therefore, need any wide-ranging acuteness to see what I have to do for my willing to be morally good. Inexperienced with regard to the course of the world, incapable of bracing myself for whatever might come to pass in it, I just ask myself: can you also will that your maxim become a universal law? If not, then it must be rejected, and that not because of some disadvantage to you, or to others, that might result," (is the abolition of the reciprocal trust necessary for the sake of the lives, needs, and business of human beings, the impossibility of passing things on to others via promise, not a true disadvantage contracted by me and others, which in fact must first be made aware to me via experience, and is this disadvantage not the only reason why the maxim to help oneself through lying promises does not qualify as a universal legislation?) ["]but because it cannot fit as a principle into a universal legislation, for which reason extracts from me immediate respect; and although I do not yet see on what it is founded, at least I understand this much: that it is an estimation of a worth that far outweighs any worth of what is extolled by inclination, and that the necessity of my actions from **pure** respect for the practical law is that which constitutes duty, to which every other motive must give way, because it is the condition of a will good in itself, whose worth surpasses everything." [4:403.18–33]

This is the outcome that is supposed to result from observing the moral sentiments and cognition of human beings, according to the author. Nonetheless, it can still be doubted: first, whether his way of representing a good will, its worth, and duty are the only ones that can possibly be compatible with these observations; and second, whether the [455] law and highest principle of morality put forward by him is formal and excludes everything material, just as he desires. Since this concerns the main issue of this new moral system, I will venture to offer a few remarks about it, and I wish to begin with the latter. Here it seems to me that the principle of morality established by the author 'act in such a way that you can will that your maxim of volition can become a universal law,' is hardly different from the claim of other moralists, that what is right is that whose universal execution is **generally beneficial**, or is in conformity with the interest of rational beings, and that what is wrong is that whose universal execution is **generally harmful**, or is counter to the interest of rational beings; which one could then express as such: act in such a way that your maxim, according to which you act, is not counter to the common interest of all rational beings, but is rather in conformity with it.—For, to remain with the above example, one can then ask: why could I not will a universal law to lie? And here it seems obvious to me that, if such a law were to have absolutely no influence, absolutely no relation to a pre-given interest of rational beings, or if these rational beings were to have absolutely no interest, either of the understanding or of the will, in a word, if they were entirely indifferent towards agreement or contradiction, towards truth or falsity, towards perfection or imperfection, towards pleasure or pain etc., and were completely lacking sensation, then it would have to be all the same to them whether a universal law to tell the truth or a universal law to lie were established. The consideration that, in the latter case, absolutely no promises would be possible any longer, would not influence a being, for whom it is of no consequence whether there are true, or false, or absolutely no promises, and its maxims, if it could even have maxims, would be able to qualify for a universal legislation by means of absolutely nothing at all. Indeed, it seems completely inconceivable to me that a law could in fact be given to such a completely uninterested being, and that such a being could be necessitated morally, i.e., via representations, to observe it. But what kind of representation can this be that binds a rational being to a law, or gives this being pure respect for the law? It is impossible for one to say: [456] the representation of the law itself, for this would be *idem per idem*,[3] since for a rational being the law itself is nothing other than a certain representation that it should act in such and such a way. Rather, we are looking here for a third representation that constitutes the necessary connection between the law and the will of the rational being, and there must be such a representation insofar as the law is supposed to be moral and not physical. Such a representation can be either the truth or the utility of the law; its harmony with the faculty of thinking or its agreement with the faculty of desire. In both cases the law would interest a rational being to the extent that it is in accordance with its nature, and the representation of this would only be the middle term [Mittelband], and indeed the only one possible, by means of which a rational being can be bound to a law and necessitated to follow it. If this being were indifferent towards utility and harm, then the interest of truth or of speculative thought would remain to us. But in this case as well the obligation or estimation [Ansehen] of the law is still grounded on an interest. But if I were to not have this interest either, then the consideration that being allowed to make fraudulent promises would, through a universal law, invalidate all promises and destroy itself, could never require anything of me [nie etwas über mich vermögen]. For, as already stated, if I am indifferent towards whether something is true or false, conceivable or inconceivable, then respect for the law can never take place because of or by means of the fact that something, e.g., a promise, becomes a law only by virtue of existing by itself or being conceivable as such.

But if this is how things are, then we will never discover what the author deems necessary in order to distinguish morality from prudence, or rightful and duty-conforming action from merely prudent and clever action, namely a so-called categorical imperative or highest command of morality that is valid absolutely and in itself, and which is in no way and in no respect hypothetical. I inquire: why then must we discover such a categorical imperative? Perhaps in order to be able to accept an absolutely good will? I inquire further: why must we admit of an absolutely good will, and what lies in our moral sentiments and common knowledge of morality that necessarily leads us to the presupposition [457] of such an absolutely good will? The author himself admits that it can never be given as actual in experience. [see 4:407.1–4] But there is still the question of whether such a

---

[3] *the same for the same*, i.e., tautological.

good will is something more than a nice but impossible idea, and whether that which is supposed to turn it into an absolutely good will, namely mere formality or the quality of conformity to law, is sufficient for this. It does not seem so to me, as I have already mentioned above, because I must always presuppose the validity or binding power of the law, by means of which a will acting in conformity with such a law is supposed to be good. And this validity must indeed be grounded in something, must be cognized from somewhere, otherwise it must be an innate, physical law effective through the constraint of instinct, not a moral law effective through representations. Now, that on which the validity of the law is grounded, or from which it is cognized, is precisely that which comprises the **condition** of its validity. Thus, there is no other moral law than a hypothetical one, and we cannot conceive of a merely formal law as valid. Similarly, I cannot cognize a will as absolutely good merely because it conforms to law, or because the law alone is the maxim of its volition. Rather, it always depends, first, on whether its law is also good. This then leads us to what I mentioned at the beginning, [namely] that the moral investigation must begin with the concept of the **good**, and the question must first be investigated whether, in relation to the conduct of human beings, anything is capable of being good other than that which is actually good for the human being as a sensing and thinking being. If something can be found in this investigation that is universally good for sensing and thinking beings in general, without exception and in all circumstances, then this must be called the highest and absolute good. If there is such a highest good, then there must be a common nature of all rational beings and a universal interest grounded therein, for only by means of agreement with the former and conformity with the latter can something be good for such a being. Accordingly, the good will would be the will whose maxim is: do that which conforms to and agrees with the nature common to both you and all rational beings, as well as the common interest grounded therein. This is the highest principle of morality, and if [458] this furnishes no categorical imperative, then none is possible. For, higher or deeper than in the common nature of all rational beings, the rule of their will and their conduct cannot be sought. This principle becomes binding and turns into a law for me through the representation that my interest and that of all rational beings is one and the same; that, consequently, a **true** collision of my true advantage and the true advantage of other rational beings cannot arise; and that in the case where I do not follow a part of my nature, e.g., a particular inclination, but rather follow my entire nature, I make not only myself but at the same time all rational beings in general into my end, and care for their interest at the same time as I do mine. As a result, the principle of morality so stated also corresponds to the **second** formulation, in which the author expresses his principle, namely this one: **act in such a way that you never use rational beings merely as a means, but always simultaneously regard them as an end**. [4:429.10–12]

It can now also be easily shown that, with this way of representing the highest principle of morality, neither is all difference between morality and prudence abolished, nor is **duty** transformed into an empty, chimerical concept. Thus, in order to preserve this distinction and duty as a real concept, we do not necessarily need a categorical imperative. Acting morally or rightfully and in conformity with duty means making the above-stated highest principle of morality into the maxim of one's will, and if apparent collisions of one's own and the common interest arise, the latter comes before the former. This is also called acting wisely, if it is otherwise true that there is a universal harmony in the kingdom of spirits or, as the author puts it, a kingdom of ends, and that I infallibly promote my own true best when I make it a maxim of my will to act in conformity with the universal interest. The opposite of this is called acting evilly, immorally, and adversely to duty, namely when I prefer my particular advantage to the universal interest or, as one could also put it, if I do not follow my entire nature insofar as it is one and the same with the nature of all rational beings, but only a part of it, [459] e.g., I follow an inclination. In such a case I also act unwisely, since wisdom and virtue are generally only different names for the same thing; the former used in relation to the understanding, the latter in relation to the will. When it comes to wisdom, however, prudence and cleverness are not the same according to the use of language, and for this reason I can simultaneously act unwisely and not in conformity with duty but still prudently, i.e., I can pay attention to the immediate consequences of my action that are to be assessed by me and, in line with this, do my best according to what I foresee. But I can also do my duty merely from prudence, when it is not the common interest of the world of spirits [Geisterwelt] that determines my will, nor the representation of the agreement of this universal interest with my own, but the foreseen, pre-calculated advantage that my right action will bring to me that determines my will, and when the maxims of my will consist in a certain business-like spirit of calculation. Admittedly, if my foresight and calculation were always infallible and correct, and if there were no hindrances in me to will that which my true advantage dictates, which I always correctly know, then this prudence would be the same as wisdom and virtue. But in this case, there would be no real duty or necessitation by means of respect for a law to do that which my wisdom or prudence infallibly and irresistibly prescribes to me, just as we cannot presume that God has a duty. However, since my foresight and calculation are very limited and deceptive, and all cleverness is insufficient for me to reliably discover what is my true best, and since I have particular intentions and inclinations that conflict with my true interest, prudence cannot be my maxim of morality. Rather, I must hold myself to a more secure maxim if I want to look after my true best, i.e., I must make it my maxim to do what is **right**. If I hold myself to this, then I act in conformity with duty, and this is obviously very different from acting prudently, or from calculating and observing my own advantage or disadvantage in a given case. The human being who acts in conformity with duty and rightly is the one who, in the above example, does not wish to extricate himself from the predicament by means of a deceitful promise, and does not do so because they are convinced that this conflicts with the following maxim: to do nothing that is against the interest of all rational [460] beings and therefore also, contained therein, his own true interest. The human being who acts prudently is the one who, without regarding the interest of the whole, refrains from making a deceptive promise merely because they fear that it would damage their reputation or bring them other disadvantages.

Finally, if we were to compare the third formulation, wherein the author expresses his principle of morality or his categorical imperative, it might also agree with our hypothetical imperative **to a certain extent**. This third formulation is: **the autonomy of the will is the highest principle of morality**. [see 4:440.14–15] "This autonomy of the will is the characteristic of the will by which it is a law to itself (independently of any characteristic of the objects of willing). The principle of autonomy is thus: not to choose in any other way than that the maxims of one's choice are also comprised as universal law in the same willing." [4:440.16–20] This is somewhat vague, but I understand it in such a way that the maxim is nothing other than the law itself. That is, considered objectively it is called the law, to which the will conforms. But if one considers it subjectively, then it is the maxim, according to which the will acts. This becomes even more clear if one contrasts this with that which the author calls heteronomy of the will. This heteronomy is supposed to take place ["]when the will searches for its determination in something other than the suitability of its maxim for its own universal legislation, thus when the will goes beyond itself and looks for the law that should determine it in the characteristic of one of its objects.["] [4:441.3–6] ["]The will does not therefore give itself the law, rather the object gives the will the law, through the object's relation to it. This relation [...] grants only hypothetical imperatives: I should only do something because I want something else. In contrast, the categorical imperative says: I ought to act in such or such a way, even if I do not want anything else. For example, the former says: 'I ought not to lie if I want to maintain my honorable reputation.' And the latter says: 'I ought not to lie, even if it did not bring me the least disgrace.'["] [4:441.7–15] ["]The will["], says the author, ["]should not go beyond itself, should not seek the law that is to determine it in the characteristic of any of its objects.["] [4:441.3–6] Nonetheless, something must determine it, something [461] must bind it to the law. If this is not the particular characteristic of the object (which includes the consequences of the will's choice of this object), then absolutely nothing remains that can and ought to determine the will other than its own nature and the general interest of every rational being grounded therein. To make a deceptive promise is against this interest. This fact alone (not the potential good or bad consequences that one's promise could have) should determine one to not make the same promise. I can ascribe no other meaning to autonomy than the following: that the will should be determined, as by a law and by a maxim, by the dual interest of truth and utility grounded in the common nature of rational beings, or by the interest resulting from both the harmony of a principle with the essential laws of our faculty of thinking and the agreement of this principle with our entire faculty of desire, or from the sum of these two things. Furthermore, I cannot conceive of or wish for a more free legislation than that which cultivates my own nature, and which the Stoics expressed by means of the following formulas: *naturam, optimum ducem, tanquam Deum sequi*; *naturae convenienter vivere*;[4] etc. This therefore agrees with the hypothetical principle of morality I have proposed. But if the author understands autonomy such that the will gives itself a law without considering whether this law is good for anything, whether it has a relation to some interest, or whether, through this formula of autonomy, a renunciation of all interest is implied by willing from duty, then this high-handed legislation seems to me to be a blind process, and not much different from that which one calls stubbornness, that is: *stat pro ratione voluntas*.[5] But, taken in this sense, this third formula of the autonomy of the will could not be united with the first: **act in such a way that you can will that the maxim of your will becomes a universal law**, for the reasons offered above. For, this formulation, as little

---

[4] nature is the best guide, follow it as if it were God; live in accordance with nature
[5] the will standing in place of a reason

as the author wishes to admit it, refers to a condition that my maxim must possess in order to be suitable for universal legislation. If one therefore compares this first formulation with our hypothetical principle, one [462] will find that both can rightly be called categorical or hypothetical. Now, the principle: I ought to do something because it conforms to both my nature and interest and those of all rational beings, seems to be even more explicit than the author's categorically obligating imperative of universal legislation, for, as I said, I must come back to the former as the only possible condition if I am seeking a ground of cognition for what passes as universally legislating, and why it does.

Seeing as I have followed the author up until this point, in that the main subject of his text is to explain that the moral imperative must be categorical and how it can be expressed in three different formulations, and seeing as I have offered a few of reasons for why I consider a categorical imperative of morality to be neither necessary nor possible, it is now just as necessary to follow him a bit further into the final section, which contains the most abstruse metaphysics and is supposed to show how such an entirely unconditioned imperative is possible, and why it is necessary. In other words, it is now just as necessary to follow him into the deepest pit of speculation, in order to retrieve from it the following barely satisfying result, instead of any profit: "that we indeed do not comprehend the practical, unconditional necessity of the moral imperative, yet we do grasp its incomprehensibility, if this is all that should be reasonably required of a philosophy that in its principles strives up to the boundary of human reason." [4:463.29–33] It may be enough to add the following: the author admits that even if no interest of any kind could drive us to submit to the principle of morality (because this must always yield a conditional imperative), we nonetheless necessarily take an interest in this [see 4:413n], and we have to see how this is the case. Here the philosopher must summon all his acuteness not only to show how this necessary 'taking an interest' in the principle of morality, which excludes all interest, is different from being driven by interest to submit to this principle, but also to make it comprehensible how this 'taking an interest' is possible in general. For this purpose, he avails himself of his problematic conception of freedom, [463] moves us out of the sensible world and into the world of the understanding, and takes, according to his other principles, from the latter world, which is entirely unknown to us, the grounds for the possibility and necessity of his categorical imperative. Since I have already explained my view of this conception of freedom, on which, in the end, the author's entire moral system rests, in the review of Schulze's *Elucidations* of the

Critique of Pure Reason,[6] I say nothing further about this and content myself with making the following remark: even if all the objections the author makes to the moral systems that differ from his own were justified, namely that such systems corrupt the science of morality in a variety of ways through the introduction of illegitimate (hypothetical) principles of morality, and is damaging to the morality of human beings, his own would heal this affliction only in theory, or only in mere speculation, but could not be of any help in practice. This is the case because his principle can neither be made sense of as a **binding** law by the understanding of common and ordinary people, and in general by those who are not versed in speculative thought, nor can it have an influence on the will of those people, for whom even the concept of happiness seems too lofty, too abstract, and too ineffectual. By means of this idea, what would we tell the people whose almost sole incentive is the inclination to pleasure and the aversion to pain? You must act rightly even if you also deny all of your inclinations, indeed, even if you ought to suppress the drive towards happiness, for you must act rightly not in order to become happy, but in order to be worthy of happiness. In fact, it is likely that if you make yourself worthy of happiness through right action, you will someday take part in happiness, but this hope cannot be a motive for you to fulfill your duty, provided that you do not want to corrupt your morality and falsify your virtue, for in that case you would, as rightful as your action may be, only ever act **prudently** but never **morally**.

---

[6] See the previous chapter of this volume.

7

Thomas Wizenmann
Introduction

One of the most significant philosophical events during the final decades of the eighteenth century was the so-called pantheism controversy, which began in 1783 in personal correspondence between F.H. Jacobi and Moses Mendelssohn and, at least on its surface, revolved around the question of whether G.E. Lessing was a Spinozist.[1] The controversy became public in 1785 when Jacobi published his *Ueber die Lehre des Spinoza in Briefen an den Herrn Moses Mendelssohn* (On the Doctrine of Spinoza, in Letters to Herr Moses Mendelssohn), in which he argued that if we embrace reason fully and consistently, then we are forced to adopt Spinozism, a code word for atheism, fatalism, and nihilism, and thereby undermine the possibility of religion and morality. The only way to save ourselves, Jacobi argued, was via a *salto mortale*, i.e., a leap of faith, by which he meant that we must believe in the existence of God, for example, not based on reason, but irrationally and based on faith or revelation alone. Mendelssohn responded in 1786 with his *An die Freunde Lessings. Ein Anhang zu Herrn Jacobi Briefwechsel über die Lehre des Spinoza* (To the Friends of Lessing. An Appendix to Herr Jacobi's Correspondence on the Doctrine of Spinoza), in which, building on his earlier *Morgenstunden* (Morning Hours) of 1785, he championed healthy human reason as the ultimate touchstone of truth and as capable of proving things like the existence of God without falling into Spinozism.

An important event that took place at the height of the controversy was the anonymous publication of a book in 1786 entitled *Die Resultate der Jacobischen und Mendelssohnischen Philosophie; kritisch untersucht von einem Freywilligen* (The Results of the Jacobian and Mendelssohnian Philosophy, Critically Examined by a Neutral Party), later revealed to have been authored by Thomas Wizenmann. This book was significant for a few

---

[1] For an extensive and detailed account of the controversy, which is still the best available in English, see Beiser (1987, Chs. 2–4).

reasons. First, it helped popularize the debate by summarizing the state of the controversy. Second, it helped people focus on the philosophical questions under discussion as opposed to the somewhat biographical issue of Lessing's Spinozism. Third, it almost certainly played a role in encouraging Kant to finally enter the debate.[2] The *Results* argues that both Mendelssohn and Jacobi were on a dangerous path that led to irrationalism. This is the case for Mendelssohn as well because, on Wizenmann's reading, he ambiguously accords final say to both reason and common sense at different times, such that common sense occasionally corrects reason, meaning Mendelssohn, like Jacobi, endorses a kind of irrational belief based on faith (in common sense) as well. The thesis of the *Results* invokes Kant's stance on the ontological argument, according to which it is not possible to demonstrate the existence of anything based on reason alone (see e.g., Wizenmann 1786, p. 83), in order to argue that only experience can give us knowledge of existence. When it comes to God's existence, Wizenmann continues, the only experience we can avail ourselves of is revelation. Thus, for Wizenmann, similar to Jacobi, there is either religion based on revelation, or no religion at all.

When Kant entered the controversy in October of 1786 with his article 'What does it mean to orient oneself in thinking?,'[3] he explicitly engages with "the acute author of the *Results*" (8:134.6), whose identity was, at the time, still unknown to Kant. In this essay, Kant not only accuses Wizenmann of "fanaticism [Schwärmerei]" (see 8:134.3), but it is also here that Kant first presents his doctrine of rational belief or faith (*Vernunftglaube*)[4] which he goes on to develop more fully in the second *Critique*, namely the doctrine that it is a need of reason to *believe* in God's existence on practical grounds, even if we cannot prove and possess *knowledge* of this on theoretical grounds; put differently, that it is a postulate of pure practical reason to believe in God's existence.

Kant's reaction to the *Results* in the 'Orientation' essay forced Wizenmann to respond and to reveal his identity in the essay translated below. Written before the end of 1786 and published in February 1787, the essay was penned as an open letter to Kant. After an introductory section where Wizenmann clarifies the circumstances surrounding his own entry into the pantheism controversy (pp. 116–20, original pagination), he

---

[2] See Beiser (1987, pp. 113–15) for details surrounding the attempts of Kant's contemporaries, including those of Jacobi and Mendelssohn, to get Kant to enter the debate.
[3] Originally published in the *Berlinische Monatsschrift*. 8. Band, October 1786, pp. 304–30.
[4] In the following translation, I have rendered '*Glaube*' as 'belief' throughout. See the Translation Notes below.

defends himself against a number of Kant's claims in the 'Orientation' essay that suggest the *Results*' conclusions were wrongheaded (pp. 12–128). In the main part of the essay (pp. 128–43), Wizenmann considers what it means to orient oneself and denies that it is possible to do so on the basis of subjective grounds of assent alone, as Kant claimed in the 'Orientation' essay. It is in this section of the text that Wizenmann presents his famous example of the lover who infers the existence of their beloved's reciprocal love, simply because the lover needs this to be the case (see p. 137 and Kant's direct response at 5:143n). In the final section of the essay (pp. 137–55), Wizenmann discusses what he takes to be the true origin of the concept of God, and argues that he and Kant disagree about the nature of reason. Kant responds to Wizenmann's essay primarily in the second *Critique*'s chapter 'On Assent from a Need of Pure Reason' (5:142–46) but also in the 'postulates' chapter (5:134–41) and perhaps in other places as well.[5]

Thomas Wizenmann (1759–1787) was born in Ludwigsburg, a city just north of Stuttgart, where he attended the local Latin school alongside Friedrich Schiller, who was just a few days younger than Wizenmann.[6] In 1775, when he was not yet 16, Wizenmann began to study at the monastery (*Stift*) in Tübingen, but only as a *famulus*, i.e., an assistant who had to serve the regular students who paid to be there. Additionally, he was only allowed to study philosophy rather than theology, the latter being that which his Pietist father initially prepared him for. But in 1777 Wizenmann was able to end his servant role, began to study theology as well, and in that same year received his *Magister* degree in philosophy from the University of Tübingen. After working as a private tutor for a few years and eventually passing his consistorial exams (but not with flying colours) Wizenmann became a vicar in Essingen in 1780 and began to publish essays in some minor Pietist journals. In 1783 he gave up his vicarship to become a tutor for a businessman in Barmen, and on the way there he stopped in Düsseldorf where he met Jacobi, who had read and was impressed by an early book Wizenmann wrote on Satan (see Wizenmann 1782). The two exchanged letters and visited each other often over the coming years and they developed an intimate friendship.

---

[5] See Beiser (1987 pp. 121 and 345) for suggestions of other places in the second *Critique* where Kant might have responded to Wizenmann. For some helpful discussion of the exchange between Wizenmann and Kant, see Willaschek (2010), Chance and Pasternack (2018), and Beiser (1987, Ch. 4).

[6] Information about Wizenmann's life and works is taken from Heinze (1898), Franz (2016), Beiser (1987), Albrecht (2015), and Zweig (1999).

Wizenmann suffered from tuberculosis, and in 1785 his declining health caused him to give up his position as a tutor in Barmen, after which he went to live with Jacobi in Pempelfort, at the time a country suburb of Düsseldorf. In Pempelfort, Wizenmann read Jacobi's preface to the *Letters*, which Jacobi was working on at the time, and it was there that Wizenmann wrote both the *Results* and the following open letter to Kant. In early 1787, Wizenmann moved to his doctor's house in Mühlheim am Rein, where he eventually died in late February of 1787, the same month in which his letter to Kant was published, at the age of 27. Wizenmann is the only one of Kant's contemporaries mentioned by name in the second *Critique*, and Kant praises him as "a very subtle and clear-headed man [...] whose early death is to be regretted" (5:143.33–34n).

Translation Notes

In preparing the following translation I have used the original, 1787 essay. Unless otherwise noted, I have translated *'Glaube'* as 'belief' rather than 'faith' throughout the essay, because although the term occasionally has religious connotations, the overall context of the essay makes it clear that it is primarily an epistemological point that is at issue. Furthermore, I agree with Chignell (2007, p. 335n) that using 'faith' to translate this term has several undesirable consequences. At the very least, I take 'belief' to be the more interpretively neutral option.

'To Herr Professor Kant' (1787)

Deutsches Museum. 1. Band, 2. Stück, February 1787, pp. 116–56.

[116]

To Herr Professor Kant
from the author of *The Results of the Jacobian and Mendelssohnian Philosophy*

Pempelfort, 1786.

I consign myself to a new investigation of some of my statements, not to even further disturb the spirit of the philosophical Israelite, nor to reignite a conflict that burned so brightly once already, but solely and entirely with the intention of discharging a duty of deference that I owe. I had resolved to keep myself out of this affair from that time onwards, and to question in silence what I had justly or unjustly been accused of. For, I too am convinced that every truth must and will support itself, and even I could [117] not expect to be understood as I wanted, given so many different interests of so many different parties, even after many explanations. Unfortunately, my weak health supported this decision strongly enough and I would have stuck to it had you, venerable Kant!, not spoken out against me.

You forced me to waver in my decision. For, as soon as you came out against me, I could no longer hope that a respectable part of the public would, at the very least, receive my views without prejudice and investigate them with sufficient precision. Your reputation was too decisive and, to many people, must have been worth more than reasons. A mass of people interested in the dispute seemed to hide behind your shield and spear and find satisfaction merely in your intervention. On the other hand, it was of the utmost importance to me to have my own concepts examined by the man who is so deeply steeped in the elementary concepts of reason; it was of the utmost importance to me to cleanse myself of the objections of blind faith [des blinden Glaubens] and of fanaticism [Schwärmerei] as soon as they were uttered. [see e.g., 8:134.3] And how much I would gain if I were to be so lucky as to cause just one of the significant truths under discussion to be examined more closely and be defended by you! It was impossible for these observations to not alter my decision, so long as only some of my powers remained.

I therefore venture, eminent man, to not only break a philosophical lance with you [mit Ihnen ... eine philosophische Lanze zu brechen], as Mendelssohn once put it, but also to ascertain whether my own efforts cannot improve upon your own.

Above all else, you must know with whom you are dealing. You can demand that I [118] reveal my identity to you, and it is a pleasure for me to make some circumstances of my situation known to you.

It has now been five quarters of a year since Herr privy councillor Jacobi took me in to his house. Three years ago, when I came to the area, a short text made him curious to meet me, and one marvellous evening, which passed us by so easily amidst philosophical conversation, I gained his friendship. I became ill and could no longer preside over my duties of educating the children of a businessman in Barmen. Jacobi took it upon himself to take care of me, and thanks to the peace that I enjoyed in the safety of friendship, I was indeed successful in recovering, to a certain extent. I was aware of **Jacobi's** correspondence with Mendelssohn concerning Lessing's views. I witnessed the confusion between the two men ensue, and I came to understand not only Spinoza's system more precisely, but also **Jacobi's** temperaments [Gesinnungen] themselves. Even though I could not entirely agree with the latter, we nonetheless came to agree that, in relation to the existence or non-existence of a God, nothing could be proven philosophically; that, in relation to all actually existing things, human cognition always begins with feeling or, if one wishes to express this in relation to reason, with belief; and that, therefore, each and every true conviction about the existence of God, insofar as this is possible for human beings, must begin with facts, and thus with perception, or feeling, or belief. Here we departed ways. By means of the analogy of the inexplicable power of the human will, **Jacobi** made a leap to the divinity as the source of this power, convinced that the [119] purer the will becomes, the more fervently the divinity reveals itself. I preferred to restrict myself to the Bible, which, for my personal knowledge, contained and documented the more sublime path of guiding humankind. I preferred to restrict myself to the history of the species in general, which most likely presupposes entirely different kinds of cognition than merely philosophical cognition of God. In the meantime, Jacobi published his letters to Mendelssohn,[1] and Mendelssohn the epistle to the friends of Lessing.[2] My familiarity with **Jacobi's** meaning, the misunderstandings his views were mistaken for, but even more so the pride, with which Mendelssohn extols his philosophical dogmatism, which seemed so inconsistent to me, and the ambiguity of at one point assigning all responsibility concerning our cognition of God to philosophy and healthy human reason, but at another praising Judaism as the pure source of the true cognition of God, and in general my conviction of the superiority of religious human history according to the Bible above everything that philosophical dogmatism might illustrate about religion, all of this, taken together, caused me to freely decide to write the *Results*. I worked on it in isolation, and only once it was as good as complete and had been worked out all the way to its conclusion did Jacobi get to see it. The clarity of its presentation surprised him. He was writing the preface of his defence against Mendelssohn[3] and, in the joy of having seen himself be displayed so clearly, he gave me all the words of praise that certain impartial parties found so exaggerated and biased.

These are the circumstances under which the *Results* came into being and were published, in which it was my aim: (1) to elaborate the foundational principles and the starting point of the investigations of two philosophers, to judge them according to reasons, and to position them against each other; (2) to destroy one philosophical system by means of another, [120] deism by means of atheism, and the latter by means of the former as a system, and in general to prove that no demonstration of the existence or non-existence of a God, and of his relation to the world, is possible; and (3) to precisely determine the concept of reason and, immediately following upon the determination of this concept, to illustrate the rationality of a belief in revelation as soon as this revelation possesses valid historical evidence. It goes

---

[1] *Ueber die Lehre des Spinoza in Briefen an den Herrn Moses Mendelssohn* (On the Doctrine of Spinoza, in Letters to Herr Moses Mendelssohn). Breslau, 1785.

[2] *An die Freunde Lessings. Ein Anhang zu Herrn Jacobi Briefwechsel über die Lehre des Spinoza* (To the Friends of Lessing. An Appendix to Herr Jacobi's Correspondence on the Doctrine of Spinoza). Berlin, 1786.

[3] *Wider Mendelssohns Beschuldigungen betreffend die Briefe über die Lehre des Spinoza* (Against Mendelssohn's Accusations Regarding the Letters on the Doctrine of Spinoza). Leipzig, 1786.

without saying that I had to pursue these aims incessantly with a view to Mendelssohn.

Judging according to the statements of various men, and according to your own as well, I was not able to achieve my aims, not even so far as to make the aims themselves clear and distinct enough. Whether the cause of this lies in a vagueness of my expression, in the hurried course of the entire text, in the unusual nature of this connection between concepts, in the deception of certain words, in pre-established opinions of the readers themselves, or in all the above together, I do not venture to say. At the same time, it will not be pointless to cite some examples.

You say on p. 322[*]: "In the dispute between Jacobi and Mendelssohn, everything seems aimed at the overturning of, I am not entirely sure, either **rational insight** alone (by means of the alleged strength of speculation) or **rational belief** [Vernunftglaubens] as well and, on the other hand, at the establishment of a different belief that any individual can make at their own discretion. One ought to come close to the latter conclusion if one considers the **Spinozistic** concept of God to be the only one that has been put forward that agrees with all the principles of reason, but which should nonetheless be rejected. For, even if it is quite compatible with [121] rational belief to concede that speculative reason itself is never in a position to have insight into the **possibility** of a being such as we must imagine God to be, it is consistent with absolutely no belief and with no assent [Fürwahrhalten] to any existence whatsoever that reason could have insight into the **impossibility** of an object but could nonetheless cognize its actuality from other sources." [8:143.11–144.7]

In order to make the argument clear, by means of which the establishment of a belief that anyone can make at their own discretion is attributed to me, I wish to make these sentences more accessible. You wish to say that for the person who pretends to have insight into the **impossibility** of a God by means of reason, such as Spinoza and his defenders, no rational ground remains for them to believe in and have faith in God [einen Gott und an einen Gott zu glauben]. Thus, if such a person asserts the **impossibility** of a God, and if they simultaneously believe in his **actuality**, then this must be a merely arbitrary belief, which mocks reason and which anyone can make at their own discretion, because neither the latter nor the former belief has a rational determining ground. This is also, without a

---

[*] See *berlinische Monatsschrift*, Oct. 1786. [i.e., Kant's 'Orientation' essay]

doubt, what you call on p. 305 the "principle of fanaticism and the dethronement of reason." [8:134.3–4]

This reproach is fair and irrefutable if things are as you have interpreted them. It all depends on whether I do in fact pretend to have insight into the impossibility of a God by means of reason. But in the *Results* I find a passage, right after the account of the Spinozistic system, which says exactly the opposite: "The atheist," it says on p. 143, "if he is well-informed, needs to prove nothing in order to win against the deist, [122] he need only analyze **his** (the deist's) **concept**: he cannot just dismiss the possibility of a God in general, but only the **God of the deist**. For, he can just as little demonstrate the **impossibility** of the infinite God on the basis of what is finite, as the theist can demonstrate his possibility. If we therefore (as I reason further) cognize a God, then you must reveal to us another source of knowledge than mere reason and demonstration."

This passage, which has gone unnoticed by many, clearly states what I have aimed at, which is to show that reason is capable of an objectively valid ground for neither the possibility nor the impossibility of a God, neither of belief nor of disbelief, and that reason therefore entitles us to search for other sources. Far from wishing to establish a belief that anyone can make at their own discretion, I am primarily concerned with avoiding any arbitrary, self-made belief, and with finding objectively valid grounds of a belief that agrees with reason, but outside the field of abstract reason. This was my intention and I said so as well, and I could therefore rightfully complain about the nonetheless nicely stated objection of having offered a "principle of fanaticism and of completely dethroning reason," if complaining were my intention.

I am just as much taken aback by the astonishment over my claim that the Spinozistic concept of God is the only one that agrees with all the principles of reason, but which should nonetheless be rejected. It is true, I consider the Spinozistic concept of God, or better, the Spinozistic view of the world (for it is well-known [123] that Spinozism existed before Spinoza, and therefore that it is not necessarily bound to all his mediate concepts) to be the most precise and consistent system of speculative reason. For, it has the following advantage over all other systems: that it is not oriented according to a singular finite form, for example the human form; that, in order to form a transcendental, i.e., objectively valid system, it does not descend from objective to subjective grounds but, in its speculative form, progresses all the way up to the necessary source of all things, forms, and changes, without paying attention to its surroundings, and thus does not explain matter from form, but form from matter, as the sum of all the laws, powers, and relations of the universe. I therefore say that if any system is valid, then the Spinozistic system must be valid above all others. But now, as you put it, the critique of reason steps in and proves that reason has its boundaries, and that every speculative system oversteps these boundaries and thereby exposes itself to fanaticism, as I have illustrated on, e.g., pp. 125 and 181 emphatically enough. This is to say that each and every healthy critique of reason incontrovertibly teaches that we can know absolutely nothing about the inner connection of things, and therefore that the person who wants to establish something about this inner connection of things, and thus about the possibility or impossibility of a God or his relation to the world, is mad in the philosophical and actual sense of the word. It is similarly fanatical and groundless, for instance, to deprive God of understanding and will because it is impossible that the first cause of things could have an understanding and will analogous to those of human beings; or to confer understanding and will upon the infinite being because for finite beings we know nothing higher than [124] understanding and will. With this retreat from speculative philosophy, what have I said or done except that which you yourself say or do, perhaps with somewhat altered mediate concepts* (for, there are various paths to this insight)?—Now, two prospects for cognizing God reveal themselves here. Either, in the absence of all objective grounds of speculative reason, facts are given to us, from which the concept of a higher being can be immediately abstracted, and this leads us to a historical cognition of God that gradually and progressively develops, or we fall back upon merely subjective grounds. I have chosen the first path. You have taken the second and have included Mendelssohn in it as well.

For, you even admit that, in essence, Mendelssohn's way of orienting oneself is just as distinct from your own as is his philosophy, even though you went to great lengths to illustrate it in a logical way suitable to you.

---

* I confess that it is incomprehensible to me as well how you could come to believe that I wanted to find "support for Spinozism" [see 8:143.19–20n] in your *Critique of Pure Reason*. I mention you twice: first as the person who destroyed the proof of a God from the idea [of one] (p. 30 and p. 83), and second as the person who cognizes the limits of reason and also compels others to cognize this (p. 172). Perhaps I was too stupid to have mentioned you even there, had I not wanted to set authority against authority, on account of certain readers. For, my own train of thought stands firm without any foreign support. In any event, it did not even occur to me to cite you for the sake of Spinozism.

You yourself say: "Who would have thought that Mendelssohn's admission that it is necessary to orient oneself in the speculative use [125] of reason would be so detrimental to his fruitful opinion concerning the power of the use of speculative reason in theological matters, which was in fact unavoidable." [8:133.28–31] You yourself acknowledge the "ambiguity, in which he left the employment of healthy reason in contrast to speculation," [8:134.1–2] and admit that "Mendelssohn, without knowing it, orients himself in speculative thinking by means of a felt need of reason, and therefore that he certainly erred in entrusting to his speculation enough capacity to, on its own, achieve everything via the path of demonstration." [see 8:139.33–140.9] In this respect, you have therefore granted everything that the *Results* denounced of Mendelssohn's philosophy, which is nothing other than the reliability that he praises in his speculation, along with the admission of having to orient oneself. For, one of the two must surely be abandoned, either the reliability of demonstration, or orientation. The necessity of the latter can only hold if the inadequacy of the former has been granted: "an admission" you add "to which his acuteness would ultimately have brought him if he had also been granted, along with a longer life, that application of mind, found more often in youth, which permits the alteration of old, habitual ways of thinking to accord with alterations in the state of the sciences. In any case," you continue "he retains the merit of insisting that the final touchstone of the reliability of judgement is to be sought in reason alone, whether, in the choice of its propositions, it is guided by insight or by mere need and the maxim of its own advantage." [8:140.11–20] I do not wish to diminish this merit by means of the remark that, according to the comparison [126] made in the *Results* on pp. 209 to 214, he lists the revealed legislation of Judaism in addition to reason as the source of supremely important and essential cognitions of God. I myself claim no special right to this merit, because I would not have thought it possible to deny this to a philosophical mind without offence, even if I have defended reason as the touchstone of truth as emphatically as anyone on more than one occasion in the *Results*, but especially on pp. 177 and 191. This merit, I say, of having sought the final touchstone of the reliability of a judgement in nowhere but in reason alone, considerably loses value, however, if one neither knows the boundary by means of which objective grounds separate from merely subjective ones, as you yourself claim of Mendelssohn, nor has a certain insight into the capacity of reason, such that it is possible for one to mistake subjective for objective grounds and orient oneself merely by means of a felt need of reason without being aware of it, in that one believes to be orienting oneself by means of cognition. And herein lies the big difference between you and Mendelssohn,* between you and all of those who [127] take a blind and unintelligent cry to be reason. For, only insight has value, and only clear consciousness has merit.

In this, eminent Kant, we therefore think entirely alike, that no objectively valid principle of cognizing God is possible on the basis of pure reason. But whether, for that reason, it is also necessary or only possible to refrain from objective grounds of any sort [128] and to let oneself be determined by merely subjective grounds, this is not yet entirely clear to me. It seems to me that this all depends on a completely distinct development of the concept, an analysis of which you have so excellently prepared

---

* The cunning [Kunstgrif] of certain people who counter reasons with mere dictums [Machtsprüche] they obtain about the standing of the immortalized Mendelssohn, and which are meant to give his opponents the spiteful appearance of completely misunderstanding Mendelssohn's merits—this cunning forces me to make the otherwise superfluous explanation that I not only respectfully admire Mendelssohn's merits when it comes to the spread and popularization of philosophical cognition, but I also count myself among those who were deeply moved by his death. On the evening that I received word [127] of this, my sentiments flowed into the following ode:

Two Apparitions [Schatten] on the Occasion of Mendelssohn's Passing

Who is the apparition, floating up so calmly
    in the sombre shimmer of the moon?
How he rises, lost in thought! How he looks up,
    as if it were not his day of judgement!
Look! . . . that is not the look of the coward, nor of the conqueror.
    O, tell me who he is!
That is the apparition of the sage who indefatigably pursued the shimmer of
                                                               truth
    on earth.
Full of God's foreboding, and full of the foreboding of immortality,
    he changed.
Aware of this change himself, he looked up
    as if it were not his day of judgement.
Listen to the lamentable tone behind him! . . .
    I hear him weep with pain.
Did he leave behind orphans, and does a widow wring her hands
    as the body is taken away?
A widow and orphans. The sighs resound far and wide
    in Germany's fields.
Boys, honourable and audacious, who console themselves in the battle over falsity,
                                                            and truth
Oh, and Germany's daughters, who derived hope from him
    of eternal life,
lament him! . . .

the ground, namely of the concept of what it means to **orient oneself**. The application of this developed concept to our object will thus in general either settle us in our dialectic or determine for us the extent and degree of our cognition in this subject, while removing all further ambiguity.

"To orient oneself in thinking means" as you say, "to determine oneself according to a subjective principle when objective principles of reason are insufficient for assent." [8:136.35–37n]—I must straightaway ask the question here of whether it is even possible to separate objective principles of reason from subjective ones in such a way that a purely subjective principle can become the determining ground of any assent.

Subjective principles of reason can only and exclusively relate to the **form** of my existence. More specifically, they do so insofar as I regard this form purely and independently of all **matter**, i.e., of everything that the form can grasp and process. It is therefore already contained in the concept **pure form** that nothing can be in it that I could affirm or deny, and thus that no judgement whatsoever takes place in the form as such. In order to produce a determination in the form, matter or objects must necessarily be added and become related to the form. Only then is the form in a position to affirm or deny. All the parts of this foundational relationship of form and matter, or all the applications of it to individual cases, must correspond to the foundational relationship itself. Accordingly, just as it is impossible [129] for a judgement to be made based on the mere form of my reason, if I were to consider it apart from all connection to its matter, it must be just as impossible for purely subjective principles of reason to be thought without any connection to objective ones.

This is exactly how things are with objective principles of reason. These are called objective because they are considered valid in themselves and absolutely, apart from all connection to the subject that thinks them or to the form of human reason. But there can be no other absolutely valid propositions and principles of this kind than identical ones (but which are absolute only as far as identity extends), because it is impossible for anything material to be intuited differently than through my form, in such a way that everything objective is subjectively modified and determined. Accordingly, there can be no purely objective principle of reason.

To elucidate, I wish to analyze a proposition that has been passed off as absolutely valid, the examination of which can occasion some other very fruitful considerations. The proposition is this: **every effect has a cause**. This proposition clearly contains two others, namely these: **every consequence presupposes something antecedent**, and **between the consequent and the antecedent there is a connection**. That which is purely objective, absolute, or necessary in this proposition is its logical connection alone, which must be expressed as follows: **if something consequent exists, something antecedent exists as well**. And the ground of its objective validity clearly lies in the identity of the idea that the consequent necessarily includes the antecedent. Everything else in the proposition 'every effect has a cause' is thoroughly empirical and [130] subjective. For, apart from logical connection, the proposition contains the two concepts: **effect** and **combination** [Verknüpfung]. Effect is necessarily linked to the form of our reason, with the manner of our intuition, and combination is a concept that comes into being by means of the way in which we combine [die Art unsers Zusammennehmens] appearances that follow in succession of one another. Accordingly, what is objective here is inseparably connected to what is subjective.

Still, it should be noted that this argument is not supposed to decide anything about the reality or ideality of any kind of object or its relation to me, rather it is merely limited to proving that neither purely objective nor purely subjective principles of reason are possible.

Allow me to pursue this further, guided by your own article.

You say: "I orient myself geographically, even with all of the objective data in the sky, only by means of a subjective ground of differentiation, namely by means of the feeling of the right and left hand. If all of the constellations were to one day, by some miracle, be reversed in their direction, but nonetheless keep the same shape and position relative to one another, such that the direction that was previously east now became west, no human eye would notice even the slightest alteration on the next starlit night, and even the astronomer, if he pays attention only to what he sees and not at the same time to what he feels, would inevitably become disoriented. But his faculty of differentiation, implanted by nature but made more familiar by frequent practice, comes to his aid completely naturally by means of the feeling of the right and left hand. And if he were to fix his eye on the polar star only, he would not only notice the change that has taken place, [131] but would be able to orient himself in spite of it." [8:135.9–22]

But in this case do you not connect the objective ground of the polar star to the subjective ground of the right and left hand?

This is also the case when I orient myself mathematically. You write: "In the dark I orient myself in a room that is familiar to me if I can touch just one single object whose position I remember. But it is obvious that nothing helps me here except the faculty for determining position according to a subjective ground of differentiation. [...] I orient myself by means of the mere feeling of a difference between my two sides, the right and the left." [8:135.25–35]—But you find it entirely necessary to **touch an object** if you want to orient yourself in a room that is familiar to you and is completely dark, thus it is not the subjective ground of differentiation by means of the right and left hand alone that puts you in position to correctly judge the position of the objects you cannot see, rather you must necessarily take an objective ground of differentiation into consideration, the object that you touch.

If there is to be a true relationship between geographical and mathematical orientation, as well as logical orientation, to which I will come presently, even if only an exemplary relationship, then, when it comes to the object, in relation to which I want to orient myself, I must have two principles, on my account, an objective and a subjective principle. For, if I only had a subjective principle, then the relationship between geographical and mathematical, as well as logical orientation, which you yourself have provided, would immediately cease.

In this regard you say: "The subjective means still remaining—if, [132] starting from familiar objects of experience, reason wants to extend beyond all the boundaries of experience and finds no object of intuition at all but merely space for intuition—is nothing other than the feeling of reason's own **need**." [8:136.12–13]

If I now draw a parallel between this **feeling of a need**, when it comes to logical orientation, and the **feeling of the right and left hand**, when it comes to geographical orientation, and if I am permitted to assume that you intend to present no further ground of orientation outside of this feeling of a need, then it is clear that the parallel you have drawn between geographical and logical orientation does not exist whatsoever. For, we have seen that it would be impossible to orient oneself geographically with respect to the direction of the constellations if no objective ground were added to the subjective one, to feeling. Since you nevertheless only ever speak of subjective grounds, it seems plausible to me that you are mistaken in one case or the other, that you either overlook the objective ground in geographical orientation, and thus have drawn a parallel that does not exist, or that you confuse subjective and objective grounds in logical orientation.

I therefore wish to discern both cases, not only because I am unclear on your meaning, but also to examine the matter from every angle, beginning with the latter case. I am inclined to accept that objective grounds occurred to you when it comes to the subjective ground of need, and that you only named the subjective ground because it is what primarily comes into play.

This is what would have to be the case if you wanted to seriously defend Mendelssohn's way of orienting oneself. For, he admittedly takes subjective grounds as his starting point but thoroughly connects them [133] with objective grounds, which the examples I set out in the *Results* sufficiently prove. However, as little as your clearest explanations fit this case, it nonetheless seems to me as if you have at least brought a trace of the objective into the discussion of your question and into the grounds of orientation, and even this small trace, if it is not removed, could confuse the skilled readers of our time.

You say: "Not only does our reason already feel a need to take the concept of the unlimited as the ground of the concept of everything limited, hence of all other things, rather, this need goes so far as to presuppose the **existence** of this concept, without which reason can provide no satisfactory ground at all for the contingency of the existence of things in the world, let alone for the purposiveness and order which is encountered everywhere in such a wondrous degree [. . .]. Without assuming an intelligent author we cannot give any intelligible ground of such things without falling into pure absurdities; and although we cannot **prove** the impossibility of such a purposiveness without a first **intelligent** cause [. . .], our lack of insight notwithstanding, there remains a sufficient ground for assuming such a cause: that reason needs to presuppose something that it comprehends in order to explain this given appearance on its basis, since everything to which reason can otherwise connect a concept does not satisfy this need." [8:137.29–139.5]

The trace of objectivity in this reasoning, I feel, has to do with the fact that you seem to ground an aspect of belief in the deity directly on the **intelligibility** of the origin of the world, if we were to assume a deity. For, the [134] mere **need** to believe in a God can also, as is well known, be regarded objectively when one infers inductively from the fact that every means has its end, and every inclination its object, to the fact that the need for God also makes the existence of the object probable.—Just how distant this line of reasoning is from your own is obvious, however.

The tinge of objectivity is laid on somewhat thicker with the practical use of reason. You say: "the pure practical use of reason consists in the prescription of moral laws. They all lead, however, to the idea of the **highest good** that is possible in the world insofar as it is possible only through freedom: **morality**. But on the other hand, they also lead to what depends not merely on human freedom but on **nature** as well, namely to the greatest **happiness**, insofar as it is distributed in proportion to the former. Now, reason **needs** such a **dependent** highest good and, for its sake, to assume a supreme intelligence as the highest **independent** good; but not, of course, to derive from it the binding authority of moral laws or the incentives to observe them [...], but rather only in order to give objective reality to the concept of the highest good, i.e., to prevent it, along with all of morality, from being understood as a mere ideal, [as would be the case] if that whose idea inseparably accompanies morality did not exist." [8:139.15–32]

Reason therefore needs to assume a supreme intelligence as highest, independent good in order to be able to regard the happiness connected to morality, and also morality itself, as a reality and not a chimera. Now, if we regard nature as legislating, then it leads us to morality [135] from all sides. However, this cannot be conceived of as possible if we do not presuppose an original source of freedom and happiness. Accordingly, because nature leads us to morality, it simultaneously leads us to such an original source, to the concept of a God.—In this way, this reasoning is simultaneously objective.

I do not want to say anything about the difficulties that are connected to this series of concepts if it is to hold objectively. Rather, I only want to remark, in general, that if something objective were to be mixed with subjective grounds, I would immediately lose my way in the field of speculation, where grounds must be weighed against grounds, and no orientation could therefore take place.

To be sure, this way of orienting oneself, for which I have criticized Mendelssohn, is completely opposed to your meaning; this case would not only contradict your definition of orientation, but your entire philosophy. You free yourself of all objectivity and orient yourself solely and entirely subjectively. You say: "Since we lack all objective grounds for the existence of a God, in that we are not in a position to determine anything about his existence, we must withdraw into ourselves and merely consider whether the concept of a God, the presupposition of his existence, is beneficial to us or not. If this presupposition is useful or beneficial to the use of reason, i.e., if we are thereby able to make something conceivable or attain some useful end according to our subjective faculty of comprehension, then we accept this presupposition. The idea that the presupposition of a God is beneficial to the use of our reason does not in the least reduce our ignorance of God, nor does it at all [136] contribute anything to making the existence of a God more probable; nothing could be further from the truth. Rather, we presuppose a God merely because it would be foolish to not make use of a usable concept, whether the concept corresponds to an object or not." You call this **orienting oneself in relation to God**.[4]

And with what example, eminent man!, with what example do you wish to elucidate this way of orienting oneself? Is it possible that you orient yourself geographically or mathematically without becoming more certain of that which you become closer to cognizing by means of the subjective grounds you make use of? At the very least, the examples that come up in your essay obviously show that we can only say to have oriented ourselves if, once the previous determining grounds have failed us, we find new subjective or objective grounds to affirm or deny the intended object itself, and on account of these grounds. I could conclude from this, without any risk of being refuted, that the expression 'orienting oneself' is misused if the grounds by means of which I orient myself change nothing about the believability [Glaubhaftigkeit] of the thing itself and rather leave me in the same uncertainty about it that I was in before. But if I consider things, along with the expression, less precisely, then it remains certain that grounds that have no relation to the believability of a thing also determine nothing in relation to the believability under discussion, and that it would be to establish a principle of fanaticism if one were to claim that, when it comes to believing in a thing, one is permitted to be determined by grounds that have no influence at all upon the thing's believability. [137]

I avail myself of the word **fanaticism** [Schwärmerei] not in order to reciprocate the objection you made to me, nor in the least to tease a man that I so very much admire with a worn-out catchword, but only because I cannot in fact find another expression for this logical phenomenon. For, if it were rational for an intelligent human being to believe in and presuppose a God, for whose existence it lacks all grounds, merely because it needs to do so in the practical use of its reason, then it must also be rational for the lover to presuppose and believe in a creature's love because this belief is a need for such a person when they lack all grounds for this love's actuality. But what is one to call the state of such a lover? And what should one call the state of such a believer?

You yourself, venerable Kant!, would not excuse me if I allowed the inconvenience of the conclusions to prevent me from speaking precisely. I must therefore attack your principle even on its final support. It is not enough to have shown that it is not orienting oneself if, when assenting to

---

[4] The long quotation in this paragraph is a paraphrase of a number of claims made at 8:136–37, where Kant talks about orienting oneself in relation to 'something supersensible' (see 8:136.34) in general. Here, Wizenmann applies Kant's remarks to the concept of God in particular.

something, one allows oneself to be determined only by subjective grounds, and that this is an obvious principle of fanaticism. I must also raise the question: is it truly a need of reason to accept and presuppose the existence of God?

Need?—Reason, which must attain certain ends in order to not lose its nature, would then only be capable of attaining and actually attain these ends or endpoints of its efficacy by means of that presupposition. For, the concept of a need expresses a striving, without whose satisfaction the nature of a being that is aware of itself cannot [138] survive, and presupposes that the object, for which this being strives, really satisfies its striving. Our question can therefore be divided into two others:

1. does reason have such a need to accept a God, such that its nature cannot exist without doing so?
2. will the need that reason possesses be satisfied by presupposing a God?

The nature of reason consists in the faculty and the aspiration to cognize relations, and to judge one relation of things on the basis of another. Thus, if one were able to abolish the relations of things, insofar as they are present to our intuition, one would simultaneously abolish reason insofar as it proves to be efficacious. Now, if reason wants to achieve secure footing, it is nonetheless a need for it to base the more variable on the less variable and to trace the former back to the latter. Indeed, in order to achieve some sort of certainty in cognition it must go back to what is completely invariable and necessary, and therefore to isolate everything variable and merely subjective and make what is invariable and necessary the touchstone and measure of all its cognition. This invariable thing that reason must place at the foundation of all its cognition is not allowed to consist in propositions that have some sort of existence as their content. For, existence itself is precisely that object of reason which reason wants to test by means of the invariable. And the **object** of the test cannot simultaneously be the **criterion** of the test. Thus, only identical and therefore absolutely true propositions, as such, constitute what is invariable. If you therefore claim: "If our reason were to feel a need to take the **concept** [139] of the unlimited as the ground of the concept of everything limited, hence of all other things, then this need goes so far as to presuppose **existence** itself, without which reason can provide no satisfactory ground at all of the contingency of the existence of things in the world, let alone for its purposiveness and order" [8:137.29–138.3]; then I say: if you claim this, i.e., if on the basis of reason's need to presuppose the **concept** of the unlimited you infer the need to accept the **existence** of the same, then you obviously take the need of reason too far, in my view. Regardless of whether or not reason is able to provide a satisfactory ground of the contingency and order of the world, no **need** can arise for it to presuppose any sort of **existence** on this basis. For, its need relates merely to order and certainty in its **concepts**; **existence** is that which it seeks. If it cannot determine this by means of objective grounds, then it is its duty to admit that it does not know it. This is a duty because every presupposition on the basis of merely subjective grounds can hamper and impede the cognition of truth.

This is the case with respect to the **theoretical** use of reason. In its practical use, I admit that the reasons, on the basis of which you infer the need of that presupposition, are even more mysterious to me. For, in the first instance, if, as you say, "neither the binding authority of moral laws nor the incentives for observing them are to be derived from the existence of a God" [8:139.24–26], then I can understand it in no other way than that morality must indeed exist without a God. But if his existence must be presupposed, as you also say, "in order to give the concept of the highest good objective reality, [140] i.e., to prevent it and all of morality from being understood as a mere ideal," [8:139.28–31] then morality is indeed first made possible by the presupposition of a God, in such a way that the reality of morality is made dependent on the presupposition of a God, and the reality of a God on the presupposition of morality. But can any kind of **need** of reason to presuppose one or the other even arise from reciprocally presupposed concepts?

At the same time, if I were to grant that need to reason, both in its theoretical and its practical use, would the presupposition of a God, insofar as we are in a position to conceive of him, satisfy that need?

If this presupposition could "**give the concept of the highest good objective reality**," [8:139.28–29] then it would have satisfied the need of reason in its practical use. For, this, namely objective reality, is the gap that the presupposition of a God is supposed to fill. To be precise, the mere presupposition, without any objective grounds, is supposed to contain and grant objective reality. This obvious impossibility is the point that makes me question whether I have completely misunderstood you, eminent man, or whether something human confronts you here. I could easily convince myself of the first option for subjective reasons if the objective appearance of things did not speak so strongly for the latter.

The same mistake arises in a different form when it comes to the theoretical use of reason. Here too the presupposition of a God cannot satisfy its need, and for the following reason: namely because the question of reason is not answered by means of this presupposition, [141] but is pushed back further. For, the need of reason arises from the following: "because without assuming God, one can give no satisfactory and at the very least no comprehensible ground of the contingency of the existence of things in the world, let alone of their purposiveness and order." [8:138.1–3] But since we cannot determine whether things are contingent or not, what remains for us to explain is only their **order** and **relationality** [Verhältnißmäßigkeit]. To this end, you want to presuppose a single intelligent cause of the world because you cannot make it comprehensible how order and the comprehensive relation of things to each other can ever exist, other than by means of the understanding. But on what basis do you then want to explain order, relation, and perfection in that first, intelligent cause? In the end, do you not either have to abandon all explanation of order and relationality and resort to a necessity, wherein nothing is comprehensible, or leave everything in general unexplained? By presupposing a God, you therefore gain only this: that you push back the question of reason one step further, but you never satisfy its need.

Accordingly, your **rational belief** [Vernunftglaube] rests on not a single tenable support, if it has just been proven: that there exists no need of reason to assume a God, as you define this need, neither in its theoretical nor in its practical use; that, even if this need were to exist, it would not be satisfied by presupposing a God; that there is therefore no subjective ground of assent in your system when it comes to the existence of God; and finally, that it is completely impossible and a principle of fanaticism [142] to allow oneself to be determined, i.e., to orient oneself, by means of merely subjective grounds of assent.

Indeed, I must admit that I do not at all comprehend how you could bestow the honourable name of **rational belief** upon the belief which, in order to be grounded, completely excludes the use of reason. For, it would indeed be to exclude the use of reason if one were to replace an inference with a mere need, and also to accept this need as the ground of assent without any connection to inference. You would be much more justified in calling this belief a **belief of need** [Bedürfnißglauben]!

To speak strictly and not figuratively, **rational belief** can only be the kind of belief that is based on actual grounds of reason, i.e., inferences. In this way Mendelssohn could have called his style of conviction about God a rational belief, and with good reason. It was **belief**, because it was really only need that he proceeded from, and because he was not in a position to elevate his argumentation to an inseparable, unbroken whole. But it was **rational belief** because he supported that need with objective grounds, that is, with inferences.

And since, with respect to believability, nothing can be determined for all time on the basis of merely subjective grounds or motives [Motiven], that is, on the basis of motives that do not relate to the believability of a thing, in accordance with the laws of reason we will be forced to either abandon all belief, for which all objective grounds are lacking for us, or to connect subjective grounds with objective ones.

I therefore agree with you, venerable Kant, that no demonstration with respect to God's existence is possible. But I cannot orient myself [143] by means of merely subjective grounds. Rather, I believe I must follow the immortalized Mendelssohn and all dogmatists here in that I must exclusively possess objective grounds if I am to be determined when it comes to assent.

The dogmatists, however, are not lacking such objective grounds for the existence of God, they are simply not purely objective and transcendentally demonstrable. But their shortcoming does not simultaneously make them unusable, as is amply admitted in the *Results*, pp. 39f. If, for example, Mendelssohn argues with the Psalmists as follows: "**Should not the person who plants an ear be able to hear?**," he does not orient himself by means of a merely subjective motive, but underlying this argument is the objective principle that there can be no relation, no power in that which is brought about that is not also present in that which brings it about. Indeed, this principle brings us a step closer to the cognition of a God. And if the other principle, namely that the ordering of all relations and powers is only possible by means of an ordering understanding and will, if this principle, which is unavoidably required to supplement the proof, is objectively valid along with the first, then the demonstration is lacking nothing further. But this latter principle is at the most only subjective, that is, valid in analogy to the human form of intuition, and this is why the proof retains its holes. Nevertheless, the proof strives for objective validity and is not entirely empty of it, and I can allow myself to be determined by it when assenting to a thing if I can think of no further reasons against it. The dogmatist only need overcome himself and admit that it is not **certainty** but only **a kind of probability** that [144] determines him to believe in the existence of a God and that, when we consider the objective grounds for and against to be equal, it is only **need** and the **generosity** of the scale in relation to the grounds '**for**' that tip the balance. Then I can continue to philosophize with the dogmatist in complete peace.

Permit me to conceive of you as such a dogmatist for a moment in order to pursue my train of thought. As such a person, you say to me that no human being can resist the **need** of believing in God, no matter how speculative their reason has become. But you trace this need back to an entirely different source than you did in your own system. The human being, you now say, is the only creature on earth that is most distinctly aware of their finitude and dependence on nature. Inseparably connected to this consciousness is the feeling of a continual insecurity about one's existence and well-being. Regardless of whether this feeling is not continually occurrent in the human being, because its inclinations and representations are alternatingly attracted by a thousand other objects, it is nonetheless often drawn into a context of external and internal circumstances in which this feeling forces itself upon the human being, and where the longing takes hold in it to give more stability to either external circumstances or its inner self, or both simultaneously. But it is impossible to annihilate the influence of external circumstances on the happiness of human beings if security about existence belongs to one's happiness. It is just as impossible for human beings to determine the external relations of things towards themselves at will. But one of the two must be possible in order to put the human being at ease. Thus, in order to soothe the human being, that is, in order to satisfy its foundational striving [145] to feel secure about its existence, no other means remains than to conceive of itself in relation to a being, to whose power and wisdom all of nature is subjected, and on account of whose goodness the human being can hope that its entire fate has been calculated for the best end, and that even the apparent destruction of its existence has been for the increase of its enjoyment and its perpetual security. How is the human being, the creature thrown onto earth and who is alone frightened by the frailty and uncertainty of things, not supposed to long for such a being, take comfort in such a being, and bring about the most beautiful fruits of humanity in conjunction with it?

The distinct consciousness of finitude and insecurity, and the incessant longing to securely know one's existence therefore brings about the longing for a God in the human being. One could claim that this longing increases at the same pace as the education of human beings because true culture advances towards that which is invariable without end. Indeed, perhaps the source, from which the philosophical concept of God (conceiving of him as invariable and infinite, for example) receives its first impetus can be found in this need.

Now, let this human being, with this longing in its heart, go out into nature. Let it perceive the benevolent, wise, and manifold relationships of things and forms to each other. It will not resist this impression. It will feel the author of nature and raise its hands to the sky.

From this moment on the human being is familiar with the idea of a God. It will not occur to the human being to try and explain the order and relationality of things in the world except by means of an ordering and creative understanding. Even the speculator's refined sense of doubt [146] will feel defeated from time to time by the total impression of the order of the world, by the sight of their own ornate body, such that they will confess that these are the traces and scenes not of a blind necessity, but of an eternal understanding. Let us stay on this flat and straight path of motherly nature; whoever verges off to the right or to the left is in danger of becoming terribly lost!

Excellent, my dear dogmatist! You have given us an account of the human being's belief in God on the basis of the understanding and the heart of human beings. We cannot demand a more complete analysis. But if you want to satisfy us, then you must also determine the logical value of this belief for us. For, it seems to me that it goes too far to say that "if we accept no intelligent author of the world, then no intelligible ground of its order can be given without falling into genuine absurdities." [8:138.6–8] For we grasp just as little of an **intelligent, first cause** as we do of the **eternal necessity of παν**.[5]

And vice versa!, you remind me: we grasp nothing more of the eternal necessity of παν than what we grasp of a first, intelligent cause. For, neither of them explains to us the beginning of an action, the possibility of something finite coming into existence. Both the necessity of things and the infinitude of their series, as well as a first, intelligent cause are, logically considered, only formulas for avoiding the confession that we know nothing and that, beyond the analogy with sensible relations, everything is obscure for us. The supposition of necessity, however, possesses the logical advantage that it is protected against all the attacks of speculation, because it excludes, of itself, all appearances as grounds of explanation. [147] This advantage, however, is also merely dialectical, precisely because it leaves all appearances unexplained.—A different and, it seems to me, more real advantage is possessed by the supposition of a first, intelligent cause.

The value of this supposition does not consist in logical succinctness, rather it possesses value because it is the thought, of which nature so gently and potently convinces us. Our consciousness is the clearest and most distinct among everything we are familiar with. It is raised to such a degree that we not only form general concepts out of particular, similar

---

[5] *pan* or 'all things'.

appearances, but we also make our consciousness itself into the idea, under which we picture the origin and order of the world. That is, because order and purposiveness as such can only be grasped by means of the understanding, we blindly take the understanding to be the only means through which they can be brought about. Below this degree of consciousness, we would be animals; beyond this degree of consciousness, there is no more firm footing for us. What would happen if nature placed us on precisely this level of consciousness in order to bring about and develop the idea that is the truest, and via the shortest path and through the easiest means, even though we cannot prove it? What would happen if nature would have given us this truth by means of a transcendental configuration [Einrichtung], the transcendental insight into which nature could not achieve for us? This approach would at least be appropriate in the mind, whose nature it is to avoid syllogisms in order to obtain its aims more quickly and more securely by means of complete impressions. For my own part, I cannot criticize the philosopher when they trust in nature in this way and supplement their lack of insight with this trust.

And neither do I do this, kind dogmatist! For how could one criticize the person who is convinced by a [148] certain amount of experience that nature always follows the best path and so seldomly deceives; who childishly throws themselves into nature's lap and, in relation to the highest and most honourable impression, takes her at her mere word? Only in this way does the human being actually become good and a child of circumspection [ein Kind der Vorsicht]. They need only not forget, and the philosopher need only firmly keep in mind, the boundary between one's belief and insight, so that one remains tolerant of others and does not oneself fall into fanaticism, that is, offend against one's belief with one's insight, and against one's insight with one's belief. In this way one can also prevent "dogmatizing with pure reason in the field of the supersensible from becoming the direct path to philosophical fanaticism" [8:138.32–33n], assuming that one does not want to get involved in an all too precise critique of the faculty of reason because one is afraid that, if evil were to be increased in this way, then one's own existence would also have to be at risk.

Nevertheless, the origin of the concept of God can also be considered from a different point of view, which at first seems less advantageous but later appears all the more excellent. The point of entry is narrow and dangerous, but perhaps it leads to a field where the sky is vast, the path lit, and the views more delightful. And it seems to me that it is not appropriate for a philosopher to shy away from the search for truth on account of prejudice or difficulty.

One can regard the premises, from which you have derived the origin of our knowledge of God as sources that come into being by means of many smaller streams coming together. For, it is undeniable that several connections of ideas should already exist in the human being; that it must already have a good idea of a considerable whole; that it must have made considerable progress in the comparison of that which is proper [149] and improper, that which is great, and that which is beautiful and true; that it must have experienced many a blow in the nexus of things as well as some fortune in connection to actions, before the sum of ideas could exist, from which a tolerable concept of God can emerge. It is undeniable that the concepts of God, whether we suppose that human beings are left to their own devices or not, are first raw, in pieces, and on the whole must have been unworthy concepts. For, when have we seen human beings progress from the universal to the particular? It is the human being's nature and for more than one reason it is necessary that it takes precisely the opposite course of action in everything that it does. Particular appearances awaken particular concepts in the human being, and its judgements must, in the beginning, be just as particular and in this way restricted to appearances alone before these appearances, concepts, and judgements receive coherence and are expanded. And if this truth, gained from merely observing nature, were ambiguous, with what nerve could I deny history this truth? Were the gods of the ancients—I exclude those who had simple concepts of the cosmogony dominant in the Orient, because they obviously come from a tradition that is equally not as easy to explain—were, I say, the gods of the ancients anything more and anything other than fantasized human beings? Were they not distributed amongst the people of the world and, even according to the judgement of the wisest people, subject to invariable fate? By examining the predicates that are conferred upon these gods, does one not see that their concepts are almost entirely composed of particular appearances of nature insofar as the human being considers these appearances in relation to itself and elevates them to the actions of freely acting beings?—I ask because I want to counter certain critics with humility, not because [150] I believe to have exposed the matter to doubt.

Thus, if the question is 'where do the seeds of the concept of gods and of God come from?,' nature and the history of human beings answer: from particular appearances that the human being perceived or conceived in relation to itself, and which the human being explains by means of itself, that is, by means of the action of a being similar to it, because their true causes are concealed from it. If, for example, a storm was brewing and the human being saw its lightning and heard its thunder, on the basis of what causes should it explain this astounding appearance if it does not yet have a compendium of the doctrine of nature at hand, except by means of the free activity of a being similar to it who caused this thunder and lightning? In this way the human being suddenly possessed the concept of a higher being who has power over it and nature: the concept of a god.

But this concept must be lacking a considerable amount of the perfection that the human race's manifold destinies, appearances, and connections during our times have helped achieve! Just as the human being lends its personality and free activity to the cause of the storm, so does it also lend its passions, its concepts of right and wrong and of happiness, its desires, and its limitedness.—One must admit that this concept of God was very imperfect, raw, and sensible.

But this concept did indeed actually exist in this way. The idea of a higher being was awakened in the human being and brought to life. From then on it was able to and had to become the principle of the human being's dispositions and actions. And that was sufficient for the time being. [151]

The example I have used of the storm can be further supplemented with many others to show how naturally the human being can be guided towards the concept of God by means of appearances of all kinds and, according to its nature and as a result of human history, how it most likely must be led to this concept! But why should this one example not be enough?

And here, eminent Kant, is where our principles diverge from each other the most. "The **concept** of a God and even the conviction of his **existence**," you say, "can only be found in and proceed from reason, and it cannot first come to us either through inspiration or through a message communicated to us, however great the authority behind it. If I experience an immediate intuition of such a kind that nature, as far as I am acquainted with her, cannot provide me, then a concept of God must serve as a guiding principle as to whether this appearance agrees with all the characteristics required for a deity. Now, even if I have no insight at all into how it is possible for any kind of appearance to depict that which can only be thought but never intuited, even if only with respect to quality, this much is still clear: that in order to judge whether it is God who appears to me and internally or externally has an effect on my feelings, I would have to hold it up to my rational concept of God and test it accordingly; not as to whether it is adequate to that concept, but merely whether it does not contradict it. In just the same way, even if nothing in what he revealed to me immediately contradicted that concept, this appearance, intuition, immediate revelation, or however else one wants to call such a presentation, nevertheless never proves the existence of a being whose concept (if it is not to be vaguely determined and hence [152] might be subject to association with every possible delusion) demands that it be of **infinite** magnitude as distinguished from everything created. But no experience or intuition at all can be adequate to that concept, hence no one can unambiguously prove the existence of such a being. Thus no one can first be convinced of the existence of a highest being through any intuition; rational belief must come first, and then certain appearances or revelations could at most provide the occasion for investigating whether we are warranted in taking what speaks or presents itself to us to be a deity, and thus serve to confirm that belief according to these findings." [8:142.9–143.6]

It is easy to see wherein the cause of our currently opposing positions lies. Namely, you can say: **The concept of God cannot enter human beings through appearances, and I am able to say that the concept of God**—for, in the first instance, I only want to talk about the concept—**can and must most probably enter into human beings through appearances**. The cause of this opposition lies in the fact that you take the complete, developed, philosophical concept of God, singularly and alone, as your basis, whereas I am only talking about the incomplete, initial concept of a deity. I trust that you and anyone who can combine representations will, presupposing my concept of God, accept my conclusion, just as I would not for a moment object to approving your conclusion if I were to presuppose your concept of God. For, it is admittedly impossible that an infinite being, as such, could ever be intuited, just as, on the other hand, the concept of a merely higher being that has power over nature [153] can easily be derived from appearances to the extent that the human being reasons about them.

This is how I would have avoided the difficulty that you presented to me. I could now continue and say: "As the human being learns to combine many appearances with one another, and derives them from a single source; as it more distinctly notices the connection among things; as it grants more room and a deeper efficacy to its God; and furthermore, as it purifies its moral properties and orders and expands them according to its own feeling of correctness and moral greatness; to the extent it does so the human being perfects its popular concept of God and, when it gradually regards this concept in connection to other sciences, it eventually raises this concept up to the metaphysical purity, by means of which it is placed outside of all relation to appearances, and by means of which all judgement concerning its ideality or reality is denied to it. But since appearances were indeed its source, and since it can no longer judge concerning the reality of the concept that has become abstract, the human being is forced to return to appearances and investigate whether they really do contain that which the concept abstracted from them. And if they do not contain this, then the concept remains indeterminate with respect to its reality. But if they do contain this, that is, if the concept has appearances which, in an unambiguous way, presuppose personality and the direct action of a higher being, then, to the extent that the whole is compatible with these appearances, it can therfrom derive an incomplete proof of the **existence** of a God and an incomplete proof of the existence of a higher being without hesitation."—This is how the difficulty would be avoided, but it would not yet be overcome. [154]

If, as you say, "the **concept** of God and even the conviction of his **existence** is only found in reason and can only proceed from reason alone," [8:142.9–10] then this concept and this conviction must certainly be taken as the standard and measure of the appearance and revelation that relate to that concept. Indeed, they disappear, as it were, as insignificant and superfluous decorations that do not deserve to be esteemed in comparison to that rational concept and that rational conviction, the height and perfection of which they can never attain. But if we take the liberty of considering the case where the concept of God and conviction of his existence cannot be found in reason alone and do not proceed from it alone, then it undeniably follows that appearances, from which the concept and the conviction of the existence of a higher and highest being can be respectively abstracted, emerge as what is essential [das Hauptwerk], and that they must be tested not through the false concept of reason, but can alone be tested in the way that all appearances must be tested.

Accordingly, what is to be investigated above all else is whether the concept of God and conviction of his existence can be found in reason, and indeed in reason alone.

In order to prevent all misunderstanding, we will proceed from definitions.

To you, reason is: the form and rule of thought. I prefer to call it, perhaps with little substantial difference: the capacity to perceive relations both between things and between concepts, and to connect them.

A concept that can be found **in reason** alone would therefore be: a concept which, considered without any [155] connection to appearances or what is material, exists merely in the form of thought.

But a concept such as this is impossible because it is impossible, in any kind of form and in any kind of power, for a change to take place or a judgement to be made if the form is conceived without any relation to its matter and the power not conceived in connection to power.

The implication that immediately follows from the real definition of reason is so clear that I do not comprehend how one can almost universally speak of reason, insofar as it is efficacious, as if it were a capacity or thing that is independent of all appearance, and thereby always preserve concepts so ambiguously.

Reason, insofar as it judges or is efficacious, must necessarily be connected to appearances, the matter of judgement, and there is no concept that proceeds from reason alone.

But there are indeed such concepts in a different sense and in accordance with a looser definition of reason.

Of this kind are all universal and necessary concepts, and even all **concepts** as such. For, where else should a concept come from, from where should it proceed, where else should it be found, except in reason? How should a concept, as universal or necessary, be cognized, except by means of reason? It is not as if reason could have concepts or make judgements independently of all appearances, but because reason alone is the capacity of converting appearances into concepts and noticing their universal and necessary relations to each other.—For this reason and to this extent I can say that concepts can be found in reason alone.

To the greatest extent, this can be said of necessary concepts or, which in my opinion is the same thing, [156] of merely logical or identical concepts. These necessary concepts, even if their matter must always be empirical (for there is no **concept** without the presupposition of **a thing**, and we cannot conceive of a predicate except as in relation to a subject), these necessary concepts, I say, go beyond all appearances. Their inner truth does not depend on appearances, but on that which is necessary, that which is identical in the relation of the predicate to the subject. They are the laws of thought themselves, and thus are to be found only in reason.

I cannot go on, venerable man!—This fragment has been on my desk for a month, and I have not been in a position to add a single line. It is also very probable that many months will go by before I am capable of any other work. Please allow this fragment (which, unfortunately, is lacking my most cherished aim, **something positive**) to appear before you earlier rather than not at all or only once the memory of the **dispute** has faded away, along with everything else! Allow me to submit this piece to you as a testament to my great admiration for you, just as great as my love of truth, and permit me to hope that you do not think of me without affection.

Thomas Wizenmann
Magister of Philosophy

PART III

The Reception of the *Critique of Practical Reason*

8

Johann Georg Heinrich Feder
Introduction

Johann Georg Heinrich Feder (1740–1821) was born in the village of Schornweißach, Bavaria, where his father, an educated pastor, was his first teacher.[1] Starting in 1757 Feder attended the University of Erlangen, where he studied philosophy, pedagogy, and theology, and where he was introduced to Wolffian philosophy. After working as a private tutor for a few years in the early 1760s, Feder completed his *Magister* thesis in 1765, which was a critical discussion of Rousseau, entitled *Homo natura non ferus* (Man is Not Wild by Nature). This granted him permission to teach and in the same year he became professor of metaphysics and logic at a *Gymnasium* in Coburg. While in Coburg, Feder wrote an extremely successful textbook for his students: *Grundriß der Philosophischen Wissenschaften nebst der nöthigen Geschichte* (Outline of the Philosophical Sciences, along with the Necessary History) (1767). Indeed, Kant used this as the textbook for all ten of his courses on Philosophical Encyclopedia that he offered between 1767 and 1782. The success of this book led to Feder being offered a professorship of philosophy in 1768 at the University of Göttingen, one of the most prestigious universities in Germany at the time, and he remained there for nearly thirty years. In 1797 he transferred to the *Georgianum* in Hanover, retiring in 1811 when the institution closed. Feder died having become a *Hofrat* (Court Councillor) and a member of the Göttingen Society of Sciences.

Feder was a well-respected and well-known philosopher, especially during the 1770s and early 1780s. In addition to the 1767 *Outline*, he published another extremely successful textbook in 1769, entitled *Logik und Metaphysik, nebst der Philosophischen Geschichte im Grundrisse* (Logic and Metaphysics, along with the Philosophical History in Outline), which

---

[1] Information about Feder's life and works is taken from Thiel (2016), Beiser (1987, pp. 180–81), Nowitzki, Roth, and Stiening (2018), Birken-Bertsch (2015), Müller (1961), and Sassen (2000, p. 16).

went through seven German editions and four Latin editions, as well as a textbook on practical philosophy in 1770, the *Lehrbuch der Praktischen Philosophie* (Handbook of Practical Philosophy). His magnum opus was a four-volume work on the will entitled *Untersuchungen über den menschlichen Willen* (Inquiries Concerning the Human Will) which was modelled on Locke's *Essay* and was meant to be an investigation into the will that would serve as a counterpart to what Locke did for the understanding. As one of the most well-known 'popular philosophers' of the period, Feder also contributed to many highly regarded journals of the time, often on issues of public interest such as the death penalty, intellectual property, and human rights with regard to animals.[2] He was also the first to review Adam Smith's *Wealth of Nations* in German, which contributed to it quickly becoming a classic among German intellectuals.

A turning point in Feder's life and career took place in early 1782 when, while working for his local academic journal, the *Göttingische Anzeigen von gelehrten Sachen*, he edited the infamous Göttingen review of the first *Critique*, which was originally written by Christian Garve and to which Kant responds in the *Prolegomena*.[3] Feder's role as editor of this review had a lasting, negative impact on his career and reputation: he became known as viciously anti-Kantian and both his students and colleagues subsequently lost respect for him. Feder attempted to vindicate himself by replying to Kant in *Über Raum und Caussalität zur Prüfung der Kantischen Philosophie* (On Space and Causality, by way of Examining the Kantian Philosophy) (1787). Although Feder's reputation was already on the decline at this point, his was still an influential voice and this work was reviewed no fewer than seven times.[4] Feder continued his assault by founding the anti-Kantian journal *Philosophische Bibliothek* with Christoph Meiners in 1788, but it sold so poorly that it closed in 1791 after just four issues.

Feder therefore has a somewhat tragic legacy: even today he is best known as being an uncharitable critic of Kant, even though he contributed much more to the scholarly and public discourse of his time than mere Kant criticism. Even his engagement with Kant is not limited to his role in the infamous Göttingen review: in addition to the above-mentioned monograph, Feder wrote a few shorter articles dealing with Kant's

---

[2] Feder (2018) reprints many of his most important essays.
[3] For an account of this affair, see Beiser (1987, Ch. 6.3), Sassen (2000, pp. 6–11), and Hatfield (2004, pp. xix–xxiii).
[4] All of these reviews have been reprinted in Landau (1991, see pp. 509–12, 564–71, 572–76, 631–32, 655–57, 681–700, and 712–22).

philosophy as well as many reviews of both Kant's own works (including the *Groundwork*[5] and third *Critique*) and other writings engaging with Kant's philosophy.[6] Furthermore, Feder is not always critical of Kant: at various points in his career Feder has positive things to say about Kant's *Dreams of a Spirit-Seer*, for instance, and even claimed that this work had a lasting influence on his thought.[7]

Feder's review of the second *Critique* consists of thirty-six numbered sections wherein he paraphrases from the book and then offers some critical commentary. Feder begins the review with the remark, made in section 2, that he never meant to deny the possibility of *a priori* cognition. Feder therefore takes the claim Kant makes at 5:12.7–8 to be directed at him, which is likely given Kant almost certainly read Feder's *On Space and Causality* prior to publishing the second *Critique*, and which contains a claim to this effect.[8] Other notable points made in the review include: the doubt raised in sections 5, 6, and 12 over whether pure reason can be practical independently of feelings and inclinations; Feder's extended discussion of the concepts of good and evil and their relationship to pleasure and displeasure, in section 17; and his claim in section 23 that respect for the moral law is just respect for ourselves as self-legislators. The review ends, in section 36, with a summary of the three ways in which Feder takes Kant's moral theory to be different from all others: (1) Kant's principle of morality concerns reason only and not the entire human being, and that for Kant happiness does not include things like self-contentment and self-respect; (2) Kant's concept of freedom is meant to be an exception to the law of causality, rather than something that is compatible with it; and (3) Kant's understanding of God and immortality of the soul are ideas that support his moral system but which we cannot theoretically cognize. As a whole, Feder's review of the second *Critique* captures the opinion of one of Kant's most well-known and infamous critics, which both Kant and his contemporaries would have been

---

[5] Kant was aware of Feder's review of the *Groundwork*; see the letter from Schütz from Nov. 13, 1785 (esp. 10:423.10–12). Feder's review of the *Groundwork* has not been included in this volume because it is quite short, other reviews convey the same points but formulated better, and because it is unclear that the second *Critique* directly responds to it.
[6] See the bibliography in Nowitzki, Roth, and Stiening (2018) for a complete list of his monographs, works he edited, articles, and reviews.
[7] See e.g., *Philosophische Bibliothek* 3 (Feder and Meiners 1790, p. 225) and Nowitzki, Roth, and Stiening (2018, pp. 1–2).
[8] See the letter from Biester from June 11, 1786 (10:457.14–15), the letter from Bering from May 28, 1787 (10:488.4–5), and the letter to Schütz from June 25, 1787 (10:490.14–17). See also Feder (1787, p. 35) for a claim suggesting that *a priori* cognition is impossible.

interested in reading. Indeed, it is likely that the review attracted a wide readership because not only did Feder's writings gain attention at the time, as mentioned above, but Feder also makes no effort to hide his identity by signing the review with his real initial, 'F.'[9]

Translation Notes

This is the first English translation of Feder's review of the second *Critique*. The basis for the translation is the original 1788 review, published in Feder's own anti-Kantian journal the *Philosophische Bibliothek*, though I have also consulted the modern reprint in Feder (2018).

---

[9] In general, and as both Sassen (2000, p. 45) and Gesang (2007, p. xii) note, the identity of the anonymous authors of reviews was a poorly kept secret.

Review of the *Critique of Practical Reason* (1788)

Philosophische Bibliothek. 1. Band, 1788, pp. 182–218.

[182]

Critique of Practical Reason. By Immanuel Kant. Riga, J. Fr. Hartknoch. 1788. 8. 292 pages.

In order to be able to pass an accurate judgement on this new product of the Kantian genius—which is more than a mere reworking of the *Groundwork of the Metaphysics of Morals*—and on its relation to the doctrines of other philosophers, it is necessary to uncover the main principles on which the author builds, and by means of which he proceeds, and to accompany them individually with comments. In order to make the occasionally necessary reference to them easier, I will number them. [183]

1) The **faculty of desire** is the faculty of a being to be, by means of its representations, the cause of the reality of the objects of these representations. p. 16. [5:9.20–22n] Or to determine itself to bring such objects about (whether the physical faculty is sufficient, or not). p. 29. [5:15.10–13]
    *) This definition does not seem entirely adequate to me. We can desire, wish, or strive for that which we cannot bring about by means of our efforts, and which depends on fortune. For example: the whole prize of a lottery. I suppress some other doubts concerning this definition because they do not concern anything important.

2) To claim that there is no *a priori* cognition at all would mean just as much as to claim that there is no reason. p. 23. [5:12.7–8]
    *) This depends on what *a priori* cognition is supposed to mean. Concepts and principles prior to all experience, all sensation, and independent of them? These do not exist and even Kant does not really claim that they do. For, the concepts that he calls *a priori*

are, according to his own definition, in themselves and without connection to experience, **empty forms of thought without any content**. And his pure **intuitions** are: **intuitions**. Consequently, whether their ground is merely internal and subjective or objective and external, [184] they are, **according to the language of other philosophers**, sensations or sense perceptions as soon as they are present, only stripped of **corporeal qualities as far as possible**. Or they are not real intuitions but only certain determinations of the faculty of real sense perception.—But if *a priori* cognition means a connection of representations to judgements and inferences, in accordance with the subjective and objective principles [Gründe] of human cognition, in relation to certain objects and events that have not occurred in experience, nor will occur in experience in the future, or preceded our experience, or which cannot otherwise be found outside of experience, then *a priori* cognition embodies the essence of reason. For, all foresight and all inference depends on it. But to whom has it occurred to deny this *a priori* cognition? At the very least not to any opponent of the *Critique of Pure Reason*, as far as I know. Rather, precisely this *Critique* restricts the ability of reason to cognize something about objects outside of experience much more than it has seemed to others, who, by means of the principles of analogy, nonetheless believe themselves able to ground, not scientific insights corresponding to certain ideals, but a rational way of thinking without first availing themselves of the good will or practical reason.

3) All practical principles that presuppose something that can only be cognized empirically can furnish only **maxims**, but not **practical laws**, [5:21.14–16] [185] because the latter must have **objective** necessity, which can only be cognized *a priori*. pp. 38f. [5:21.36–22.1]

   *) So, it once again depends on nominal definitions? In the end, however, it will only depend on: (a) **in what sense** the author can **prove** that some kind of **objective** necessity is cognizable *a priori*; and (b) whether all the things that moral science can and should set as its end can, as far as possible, be achieved by means of principles, the correctness of which the human being can convince itself of, whether one calls them **laws** or **maxims**, and their ground objective or subjective.

4) All practical rules that are grounded on the principle of self-love, thus on feelings, place the determining ground of the will in the **inferior**[1] **faculty of desire**. And if there were no other (merely formal) laws (those alone which, as reason plainly sees, contain the general essence of a law without application to a particular object known through experience), which **sufficiently** *) determine the will, then no **superior faculty of desire** could be admitted. [5:22.27–31]—**It does not at all depend on** where the representations, which affect the will with pleasure [Lust] or displeasure [Unlust], come from, etc. **) p. 41. [5:23.2–6]

> *) **sufficiently**? And there are such [laws]? Subsequently, the author seems to explain this differently. [186] Or what does this **sufficiently** mean here?
> **) One should think, however, that quite a lot depends on this.

5) Either there is no (superior) faculty of desire at all, or pure reason must be practical of itself and alone, that is, without presupposing any kind of feeling, thus without representing the agreeable or disagreeable as the matter of the faculty of desire. [5:24.35–38]—The smallest admixture of the impulses [Antrieben] of feelings and inclinations would lower and **destroy** its dignity and force [Nachdruck]. pp. 44[–45]. [5:25.3–4]

> *) All terminological disputes aside, every psychologist would gladly grant to the author that reason is certainly practical in itself to a certain degree or is capable of affecting the will. In that we comprehend relations, agreement, and contradiction by means of reason, and cannot think contradiction, neither can we will that which leads to a contradiction in our representations. Reason would oppose itself, it would be offended, if the person we recognize as innocent were to be represented or treated as guilty, slandered, bad-mouthed, or otherwise mistreated. It would be the same if we were to treat something as not belonging to another person, which does indeed belong to them according to our concepts, or if we were to withhold their property from them or ruin them. It would be the same if we were to consider ourselves [187] to be parts of the world and of the human community and consider our neighbours to be just as good as and equal to us, but we were to make ourselves the

---

[1] The Cambridge Edition of Kant's works adopts 'higher' and 'lower' for the '*ober*' and '*unter*' faculties respectively. I have adopted 'inferior' and 'superior' to remain consistent with Wolff's and Baumgarten's Latin terms of '*inferiori*' and '*superiori*', on which Kant's German terms are based.

centre of creation and sacrifice everything for our own sake and subordinate everything to ourselves. **To what extent** this opposition of reason is capable of controlling the opposing, sensible stimuli and inclinations on its own is still a question. And what Kant says about this will become clear in the following. And whether or not we can call that which we perceive in ourselves when reason expresses itself in this way a feeling (agreeable or disagreeable); whether the will's compliance with, receptivity to, and determinability by reason is to be called **inclination** or **respect**; this is, again, not something I want to argue about much with anyone. In the meantime, it has become customary, at least in common and scientific language, to acknowledge **rational** inclinations and **sensible** inclinations and drives, and to separate them from one another.

6) To be happy is a necessary striving of every rational, finite being and therefore an unavoidable determining ground of its faculty of desire. p. 46.[2] [5:25.12–14]

   *) The **prescriptions** and doctrines of moral science, whether Kant calls them maxims or laws, must therefore take this necessary striving, this unavoidable determining ground, into account as well. And **the smallest admixture of the impulses** [188] **of feelings and inclinations** into the principle of pure practical reason does not have to be so ruinous as the author just (no. 5) presented them to be.

7) In the case of merely subjective practical principles it is expressly made a condition that they must have as their basis not objective but subjective conditions in the power of choice [Willkühr], [5:26.27–29] for otherwise the rules of uniform appearance, in the corporeal world for example, when they are not in fact cognized *a priori*, are only called **natural laws** because one assumes (as for chemical laws) that they would be cognized *a priori* from objective grounds if our insight went deeper. pp. [47–]48. [5:26.23–27]

   *) What is inserted into definitions can surely be deduced from them in turn. But when the question concerns that which actually exists in nature, and that which can and must happen according to it, nothing in the least can be decided and proven

---

[2] Feder cites the incorrect page here. This claim is made on page 45 of the 1788 edition of the second *Critique*.

with all these terms and determinations of words. What compels or justifies us to these mutual conditions? That the determinations of the will grounded in inclinations and feelings all have **merely** subjective ground, but not also objective ground in the relation of our nature to the remaining things in the world and to the will of the creator? And that, on the other hand, the laws of nature, with which we are concerned in theoretical philosophy, are cognizable *a priori*, in a sense [189] of the expression that ought not be possessed by the prescriptions for correct action that apply to inclinations? Without borrowing concepts from experience, whether internal or external, **nothing**, not a single natural law, can be proven about the nature of things. But in relation to given or borrowed concepts, all of moral science and the entirety of natural law can be demonstrated *a priori*, and both of them have been proven this way often and for a long time. However, if something is to be achieved with these *a priori* demonstrated systems of natural necessity, we must first refer to experience (whether internal or external), to how they relate to actual nature. And it is precisely that foundational principle of self-love or happiness that Kant claims is not valid as a practical law but only as a maxim of prudence that ancient philosophers considered to be a natural law cognizable on the basis of concepts. *Omnis natura conservatrix est sui*[3] was for them an axiom. How is a power supposed to be directed against itself, or a will able to desire that which is contrary to itself? Thus, if it is to depend on this kind of *a priori* cognition, and from objective grounds, then the moral systems that Kant disputes might still be saved.

8) The maxim of seeking one's own happiness cannot hold as a law because each person has their own happiness as an object, [190] which is distinct from and often conflicts with that of everyone else, thus there is no universal law there. p. 50 [see 5:28.4–17]

*) The principle of following **reason**, of determining oneself in one's will according to the **truth**, of seeking the promotion of the **highest good** (one can choose any of the other expressions that Kant employs to designate the foundational principle of practical reason, or one similar to them) cannot hold as a law, because

---

[3] *all nature preserves itself*

everyone has their own reason, truth, idea of the common best and the highest good, etc., which is different from and often conflicts with that of everyone else.—Thus, it seems to me that we can reply to the first with *kat'anthropon* or *ex concessis*.[4] But just as human beings nonetheless seem to agree about certain common concepts and principles despite all the individuality and divergence with respect to their concepts and judgements, so do their inclinations and intentions also initially agree in some respects, and over time they agree in ever more respects in relation to the **common good**, despite all their egoism and self-love. And this is precisely the point of moral science: to, where possible, bring human beings to the point where they envision and seek their well-being, their contentment, and their highest good in the promotion of the common best according to the best possible knowledge, and thus in the true performance of their duties.

9) A will, for which the mere **legislating form** of maxims alone can serve as a law, [191] must be a **free** will, that is, one independent of the empirical law of causality. [see 5:29.4–9] Such a will has **autonomy**. **Heteronomy**, on the other hand, is when the inclinations and the **matter** of the law connected to them determine the power of choice. pp. 51ff. [see 5:33.25–28] Thus, freedom of the will consists in the fact that the will is determined by the law not merely without the cooperation of all sensible impulses, but with rejection of them all and with infringement upon all inclinations **insofar as** they are capable of opposing that law. p. 128 [5:72.29–32]

   *) This is a main point of our author's system. We first want to examine his **concept** of the freedom of the will. It is in no way completely new or opposed to otherwise common concepts, rather, **considered in itself** it can be identified with that which the Stoic calls freedom and what is otherwise called **higher moral** freedom. For, this consists in nothing other than complete dependence of the will on the representation of duty known through reason and independence from sensible stimuli and impulses. Thus, the will alone is free and the vicious fool is a slave of his body and his passions. However: 1) Is the essence of the law of causality restricted by this freedom of the will? 2) Is it

---

[4] Both of these expressions are synonyms for *ad hominem*, and the way in which they are used here implies an argumentative strategy whereby one uses the beliefs or line of argument of one's opponent against them. For information on the former expression, see Campe (1801, p. 437).

an **error of language** to call [192] the stirring of the will in relation to the rational representation of **duty** (*in sensu composito*[5] or according to form) not just **respect**, along with the author, but also a **rational inclination** and to accept an **internal moral feeling**, the latter being something which the author himself accepts? p. 142 [5:80] 3) How strong or weak is this stirring, respect, and inclination according to the **original** predispositions of human nature, to the extent that we know it philosophically? And to what extent is it necessary that this stirring become aroused and strengthened by means of a connection to the interest of other inclinations that relate to particular objects, and in general by means of a connection to the striving for happiness, well-being, and contentment? These are questions which, at the very least, cannot be settled by means of definitions.

10) Even though freedom does not immediately present itself to us in experience, rather the latter (all appearances) is subjected to the law of causality (to **mechanism**, the author also says), the consciousness that there are moral laws nonetheless proves to us that there is such a transcendental freedom (not bound to the law of causality). pp. 57f.[6] [5:29.30–30.3] Compare p. 169. [5:94–95]

    *) In this Kant distinguishes himself with his concept of freedom from others in that he conceives of this freedom as not immediately cognizable on the basis of experience, but provable only on the basis of the existence and nature of the moral [193] law, and at the same time as diverging from the law of causality. But **the** freedom that is provable on the basis of the existence and nature of a moral law contains no exception or divergence from the law of causality and is immediately cognizable on the basis of experience. Not only has it been irrefutably shown by many thorough philosophers, who are well enough known and do not need to be named, that even if **everything** were to follow from decisive grounds, the moral concepts of duty, merit, blame, and punishability would still be able to coexist in their entirety, but I also do not understand how the author, according to his own concepts and foundational principles of morality and moral laws, can deduce a freedom that is not

---

[5] *in the composite sense*
[6] Again, this is the incorrect page. This is a paraphrase of statements made on p. 53 of the 1788 edition.

subjected to the law of causality and is not to be immediately cognized on the basis of experience. According to his system, as is clear from what has already been said, and as will become even more clear in the following, morality is based on the fact that the will is determinable by, or at least has **respect** for, the **form** of the moral law or the representation of **duty as duty**, independently of the other interest of the inclinations. If we accept this, what follows? That the will does not therein stand under the law of causality? Is the **representation** of duty here, along with the **nature of the will**, not the **cause**, and respect, if not an inclination and decision to determine oneself according to duty, the **effect**? And [194] is this causality not cognizable on the basis of experience just as well as any other? The more distant and ultimate ground of this representation of duty and this nature of the human will is obviously not yet clear. This is the reason why many have hesitated to judge deterministically in the metaphysical dispute concerning freedom when it comes to **ultimate** grounds. But if it were permitted to suspend judgement on this issue, then I do not see on what basis it can be claimed that the existence and nature of the moral law **proves** a freedom of the human will that is independent of the law of causality and is not to be immediately accepted on the basis of experience. I know that Kant wants to restrict the principles of the human understanding of causality merely to objects of experience alone. And on this basis, it obviously follows that they prove nothing in relation to that which is completely outside of our experience. But that restriction of the use of the concept and of the principles of causality, with its justification or lack thereof, does not belong here. For, here Kant wants to prove something on the basis of the nature of the moral law. It is therefore only a question of what can be proven on this basis and not whether we can prove something in relation to that concerning which we have no immediate experience, with principles that originate from experience and the nature of our understanding taken together. [195]

11) The fundamental law of pure practical reason is: act in such a way that the maxim of your will could simultaneously hold as a principle of universal legislation. [5:30.37–39]—This foundational law is not a prescription, by means of which an **action** should happen, rather it is a rule that merely determines the will *a priori* with respect to the

Review of the *Critique of Practical Reason* (1788)

form of its maxims. [5:31.17–21]—One can call the consciousness of this law a **fact of reason**, because one cannot infer it from antecedent data of reason and because it forces itself upon us as a synthetic proposition *a priori* that is not grounded in intuition, neither pure nor empirical. p. 54. [5:31.24–28]

*) In the first instance, one must be careful here not to confuse or confound two things with one another, namely the **hypothetical proposition: if** my maxims are to be laws (in line with the concept of a law, according to which it is a universal decree, a prescription of objective necessity), then they must be of universal validity; and the **categorical proposition**: the maxims that determine my rational will must be such laws. The first is an identical proposition, which in essence says no more than that a law must be a law, and which forces itself upon us just like everything that is contained in the principle of contradiction. The categorical proposition is indeed true when it is understood correctly. But its ground is all the more intermixed the more it [196] is really practical. Understood correctly, it does not in fact say that there could not be particular, individual laws of nature and prescriptions of reason. Rather, it only says that: reason takes its cue from **grounds in the nature of things**; thus, when it comes to identical grounds, it must always define the same thing as true, right, duty; the rational will is that which is determined by reason (not by imaginings, illusion, and passion); thus, it must comply with maxims that are capable of always holding in the same circumstances. Thus far, all of this is only hypothetical and analytic. But reason is nonetheless practical and, as Kant expresses it, **categorically commanding**. It **forces** and **urges** us to act according to those maxims that are grounded in the nature of things, and thus those that are to be regarded as valid or justified in every similar case. It cannot tolerate or calmly regard the **contradiction** of wanting to have a **reason** for our actions, presumptions, rights, etc., and of not always allowing these same actions, presumptions, rights, etc. to be valid where the same reason exists. Whence the rule of right: *Quod quis iuris in alterum statuerit, ipse sibi statuisse censendus est*;[7] and the common feeling of **approval** (*sensus aequi*[8]), a main part of moral feeling. I do not want to argue about whether it is better to call this a **fact of reason** or an **internal sensation**. But how much the reason that is

---

[7] *the law that one has decided for another is the one decided for oneself*   [8] *sense of fairness*

practical in itself **accomplishes** [197] in human nature by itself alone, this must be decided on the basis of experience. And whether or not everything it accomplishes, be it a lot or a little, should be included under the principle of **rational self-love**, this can be decided by those who conceive of this principle, not according to one-sided concepts and prejudices, but just as it is actually accepted and developed in the most well-known moral systems.—But as for our author, he continues:

12) As soon as the maxim is determined by the relation of the object to **inclinations** and **impulses**, it establishes no **obligation** and is rather opposed to the **moral disposition**, even if the **action** that results from this is **in accordance with the law**. p. 59. [5:33.28–33]

   *) Nobody who has any understanding of moral philosophy will object to the principle that an action can be in accordance with the law without being morally good, and that the latter depends on the disposition underlying it. But to oppose all inclinations and impulses to the moral principle is nothing other than to dispute over words by means of high-handed, arbitrary definitions. (see no. 5) Until now, all moralists have understood, and nobody has objected, when virtue has been spoken about as a prevailing inclination towards cognized duty, and about impulses of reason and of conscience, etc. And [198] now, all of a sudden, the will is supposed to be efficacious **without** inclination and impulse if it is to be morally good, and obligation and inclination should completely exclude one another!

13) A practical prescription that has a material and hence empirical **condition** must therefore never count as a practical law, even if the **object** is empirical. [5:34.2–3] Thus, with respect to the law of **promoting the happiness of others**, this object, the happiness of others, is not permitted to be the determining ground of the **pure will**, rather it is merely the lawful form alone that restricts the maxim grounded on inclination and produces obligation. pp. 59f. [see 5:34.32–35.5]

   *) That sensible kind-heartedness it not yet true love of human kind; that the former must be regulated and shaped by reason; and that, in general, reason produces obligation, not inclination, **whether without reason or in opposition to it**: these are familiar foundational principles of all moralists.

14) **There would be little to object** to a **false testimony**—given prudentially and reliably—if someone directed their principles solely towards their own happiness. p. 62. [see 5:35.19–29]

*) And Kant wants to make use of such arguments and turns of phrase in order to present all previous moral systems as faulty, [199] and to make his *Critique of Practical Reason* significant?

15) The objective reality of the moral law cannot be proven by means of a **deduction**, by means of all the efforts of theoretical, speculative, or empirically assisted reason, and is nevertheless firmly established of itself. pp. 81[–82] [5:47.15–20]
  *) As a fact of reason?

16) But something different and quite **paradoxical** takes the place of this vainly sought **deduction** of the moral principle, namely that, conversely, the moral principle itself serves as the principle of an inscrutable faculty which no experience can prove, but which speculative reason must at least accept as possible—in order to not contradict itself in cosmological ideas—namely that of **freedom**, not only the possibility but the reality of which the moral law proves. p. 82 [see 5:47.21–29]
  *) See no. 10.

17) The only objects of a practical reason are those of the **good** and the **evil**. The first is a necessary object of the faculty of desire, the second of the faculty of aversion, but both according to a principle of reason.—The concept of the good must [200] be derived from an antecedent law and not serve as the foundation of this. [5:58.6–11] The use of language distinguishes the **good** from the **agreeable**. pp. 101ff. [5:58.24–26] The cause of **all the errors** of philosophers in moral science is that they sought to derive the foundational law of **morality** from a preceding concept of the good, rather than the other way around etc. p. 112. [5:64.7–15]
  *) Everything that arouses satisfaction [Wohlgefallen], **insofar as** it does this, agrees with nature and, insofar as it does this, it **must** therefore seem good (*quidquid appetitur, appetitur sub specie boni*[9]) and **be called** good in the most general and broad sense of the word. The same goes for what **tastes** good, **smells** good, etc. If it **entirely** agrees with nature according to all its parts, qualities, effects, and other relations, and therefore arouses satisfaction or approval in all respects, when represented correctly, then it is a **pure** and **complete** good. But if it does not agree with nature *a potiori*[10] and thus arouses dissatisfaction [Mißfallen] when represented correctly, then it is a mere

---

[9] whatever is desired, is desired under the guise of the good   [10] for the most part

apparent good and a **true** evil. If it does not agree with nature in all respects but nonetheless *a potiori* and arouses satisfaction and approval *a potiori*, when represented correctly, then it is a true but **imperfect**, inadequate good. If something pleases immediately in itself, then it is called **agreeable**, and **disagreeable** when it displeases in itself. If it induces satisfaction or desire by [201] preventing or removing what is disagreeable, or by procuring or retaining what is agreeable, then it is **useful**. On the basis of these concepts, which are solidified in common speech, the following results:

1) That the concepts of the **good** and the **agreeable** are not distinct as *opposita*[11] that exclude one another, but rather as *coordinata*[12] and *subordinate*.[13] That is a) under the general and broad concept of the good, or the **desirable**, stand the concepts of the agreeable and the useful as species. b) Under precisely the same concepts stand, according to a different ground of division, the concepts of the true good and the apparent good, and under both of these the agreeable and the useful can appear again as *subdividentia*.[14] In a table:

The Good (Desirable)

With respect to the reason why it pleases or is desired		With respect to its quantity	
agreeable	useful	true good	apparent good
		In all respects or very predominantly agreeable	In all respects or very predominantly useful	apparent pleasure [Vergnügen]	apparent advantage

2) That, even though the concept of the good is in the table as *genus*, the **element** of all concepts of the good is nonetheless the agreeable or well-being. Just as **animal** would be at the top of a table and 'human,' 'horse,' etc.

---

[11] *opposites*   [12] *coordinates*   [13] *subordinates*   [14] *subdivisions*

under it, the concept of animal [202] is nonetheless abstracted from the particular representations of human, horse, etc.

3) That the **absolute** good or the good **in itself** (*per se bonum*) is the agreeable is clear from concepts. One only confuses the following questions here: a) Which are the first feelings of pleasure [Lust] and pain and the first **goods** of the human being in the **temporal order** of the development of human drives and activities? b) How many of these are **foundational feelings**, and which arise from the separation and connection of others, and how many things have an absolute value for human beings? c) What is the first or **highest good** of human beings in the **ranking** of reason?

4) And now it will be possible to see **the extent to which** the concept of the **good** has to be derived from an antecedent **law** and not serve as its foundation. a) A **law of nature** lies at the foundation of all goods; the ground of the agreeable and disagreeable lies in the nature and in the relations of things. b) Thus, a law of nature also lies at the foundation of **respect** and **approval**, to which the **true** and the rational determine us, when they are known; the law, namely, by means of which the contradictory cannot be represented and thus also cannot be approved or desired, but the consistent, possible, and real can. c) Laws of reason in particular therefore lie at the foundation of the representations of the highest good [203] and of true goods. d) But when it comes to all positive **prescriptions** of reason of a particular, objective content, whether they concern duties to ourselves or to others, concepts of the good lie at their foundation and must so lie. The relation to the well-being of the individual or the whole is the *ratio legis*,[15] on the basis of which the suitability or reprehensibility of all prescriptions and laws are and must be judged. Kant himself says further:

18) Our well-being and woe count for a very great deal in the appraisal of our practical reason and, as far as our nature as **sensible** beings is concerned, **all** that counts is our happiness if this is appraised, as

---

[15] *rational law*

reason especially requires, not in terms of transitory sensation but in terms of the influence this has on our whole existence and satisfaction [Zufriedenheit]. But it is not the **only** thing that counts. Namely, the first is true insofar as the human being is a being **with needs**. But the human being is not so completely an animal so as to be **indifferent** towards all that reason says on its own. pp. 107[–8] [5:61.18–32]

> *) What distinctions and expressions these are! And just in order to lend the principle of happiness some appearance of dubiousness! But what does this principle have to do with the claim that the human being is entirely an animal and is indifferent to everything that reason says [204] on its own? The consciousness of having reason and truth, in itself and at the foundation of all of one's strivings and actions, comprises the most essential, i.e., the most durable and invariable, if not the most primary and most prominent part of contentment and happiness. The human being will always be a being with needs, and insofar as the human being possesses a rational spirit, it is an **internal need** for the human being to have truth, conceivability, and consistency at the foundation of its strivings and actions.

19) The moral law, as determining ground of the will, must, **by thwarting all of our inclinations**, effect a feeling that can be called pain. p. 129. [5:73.3–5]

> *) It need only thwart **some**, not necessarily **all** of our inclinations, in order to effect such a feeling.—But in that the moral law demands nothing that is contrary to our true welfare, it thwarts the inclinations only in their contingent, variable form, and not the essential, foundational drive, the striving for well-being.

20) All of the inclinations taken together constitute **regard for oneself** [Selbstsucht], *solipsismus*, in which one can further distinguish **self-love** [Eigenliebe] and **self-conceit** [Eigendünkel]. **Rational self-love** can arise by means of the moral law. [p. 129.] [5:73.9–18] [205]

> *) Thus, there is absolutely nothing good in the foundational predispositions of the **inclinations** and **impulses**!

21) Respect for the moral law is a **feeling** that is not of an empirical origin but is rather produced by an intellectual ground.—It is the only feeling that we cognize completely *a priori* and whose necessity we have insight into. pp. 130. [5:73.32–37] 134. [5:75–76]

*) A feeling indeed. But a feeling is, insofar as it is felt, something empirical and belongs to experience. **Supposing** that we could know something of reason and rational will without inner sense [inneres Gefühl], we could admittedly cognize this feeling, this respect for the moral law, *a priori*, namely from the concepts of reason and rational will, in which it is contained. But what kind of *a priori* cognition is this such that we must soon say that we have our concepts of reason, will, and our entire soul solely on the basis of inner sensation?

22) Respect for the law is not the incentive to morality, rather it is morality itself. p. 134. [5:76.4–5]

    *) The latter *in abstracto*. But in a particular application, this respect is nonetheless the incentive to morally good conduct. Compare no. 24.

23) Respect is so little a feeling of pleasure [Lust] that one only reluctantly gives way to it **with regard to a human being**. p. 137. [5:77.19–20] [206]

    *) One can easily see where this is going. However: a) According to my experiences and observations I cannot find that the feeling of respect is always so constituted. Disagreeable feelings, of fear, of jealously, of one's own imperfection, can easily be attached to respect. But respect **in itself** is an agreeable, uplifting, strengthening feeling. b) Furthermore, we cannot infer the nature of respect in general or of respect for the moral law from that which we feel when we respect another person. Basically, this is just respect for our own reason, thus for the better part of ourselves. When our reason prescribes laws to us, we prescribe them to ourselves. c) Even if this respect for the law brings about disagreeable feelings in relation to the remaining disorderly dispositions of our nature, it can still determine the will by means of the drive for happiness, namely when the reproaches that reason makes of us and the discontent and self-contempt that are connected with the contempt of its commands become an even more extraordinary feeling than that which arises from the limitation of the inclinations that are contrary to the law.

24) Respect for the **moral** law is therefore the sole and undoubted **moral incentive**. p. 139. [5:78.20–21] [207]

    *) Granted. But the same is without a doubt also contained in the following words: "Virtue is first and foremost founded on a single internal property or determination of the will, namely the prevailing, active resolution to always assign the cognition of duty to the will's highest, most decisive motive."—Every other impulse towards right conduct that is not based on this universal drive and resolution is not true, **moral virtue**, but something like the virtue of temperament or political virtue. See my *Foundational Doctrines of Practical Philosophy*, p. 172.[16] I have never believed that these principles teach something unique and have an advantage over other terribly good moralists. Whether this virtue is **innate** in human beings by means of reason or must be gradually **brought about** through representations and practice, this is not currently the question.

25) Moral interest is a pure, sense-free interest of practical reason alone. [5:79.23–24]—Interest is in general an incentive of the will insofar as it is determined by reason. p. 141. [5:79.19–22]

   *) If one does not wish to include **inner sense** in sensibility, then I have nothing to object to this definition.

26) The principle of one's own happiness is in striking contrast to the command: love God above all else and your neighbour [208] as yourself. The former would be as follows: love yourself above all else, but God and your neighbour for the sake of yourself. [pp. 147–48] [5:83.33–36n]

   *) Once again, an argument not to be expected from such an insightful philosopher. Compare no. 14. For most readers it might be superfluous to respond to this. But I will do so for the sake of some. a) The love of oneself that the principle of one's own happiness bids us and the love that we are to show God are very different things under the same name. The human being can love itself above all else, i.e., place more importance on its own happiness than on the happiness of any other being, but still love God above all else, i.e., experience unlimited gratitude towards God as the author of its existence and find the purest and the highest pleasure [Vergnügen] in the representation of God as the representation of the highest perfection. It would be pure nonsense to subordinate the promotion of one's own happiness to the promotion of divine well-being. The author himself soon makes remarks that imply this. b) Other formulas must be used if

---

[16] Feder is referring to his *Grundlehren zur Kenntniß des menschlichen Willens und der natürlichen Gesetze des Rechtverhaltens*. Göttingen, 1782. See Book II, Part II, Ch 1, §40, pp. 171–72.

we are to illustrate the **genealogy of drives** in the order of nature as well as the procedure with human beings who are at the lowest levels of moral education, and other formulas if the ideal of moral perfection is to be made clear. [209] (see p. 149. [5:83–84]) The truly virtuous person serves their neighbour, is just, and is fair merely from duty, without further view to themselves. This is not true of the human being who is to first become virtuous. c) If the human being does not love itself and its own existence, not much would come of its love of God. The fanaticisms of a Guyon[17] are surely not healthy philosophy. d) That the human being strives for its own welfare and perfection more persistently and strongly than for the happiness of others is such a wise and necessary arrangement of nature that the moralist who says otherwise betrays a lack of insight. For, α) the first and most essential condition of the possibility of being happy is that one wants and searches for it oneself. Nobody can be made happy and more perfect by force. β) A person can promote the perfection and well-being of others to the extent of their own power, understanding, and cheerfulness of soul; put briefly, to the extent of their internal and external ability. γ) Thus, it is clear that loving one's neighbour as oneself might express something far different and more than loving others for one's own sake, but nonetheless fit into the system of a moralist who takes the principle of self-love as their starting point, as the **most powerful, foundational law** of nature.

27) The consoling and uplifting feeling of having acted in such a way that one cannot [210] despise oneself in one's own eyes, the consciousness of having preserved and honoured the humanity in one's own person in its dignity—this is not happiness, **not even the smallest part of it**. p. 157. [5:88.4–10]
  *) If this involves the author's concepts of happiness then I am not for it. For me and many others this is an essential part of happiness. The reason that he provides is: "For, no one would wish upon themselves the occasion for it, nor perhaps even a life in such circumstances." [5:88] No one? Not even the person who has already felt how immediately rewarding it is to have

---

[17] Jeanne, or Madame, Guyon (1648–1717) was a French mystic who was accused of advocating Quietism, a set of beliefs Pope Innocent XI condemned as heresy.

been true to cognized duty, to sacrifice sensibility for reason? The author might like to justify this claim. And as far as it concerns those who do not yet know the pleasure of self-mastery, of the triumph of reason over passion, who only obey the law of reason "because they cannot bear to be unworthy of life in their own eyes" [5:88], it is just as in accordance with the principle of happiness to act in such a way that one saves oneself from predominant, intolerable evil, to which self-contempt and pangs of conscience belong, as it is to partake in agreeable sensations.

28) The inner tranquility of the upright person in the consciousness [211] of having acted, and of acting, in accordance with their duty is the effect of a respect for something completely different than **life**.— Such a person lives only from duty, not because they have the least taste for living. p. 157. [5:88.13–20]

   *) This can occasionally be the case and the state of mind of the upright person, but it does not belong to the essence of an upright cast of mind [Denkart]. And when this obtains, **existence**, their being in general, is certainly not indifferent to or detested by the upright person, if we are talking about this earthly life. It lives on in the inside of the human being, even if it has died out from the outside.

29) The incentives of happiness may well be connected with this (purely moral) incentive (respect for the law).—A reflective Epicurean must declare themselves in favour of moral conduct.—It can even be advisable to connect the prospect of a cheerful enjoyment of life *) to that supreme motive [Bewegursache]. [p. 158; 5:88.27–33]—The distinction between the principles of duty and of happiness is not that of an opposition. **) **In a certain respect** ***) it can be duty to attend to one's happiness. [p. 166.] [5:93.11–16]

   *) Even better: **of complete existence** in time and eternity.
   **) I thought so too, and now we are no longer so different from each another.
   ***) What is this cautionary qualification supposed to mean? [212]

30) **Happiness in virtue**, the latter as **the supreme condition** of the former, is the highest or complete good of a person and also of the world. *) [p. 199] [5:110.29–35]—These two elements of the highest good, happiness and morality, limit each other quite considerably within the same subject and infringe upon each other.

Review of the *Critique of Practical Reason* (1788) 221

**) [p. 202] [5:112.27–32] They cannot be analytically deduced from each another but are connected synthetically according to the relation of causality. [p. 204] [5:113.20–22]

>*) This has always been a main principle of all moralists, and especially of those who take the principle of happiness as their starting point.
>
>**) Actually and on the whole or only apparently and in particular instances? Can one really lose happiness in virtue, and can happiness be promoted without virtue? Does the author mean this? Certainly not. Otherwise he would not be able to make virtue the supreme condition of happiness and assume there to be a causal relation between the two.

31) **Self-contentment** [Selbstzufriedenheit] is the correct name for a **satisfaction** with one's existence, which is not an **enjoyment** [Genuss] like happiness and is, at the most, only an **analogue of happiness**. In fact, it is a **negative satisfaction** with one's existence, in which one is conscious of needing nothing. pp. 211[–12] [5:117.25–31]

>*) I do not wish to any further anticipate readers' observations about the fuss the author makes over words and distinctions [213] in order to distance himself from the common system of morality. One can compare here no. 29.

32) **Holiness** or complete conformity of the will to the moral law is a perfection, of which no rational being of the sensible world is capable at any point in time of its existence. Since it is nonetheless still required by pure practical reason, it can only consist in a progress that goes on to infinity. [5:122.9–14]—Immortality of the soul is therefore a postulate of pure practical reason. [5:122.20–23]—The infinite being, to whom the temporal condition is nothing, sees in what is to us an endless series the holiness that his command inflexibly requires—wholly within a single intellectual intuition of the existence of rational beings. pp. 220ff. [5:123.7–13]

>*) This is all marvellous, especially the last part!

33) Pure practical reason commands virtue as the supreme condition of the highest good, the second element of which is well-being. This relation of well-being to worthiness or virtue cannot be claimed without presupposing an all-powerful and just being who rules nature. The existence of God is therefore a second postulate of pure practical reason. p. 224. [5:124.12–19]

*) Which would be all the more true if theoretical reason could not be denied all of the [214] reasons for believing in such a cause of the world.

34) God's final end in the world is the highest good, i.e., happiness under the condition of morality. p. 133.[18] [5:130.29–34]
  *) Assuming that there are animals without reason, as seems to be the case, the final end of the world might not be completely restricted to the well-being of moral beings.

35) If the cognition of God and eternity were granted to **theoretical reason**, which lacks such cognition, then the inclinations, which always have the **first word** *), would first demand their satisfaction [Befriedigung] under the name of happiness. [5:146.29–147.3] And because God and eternity with their frightful majesty would unceasingly stand before our eyes [5:146.8–10]—the majority of actions in conformity with the law would originate from fear, only a few from hope, and none from duty. [5:146.18–20]—Human conduct would therefore be transformed into a mere **mechanism**, where, as in a **puppet show**, everything would gesticulate quite well but no life would be encountered in the figures. **) pp. 264[–65] [5:146.22–26]
  *) What does this actually mean in the author's system? There it seems that reason has the first word, since it commands categorically. [215]
) Is there therefore absolutely no cognition of God among us, from any kind of source, or is the above judgement really supposed to be valid of all religious virtue? This is not asked *ad invidiam*,[19] but only in order to see whether everything can coexist and is consistent.—As much as I would like to admit that only so much cognition is made possible for us as serves us, I am nonetheless not in a position to understand the ground of the implications that the author piles on top of one another. The idea of God is indeed efficacious according to its nature, not merely by means of **fear and **hope**, but also by means of gratitude, respect and trust, and obedience to its laws. Reason, all the laws of nature, and all good impulses in human nature acquire more authority and weight when theoretical reason does not leave it doubtful whether they are the work of chance,

---

[18] The correct page is p. 235 of the 1788 edition.
[19] *in appeal to the prejudices of the person addressed*

of a blind necessity, or of the highest wisdom and goodness. Belief in God and another life moderates dependence on the goods of this earth and thereby removes a main obstacle of virtue, without thereby making them selfish and dependent on the fear of punishments or the desire of reward. And if the author does not want to deny all of this **in general**, how can he do so under the assumption that being convinced of the foundational truths of religion is brought about by theoretical philosophy? I do not at all see how the ideas of **mechanism** and a **puppet show** are involved here. [216]

36) One cannot deny that, in order to first bring either a yet uncultivated or even a dissolute mind onto the track of the morally good, **some preparatory guidance** is needed to entice it by means of its own advantage or frighten it by means of harm. But as soon as this has had only some effect, the pure moral motive must be thoroughly brought to bear on the soul. p. 271. [5:152.19–25]

If one now looks back upon all of the main principles of this *Critique of Practical Reason* that have been extracted and explained up to this point, or otherwise has its contents before one's eyes, then one easily sees that all of the ways in which the author distinguishes himself from other moralists, or seems to distinguish himself, come down to three points.

1) The **principle of morality**. But in this respect, all the difference has to do with the fact that Kant a) focuses on **pure reason** (no. 4. 5. 10.) and the other moralists on the **entire human being** with all of its inclinations. b) That he does not include self-contentment and self-respect in happiness and applies the names of **inclinations** and **impulses** exclusively to those determinations of the will that do not have their ground in reason and are able to oppose the moral principle (no. 20. 22. 23. 27. 31.). The others, by contrast, consider self-respect, self-contentment, and consensus among inclinations and drives to be one of the [217] most essential aspects of happiness, and they divide the inclinations into good and evil, rational and irrational ones, or, with respect to the drives, they distinguish **what is essential** and invariable, and which is also not evil, from the **contingent**. On the one hand, he nonetheless admits that morality is the **supreme condition** of happiness. And on the other hand, it is a common doctrine that the will is first moral and virtuous when the representation of duty as such is the

decisive and ruling motive. Similarly, Kant explicitly admits that respect for reason and some kind of feeling of approval exist in the human being by nature. He also explicitly admits that consideration must be given to advantage and well-being in order to make the inclinations completely moral, and that being happy is a necessary endeavour and an unavoidable determining ground of the faculty of desire. (no. 6. 18. 30. 36.)

2) **Freedom of the will**. For, a) there would be no dispute if Kant wanted nothing other than for freedom of the will, in the moral sense, to consist in its determinability by means of representations of reason. For, we all know and teach this, and we know that this attribute of humanity is improved by means of practicing wisdom and is weakened by following sensible drives. However, b) this freedom is supposed to α) be an exception to the law of causality and, as such, [218] β) follow from the essence of morality. (no. 9f.) But Kant has not yet proven this.

3) The **grounds for believing in God and another life**. Kant considers these, as we do as well, to be the essential conditions of supporting the system of morality or pure practical reason. Only a) he denies that **theoretical** philosophy contains sufficient grounds for this and rather finds these merely in the moral nature of the human being, or in practical reason; b) it seems that he does not want to extract **motives** to virtue from them, rather, he only regards them as presuppositions, without which practical reason would be inconsistent or inexplicable. (no. 35.)

As he says in the Preface [see 5:10.23–25], the author believes that he need not concern himself with objections to the **language** [used]. In fact, I encountered no new word other than *solipsism* for egoism. Admittedly, practical philosophy does not provide as good material for the arbitrary alteration of language and self-created words as the abstractions of logic and metaphysics. Readers will have nonetheless noticed some **unnecessarily extravagant** expressions in the extracts and might notice still others in the book.

F.

9

August Wilhelm Rehberg
Introduction

August Wilhelm Rehberg (1757–1836) was born in Göttingen and was the son of a civil servant.[1] Although Rehberg himself ended up spending most of his career in the civil service as well, his early interests were in philosophy and literature. Rehberg studied medicine, philosophy, and law at the University of Göttingen between 1774 and 1779, where he was not very impressed by the popular philosophy dominant there at the time, so he taught himself the philosophy of Leibniz and Spinoza and he came to admire Hume's skepticism as well. After finishing his studies, Rehberg's initial ambition was to become an academic. In 1779 he wrote a response to a prize essay question from the Berlin Academy on the topic of *Das Wesen und die Einschänkungen der Kräfte* (The Nature and Limitations of Forces). Although Rehberg came second, the Academy's secretary, Jean-Bernard Mérian, was so impressed with Rehberg's contribution that he put Rehberg's name forward to become Johann Georg Sulzer's successor as professor of philosophy at the *Ritterakademie* in Berlin. Unfortunately, Mérian's efforts failed, allegedly because Prussia's Frederick the Great insisted on his cooks coming from Hanover and his philosophers from Switzerland (both Sulzer and Mérian having been Swiss). Thus, after teaching German privately to Englishmen for a few years, Rehberg became secretary to the Duke of York in 1783 and then entered the civil service in Hanover in 1786, where he would stay for the remainder of his career in various capacities, making important contributions to Hanover's domestic affairs. Rehberg retired in 1826, and after moving to Dresden for a time and travelling in Italy, he returned to his hometown of Göttingen, where he died in 1836.

Rehberg's occupation as a statesman did not prevent him from making several important contributions to the philosophical debates of his time,

---

[1] Information about Rehberg's life and works is taken from Beiser (2020), Böning (2016), Henrich (1967, pp. 18–20), Gregory (2022, pp. 566–68), and Kraus (2003).

nor from being a productive and successful writer in general. Early in his career, for example, he wrote two dialogues: one on the topic of 'the vocation of man' (Rehberg 1780), and another on the nature of pleasure (Rehberg 1785). He also made important contributions to the pantheism controversy in the form of both reviews[2] and in a 1787 book entitled *Über das Verhältniß der Metaphysik zu der Religion* (On the Relation of Metaphysics to Religion), in which he took the unique position of endorsing neither theism nor pantheism but skepticism, while occasionally engaging with Kant's philosophy as well. Rehberg is best known, however, as an influential critic of the French Revolution: after publishing several essays on the topic in the early 1790s, Rehberg collected these in a two-volume book entitled *Untersuchungen über die französische Revolution* (Inquiries Concerning the French Revolution), published in 1793. These essays were widely read and gained him a national reputation, so much so that he has been called the 'German Edmund Burke,' as well as the founding father of German Conservatism.[3] Later in life, Rehberg wrote on historical topics such as a history of Hanover (Rehberg 1826) and devoted himself to editing his own collected works, which he left unfinished (see Rehberg 1828–31).

Most important for present purposes is that Rehberg was a critical admirer of Kant, and thus heavily engaged with both Kant himself and the discussion surrounding the critical philosophy. In addition to his 1788 review of the second *Critique*, to be discussed in more detail shortly, Kant and Rehberg corresponded directly in 1790 on the philosophy of mathematics. (see 11:205–10) Rehberg also wrote a response to Kant's 1793 'Theory and Practice' essay, entitled 'Über das Verhältnis der Theorie zur Praxis' (On the Relation of Theory to Practice), which was published the year after Kant's and in the same journal, the *Berlinische Monatsschrift*.[4] Rehberg also occasionally defended Kant's philosophy, such as in a review of Johann August Eberhard's *Philosophisches Magazin*,[5] which was a journal that offered an outlet for pro-Leibniz-Wolffian reactions to the critical philosophy. Indeed, Rehberg even advanced what he took to be Kant's true position in his frequent engagements with Karl Leonhard Reinhold, such as

---

[2] Rehberg reviewed works by both Herder (1788b) and Jacobi (1788c), and Jacobi responded to the latter review in Supplement III of the second edition of his *Letters* (see Jacobi 1789 and di Giovanni 2005, p. 125).
[3] On Rehberg's role in the history of conservatism, see Epstein (1966).
[4] See Gregory (2021) for an English translation of Rehberg's essay as well as Gregory (2022) for an introduction.
[5] See *Allgemeine Literatur-Zeitung*, 1789, 1. Band, Number 90, Sunday, March 22, 1789, pp. 713–16.

in a 1791 review of the first volume of Reinhold's *Beyträge zur Berichtigung bisheriger Missverständnisse der Philosophen* (Contributions to the Correction of Philosophers' Previous Misunderstandings), which Reinhold read and to which Reinhold later responded.[6]

Rehberg's review of the second *Critique* was published in August 1788, approximately seven months after the book's first appearance in late December 1787.[7] The review gained a wide readership:[8] Reinhold, for example, read the review and referred to it as "remarkable" in the preface to the second volume of his *Briefe über die Kantische Philosophie* (Letters on the Kantian Philosophy), adding that it had influenced his own understanding of freedom (see 1792, p. ix). This reference to the review in particular, four years after its initial publication, likely inspired readers to revisit it and could have influenced Fichte to read it as well (see Schulz 1975, pp. 208ff.). Kant himself certainly read Rehberg's review, because Christian Gottfried Schütz, one of the editors of the *Allgemeine Literatur-Zeitung*, the journal in which the review was published, sent Kant the review in advance to get his opinion of it and to ask whether he might like to submit a response (see 10:541.9–19). Kant never published an essay in response to the review, and if Kant ever responded to Schütz's letter, it no longer exists. Kant is thought to have responded to many of the points raised in the review in several of his later writings.[9]

After providing a concise summary of the main sections of the second *Critique* (pp. 345–50, original pagination), Rehberg asks whether it is even possible to conceive of pure reason as practical (p. 352). He then goes on to criticize Kant's definition of the faculty of desire and claims that his definition is better suited to the will, because we desire many things that we know we cannot bring about (p. 352). Kant responds to this charge in the third *Critique* (see 5:177.29–35n). Rehberg then makes one of the most important statements of the review: that the feeling of respect must be something sensible and, as such, must contain an element of pleasure, despite what Kant says (p. 354). Rehberg even goes on to say that Kant's claim that the incentive of morality cannot be a pleasurable sensation leads to a dangerous kind of fanaticism (*Schwärmerei*), namely "the deadening of

---

[6] For a discussion of Rehberg's relation to Reinhold, see Beiser (2020) and di Giovanni (2005, pp. 126–27 and 135–36).
[7] An additional source of information for many points in the present paragraph is Walsh (forthcoming), whom I thank for sharing his unpublished research with me.
[8] See Rehberg's own remarks to this effect in his *Sämmtliche Schriften*, 1. Band, 1828, p. 84.
[9] In addition to the references listed below, see also Kant (1996a, p. 460, note 42) and compare 6:57.26–58.15–40n with p. 358 of the original review.

the senses" (p. 355). It has been suspected that Kant responds to this charge in at least two of his later works.[10] Other notable claims include the following: that the idea of a deity is necessary to explain the connection between the intelligible and sensible worlds (pp. 356–57), that the idea of morality is only connected to a comparative rather than an absolute concept of freedom (p. 357), that Kant's system is only a better version of the perfectionism we find in Wolff's philosophy (p. 358), and that the postulates of immortality and God contradict that of freedom (p. 359). A main conclusion of the review is that there is no such thing as pure practical reason, but only the application of pure reason to an empirical faculty of desire (p. 357).

Translation Notes

In preparing this translation I have primarily used the original 1788 review, but I have also consulted the version edited by Rehberg himself in his collected works (1828–31), as well as the critical edition included as an appendix in Schulz (1975). When two German terms are given in square brackets, separated by a forward slash, they represent the original terms used in the 1788 and 1828 editions of the review, respectively. As has been my practice throughout this entire volume, '*Schwärmerei*' has been translated as 'fanaticism' in the following review[11] but I have noted where Rehberg uses other terms, such as '*Fanaticismus*'.

---

[10] See the footnotes in the *Religion* at 6:6–8n and 6:170.20–38, as well as the editorial notes by Wood and di Giovanni in Kant (1996a, p. 456, note 2 and pp. 468–69, note 167). Di Giovanni suggests that this charge is also working in the background of Kant's essay 'On the Miscarriage of all Philosophical Trials in Theodicy' (see Kant 1996a, pp. 22–23).

[11] See Clewis (2018, p. 184n) for an excellent discussion, and further sources, on why 'fanaticism' is the preferred translation for '*Schwärmerei*'.

Review of the *Critique of Practical Reason* (1788)

Allgemeine Literatur Zeitung. 1788, 3. Band, Numbers 188a and 188b, Wednesday, August 6, columns 345–60

[345]

Riga, Hartknoch: *Critique of Practical Reason*, by *Immanuel Kant*. 1788. 8. 292 pages.

In the *Groundwork of the Metaphysics of Morals*, the author analytically explicates the following from the common, confused concepts of morality: that it is absolutely necessary to arrive at one ultimate practical principle that can be known *a priori*, and thus make reason alone the source of the human being's moral capacity if such a being does not want to entirely renounce all morality and surrender itself to only those sensations that are part of its animal nature; that this practical law of reason concerning human moral conduct, when conceived purely, leads to the idea of metaphysical freedom, and thus discloses the human being to itself in a higher form entirely independent of the sensible world and its laws, as well as in a very particular dignity, as the member of a distinct, intelligible world.

The author now works out these ideas about the moral nature of human beings synthetically in the first part (the Doctrine of Elements). First, the Analytic contains an explication of the fundamental practical law of reason. The sensible world enables me to cognize objects; a law of reason cannot, therefore, contain any object, but must be merely formal. In application to a *given* object it becomes a maxim. All objects that can be so given relate to the sensible nature of human beings, and thus to the principle of self-love or of one's own happiness. The law of reason, on the other hand, cannot contain a determining ground of the will by means of an object, but only by means of its form, for it would cease being efficacious as a law of reason as soon as this efficacy is tied to a concept of sensible objects. A will determined merely by form is free, for metaphysical freedom consists in complete independence from all laws of the sensible [346] world. Indeed, a free will of this sort can be determined by nothing other than the law, by virtue of its form. The fundamental law of pure practical reason is therefore this: act in such a way that the maxim of your will could always hold as a principle of universal legislation. This law is in fact that which lies at the foundation of all the moral judgements of human beings, and it follows from this fact [Facto/Factum] that pure reason really is practical. (This is also the reason why this work is not entitled *Critique of Pure Practical Reason*, but *Critique of Practical Reason*, because this critique of the practical rational faculty proves that it is pure.) This one principle of all moral laws is therefore identical to the autonomy of the will, that is, the will's complete independence and freedom.

These principles of pure practical reason do not permit the kind of deduction of their correctness in application to real objects as that permitted by the principles of pure reason in its speculative use. For, in the latter case the question is: what are the objects, to which the ideas of pure reason are permitted to apply or even must apply? But in the present case the law, as soon as it is actual (which has already sufficiently been proven by means of its conceivability), produces its object itself and therefore serves as the principle of a deduction of an otherwise inscrutable freedom that was established as possible, but only as possible, by speculative reason. It is precisely because this practical reason produces its object itself that this object is just as real as practical reason itself, and this grounds its warrant to extend beyond itself in its practical use, which it cannot do in its speculative use without passing into a world of ideas whose objective reality can in no way be proven.

The object of a pure practical reason cannot therefore be determined before the moral law (empirical moralists tend to even base the moral law on the object), rather this object must be determined after the law and by [347] means of it. (2nd Chapter) This object is therefore moral (that is, in itself and without any subjective conditions) *good* and *evil*, words which are already determined to express these ideas by means of the common use of language, which distinguishes them from well- and ill-being or woe. Freedom, worked out by means of all the categories and with respect to the concepts of good and evil, therefore shows the path to a complete investigation of the entire moral capacity of human beings (which we await with the greatest longing in the promised Metaphysics of Morals).

It might be permitted here to insert a remark about the table of the categories of freedom. The thread, along which the categories of modality proceed, is not clear. According to the author they are: the permitted and the forbidden, duty and what is contrary to duty, perfect and imperfect duty. It seems to the reviewer, however, that they must be characterized in the following way: (1) the permitted (that which *can* coexist with duty) and the forbidden; (2) that which is in accordance with duty or is virtuous (that which is *actually* determined by duty) and its opposite; and finally the holy (that which stands in an absolutely *necessary* agreement with the moral law because it is nothing other than a pure expression of it) and the unholy. The division into perfect and imperfect duties, on the other hand, counts more as subjective and objective determinations according to their common meanings and therefore belong to the categories of quantity.

These laws of freedom (as the author continues under the title: Of the Typic of Pure Practical Judgment) cannot be represented in the sensible world by means of a schema (of the pure form of intuition) like the concepts of the pure understanding, for they are entirely distinct from the laws of nature; indeed, they are opposed to them. As laws, however, they can be portrayed as laws of nature (not as objects of nature) as if a type [Typo/Typus], and this type [Typus] is the rule of actions, according to which they ought to be capable of holding as a universal law of an intellectual nature, of which one is oneself a part. This rule is in fact the one according to which the common understanding judges the moral goodness of actions (in accordance with the everyday question: what if another were to do that?). It is therefore essential to this concept of moral goodness that it relate to reason as effect to cause, and consequently that the moral law immediately determine the will. Morality can therefore admit of absolutely no other incentive than itself. (3rd Chapter) Any given action that springs from other incentives is only in accordance with the law; legal, but not moral. On the one hand, [348] the moral law infringes upon these other sensible incentives as determining ground of the will, and on the other hand it itself thereby creates space for its own efficacy. In the former regard it is therefore an object of fear, in the latter an object of the greatest respect of human beings, and these feelings (moral feelings) generated by pure reason alone are the moral incentives of human beings; not the incentive to morality but morality itself as incentive. In the constant struggle with sensible inclinations (i.e., in finite beings) it is virtue, in infinite beings on the other hand, where the moral law is thought to be freely efficacious without any hindrances, it is holiness.

At the conclusion of the Analytic, under the title *Critical Elucidation of Pure Practical Reason*, there follows a justification of the procedure that has been adopted in the entire undertaking, and of the use of the idea of freedom as the main idea that underlies the whole, in order to avoid the misunderstanding and misuse of it that are so common in philosophy. Freedom in the metaphysical sense, absolute freedom—in contrast to comparative freedom, which indicates only dependence on internal causes but according to the same laws of natural necessity, to which mechanical dependence on external causes is subjected—this freedom is a transcendental capacity, not a psychological quality. But if one now considers time, by means of whose mediation the necessity of the entire world of natural appearances subjected to time is demonstrated, to be a quality of things in themselves, then it is completely impossible to unify that transcendent freedom, to which the moral law (and, the reviewer adds, the speculative need of reason) unavoidably leads, with the demonstrable necessity of all appearances in time; and thus the great value of the investigation of this concept, of time, that is undertaken in the *Critique of Pure Reason* is proven here. And in this way the solution to another problem is provided which threatens the concept of freedom from the side of the loftier concept of God as the creator of all things. For, if this creation concerns things in themselves but not their appearances in time, then it indicates no relation to the sensible world at all, and no determining ground of appearances can therefore be sought in the deity. The author himself nonetheless seems to feel that a difficulty still lies here that he is not yet in a position to solve, and which he prefers to honestly admit instead of just pleasing the majority of philosophers of this supposedly good topic, which is really only the interest of their self-love, [349] and concealing the deeper-lying difficulties in the hopes that others will overlook them. (In fact, this difficulty is very closely connected to the foundation of the author's entire system and to the way in which he deduces the objectivity of the intelligible world from a practical point of view, as the immediately following elaboration of the remarks that the reviewer intends to make will show.)

Second Book. Dialectic. The business of reason is to at all times seek the unconditioned for the conditioned objects that are given in sensibility. This is to be found nowhere else than in things in themselves. Our cognition, however, extends no further than to appearances. Hence the illusion that induces reason to take appearances for things in themselves, until the conflict of reason with itself that unavoidably emerges from this leads reason to that necessary investigation, the ground of which is developed in the *Critique of Pure Reason* under the name Dialectic. In its practical use, reason seeks an unconditioned of this kind as object under the name of the highest good. An unconditioned good is indeed virtue, but it is not yet a complete good. For, happiness also belongs to such a good as the object of the *entire* faculty of desire of a finite being, and the Analytic showed that the connection between these two concepts, between virtue and happiness, cannot be analytically cognized in a single concept as an identity, as Epicurus and the Stoics maintained, the former of whom wanted to reduce virtue to the consciousness of striving for happiness, and the latter happiness to the consciousness of virtue. On the contrary, this connection is synthetic. The desire for happiness must therefore be the motive [Bewegursache] to virtue or virtue the efficient cause of happiness. The former, however, annuls all virtue, and the latter is impossible because the appearances of the sensible world do not take their cue from moral dispositions but from physical circumstances.

This antinomy is resolved in the same way as the antinomy of freedom and natural necessity in the *Critique of Pure Reason*. Happiness as the necessary consequence of morality can very well be thought, namely in an intelligible world, and the rational being already experiences an analogue of it in its sensible appearance in the feeling of self-contentment [Selbstzufriedenheit]. A necessary requirement for the realization of the highest good is complete conformity of dispositions to the moral law, or holiness. This is not possible at any moment for a rational being of the sensible world and can only be found in a progression towards perfection extending into infinity. [350] The immortality of the soul is therefore a postulate of pure practical reason. The second thing that belongs to the completion of the highest good is happiness in exact proportion to holiness, or the concept of a whole, in which moral perfection stands in a perfect relation to the degree of happiness. (According to what has been said previously, this is only conceivable in the entire existence of things themselves, not merely in their appearance in time and space, thus in a best world, but one entirely distinct from that which teaches us to fantasize that the present sensible world contains the greatest quantity of happiness that its form allows; for, the hindrance lies in the matter that God shapes, does it not?) This happiness in exact proportion to the degree of morality can only be conceived by means of a concept of a holy intelligent being as the ultimate cause of the world. The existence of God is therefore the second postulate of pure practical reason. (In the final section the author adds that the impossibility of conceiving of the agreement of the world with the moral law without God is only subjective, thus in a being who comes to have consciousness of its morality, disbelief is not possible, but doubt, *epoché*, is.)

It is in fact with reluctance that the reviewer presents the content of this section (of one of the most magnificent treatises he has ever read) in so few, meagre lines, but he sees so much more still to say in front of him that we must hurry ahead.

Thus, although practical reason is held up by its postulates—immortality, an intelligible world of free powers, and the theological ideal—the objective reality of which speculative reason was only capable of proving by means of deception, nonetheless no cognition of these objects is thereby established, for the only thing that the need of the moral law proves is this: that those thoughts have objects. Practical reason does not further require insight into the nature of these objects, and it does not open a source of insight either. All theoretical cognition of the nature of God and the soul thus remains merely playing with empty words or obviously false representations.

The second part, *Doctrine of Method*, contains a short, very illuminating, and exceptionally clear explanation of the way in which one must provide the law of reason with access to the human mind. To be precise, respect for the law is established by displaying the practical law in its purity, and virtue is thereby generated and strengthened. A great contrast to the popular methods of recent educational science, which places so much importance on the arousal of passionate feelings and thereby moulds only weak and haughty creatures. [351]

Similar to the other works that the public has received from the author several years ago, this one too affords the inquisitive mind, which is not satisfied with singular lucid views and disconnected opinions of individual pages of its subject matter, and which longs to understand the final ground of all its judgements and their complete coherence, with the following: complete satisfaction, which can only be achieved by means of a scientific discourse built on the ultimate foundational ideas of metaphysics and which illustrates the entire extent of its application. Similar to his other works, and by means of the sublime beauty of this discourse which is pursuant of its own end, and only its own end, and which is free of all coveted, foreign ornamentation, this one affords the great sensation of wonder towards the spirit that presents itself in every line as master of its subject matter, and which clearly portrays the thoroughly considered occurrent thought without effort and always in its entire extent. By means of the power of expression that says no more than what the author wants to say, but which also says this in entirety, it also affords the pleasure of distinct cognition united with the lively sensation of the complete dignity of its subject matter. But this work has the following very great merit over and above the author's earlier works when it comes to the great majority of readers: that this explication is much easier to understand because the much simpler subject matter, compared to that treated in the *Critique of Pure Reason*, does not require the great effort of holding on to so many and so various complicated ideas simultaneously, and because this subject matter does not require as many unusual expressions as the other. It is therefore to be hoped that this investigation of the ultimate foundation of morality, unique in its kind, will contribute much to the correction of prevailing scientific ideas, which are in fact in need of such a correction. Nevertheless, in the opinion of the reviewer something indemonstrable has creeped into the system elaborated here and it runs throughout the entire treatise, in consequence of which only a small change of expression is required to make the treatise perfectly convincing, but for this reason its discussion is of the utmost importance.

The fundamental laws of morality must be categorical if there is a moral science at all, and these should not be reduced to a doctrine of prudence. Necessity can only be found in rational cognition, thus pure reason alone is the source of cognition of a pure doctrine of morals. None of this is subjected to doubt, and the defenders of an empirical moral science as the only one possible can view themselves however they want, they will never escape the justified objections that are so forcefully made to them in this *Critique of Practical Reason* in many places with the most concise arguments. [352]

The question now, however, is whether pure reason of itself and alone can find a synthetic principle of its efficacy, and what kind of relation this principle, as the moral law, has to the sensible human being.

First, is it even permissible to conceive of a pure practical reason? Although the reality of the categories can only be proven of objects of the senses by means of intuitions of the pure form of sensibility, noumena can also be thought under the categories even if not cognized. It is therefore permissible to think of pure reason (a noumenon) as a cause or power, and to call that which corresponds to the effect *good*. The relation between pure reason as cause and this *good* as effect is a pure will. We can therefore also conceive of synthetic principles of the connection between pure reason as cause through freedom and an (entirely unknown) object, and none of this can be rejected in so far as it belongs to the realm of ideas (but not the realm of chimeras, which are unauthorized sensible envelopments of such ideas). We can only ask how its connection to the sensible world and its reality in it can be proven. This can happen directly in no way other than by means of the consciousness of oneself as pure reason, as free will, and as the possessor of absolute value. As the author himself says at the beginning: pure reason, if it really is practical, proves its reality by means of what it does [durch die That]. [5:3.10–12] But the first thing, consciousness of oneself as pure reason, exists nowhere. The second thing, consciousness of free will, depends on the first. The author seeks to facilitate the representation of this (in the 2nd section of the 1st chapter [5:21–22]) by means of the remark that the understanding, aside from its relation to objects, also has a relation to the faculty of desire. But the definition he offers of this faculty of desire (p. 16 of the Preface [5:9.20–22]) is a definition of the will. The definition is: the faculty to be, by means of representations, the cause of the reality of the objects of these representations. We desire many things, concerning which we ourselves know that we cannot be the cause of their reality. According to the common use of language, that definition is thus well suited not to the faculty of desire, but to the will, which indicates the relation of the understanding to the faculty of desire, and which thus cannot be a correlate of the understanding in such a relation. (In order to avoid all ambiguity and the admixture of sensible determinations, and so that the provided definition very clearly includes a transcendent thelematology, the reviewer would conceive of it as follows: the power to make possibility into actuality. In this way it would actually contain only categories.) [353]

Finally, and third, if one asks for the definition of the idea of the absolute good (which is vainly sought in the 2nd chapter of the Analytic), absolutely nothing else can be offered than that which is in conformity with reason. Should this good be thought of as a transcendent object, then nothing but fanaticism results, since our transcendent cognition concerns only that which is formal, and that which is formal about any given transcendent object can be nothing other than the law of reason. Thus, it is confirmed here that, as in its speculative use, reason only revolves in a circle around itself[1] and can in no way think outside of itself and discover synthetic principles for itself. But if it can in fact be conceived for the purpose of a pure legislation of the doctrine of morals, then one can ask whether or not pure reason, even if no immediate consciousness of it takes place in sensibility, is nonetheless capable of being connected to the latter. The necessity of such a transition from reason to sensibility for the purpose of morality is allegedly proven (p. 53 [5:29–30]), in that without morality the problem of freedom would not at all be raised. But this is false. The metaphysics of nature also contains the occasion for the idea of a power determined entirely through itself, and it is only the subjective interest of happiness that makes the question so much more important

---

[1] See A366.

for us with respect to morality. And by what means is that transition supposed to take place? If the action of a sensible being is regarded as the effect of reason, then this process is entirely similar to that which is so fittingly presented with all its shortcomings in the *Critique of Pure Reason* under the title: On the Amphiboly of the Concepts of Reflection. That transition must [354] therefore take place via something similar in kind to sensibility, by means of which pure reason is subjected to the determination of time without becoming sensible. This is moral feeling; respect for the law. But is this respect not a sensation? Kant twists and turns himself in the most diverse way in the 3rd chapter of the Analytic in order to show that it is not a sensible feeling. But here he is most unsatisfying. All that can be inferred from his arguments is this: the pleasurable sensation that is connected to the cognition of the rational law deserves to be separated from these sources of happiness, precisely because it is connected to the absolute interior of cognition, in contrast to all its objective contents. (Just as, for example, Plattner has explained and proven in a very excellent treatise on the partiality of the Stoic and Epicurean systems with respect to the explanation of the origin of pleasure, in the first part of the 19th volume of the *Neue Bibliothek der schönen Wissenschaften*.[2]) It is therefore entirely fitting that Kant reserves the expression of respect solely for the feeling connected to the cognition of the law of reason, but this respect nonetheless still remains a feeling of pleasure, as is illustrated very clearly by the most disinterested observation of great human characters. For, the uneasiness that is connected to this in line with the author's remark (p. 137 [5:77.19–23]), results solely from the feeling of one's own weakness, which is often aroused by this and other subjective auxiliary circumstances. He accuses those of fanaticism who turn this feeling of pleasure in the law into the moral incentive, since this must consist in the law itself. He finds this moral fanaticism very pernicious and sets it apart from religious fanaticism (p. 150 [5:84.23–24]), just as he earlier (p. 125 [5:70–71]) sets it apart from mysticism, because these are compatible with the purity of the moral law. The latter is indeed grounded in abstraction [in der abstracten Idee] and is true in speculation. But surely there must be a Fenelon[3] somewhere (if it is even permitted to offer real human beings as examples, whose [355] infinitely complicated moral incentives are not capable of an entirely pure determination),

---

[2] Rehberg is referring to Ernst Plattner's essay: 'Versuch über die Einseitigkeit des stoischen und epikurischen Systems in der Erklärung vom Ursprunge des Vergnügens' in *Neue Bibliothek der schönen Wissenschaften*. 19. Band, 1. Stück, 1776, pp. 5–30.
[3] For an introduction to Fenelon and his conception of love, see Hanley (2020, introduction and Ch. 7).

who transfers his love of the beauty of the moral law to an object, to the ideal of reason, and in this way becomes, as a religious fanatic, the most sublime human being. But this is not at all the path that human passion tends to take. On the contrary, this object of religious fanaticism pulls the majority of those who are devoted to it away from the real world and makes them completely forget that true morality consists solely in the application of its laws to the sensible world. Mysticism therefore tends to be only the innocent last resort of the unfortunate people who have become incapable of all efficacy in the world on account of hardship and atrocity; or it tends to be the disgraceful disguise of immoral characters who permit everything in the sensible world, which can never correspond to the ideal, and on this account transfer morality into an intelligible world, and on the basis of whose feelings they ground only the most despicable of all kinds of pride, namely super-sensible, theological pride. For all these reasons so many great people of the earth love fanaticism, thus all the efforts of priestly souls, no matter the denomination they may be, to either heal or console the minds of such people by means of fanaticism, are either futile or loathsome.

The idea that the law itself but not pleasure in the law has to be the incentive of morality is itself fanaticism. For, what else can it be but fanaticism (which amounts to the fabrication of super-sensible objects), if respect for the law is said to be a feeling but not a sensible sensation? And this fanaticism leads directly to a distinct and the most dangerous fanaticism [Fanaticismus], to the deadening of the senses. If the only thing that is morally good is that which happens directly for the sake of law, and respect for the law infringes upon *all* sensible incentives, then pleasure in the law would be restricted by respect and we possess the unfortunate scrupulosity that is destructive of all morality belonging to those who punish themselves because they find pleasure in God's love, and thus do not love him unselfishly and for his own sake, but for the sake of the happiness that is thereby brought about.

The relation of the ideas of pure morality and freedom to human nature is therefore the following: they stand, as the author says quite well (p. 75 [5:43.35–36]), to the determinations of our will as a pattern to be imitated, as it were. Thus, as idea, but not as cause, the transcendent use of pure practical reason is [356] immanent, and this is completely sufficient even for morality. For, imputation, which on the author's view would completely disappear along with transcendental freedom, does not really concern (in line with the rational psychology in the *Critique of Pure Reason*) the entirely empty transcendental I, but empirical consciousness.

I am the one who, in my appearance in the sensible world, accuses and despises myself for my injustices. And what would this imputation look like if it were to concern the transcendental I, the noumenon, whose essence is pure reason, and which necessarily presupposes absolute freedom? This is the place to discuss the difficulty that the author himself brings up, as mentioned above, and which he in a certain respect splendidly solves. Just as reason can be thought of as a *causa noumenon*, so is it permissible to think of it under the category of effect, and to inquire about the ground of its existence. Thus, with this question one encounters (though not necessarily immediately) the idea of God as the creator of all existing things. But if the deity is conceived as the cause of the soul, as a thing in itself, then the pure effect of this thing is an effect of the deity. To this Kant says: creation only concerns the noumenon, thus not its effect in the sensible world. The reviewer would go even further and require the proof of the reality of that concept of metaphysical creation, which, as an idea, *can* always be thought, but whose application to noumena is not clear. But does Kant's response really solve the difficulty? If we make use of the concept of the deity only so that the representation of finite noumena and their conceivable relations is complete, then of course. But the true metaphysical occasion for the idea of a deity, and the metaphysical need of reason to assume an original being, does not at all lie here, but in the connection of reason to sensibility that is given through experience but is incomprehensible to reason. This is the ultimate, insoluble problem of all philosophy, of transcendental psychology as well as cosmology. Concepts of the understanding and ideas of reason can be thought, and sense perception can be intuited, but how it happens that sense perception becomes subsumed by concepts of the understanding, how intelligent beings intuit sensible objects, and thus how the world of ideas can be connected to the real world and is actually so connected, this is a problem whose insolubility gives rise to the idea of an ultimate, infinite, original being, in which the connection between the intelligible world to the world of appearances is grounded. The [357] idea of the deity is therefore indispensable for conceiving of the possibility of how noumena sensibly appear, and if creation in time is an absurd notion, then the existence of appearances in time requires an idea in order to make it comprehensible how this appearance can be thought. But a part of this significant problem, which requires the idea of the deity to be solved, is the question of how the efficacy of an intelligent being (which can be conceived as a cause but cannot be known as one) becomes a sensible action. It is therefore entirely impossible to completely separate this appearance in the sensible world from the relation between the power itself and the deity. As unphilosophical as not only the atheistic but also the deistic fatalism of nature is, we cannot rid ourselves of a distinct intelligible fatalism of nature without simultaneously dispensing with the idea of the highest original being. But morality is not at all harmed by this system of intelligible necessity, for the latter depends entirely on reason. And the latter remains reason whether it exists independently or depends on another being for its existence, and as such the idea of morality is inseparably connected to a comparative concept of freedom (which indicates independence from inner determining grounds), but not to the absolute concept of freedom, which can never be proven even by reason as noumenon, as has just been shown.

From all this the reviewer believes himself justified in drawing the following conclusion: that there is no distinct pure practical reason; rather that this only consists in the application of pure reason to the empirically given faculty of desire: that, consequently, (to avail myself of Kantian expressions) the transcendent principles of this *Critique* must be modified into transcendental ones; that, as transcendent principles, they are suitable only as regulative ideas, but as transcendental principles, on the other hand, they become constitutive principles of moral science; and that the problem, indicated later on (p. 162 [5:91.3–4]), of the unity of the pure rational faculty, of the theoretical as well as the practical, is hereby already solved.

Accordingly, the principle of contradiction is the supreme *principium cognoscendi* of pure morality. But its prescriptions are in fact originally only prohibitive, and all of reason's original efficacy consists in cancelling actions, just as the contradiction experienced in a thought eliminates the illusion, by means of which it was taken to be true. Now, the foundational law of morality given in the *Critique of Practical Reason* is in fact: act in such a way that the maxim of your will could always simultaneously become valid as a principle of a universal legislation, that is, conceived as a maxim that includes rules for other beings similar to us, it is synthetic; but only conceived as such. On the other hand, as the supreme law of pure practical reason it has only a false appearance of a synthetic principle. That is, it appears as if, by means of the word *universal* law that the law is to include more in it than the action itself, to which it is adapted in each case. But this universality only indicates (as the reviewer has stated in another place[4] in

---

[4] Rehberg is likely referring to his *On the Relation of Metaphysics to Religion* (1787). See especially pp. 130–32.

more detail) a negative determination, a withdrawal from all possible subjective auxiliary determinations.

In the same way, if *freedom* is only supposed to denote independence from all conditions of the sensible world, then the solutions to both problems, of finding the nature of a will determined by the moral law, on the one hand, and of finding the nature of the determining ground [358] of a free will, on the other hand, are identical propositions (as the author himself says in the remarks to the 2nd problem, namely that the self-consciousness of a pure practical reason is identical to the positive concept of freedom).[5] For, the mere legislating form of subjective maxims is the law of reason, and there can be no other definition of reason than the human being's non-sensible faculty of cognition. The will, whose sufficient determining ground is reason, is therefore independent of the conditions of the sensible world. But if freedom indicates the power of being determined entirely through oneself, concerning which there is no regress of the question of even higher determining grounds, then, as we have seen, this idea can be conferred upon no other noumenon than the deity.

The relation of this theory of morality to other, common theories therefore appears to be something distinct. In a very nice remark (p. 69 [5:40]), a table is drawn up of all possible material determining grounds of moral science. Among these, two are objective: perfection according to Wolff and the Stoics, and the will of God according to the theological moralists. The latter is to be counted among the internal subjective determining grounds if, according to the usual way of thinking, it is only supposed to imply compliance with our master who governs us by means of the fear and hope of future punishment and reward. If it is supposed to imply sublime theological moral science, on the other hand, where God, as the most perfect being, comprises our norm of perfection, then it teaches precisely that which the law of perfection contains by means of a detour.

This principle of perfection, however, is in essence a formal principle and not a material one, because perfection can be defined by means of nothing other than agreement, and thus by means of the law of reason; and because all relative perfection in relation to a given end already presupposes an absolute perfection, and without it becomes meaningless when we are talking about one's own perfection and thus of the subject that has no other end than itself. The system put forward in the *Critique of Practical Reason* is thus in essence only a better and thoroughly more satisfying version of the system that takes perfection as its basis (at least for those who

---

[5] See 5:29.6–8.

find the remarks presented thus far to be well-founded and modify the system accordingly).

The author will not believe that, by means of this remark, the reviewer wishes to subtract only the most negligible amount from the value of the work. But for the sake of the reader, an excellent remark in the preface (p. 14 [5:8.28–37n]), in which a reviewer is answered, must be employed here: "A new and correct formula is nonetheless something extremely important. Entirely new and unprecedented principles presuppose an entirely new previously unknown world. All of our scientific efforts are nothing other than the seeking out of formulas."[6]

The reviewer would like to vindicate the Stoics, however, who are sometimes cast in a somewhat disadvantageous light in comparison to more recent moral science (in comparison to platonic moral science, in fact, insofar as it is cleansed of the fanatic positions appended to it and all the beliefs derived from it) by means of the remark that the perfect, merely formal purity of the law is indisputably satisfying all on its own as the foundation of moral science, albeit in the speculative system. But the Stoics (whose ideal of the sage was also a model unachievable in this world) invested everything in the actual human being, as far as we know (for we have never possessed their famous theoreticians), and thus closely connected their presentation of the moral law to the sensations that are the most [359] conducive to it, and which have been weakened by the modern civil and intellectual arrangement of the world.

There is not much more to say about the subjects of the Dialectic. The two postulates it deals with, by virtue of which immortality and the deity must be conceived as objects, contradict the postulate of freedom, from which they are derived. For, freedom could only be justified by means of the fact that creation is said to concern only the intelligible but not the sensible existence of things. But since sense perceptions must be included in the happiness of intelligent beings (if the author does not want succumb to the argumentation, for which he criticizes the Stoics), then happiness is nonetheless also a part of the highest good, even if a very negligible one, and thus also a part of the world whose ultimate cause is God; one can call this relation (which is in fact only improperly called a cause) creation, or however else one wants. The principles of the dialectic of pure speculative reason are thus proved here as well. And since reason, by virtue of its

---

[6] In the footnote Rehberg paraphrases here, Kant is answering G. A. Tittel's claim that, in the *Groundwork*, Kant does not offer a new principle of morality, but only a new formula of a principle we have long been familiar with. See Chapter 4 and Walschots (2020) for a discussion.

nature, works towards a highest unity among its principles, all of its futile efforts to think of its ideas as actualized turn out to be a Spinozism, which, as Kant (p. 182 [5:102.1–2]) very rightly says, is not the only way in which the actual world can be thought, if space and time are supposed to be valid as determinations belonging to it, but which also, cleansed of these false representations of space and time, is the only way in which theological ideas can be thought at all if objective reality is to be imputed to them; the same sort of objective reality that they absolutely cannot have *for our present* understanding.

However, if, according to the reviewer's analysis, pure reason is not practical, then the highest good can also be thought through the category of community, and because in this case all incentives of the will must completely harmonize with objective laws, the idea of a best world can certainly thereby be imagined, with which the real world makes the most terrible contrast. Furthermore, and this is extremely important, since morality is just as much based on reason according to the theory constructed by the reviewer, which no human being who is conscious of it can renounce, the difference between taking the necessary ideas of reason to be objectively grounded and taking its principles to be constitutive, on the one hand, and ascribing an ideal reality only to the former and taking the latter to be regulative, on the other hand, is in essence not very meaningful. But those ideas may not at all be used as the incentive to an increased cultivation of reason, which the human being finds itself motivated to seek out regardless, because heteronomy of the will would unavoidably arise, and all true dignity of moral science would thereby be lost. The latter is indisputably the greatest corruption that human nature is exposed to, as the incomparable author who occasioned all these observations has so fittingly stated. The effect of this naive, materialistic atheism is corruptive in the sensible world that is governed solely by passions; passions which lead the human being to the empty delusion that the passions themselves are happiness, and that virtue, as well as reason, from which virtue arises, is an empty name. As corruptive as this is, the influence of speculative atheism in the realm of the cultivation of reason is just as restorative, in that it drives back [360] the presumptions of a dogmatic-metaphysical religion by means of constant oppposition. These presumptions make their mark at all times and without fail, and they corrupt morality as well as everything else that rests on a fundamental insight useful for science, so long as these presumptions are not kept within their boundaries by that constant opposition, and those boundaries are misjudged to be on its side.

The misuse of theological ideas is not merely dangerous to the human being considered as a rational, speculating being, however, but also to the sensible, weak, unintelligent, passionate human being, and particularly where the human being is especially dangerous to itself by means of all these qualities, namely in the large group of people that is bound together by the civil constitution in nations. The spectacle of a group of people who are stripped of all morality and surrender themselves to the sensible passions only, and who wipe each other out by means of the desire for this kind of pleasure, would be terrible. And yet, because even this could not eliminate every positive expression of every power, and in particular could not destroy all reason, it would still be a divine spectacle compared to viewing this same group of people if, in addition to all the physical evils that plague it, it were to be transformed into a group of fanatics [Fanatikern] by means of the horrors of a power of judgement confused by reason overstepping itself. These fanatics, who are said to be ruled by reason, strive to destroy each other and themselves by means of reason in order to bring about the bliss [Seligkeit] of their intelligible personality within the hell of their sensibility.

Religion, as the fruit of the moral disposition, is the most sublime product of the human spirit; couching its principles in the laws of appearances is the most beautiful poetry of the understanding; and couching them in the form of real beings is the most beautiful flower of the imagination. In his work, Kant has superbly shown that without religious ideas the moral system cannot be completed. But because the group of people that appears holy or is fearful will only endeavour to confirm old prejudices on the basis of this avowal, it must also be added that the system of morality erected in this *Critique of Practical Reason* is simply the only way to unite religion with the principles of a real and pure moral science, if religion is to be included in the *principio cognoscendi*. This point is added in order to warn other philosophers who might like to utilize all of this in order to reinstate the general approach of constitutive principles of moral science which have their origin in a source other than reason, or in order to appease themselves in this way.

In conclusion, the reviewer adds [a final remark], but not for the sake of the great spirit who, in the Preface to the second edition of the *Critique of Pure Reason*, has embraced the interest of science by means of the statement that it does not *mind* being refuted, something which is only a danger to the self-loving writer,[7] and not for the sake of the researcher who

---

[7] See Bxlii–xliii.

seeks truth or the teacher who promotes cognition, but on account of other readers. The remark is that the reviewer believed himself able to illustrate his unlimited admiration of this author's efforts by means of nothing else suitable than a well-considered examination, by means of which the interest of the science that we both love must always prevail, even if it could not turn out to be entirely favourable.

10

Christian Garve
Introduction

In February of 1792, Kant sent an essay entitled *Vom radicalen Bösen in der menschlichen Natur* ('On the Radical Evil in Human Nature') to J. E. Biester, the editor of the *Berlinische Monatsschrift*, which was an important organ of the Enlightenment in Germany and where Kant had previously published many of his shorter essays.[1] Kant initially intended the essay to be the first of a four-part series to be published in the journal, all of them dealing with the relationship between religion and reason (see 11:430). Unfortunately, Kant's plans were forced to change: although the first essay was approved by the censors in Berlin who were responsible for overseeing the publication of texts engaging with theological matters, among others, the second essay was not. Upon hearing the news, Kant wrote to Biester and requested that the manuscript of the first essay be returned, because Kant believed that "the previous essay must create an unfavorable impression in your journal without the succeeding pieces" (11:349.26–28). Kant eventually published the four essays as a book under the title *Religion within the Boundaries of Mere Reason*.[2] In exchange for withdrawing the first essay, Kant offered to send Biester a different one "very soon," this time "something entirely on moral philosophy, namely on Herr Garve's recently expressed opinion about my moral principle, in his *Essays*, Part I" (11:350.16–19). Kant is referring to Christian Garve's *Versuche über verschiedene Gegenstände aus der Moral, der Litteratur und dem gesellschaftlichen Leben* (Essays on Various Topics from Moral Science, Literature, and Societal Life), the first part of which was published in the first half of 1792. Garve engages with Kant's moral philosophy in an extended footnote printed at the end the book's first essay, entitled *Über die Geduld* ('On

---

[1] Kant's original letter to Biester, which would have accompanied the essay, is lost, but we learn about it from a letter of Kant's to C. F. Stäudlin a year later, on May 4, 1793 (see 11:429–30).
[2] For an excellent account of the origins of the *Religion*, as well as more information on Kant's complicated relationship to the censors at the time, see George di Giovanni's introduction to the *Religion* in Kant (1996a).

Patience'). Kant's response to Garve was eventually published as the first part of his essay 'On the common saying: That may be correct in theory, but it is of no use in practice,' which was published in the *Berlinische Monatsschrift* in September 1793.[3] What follows is the first English translation of Garve's footnote that occasioned the essay.

Christian Garve (1742–1798) was born and died in Breslau, and the course of his life was influenced by two main factors: a close connection to his mother and poor health.[4] In his early life he was educated at home before moving to Frankfurt an der Oder in 1762 to study theology with Alexander Gottlieb Baumgarten. Baumgarten died shortly after Garve's arrival, so in 1763 he left for Halle to study with Baumgarten's disciple Georg Friedrich Meier, among others. In 1766, Garve completed his *Magister* degree with a dissertation on the logic of probability (see Garve 1766), and in the same year he moved to Leipzig, where he lived in the house of Christian Fürchtegott Gellert,[5] who exerted an important influence on Garve by introducing him to British philosophy. In 1767 Garve returned to Breslau to be with his mother, before moving back to Leipzig in 1768 and receiving his habilitation for a thesis on writing the history of philosophy (see Garve 1768). He began to lecture in Leipzig and was appointed junior professor (*außerordentlicher Professor*) there in 1770, but he was forced to give up his position because of persisting health issues and once again returned to Breslau in 1772. Garve then remained in Breslau for the rest of his life, working as a private scholar and translator. Garve's mother died in 1792, and after suffering from a type of facial cancer in the later years of his life, he died in 1798.

Garve was a well-respected writer and translator in late eighteenth-century Germany. His 1772 translation of Adam Ferguson's *Institutes of Moral Philosophy* (1769), for instance, to which he attached a commentary, was praised by figures like C. M. Wieland and Friedrich Schiller.[6] He translated many other works, including Henry Home's *Elements of Criticism* (1772), Edmund Burke's *Philosophical Inquiry into the Origin of our Ideas of the Sublime and the Beautiful* (1773), and Adam Smith's *Wealth of Nations.* (1794–96). Particularly influential was his translation and extensive commentary on Cicero's *De officiis* (On Duties), which he was

---

[3] For a similarly excellent introduction to the origins of the 'Theory and Practice' essay, see Heiner Klemme's introduction in Kant (1992). See also the introduction to the essay in Kant (1996b).
[4] Information about Garve's life and works is taken from Wölfel (1964), Wunderlich (2016), Oz-Salzberger (1995), and Roth and Stiening (2021).
[5] On Gellert's philosophy and its potential importance for Kant, see Kuehn (2009).
[6] See Oz-Salzberger (1995, p. 190).

commissioned to complete by King Friedrich II. The King was so pleased with the translation that he awarded Garve a generous pension.[7] It is also no exaggeration to say that Garve played an important part in the development of Kant's philosophy. In addition to his role in the genesis of the 'Theory and Practice' essay described above, it was Garve who wrote the infamous *Göttingen* review of the first *Critique*, heavily edited by J. G. H. Feder and to which Kant replies in the Appendix to the *Prolegomena*, as has already been mentioned in previous introductions. There is also reason to suspect that Kant originally intended the *Groundwork* to be a response to the remarks Garve attached to his translation of Cicero.[8] However, precisely which parts of these extensive remarks were influential upon Kant and in what way, as well as whether or not and how the *Groundwork* might respond to them, is a matter of debate.[9]

Garve's aim in 'On Patience' is to offer a general account of the nature of patience as a moral virtue. He focuses on three topics in the essay: (1) the 'difficulty' of patience, that is, how much strength and effort is required to be patient; (2) the 'general utility' of patience or how much it contributes to the well-being of society in general; and (3) the causes and aids of patience or the things that make patience easier to perform. The essay as a whole can be neatly divided into three sections: in the first section (pp. 5–51, original pagination), Garve defines the nature of patience and outlines both its difficulty and general utility; in the second (pp. 51–95), he outlines the causes and aids of patience; and in the third (pp. 95–110), he offers a general observation that he claims illustrates the overall value and utility of patience. The footnote engaging with Kant's moral philosophy is made during the second section of the essay, but the footnote itself is printed at the end of the essay (pp. 111–16) because of its length.

During his discussion of the causes and aids of patience, Garve clarifies that the aids he has listed, such as practicing being patient, are only the means of promoting patience. The principle, he claims, from which such means arise is the idea that patience itself is a moral duty or something that we ought to do. He then goes on to list three 'preparations' of patience, that is, things we can do to make ourselves better suited to being patient. The first is frequently reminding ourselves that patience is a moral obligation and that being patient belongs to a good character. The second is frequent and

---

[7] For a list of Garve's publications, see the bibliography in Roth and Stiening (2021).
[8] See the General Introduction above as well as Kuehn (2001, pp. 277–83).
[9] See Gilbert (1994), Wood (2006), Dyck (forthcoming), Baum (2020), Allison (2011, pp. 80–86), and Reich (1939).

voluntary practice being patient in relation to small, everyday evils. The third and most important preparation, which goes along with conceiving of patience as a moral duty, is knowledge of religious virtue and resignation to the will of God, which he says comes from our belief in the existence of God and the hope for a better future (p. 80). It is over the course of offering further details on this third point, namely the idea that believing in God involves acknowledging that the world has an end or purpose and that this end is the happiness of sensing creatures, that Garve is led to append an extended footnote to the text engaging with Kant's take on the matter.

Kant reacts to Garve's "objections" in the 'Theory and Practice' essay by arguing that they "are nothing but misunderstandings" (8:281.14). Interestingly enough, Kant was not the only one who thought that Garve misunderstood him: in a review of Garve's *Essays* it is claimed that it might be worthwhile for Garve to undertake "a new investigation of the *Critique of Practical Reason*" to correct his misunderstandings.[10] Garve appears to have listened, for in his 1798 *Uebersicht der vornehmsten Principien der Sittenlehre* (Overview of the Leading Principles of the Doctrine of Morals), which was dedicated to Kant, more than half of the book's approximately 400 pages are devoted to summarizing and evaluating Kant's moral philosophy. Although Garve now admits that he agrees with many of Kant's views, he repeats the criticism that Kant's rejection of the principle of happiness deprives his moral theory of the proper motives for moral action.[11] While Garve's claims in the *Overview* can be regarded as his response to the first part of Kant's 'Theory and Practice' essay, Garve also responds to the second part of 'Theory and Practice' in an essay entitled *Über die Grenzen des bürgerlichen Gehorsams* ('On the Boundaries of Civil Obedience') (see Garve 1800).

Translation Notes

In preparing this translation I have primarily used the original, 1792 edition of Garve's *Essays*, but I have also consulted the reprint of the footnote contained in Henrich (1967). Interesting to note is that Garve uses the term '*Motiv*' instead of '*Bewegungsgrund*' (motive) in the following, and the 'Theory and Practice' essay is the only one of Kant's texts where he uses '*Motiv*' instead of his usual '*Bewegungsgrund*' or '*Triebfeder*' (incentive), presumably because he is in conversation with Garve (see Klemme 2006, p. 121).

---

[10] *Allgemeine Literatur-Zeitung*. Number 21, Thursday, January 19, 1979, pp. 161–64, here p. 164.
[11] See Garve (1798, pp. 276, 282, and 388f.), as well as Stern (1884, pp. 74–75) for a discussion.

'On Patience' (1792)
Essays on Various Topics from Moral Science, Literature, and Societal Life: Part One

[80]
[...]

I come to the final and, indeed, most important aid [Hülfsmittel] of patience, which is related to the preceding one—conviction of its accord with duty—in the most precise way. This aid is religious virtue, resignation to the divine will, which emerges from belief [Glauben] in God and from the hope of a better future.

When the arrangement of nature commands something of us, this command is mere constraint so long as we regard nature as lifeless or [81] keep to mediate causes. But if a spiritual and, furthermore, a charitable and wise being created that arrangement, then the rule residing in it for us is a moral law; it is the guidance of a higher leader—the advice of an insightful friend. The duty to obey it becomes greater and the reward more certain.

The person who says that there is a God simultaneously says that the world has an end, and this end is the happiness of perceiving creatures.[*] To the thing that perceives nothing, everything is indifferent. Accordingly, there is no intention in such a thing. That we find the end of creation to be in ourselves and in beings similar to us—that is, in those that are conscious of themselves and have representations of other things—therefore has nothing to do with self-love but is reason and truth. [...]

[111]

---

[*] See the note at the end of this treatise.

Note to page 81. *

I do not believe that I have reason, within this entirely practical subject, to get involved in the theoretical dispute of whether moral perfection or happiness is the final end [der letzte Zweck] of creation. Those who maintain the first certainly do not dare separate happiness from virtue forever. But they do claim that the observation of the moral law, entirely without taking happiness into consideration, is the sole end for the human being; that it is to be regarded as the creator's sole end. But they nevertheless regard virtue from **the** point of view that confers upon the rational being, who thereby sets itself apart, the **worthiness** to be happy. They are even in agreement that the virtuous person, in their selfless obedience to the moral law, cannot and may not ever lose sight of that point of view. May not, I say, because otherwise the virtuous person would completely lose track of the path into the invisible world, which leads to being convinced of God's existence and of immortality, and these convictions, according to the theory of these philosophers themselves, are absolutely necessary in order to give the moral system support and stability. The virtuous person therefore ceaselessly strives to be worthy of happiness, according to these principles, but [112]—insofar as they are genuinely virtuous—never to be happy. To be sure, such a person always conceives of their obedience to the moral law as related to **well-being** [Wohlseyn], to which this obedience has a natural connection that is grounded in reason, but they completely exclude this well-being from their ends if they actually evince that obedience.

For my part I confess that I comprehend this division of ideas with my head quite well, but I do not find this division of wishes and strivings in my heart—that it is even incomprehensible to me how anyone can be conscious of their striving to be worthy of happiness as purely separated from the striving for happiness itself, and thus of having performed duty entirely selflessly. Such fine distinctions of ideas become obscure as soon as one reflects on particular objects. But they disappear altogether when it comes to action; when they are to be applied to desires and intentions. The simpler, the faster, and the more divested of clear representations the step is, by means of which we proceed from the consideration of motives [Motive] to actual action, the less is it possible to precisely and reliably recognize the specific weight that each motive contributed towards guiding the step in a certain way and not otherwise. On the other hand, some additional considerations of this issue, distinct from those just listed, suggest themselves to me, which prevent me from completely agreeing with the way in which the Kantian philosophy represents things, even if I believe that a thorough elaboration of our ideas in their most important respects [113] would reveal a vastly smaller dissimilarity than their designations indicate.

It seems to me that the first and most general thing that must obtain where one is to adopt an end and determine one's will according to ends is: [first,] that the being in whom the end is set actually possesses the capacity to become aware of its states [Zustände]; second, that this being has at one point in time perceived the state which is to be regarded as an end, or a similar one; and, third, that, when this being perceived this state, it preferred it or liked it better.

Unfortunately, language does not have enough expressions for concepts of this generality, and one must make use of words that are already devoted to more particular and more concrete sensations and desires to describe these ultimate origins of all sensations and desires—a subject, from which much misinterpretation arises in precisely this part of metaphysics.

Supposing further, however, that in the actual series of alterations of living and self-active [selbstthätigen] beings, the **sensation of present** states is not permitted to precede the **striving** for a certain **future** state (a matter which is not to be disputed here), then it would be certain that, in the order of concepts, perceiving and distinguishing states, by means of which one is preferred to another, must precede the choice of one among them, and therefore precede the prior determination of a certain end. But a state that a being endowed with consciousness of itself and of its states prefers to other modes of existence when this state occurs to and is perceived by it, is a **good** [114] state. And a series of such good states is the most general concept that the word happiness expresses.

In such a being, this concept therefore precedes that of an end, and that of striving towards this end, and underlies its striving. It is therefore also earlier and more original in the understanding than the concept of **moral** ends. In the succession of our ideas, the progression from happiness to virtue is thus far more natural than the other way around, according to which the concept of virtue is said to first lead us to that of happiness. A law presupposes motives, but motives presuppose a previously perceived difference between a worse state and a better one. This perceived difference is the foundational component [Element] of the concept **happiness**, which is gradually broadened by means of the quantity of such perceptions and is modified by means of their diversity. The motives for every endeavour, and thus also for following the moral law, spring from happiness in the most general sense of the word. I must first know that something is good before I can ask whether satisfying moral duties falls under the rubric of the good. The human being must have an incentive that sets it in motion before one can attribute a goal [Ziel] to it, towards which this motion is to be directed.

I infer from this, (1) that it is permissible to speak of happiness as the sole conceivable end of things, namely because a state of the following kind cannot be regarded as an end from any point of view: a state that belongs to a being that is incapable of consciousness and perception; a state that exists in a being that is conscious of itself but which has never actually been perceived by that being; or finally [115] a state which, when it occurred in such a being and was perceived by it, made no impression such that the state was preferred by this being to other states. But a state that is perceived by the being to which it belongs and, by virtue of what is characteristic of this consciousness, is preferred to other states is, according to my concepts, the foundational component [Grundstoff] of happiness.

I infer (2) that not only thinking beings, but all sensing beings and those that differentiate their states as good or evil are capable and worthy of being regarded as ends by an author of any kind of work who is rational and acts morally, and thus also by the artificer or creator of the world. Just as, on the one hand, I find nothing in lifeless and sensation-less beings, considered in themselves, that deserves to be called good or bad, beautiful or ugly, perfect or imperfect, and nothing that deserves to be described by means of an expression of preference or disparagement of any kind; just as I believe to understand that all epithets of this kind that we bestow upon singular things from the corporeal world, or upon all of lifeless nature, befit such things merely in **the** relation that they have to living beings capable of representation and consciousness (that is, whether they contribute to the preservation or destruction of such beings or whether they have an effect on the senses, understanding, or imagination of such beings that is in accordance with or in opposition to the nature of these powers); so does it seem to me, on the other hand, that the entire kingdom of living and sensing beings without distinction—may their representations be raised to a higher or lower degree of distinctness, [116] may their drives have been developed to a more or less perfect morality—constitutes the domain characteristic of the ideas of good and evil. Where there is one being who regards one of its states with satisfaction and the other with aversion, there are also other rational beings who notice this and are justified in regarding the former state and its causes as **good**, and in counting the latter, along with that which brings it about, under the category of what is **evil**; indeed, they are obligated to adopt the promotion of the former good and the prevention or reduction of the latter evil as their ends. This theory, which is derived from the very first concepts of the good and of an end, also agrees with the common concepts and natural perceptions of good human beings. These human beings, in that they burden themselves with certain duties towards animals and they take an interest in the fates of such animals, similar to compassion and sociable joy, illustrate that they do not exclude animals and their weal and woe from their ends, and that they include the existence and well-being of animals in the system of happiness, on the basis of which they also judge the end of the world.

The discussion of these concepts would be out of place here if, without an added justification, an obvious deviation in manner of expression from that of the most recent philosophy which is now generally and quite rightly esteemed did not earn the author the reproach that he has ignored the more recent developments in this science, a reproach which might have pulled the attention of the admirers of this science away from that which is true and useful in what had been said.

11
Hermann Andreas Pistorius
Introduction

What follows is the third and final review authored by Pistorius in this volume, and it completes a fascinating exchange between him and Kant. Their dialogue begins with Pistorius' reactions to the first *Critique* and the *Groundwork*[1] (contained in the reviews translated in Chapters 5 and 6 of this volume), continues with Kant's responses to these reviews in the second *Critique*,[2] and ends here with Pistorius' review of the second *Critique*. It is unfortunate that, as Pistorius explains in the first footnote, the review was "misplaced [verlegt]" and only published in 1794, years after it was initially written, for, had it been published earlier and had Kant read it, Kant might have again responded. The review nonetheless represents an important piece of the second *Critique*'s early reception, and indeed one authored by a contemporary whom Kant respected and with whom he was already in dialogue.[3]

After providing a relatively thorough summary of the contents of the second *Critique* (pp. 78–88, original pagination), Pistorius returns to some of the same points made in his previous reviews. Pistorius acknowledges, for instance, that Kant seems to have taken his earlier 'priority of the good' objection into account (see p. 96 below and p. 449 of his review of the *Groundwork*), but he again argues that logical consistency and absence of contradiction are insufficient when judging whether a maxim can be willed

---

[1] Strictly speaking, Pistorius wrote a number of other reviews that deal with Kant's philosophy and which would need to be considered if one were to fully appreciate Pistorius' assessment of Kant's philosophy. The most important of these that are not included in this volume are his review of the *Prolegomena* (Pistorius 1784), his review of the second edition of the first *Critique* (Pistorius 1788a), and his review of Jakob's *Prüfung der Mendelssohnschen Morgenstunden* (Pistorius 1788b). The three reviews included in this volume, however, are by far the most important for understanding Pistorius' reaction to Kant's moral philosophy.
[2] For information on how Kant might have responded to Pistorius in the second *Critique*, see the Introductions to Chapters 5 and 6.
[3] For some brief discussion of the importance of this review in the early reception of Kant's second *Critique*, see Klemme (2003).

255

as a universal law (see e.g., pp. 89–91), and thus again stresses that we need to take the results or consequences of universalizing a maxim into consideration (see p. 91 below and p. 455 of his review of the *Groundwork*). In this context Pistorius argues that not only the principle of contradiction but also the second fundamental law of reason, i.e., the principle of sufficient reason, which Pistorius calls "the principle of the ground and the grounded" (pp. 93–94), should play a role in moral judgement, and thus that this latter law should be capable of being a 'fact of reason' and of issuing a categorical imperative as well (see pp. 93–96). A major theme of the review is Pistorius' inability to accept Kant's distinction between the empirical and intelligible character of human beings, which he here calls "the most obscure and inconceivable thing in the entire critical philosophy" (p. 102), and which is reminiscent of his objections to Kant's distinction between appearances and things in themselves throughout his review of Schultz's *Elucidations*. Other noteworthy topics in the following review include a discussion of happiness and the highest good, which involves a comparison between Kant and the Stoics on these issues (see pp. 96–100), a critique of Kant's theory of freedom (p. 101), and an additional objection accusing Kant of inconsistency, namely, on the one hand, that Kant denies that the sensible side of human beings can be taken into consideration when determining the content of the moral law, but on the other hand that Kant implies that it must be taken into consideration in the doctrine of the highest good, a doctrine supposedly resulting from the moral law (see pp. 99–100).[4]

Translation Notes

This is the first English translation of Pistorius' review of the second *Critique*. In preparing it, I have referenced both the modern edition included in Gesang (2007) and the original review (1794). As was the case for Pistorius' review of the *Groundwork*, he often paraphrases or even directly cites from the second *Critique* without indicating that he is doing so. I have placed these passages in double quotation marks within square brackets and have noted the corresponding passage from the second *Critique* to make it clear when Pistorius is doing so.

---

[4] Pistorius' review of the second *Critique* is only seldomly discussed in the secondary literature. For some introductory but nonetheless helpful remarks, see Guyer (2021 and forthcoming), Gesang (2007), Timmermann (2022, p. 44), and Gesang (2016).

Review of the *Critique of Practical Reason* (1794)

Allgemeine Deutsche Bibliothek. 117. Band, 1. Stück, 1794, pp. 78–105.

[78]

Critique of Practical Reason, by Immanuel Kant. Riga, Hartknoch. 1788. 8. 292 pages.*

In this work the author further elaborates on the ideas, to which he had given an introduction in his *Groundwork of the Metaphysics of Morals*, and which at the same time can serve as a brief outline of his doctrine of morals, insofar as he here thoroughly deals with the following questions: whether and in what way pure reason is practical, whether it has any relation to the faculty of desire, what kind of relation this is, and how we can conceive of the relation as possible and actual.

The reviewer was at first willing to give a detailed summary of this book according to the various titles under which the author has treated his material, but he soon realized that, given the precision and necessary brevity with which the author has presented his ideas, such a summary would have to be much too long-winded for a review in order to be suitably intelligible and useful. He abandoned this intention all the more because the present text, with its rich and important content, is so concisely formulated that every admirer will gladly read it through themselves more than once, and simultaneously because the text has the following advantage over the rest of the author's recent writings: that it is on the whole much easier to understand and is not so much in need of an explanatory summary as his *Critique of Pure Reason* in order to be

---

* This article was already completed many years ago and had been sent in for printing, but it was misplaced and could not be found. Since someone has finally obtained it once again, one preferably wishes to offer it so unusually late than to want to admit that such an important product of the German philosophical spirit remains unannounced in the *Allgemeine deutsche Bibliothek*.

reasonably well understood and assessed. Following the guideline of the above listed questions, I will therefore content myself with concisely presenting the most important aspects of what Herr Kant has offered in answer to them, [79] whereby, I hope, not only what is characteristic of the Kantian doctrine of morals can to some extent become clear, but also whereby the remarks that I venture to make in relation to this doctrine become intelligible to readers.

One already knows from the *Groundwork of the Metaphysics of Morals* that Herr Kant adopts a practical reason in the important sense that he ascribes all moral legislation, the judicial office of morality, and the necessary standing and capacity to obey to pure reason alone to the exclusion of sensibility and experience. He also takes this claim as his starting point here and formulates it into the following theorems: (1) "All practical principles that presuppose an object (matter) of the faculty of desire as the determining ground of the will are, without exception, empirical and can furnish no practical laws." [5:21.14–16]; (2) "All material practical principles as such are, without exception, of one and the same kind and come under the general principle of self-love or one's own happiness." [5:22.6–8]; (3) "If a rational being is to think of his maxims as practical universal laws, he can think of them only as principles that contain the determining ground of the will not by their matter but only by their form." [5:27.3–6] On the basis of these the following two problems will be solved: first, "supposing that the mere legislating form of maxims is the only sufficient determining ground of a will, to find the constitution of a will that is determinable by it alone" [5:28.31–33]; and second, "supposing that a will is free, to find the law that alone is competent to determine it necessarily." [5:29.12–13] — The first problem is solved in the following way: such a will must be conceived as entirely independent of the natural law of appearances, namely the law of causality, or as in conflict with it, from which it follows that the second can be solved in no other way than as follows: "Since the matter of a practical law, that is, an object of the maxim, can never be given otherwise than empirically, whereas a free will, as independent of empirical conditions (i.e., conditions belonging to the sensible world) must nevertheless be determinable, a free will must find a determining ground in the law but independently of the matter of the law. But, besides the matter of the law, nothing [80] further is contained in it than the legislating form. The legislating form, insofar as this is contained in the maxim, is therefore the only thing that can constitute a determining ground of the will." [5:29.14–22] — ["]Freedom and unconditional practical law therefore reciprocally imply each other.["] [5:29.24–25] — Here it is a question of where our cognition of the unconditionally practical begins, whether from freedom or from the practical law. [5:29.28–29] Not from the first, for we can neither be conscious of it immediately, because the first concept of it is merely negative, nor conclude to it from experience, for experience offers only the law of appearances, and therefore the mechanism of nature, the direct opposite of freedom. [5:29.29–33] ["]It is therefore the moral law, of which we become immediately conscious (as soon as we draw up maxims of the will for ourselves), that first offers itself to us and, inasmuch as reason presents it as a determining ground not to be outweighed by any sensible conditions and indeed quite independent of them, leads directly to the concept of freedom. But how is consciousness of that moral law possible? We can become aware of pure practical laws just as we are aware of pure theoretical principles, by attending to the necessity with which reason prescribes them to us and to the setting aside of all empirical conditions to which reason directs us.["] [5:29.33–5:30.7] The fundamental law of pure practical reason thus reads as follows: **Act in such a way that the maxim of your will could always hold at the same time as a maxim** [Maxime] **of universal legislation.** [5:30.38–39] This rule says: one ought absolutely to proceed in a certain way, it is therefore ["]-unconditional and is represented as a categorical practical proposition *a priori*, whereby the will is objectively determined absolutely and immediately by the practical rule (which is therefore a law here).["] [5:31.6–9] ["]One can call the consciousness of this fundamental law a fact of reason, because one cannot reason it out from antecedent data of reason, for example from consciousness of freedom, rather it forces itself upon us as a synthetic proposition *a priori* that is not based on any intuition, either pure or empirical. [...] However, in order to regard this law as given without misinterpretation, one must indeed note that it is not an empirical fact but the sole fact of pure reason which thereby announces itself as originally [81] legislating (*sic volo, sic jubeo*[1]).["] [5:31.24–34] From all of this the conclusion is now drawn: ["]Pure reason is practical of itself alone and gives (to the human being) a universal law which we call the moral law.["] [5:31.36–37] And now this fourth theorem is established: "Autonomy of the will is the sole principle of all moral laws and of duties in keeping with them. All heteronomy of choice, on the other hand,["] (that is, when the will takes its determining grounds from somewhere else, or from the matter of the law, from the consequence of the action) ["]does

---

[1] *what I will, I command*

not ground any obligation at all but is instead opposite to the principle of obligation and to morality." [5:33.8–11] ["]The sole principle of morality consists in the independence from all matter of the law (i.e., from a desired object) and at the same time in the determination of the power of choice through the mere universal, legislating form, of which a maxim must be capable. But this independence is freedom in the **negative** sense, self-legislation of pure and practical reason as such is freedom in the **positive** sense. Thus, the moral law expresses nothing other than the autonomy of pure practical reason, i.e., of freedom, and this is itself the formal condition of all maxims, under which they alone can accord with the supreme practical law. If therefore the matter of volition, which can be nothing other than the object of a desire, which is connected to the law, enters into the practical law as **condition for the possibility** of the law, then heteronomy of the power of choice arises, namely dependence upon the law of nature, to follow some sort of drive or inclination, and the will does not give itself the law, but only instructions for rationally following pathological laws. The maxim, however, which in this way can never contain within itself the form of universal legislation, thereby establishes not only no obligation, but is itself contrary to the principle of a **pure** practical reason and therefore to the moral disposition as well, even if the action, which springs from it, were to be in conformity with the law.["] [5:33.12–33]

From the Analytic, wherein the author presents a deduction of the principles of pure practical reason, and wherein the previously stated moral system is further elaborated according to its foundations, we note only the following: if the [82] concept of freedom, which is merely possible or problematic according to speculative reason (in the sense in which it has been considered up until this point) is realized through pure practical reason, or is represented as **actually given** in the rational law, this is understood under the assumption that the human being is regarded not merely as a being in the sensible world (for as such a being it is subjected to natural necessity) but as a noumenon or member of a world of the understanding. In this latter character the human being can be regarded as a freely acting cause in that it can be shown that it is not contradictory to regard all the human being's actions as physically conditioned, insofar as they are appearances, on the one hand, and at the same time to regard the human being's causality, insofar as the acting being is an intelligible being, as physically unconditioned, on the other, and thus to make the concept of freedom into a regulative principle of reason.

Under the title: **On the Warrant of Pure Reason in its Practical Use to an Extension which is not Possible in its Speculative Use**, the main ideas are the following: the categories in themselves have application, and thus so does that of causality; a concept that is admittedly empty in itself, but is not impossible and inadmissible, cannot in theory be applied to noumena, such that through this application the cognition of noumena is expanded; but this can happen in [pure reason's] practical use, because the reality of the concept of causality is determinately given to us in the moral law; **the concept** of causality can therefore be united with freedom, not in order to cognize something of such a being, but in that we are permitted to regard such a being as determined through freedom. [see 5:54–56] ["]The concept of an empirically unconditioned causality is indeed theoretically empty; but it is nevertheless possible, and refers to an undetermined object,["] and [significance] is given to it despite intuition, which here does not take place, through the moral law, and by means of this ["]it has nonetheless real application, which is exhibited *in concreto* in dispositions and maxims, that is, it has practical reality, which can be specified, which is thus sufficient for its justification even in relation to noumena.["] [5:56.19–27]

From here the author proceeds to consider the object of pure practical reason. This object is [83] nothing other than the concepts of **good** and **evil**. ["]By the first is understood a necessary object of the faculty of desire, and by the second of the faculty of aversion, but both according to a principle of reason.["] [5:58.7–9] Here the question arises of whether the concepts of good and evil can be established or determined provisionally and without regard to the moral law, or whether these concepts are first to be determined after this moral law has been laid down. The latter is claimed here, and it is shown that in the former case good and evil can be determined in no other way than empirically, and consequently that the moral law, the objects of which would be these empirically ascertained [concepts of] good and evil, could not be a universally necessary law of reason *a priori*, thus only the latter case remains, namely that good and evil are first determined by and after the moral law, or that these concepts must be derived from an antecedent practical law, but cannot relate to the law as ground.

The point of the **third chapter on the incentive of pure practical reason** is to answer the following question in particular: how are we supposed to conceive of the stated relation of pure reason to the faculty of desire? The most important aspects are the following: ["]What is essential to all moral worth of actions depends on the moral law determining the will immediately. If this determination happens in conformity to the moral law, but only by means of a feeling, of whatever kind it may be—therefore not for the sake of the law—then the action will indeed contain legality, but not morality.["] [5:71.28–34] The divine will has and needs no incentives, nor any subjective determining grounds of the will. [5:72.4–5] ["]The incentive of the human will can never be anything other than the moral law, therefore the objective determining ground must always and entirely alone be also the subjectively-sufficient determining ground of action, if this is not to merely fulfill the **letter** of the law, without containing its **spirit**.["] [5:72.5–11] Since the way in which the moral law becomes an incentive is to be determined here, it must be admitted that to determine ["]how a law can be of itself the immediate [84] determining ground of the will is for human reason just as insoluble a problem as to explain how a free will is possible.["] [5:72.21–24] All that can happen in this case is that ["]one can show *a priori*, insofar as the law is such an incentive or determining ground of the will, what it must effect in the mind.["] [5:72.26–27] The effect of the law is in part only negative, and as such can be cognized *a priori* insofar as it effects a feeling, which can be called pain, and it effects this by infringing upon all inclinations, and silences regard for oneself [Selbstsucht], which is comprised of these inclinations taken together. But in this way this law is thus ["]an object of the greatest respect, and therefore a ground of a positive feeling, which is not of empirical origin and is cognized *a priori*.["] [5:73.30–34] — Now, the moral law, which is alone (namely in all respects) truly objective, excludes the influence of self-love on the supreme practical principle altogether, and unendingly infringes upon self-conceit [Eigendünkel], which prescribes the subjective conditions of self-love as law, and humiliates every human being. [5:74.19–25] That which humiliates us in our self-consciousness when represented as a determining ground of our will awakens respect for itself insofar as it is positive and a determining ground. [5:74.26–29] The moral law is thus also subjectively a ground of respect. [5:74.29–30] — Absolutely no particular kind of feeling, under the name of a practical or moral feeling, can be accepted here as preceding the moral law and underlying it. [5:75.3–5] — ["]The incentive of the moral disposition must be free from all sensible conditions.["] [5:75.28–29] ["]Respect for the law is thus not the incentive to morality, rather it is morality itself, subjectively considered as an incentive, in that pure practical reason, by rejecting all the claims of self-love in opposition to its own, supplies authority to the law, which now alone has influence.["] [5:76.4–8] ["]It is of such a peculiar kind that it seems to be at the disposal of reason alone, and indeed of pure practical reason.["] [5:76.22–23] ["]An action takes place from duty when it occurs merely from pure respect for the law or for the sake of the law. Morality merely consists in this as well.["] [5:81.17–19] — ["]The moral law is for the will of a most perfect being a law of **holiness**; but for the will of every finite rational being a law [85] of **duty**, of moral necessitation [Nöthigung], and a law of the determination of the will by means of **respect** for this law and from reverence [Ehrfurcht] for its duty. A different subjective principle must not be adopted as an incentive, otherwise the disposition is not moral, which is what really matters in this legislation.["] [5:82.8–17] — Acting from love of human beings, of order, etc. is beautiful, but that is not yet the genuine moral maxim of our conduct. [5:82.18–20] — ["]We are subjected to a discipline of reason.["] [5:82.25–26] — ["]The possibility of a command such as: **love God above everything and your neighbour as yourself**, agrees with this very well, for as a command it requires respect for a law that commands **love**, and does not leave it to arbitrary choice to make this into a principle.["] [5:83.3–7] ["]The principle of one's own happiness, which some wish to make into the supreme foundational principle of morality, is in stark contrast to this law. This would read as follows: love yourself above everything, but God and your neighbour for your own sake.["] [5:83.35–36n] ["]That law of all laws, like all moral prescriptions of the Gospel, represents the moral disposition in its complete perfection, in such a way that, as an ideal of holiness, it is reachable by no creature, but is nonetheless the model we should strive to approximate and resemble in an uninterrupted and unending progress.["] [5:83.22–27] — ["]The moral level, on which the human being stands, is respect for the moral law, and its moral condition, in which it can be at all times, is **virtue**, i.e., moral disposition in **conflict**, and not **holiness** in the supposed possession of a perfect purity of the disposition of the will.["] [5:84.27–35] — ["]The genuine incentive of pure practical reason is therefore nothing other than the moral law itself, insofar as it allows us to notice the sublimity of our own supersensible existence, and in human beings who are simultaneously conscious of their sensible existence and the dependence of their heretofore very pathologically-affected nature connected with it, it subjectively effects respect for their higher vocation.["] [5:88.21–26]

From the second book on the dialectic of pure practical reason we only note the interesting investigation into the highest good. The most important aspects belonging here consist in the following: ["]The concept **highest** is ambiguous insofar as it means the **supreme** (*supremum*) or the **complete** [86] (*consummatum*). That virtue (as the worthiness to be happy) is the supreme good results from the preceding; but it is not yet, for that reason, the whole and complete good, as object of the faculty of desire of rational finite beings. For, in order to be that, **happiness** is also required, and not merely in the partial eyes of the person who makes themselves an end, but in the judgement of an impartial reason that considers such a person in the world generally [as an end in itself]. For, to need happiness, to be also worthy of it, and yet to not participate in it cannot coexist with the perfect volition of a rational being that simultaneously possesses all power, even if we conceive of such a being only for the sake of experiment.["] [5:110.12–31]

On this occasion the author makes remarks concerning the various attempts of the Epicureans and Stoics to unite virtue and happiness with one another. Both derived this union from an identity of the two concepts, albeit in different ways. As a result, according to their style of teaching the union was analytic, not synthetic, seeing as the concepts related to each other inversely. ["]The connection between virtue and happiness is [cognized] as *a priori*, and thus as practically necessary.["] [5:113.56] ["]It is *a priori* (morally) necessary, to bring about the highest good through freedom of the will; the condition of its possibility must therefore be based solely on grounds of cognition *a priori*.["] [5:113.9–12] This leads the author to the antinomy of practical reason and to the attempt to critically resolve it. We note the following on this topic.

The connection between virtue and happiness is not analytic, thus it must be synthetic. But this is also impossible, ["]because every practical connection between causes and effects in the world as the result of the determination of the will does not take its cue from moral dispositions of the will, but from the cognition of natural laws and the physical ability to use them for one's purposes, thus no necessary connection between happiness and virtue in the world sufficient for the highest good can be expected by the meticulous observation of the moral law.["] [5:113.30–114.1] — ["]Therefore, if the highest good is impossible according to practical rules, then the moral [87] law, which commands that it be promoted, must also be fantastic and directed towards empty, imagined ends, and therefore be false in itself.["] [5:114.6–9] The author attempts to resolve this antinomy in the following way: ["]the first of the two propositions (by means of which we can express the potential connection between virtue with happiness), that the striving for happiness brings forth a ground for virtuous dispositions (according to Epicurus) is **absolutely** false; but the second, that the virtuous disposition necessarily brings about happiness (according to the Stoics), is not **absolutely** false, but only insofar as the disposition is regarded as a causality in the sensible word, thus it is only **conditionally** false if I assume existence in the sensible world as the only **way of existence** of a rational being. But since I am not only authorized to think of my existence as a noumenon in a world of the understanding, but also to have in the moral law a purely intellectual determining ground of my causality (in the sensible world), it is thereby not impossible that the morality of dispositions has a, if not immediate then mediate (by means of an intelligible creator of the world) and indeed necessary, connection to happiness in the sensible world, a connection which, in a nature that is merely an object of the senses, can take place only contingently, and is not sufficient for the highest good["] [5:114.27–115.8[2]], in that self-contentment [Selbstzufriedenheit] is not yet happiness, ["]which consists in the condition of a being, for whom, in the whole of its existence, everything goes according to wish and will.["] [5:124.21–23] — The postulates of pure practical reason are connected to this solution of the antinomy. There are three: first, **freedom**, ["]on account of the necessary presupposition of independence from the sensible world and natural necessity, and of the capacity to determine the will according to the laws of an intelligible world,["] [5:132.23–26] which is itself freedom. Second, **immortality of the soul**: ["]The production of the highest good in the world is the necessary object of a will determinable by the moral law. But in such a will the complete **conformity** of dispositions to the moral law is the supreme condition of the highest good. This conformity must therefore be just as possible as its object, because it is contained in the same command to promote this object. This complete conformity, which is practically necessary, can only be encountered in an unending **progress** towards that complete [88] conformity, and in accordance with principles of pure practical reason it is necessary to assume such a practical progress as the real object of our will. This unending progress is, however, only possible under the presupposition of the existence and personality of that same rational being lasting into infinity (which one calls the immortality of the soul).["] [5:122.4–20] Third, the **existence of God**: ["]The moral law must also lead to the possibility of the second element of the highest good, namely to **happiness** proportionate to morality, and just as unselfishly [as before], solely from impartial reason, it must lead to the presupposition of the existence of a cause adequate to this effect, that is, it must postulate the existence of God as necessarily

---

[2] The bracketed sections of this paraphrase are Pistorius' own remarks and are not in the second *Critique*'s original text.

belonging to the possibility of the highest good.["] [5:124.12–19] The happiness of the human being ["]is based on the agreement between nature and the human being's whole end, and also the essential determining ground of its will,["] [5:124.23–25] ["]consequently, the postulate of the possibility of the **highest derived good** (the best world) is simultaneously the postulate of a **highest original good**, namely the existence of God.["] [5:125.22–25] But this moral necessity to assume a God is only ["]subjective, i.e. a need, and not objective, i.e., itself a duty, for there can be no duty whatsoever to assume the existence of something (because this only concerns the theoretical use of reason), and so it is not to be understood by this that the assumption of the existence of God is necessary as a **ground of all obligation**, for this rests solely on the autonomy of reason itself.["] [5:125.31–126.1]

This is an approximate characterization of the author's theory of morality, admittedly only some of its essential features, but from which, or so I hope, a morality reveals itself that is pure, if any theory deserves to be so called; a morality, so strict in its demands, so noble in its features, so unselfish in its motives [Bewegungsgründen], and so sublime in the prospects that it opens, that it must recommend itself to every true friend of virtue, and what remains is only the wish that this sublime doctrine of morals, freed from all the obscurities that still rest upon it, and from all the difficulties that still appear to vex it, may be vindicated as true, as fit for human nature, as usable in practice, and as applicable [89] to life. The reviewer has not been able to ward off some doubts and uncertainties concerning the above, which he here wishes to present along with their reasons.

The question is not only whether we are permitted to call reason, as the most supreme and only legislator of human beings, practical to the extent that it can provide human beings with the true principle of morality, but simultaneously also whether reason's high rank, and its capacity to gain respect and obedience merely on its own, can be suitably proven. The author grants all of this to reason. But since pure reason can in no way be cognized as practical, as the most supreme and only legislator, or as the founder of all morality by means of immediate consciousness, and thus not in the Kantian sense either, (because our consciousness itself, as well as everything we perceive by means of it, is only empirical and the self-consciousness of a sensible-rational object), pure reason's high legislating rank cannot be illustrated by means of a rationalizing [vernünftelnde] analysis of our powers of the soul, such as that of freedom. Thus, nothing else can serve as a proof here except that which the author calls the fact of pure reason, namely that we must distinguish an imperative of morality from the imperatives of prudence, and an absolute law that only pure reason can provide from all the rules and hypothetical laws of self-love, the inclinations, and the sensible drives and needs more generally, and accordingly acknowledge an unconditionally good will whose worth is above all else. The entire Kantian moral system is grounded on this, as if on the ultimate and sole foundation; that is, the necessity of acknowledging a merely formal principle of morality in opposition to all material principles is grounded on this. If it can now be shown that this formal principle of morality, most precisely understood, cannot be called a categorical imperative (because a ground of cognition [Erkenntnissgrund] for why precisely this or that particular maxim passes for a universal legislation must always be available), and if it can then be further shown that this ground of cognition, if it is not the principle of contradiction itself, can be nothing other than the conformity or agreement of the maxim with the nature [90] of the subject whose maxim it is supposed to be. But none of this prevents a maxim that we cognize as being fit for universal legislation on account of its agreement with nature from being similarly formal, and to this extent agreeing with the Kantian principle of morality. The latter is and can be nothing other than **that which is in conformity with reason** [das Vernünftmäßige], and according to all the examples that are given to explain it, it consists in that which is self-consistent [das Selbstbestehende], the consistent aspect in a maxim, or the state of affairs in which I do not contradict myself when following the maxim, or in which I do not simultaneously **will** and **not will** the very same thing. The opposite, however, or the circumstance that causes a maxim to not be suitable for universal legislation, is that which is contradictory in the maxim, that which is self-defeating and -destroying, and which would be unavoidable when following it. The ground of cognition, on the basis of which, according to the author, we can judge whether a certain maxim of the will or its opposite is fit for universal legislation, extends no further than this. And if there are maxims whose suitability or unsuitability for universal legislation cannot merely be cognized and decided on the basis of their apparent conformity or non-conformity with reason, as there indisputably are, then it seems that we need some sort of condition or higher consideration in order to settle this, and in this case the Kantian imperative would neither be categorical, nor the highest law of morality. But whether there are such cases depends on being able to produce examples in which the validity of a maxim for universal legislation, or its opposite, cannot merely be judged on the basis of its conformity or lack of conformity with reason; and it may not be very difficult to find such examples. Suppose that one has to decide which of the two opposing maxims that we observe in relation to our conduct towards our enemies is fit for universal legislation, namely that which Christianity prescribes and that which the Hurons follow, the latter of which can be expressed as follows: never spare your enemy, but hunt them until you have removed them from the position of ever injuring you, even if this is possible in no other way than by killing them. It seems obvious to me here that the mere conformity with reason or consistency that is supposed to lie in the one, [91] and the contradiction that is supposed to lie in the other, cannot be used as a ground of cognition, because I neither act consistently when I follow the one, nor do I contradict myself when I put the other into practice. Things are not at all the same in this case as they are in the one given by Kant, namely that of whether or not I may extract myself from a difficult situation by means of a false promise, nor as in the case of whether or not I should steal, for in both of these cases I would contradict myself; I would simultaneously will and not will something, namely I would will that promising should be valid and also not be valid; that property both does and does not exist. But whether I deal with my enemy as a Christian or as a Huron, in each case I neither act more consistently nor more contradictorily than in the other. Thus, the ground of cognition that pure reason could provide me with here, or its mere *sic volo, sic iubeo*,[3] escapes me, and I must either remain forever undecided between my two maxims or, if it is important to me to choose between the two, search for a higher consideration on the basis which I could decide the legislative value or disvalue of my maxims. It seems obvious to me that this consideration or ground of cognition can no longer be found in pure reason, for if one were to say something such as: in order to judge the moral value or disvalue of an action or maxim, one must ["]ask oneself, whether one could indeed regard the action as possible through one's will if it were to take place according to the law of a nature, of which one is oneself a part["] [5:69.21–22]; or ask oneself whether the maxim of an action is constituted in such a way ["]that it could qualify as a universal law of nature["] [5:28.1–2]; or, finally, ask oneself: what would happen if everyone were to act in such a way?; then it would undeniable that, if one wanted to know more about these questions than that which is consistent or not, but also wanted to know that which is in conformity with nature and the universal interest of rational beings grounded therein, then one must make use of knowledge from experience

---

[3] *what I will, I command*

in order to answer them, and one must also take the consequences of the actions or, even better, the maxims into consideration, and thus that **pure** reason is not in a position to answer them on its own. Indeed, this guideline for calculating the value of a maxim indicates to us the Stoic principle of morality as the more superior [92] ground of cognition and decision in morality. Similarly, it seems undeniable to me that, if the above is correct, then the author's highest principle of morals does not in fact suffice to determine in all cases which of two opposing maxims of the will is to be preferred as fit for universal legislation.

Setting this to the side, however, the objection can be made to the entire Kantian moral system that, regarded solely as a pure intelligence, only the rational part of the human being's nature is taken into consideration and not the sensible part and its needs and inclinations. But if morality and the laws of morality are to be given to the human being as a sensible-rational subject, their entire nature should be taken into consideration. The human being is not a pure intelligence, and neither can it ever become one; rather it always remains a member of the sensible world insofar as it is to be a being capable of morality, and thus a being capable of change. Morality is indeed nothing other than a particular way of willing and acting, and presupposes: that the subject who is capable of morality can will and act in various ways; that it can, to a certain extent, determine its own constitution and condition; that there is one variety of this self-determination that is to be preferred over every other; and that this being must have an original, foundational constitution [Grundbestimmung] or an original predisposition that precedes all self-determination. For, if this being did not have such a constitution, then we could not conceive of there being a better and more fitting way for such a being to determine itself and to act, and even less could we conceive of there being a best and most fitting way, just as we cannot say of a body of matter that is in itself unformed and also passively resists all the forms that could be given to it, that this or that form is the most fitting or the best for it. Thus, the best and most fitting way for such a being to determine itself, i.e., the way that is in conformity with duty, is none other than the one that agrees with this being's foundational constitution or original predisposition, and which therefore aims at making out of this being precisely that which could and should arise from its foundational constitution. A being that is capable of morality must therefore be one that is not that which it can and should be all at once, nor one that becomes this [93] merely and solely by means of its foundational constitution or via foreign determination. Such a being must rather be one that can and should determine itself, at least partially, and thus a being that progresses towards the fulfillment of its original predisposition and the completion of its foundational constitution, i.e., progresses towards its moral education. This being must therefore be and remain a changeable being, for if it could ever become entirely complete or perfect, then it would have to stand still and could not go beyond the achieved point of perfection; it would stop being a **moral** being and thus would be, according to the concept adopted by the author, a **holy** being. But if we absolutely cannot conceive of progress from one condition to the next without the concept of time, and if the concept of time belongs exclusively to the world of the senses and appearances, then the moral human being, insofar as it should remain moral, can never become a pure intelligence, nor escape from the world of appearances. And from this it follows that such a being can never possess transcendental freedom, whether we regard it as negative or positive, i.e., it can never actually attain this freedom, even if it can nonetheless approximate it in an indeterminate way. All of this seems to prove that we should not ignore the sensible part of human nature when determining that which is moral for such a being and what morality is. Precisely this point will now be further confirmed when we return to our question of the extent to which our reason can be regarded as practical.

In general, reason is practical insofar as it concerns itself with the faculty of desire and exerts an influence on the actions and omissions of human beings in particular. This involves reason bringing the effects of the faculty of desire before its court of judgement [Richterstuhl] and approving or disapproving of them. It is therefore natural for reason to do the former insofar as and because reason finds both the maxims and ways of acting to be in agreement or consistent with its own foundational law of agreement and contradiction, and the latter insofar as reason finds these maxims and ways of acting to be contradictory or inconsistent with this, its great foundational law. Only from this point of view and in this relation does the author wish to conceive of reason as practical. Nevertheless, it is not to be denied that reason also judges actions according to its second foundational law, namely the principle [94] of the ground and the grounded, and approves of actions when they are in conformity with this principle, i.e., grounded and purposeful, and disapproves of them when they are opposed to this principle, i.e., ungrounded and unpurposeful. Indeed, according to the common use of language, grounded and purposeful action is attributed to reason in particular. Why then, one might think, should this second foundational law of reason not produce an imperative of morality just as good as the one yielded by the principle of agreement and contradiction?

Perhaps because no such fact of pure reason, on which the validity of the Kantian imperative of morality is supposed to rest, can be given for an imperative that invokes and is grounded in the principle of causality. However, regardless of how things stand with this fact of pure reason, the principle of causality belongs just as much to the essence of pure reason as that of contradiction, and the approval of reason in relation to that which is consistent is attained through precisely the same empirical consciousness by means of which we perceive that same approval in relation to that which is grounded and purposeful. The one therefore seems to be a fact of pure reason just as much as the other, and as such is capable of serving as the foundation for an imperative of reason. Just as consistent volition and action is to be preferred over inconsistent volition and action, and this consistent volition and action is to be distinguished from merely grounded and purposeful action, so is willing something and acting for a reason, i.e., purposively, to be preferred over willing something and acting without a reason or unpurposively; both of these are a decree, not of reason, for this cannot be immediately determined by our merely empirical consciousness, but of healthy human reason, in the exact same way. If reason's decree should completely apply to us in the one case, then it is appropriate for us to show the same respect for reason in the second case, where it speaks just as loudly. An example would be if circumstances were to arise, such that following only one of the following two maxims would be possible: *fiat iustitia et pereat mundus*,[4] or *salus populi suprema lex esto*.[5] The choice would therefore be left to a population or its regents to either offend against justice or sacrifice communal welfare. [95] A regent may have it in his power to either break a publicly and solemnly given promise or remove his people from their state of well-being and plunge them into the most depraved slavery and limitless misery, whether forever or for an unforeseeable amount of time. What does his duty require of him here? Or rather: what does healthy human reason say here? Should he let his people perish and therefore act against his highest purpose, or break his word? And if he breaks his word and thereby saves his people, would he not, according to the judgement of reason, act better than the dishonest gambler who gets rich by cheating? Would he not have to regard the preservation of his country, brought about by the breaking of his word, as something by means of which he would become disdainful in his own eyes? I doubt very much that, in accordance with the decree of simple

---

[4] *let there be justice even if the world perishes*, cf. 8:378.35
[5] *let the welfare of the people be the supreme law*

human understanding, he would severely punish himself for injuring justice. But let us assume the opposite case: he sacrifices the present and future happiness of his people so that justice can be done. Considering the inevitable objections that he himself, his people, and the world would make to him, as well as the ruins of his fatherland, would he be able to content and justify himself merely by means of saying: 'I have at least followed the maxim that I am able to will as a universal law'? — How the great Fredrick decided this case of conscience cannot be unknown to any reader of his surviving writings.[6] And if nearly all regents and non-regents, if an exception can even be made here, of older and more recent times should agree with this decision, which departs so significantly from the Kantian moral system, then, as a fact, this would at least prove that, even if plain human understanding recognized a difference between right [Recht] and advantage [Nutzen], between action in accordance (consistent) with duty and prudent (purposeful) action, and normally does not approve of conduct where the latter is preferred to the former, there could still be cases (to which the above-mentioned case belongs) where the advantage is so exceedingly large and expansive, the opposing disadvantage so significant and irreplaceable, the need so urgent, so overbearing, that, according to the utterance of precisely this healthy human reason, the person who allows all of this to be outweighed by mere respect for [96] rationally consistent action would, if not in his own eyes then in the eyes of all remaining human beings, appear to be a super-sophistical fantast. It therefore seems to me that it can be rightfully inferred from this fact that it is not only human nature to consider whether or not the maxim one acts in accordance with is consistent, and as such whether it is fit for universal legislation, but also whether one's action is grounded and purposeful or not. And if this is true only as a fact that is grounded in the common sense of truth, then, in my opinion, consideration of the final end or the entire natural predisposition of human beings cannot at all be excluded from the investigation and establishment of that which the human being ought to do or omit, i.e., of that which is right, dutiful, or proper for the human being. Neither can it be claimed that morality is corrupted by means of considering that which is purposeful, nor that a will that considers the purposeful to some degree is thereby made immoral. To my knowledge, this has never been claimed by a philosopher with such severity and generality before **Kant**, and if we exclude the fanatic defenders of the pure love of God, then

---

[6] Frederick II (the Great) was known to prefer the welfare of the people above all else. See e.g., his *Anti-Machiavel* (Frederick 2021, p. 20).

neither has a doctrine of morals ever denied all moral worth to the will that determines itself to action in accordance with the law from regard for the final and highest end of human beings.

We now come to the author's concept of good and evil, or the object and end of the moral law. What the author says about this seems to warrant some remarks as well. The reviewer of the *Groundwork of the Metaphysics of Morals* (*Allgemeine Deutsche Bibliothek*, Band 66, p. 449)[7] has claimed that the investigation of what is moral must begin with the establishment of the concept of the good. The author appears to have taken this into consideration insofar as he attempts to show, in opposition this claim, that, because the highest principle of morality cannot be material but formal, the concept of the good and evil cannot provide or determine the highest moral law, but exactly the opposite, namely that the moral law, which is to be sought out first, allows us to locate the absolute or highest good in that which is the end and object [97] of this law for the very first time. If we were to seek out a highest good in this way and then find that it is nothing other than the proficiency in willing and acting in accordance with reason, i.e., consistently, and if we were to locate virtue in willing and acting in this way, along with the author, then there can be no doubt that virtue should be considered the highest good. Stoic Philosophy came to this same conclusion, in that it made the principle '**act in accordance with nature**' into the highest principle of morality; and this is precisely that which the mentioned reviewer of the [*Groundwork of the*] *Metaphysics of Morals* assumed to be just as formal and not material, when considered carefully. Stoic moral philosophy agrees with the Kantian even with respect to the object and the end of this principle. Virtue is the highest good according to both philosophies; it is only with respect to the second or integral part of the highest good, namely happiness, which both **Kant** and the Stoics include in the highest good, that the two diverge from each other, and this divergence seems primarily to stem from the different concepts they have of happiness. The Stoics notoriously place happiness in the execution of virtue, and seek to identify the two according to the well-known expression *ne putes alium sapiente bonoque beatum*[8] or *sola bona quae honesta*;[9] and as such they needed to provide no special proof that happiness belongs to the highest good or consists in a component part of

---

[7] This is Pistorius himself, but because he published his reviews anonymously, he refers to himself in the third person.
[8] *lest you consider someone other than a good and wise man to be happy.* See Horace (2011), Epistle XVI.
[9] *those things alone are good which are honourable*

it—a proof which they could have in any case easily provided according to their concept of happiness, since they also take the sensible nature of human beings into consideration when establishing their principles of morality and that which belongs to virtue (regardless of it being in permanent subordination to the rational part). For, it is self-evident that the final end of all of human nature, the sensible and rational parts taken together, leads to happiness. But **Kant**—who does not wish to accept the Stoic connection or coalition system, as he also calls it, between virtue and happiness, but claims, on the contrary, that reason and virtue only cause human beings to be worthy of happiness and not to partake in it—must rightly provide the proof that happiness also belongs to the highest good, at the very least as an integral part of it, insofar as it is also an object, need, and therefore also an end of pure practical reason just as much as virtue. [98] If he were to undertake such a proof, it seems that it could be valid for the kind of happiness that is suitable for a pure practical reason, and this is none other than a happiness, by means of which reason's single need and purpose, to have consistent maxims of the will that can pass as a universal legislation of pure intelligences, is satisfied and achieved. If happiness consists in the satisfaction of this single need, in the achievement of this single end and desire, according to Kant's own definition of it, then reason can, in and of itself, strive for no other happiness than the one that results from the fulfillment and satisfaction of its one single need and end. But Kant does not seem to have this kind of happiness in mind, rather he seems to have one in mind that is called happiness in the popular sense, namely one that presupposes sensible needs, drives, and inclinations, and which at least in part arises from the satisfaction of these things. That is, happiness should be, as Kant says, ["]the condition of a rational being, for whom in the whole of its existence everything goes according to wish and will["] [5:124.21–23], which is why it is based on the agreement of nature with the human being's entire end as well as with the essential determining ground of its will. Now, if the connection between this happiness and virtue is not analytic, as both the Stoics and the Epicureans claim (although in different ways), but is, as Kant supposes, synthetic, then one can always still ask: what justifies him in connecting happiness to virtue in the concept of the highest good, or in requiring that a degree of happiness proportionate to the degree of virtue must be included in the highest good, that is, a kind of happiness required not only by the rational but also the sensible nature of human beings? That Kant is calling for the above concept of happiness is clear not only from the above given definition of it, but also from his entire argument against the Stoic coalition system. And if more proofs of this are still needed, then one could, among other things, refer to his claim that self-contentment [Selbstzufriedenheit] and self-approbation [Selbstbilligung] are not quite happiness, as well as to his claim that, in willing, happiness is the object of the good will not insofar as it, happiness, is something pleasant and flattering to the inclinations, but insofar as it is appropriate to virtue, [99] precisely because it is of a mixed nature and would make something into the end of the good will which in fact should not be its end. All of this illustrates clearly enough that the author understands happiness as, in essence, including external well-being and sensible enjoyment. If a happiness of this sort is included in the highest good and is thereby considered to be the object and end of the moral law (even under the restrictions and modifications noted here), then it is obvious that the author takes the current sensible nature of human beings into account when determining the concept of the highest good. This is the case because he also includes that which only the human being's sensible nature demands (external well-being and sensible enjoyment) in the highest good. And now it must seem very inconsistent that he does not likewise consider the sensible nature of human beings when determining the law and the will that is in accordance with the law, and which is supposed to produce the highest good. Accordingly, it must seem as if he demands more from the cause than it could and should possibly achieve; in a word, that he does not adjust his doctrine of happiness and his doctrine of virtue to fit one another, but places them in a striking misrelation and in a kind of disagreement with one another, and that in the doctrine of virtue he appears to be stricter than **Zeno**, and in the doctrine of happiness laxer than Epicurus. The very accurate remark of Herr **Garve** in his comments on **Ferguson's** moral philosophy seems to apply to the present case, namely that it is absurd to assign such goods and enjoyments to virtue as its rightful reward in a future state of life, and in general to assign to virtue the kind of happiness which one here establishes as a **duty** for us to defy and sacrifice for the sake of virtue.[10] This aside, the more we approximate pure morality and absolute freedom or independence from natural necessity, and thereby also independence from the impression of external objects and the charm of sensible pleasures, the more dispensable, the more indifferent, and the more unappealing these things and pleasures become for us; and yet, they are always supposed make up an indispensable ingredient of our happiness once we have reached a very high degree of pure morality? And they are never supposed to be missing insofar as

---

[10] Garve makes this claim on pp. 400–1 of his remarks to Ferguson (see Garve 1772).

impartial reason is said to decree that our highly elevated virtue is to be accorded a happiness that is proportionate to it, [100] that is, a happiness it is worthy of? In this connection one immediately notices that, if external and sensible happiness is always supposed to be included in the kind of happiness that is depicted by the highest good when it is complete, then we must presuppose that the human being always remains a member of the sensible world, and that it follows from this that the human being has to be considered as a sensible being when designing a moral principle and a moral law. Stoic philosophy was safeguarded against this objection of inconsistency by means of the correct relation and the harmony between their doctrine of virtue and their doctrine of happiness, and the Stoics also took the entire nature of the human being into consideration in their doctrine of virtue, both the rational as well as the sensible part. Virtue, for them, consisted not only in justice and in that which is included in it, but also in prudence, moderation, and courage; **prudence**, that is, possible knowledge of and insight into both the nature of things in general as well as human nature in particular, was necessary for the sage primarily in order to distinguish between that which is in the human being's power and that which is not in its power, and also in order to learn, via the cognition of nature, how the will can subdue and reign over nature as much as possible; **moderation**, or the endeavours and attempts to weaken and eventually suppress the inclinations and wishes that the sage recognized as being beyond the reach of human powers; and finally **courage**, or the striving and attempt to endure unavoidable evils and burdens, to acquire an ability to make oneself continually more insensible to them, and to raise oneself above fear and fright, just as moderation and practicing moderation should raise the sage above the appeal of the goods of fortune and the pleasures of sensibility. The doctrine of virtue has an obvious relation to the location of the rational human being in the sensible world and is aimed at bringing it closer to its happiness in precisely those circumstances in which it approximates virtue and its foundational constitution of elevating reason to master over sensibility. And if this virtue is in general attainable for the human being, then neither would it lack the happiness proportional to it. [101]

Finally, there would still be much to note about the so-called postulates of pure reason, but since this article has already turned out to be quite long-winded, I must content myself with adding a few ideas about the postulate of freedom. I note, first, that that which the author says about so-called transcendental freedom does not seem clear to me, but ambiguous. That is, it is ambiguous whether he means freedom of indifference or the kind of freedom the indeterminists call for in opposition to the determinists, or merely that which a Leibnizian philosopher would call absolute freedom. According to the description that he gives of this freedom, he partly calls it an independence from natural necessity or from all influence of external things on the determination of the will, and partly a capacity of practical reason to determine the will by means of its own laws. Because of this, it seems not only not necessary to think of an indeterminate freedom, but one must rather assume the opposite, for the will is always determined and must always be determined, even if not by external things, then by reason and the law that reason prescribes to the will. On the other hand, however, it seems as if the author takes indeterministic freedom to be necessary for the concept and possibility of moral imputation and claims that wherever there is a kind of necessity (which is always contained in the concept of deterministic freedom) absolutely no imputation exists. It could be that he only has a kind of necessity in mind, according to which the will is determined externally but not internally by means of itself, and thus a certain more considerable rational fatalism, and therefore that he is only claiming of the former that, where it is to be found, no imputation could take place. Assuming that the latter is his opinion, none of the human being's actions could be imputed to it insofar and as long as the human being is subjected to natural necessity. And I do not see how one can get out of this situation by attributing an intelligible character to the human being who is subjected to natural necessity, or by simultaneously regarding the human being as both a member of the sensible world and of a world of the understanding, and thus by means of simultaneously attributing transcendental freedom to the human being, by virtue of which it is responsible for its actions. For, [102] one and the same subject cannot possibly possess and express both kinds of freedom at the same time, because they are contradictory and cancel each other out. It is just as incomprehensible that the human being, who is indeed only one person, is supposed to actually possess a double and conflicting character, the sensible and the intelligible, at the same time, as a member of two different worlds, and in reality be made up of two conflicting **selves** [Ichs]. I happily confess that this double character of the human being, these two **selves** in the simple subject, is the most obscure and incomprehensible aspect of the entire critical philosophy, despite all of the explanations that **Kant** himself and his disciples have given of it, and despite all the applications they have made of it, especially in relation to the solution of the notorious antinomy of freedom. I confess that if I were to relate this hypothesis of the double character and the two **selves** in the human being to the common opposition between that which is spiritual and sensible in the human being, or to that which **Paul** calls the law in our mind and in our **body**,[11] or to that which is misleadingly attributed to **Araspes** by **Xenephon** in the *Cyropaedia*,[12] i.e., attributing two souls to oneself, one good and one evil, then this hypothesis seems to be something familiar and understandable, aside from the new terminology. But then I can sufficiently explain neither the solution to the antinomy, nor that which is based on it in the critical philosophy. The idea that the human being is to be regarded as an appearance according to its sensible character or empirical self, and as a thing in itself according to its intelligible character and intelligible self, this could provide me with the necessary light to explain things. For, if I were to regard the human being as a member of the sensible world, along with its actions and its natural necessity, always as an appearance, then it would always remain a morally acting being, its actions would always remain subjected to natural necessity and imputable, and its slavery to natural necessity would not be illusory but real. But if one were to imagine the double character of the human being and its two selves not as existing alongside one another at the same time, but as following upon one another, such that the human being in the sensible world possesses nothing more than the predisposition to become an intelligible character, or the constitution to become a pure intelligence at some point in time, [103] and if what has been noted above is true, then one can assume the following: that the human being approximates this intelligible character and all of the properties and qualities connected to it only in infinitesimal proportions, but will and can never attain it. If the human being were to actually attain this, then it would in fact be raised to the ranks and qualities of a deity, because according to how the properties and qualities of such an intelligence are described, all of the human being's volition and action (since it would no longer be able to act now in one way and then in another, as in the sensible world, and would be subjected to no alteration) would have to become nothing more than a single invariable act of its will (just as one must conceive of this for the infinite, invariable being), and the human being itself would have to be regarded as entirely invariable in relation to every causation of the variation that is ascribed to it.

With all these difficulties, obscurities and, to put it as mildly as possible, apparent contradictions, one can ascribe to the human being no more than a single character, namely the sensible-rational character, only one self, and only one very limited freedom or rational self-activity. But one can assume

---

[11] See Romans 7:23–24.
[12] See Xenophon, *Cyropaedia*, Book 6, Ch 1, 41 (Xenophon 1914, p. 141).

about this freedom that it always becomes less restricted and approximates absolute freedom in an unending progress without ever attaining this, insofar as the human being is to never stop being a finite being. Otherwise one would have to assume that the human being has a freedom that it surely possesses but which it could never use, and which in fact is of no help to the human being because it is still forever subject to natural necessity, such that it is still always determined to actions that are in fact attributed to it, and for which it always remains responsible, even if, after casting off its apparent being and as a pure intelligence it were to be transferred from the sensible and into the world of the understanding. How, then, does this entire distinction help the human being if we can apply to the human being's double character or two-fold self the same answer that the farmer is said to have given his regent, an archbishop: on account of the regent's exaggerated inclination for hunting with dogs, the farmer complained to the regent that it is not fitting for the regent, as a spiritual man, to allow the fields of his subjects to be decimated by a wild animal; [104] the regent replied to the farmer with the objection that the farmer must consider that the regent is not only a spiritual, but also a worldly man; and the farmer answered: "but, noble Sir, if the devil takes the worldly man, where does the spiritual one remain?"

In the end, how are we supposed to conceive of the possibility of the unification of these two characters that are so different in kind in one and the same subject? Is this unification essentially necessary, such that the rational character can be conceived in absolutely no other way than as bound to the sensible character in a finite subject? If this is the case, then they cannot be so opposed to each other such that one can conceive of them as two persons, as two selves in the very same subject; then just as the human being never has been a pure intelligence, so can it also never become one; then the one-of-a-kind abstraction of reason from sensibility, or rather the violent separation of the two that one rightly blames the critical philosophy for doing, cannot at all be justified. If this unification has its ground in an arbitrary design of the deity, and if one does not wish to call upon the claim of the critical philosophy, namely that the ground of the world of appearances, to which the sensibility of the human being belongs, is not to be sought in the deity, in whom only the cause of what is real lies, then we cannot very well comprehend that God wants to rob reason of the freedom characteristic of it by means of voluntarily attaching reason to sensibility, and wants to degrade reason from the autocracy appropriate to it to a slave under a tyrant, who is so unworthy of usurping rule, by means of making it dependent on natural necessity. Finally, if we were to assume that the human being, as pure intelligence, voluntarily united itself with sensibility, this hypothesis would appear similar to the dreams of certain oriental philosophers who alleged that higher spirits fell from their high dignity, made themselves sensible, and made themselves worse, by sinking into earthly bodies; so similar that it would not be worth the trouble to spend one's time analyzing the absurdities of this hypothesis any longer. In fact, the voluntary unification of reason with sensibility would be the first and only sin of humankind: it would be the first sin because all other sins would have their source in this one, and it would be the only sin because all others could be referenced back to this one, [105] in that every other action would take place under the dependence of natural necessity, and as such would no longer be imputable. This first sin would therefore have much in common with the so-called fall of man [Sündenfall], only it would be more improbable, because one would have to imagine that it be initiated by every single intelligence and not, like the fall of Adam, be initiated by him alone in order to be passed down to all his descendants or be valid for them all.

By presenting these doubts and uncertainties, the reviewer is content with the fact that they might be slightly disruptive, on account of the fact that he was not successful in clarifying the above aspect of the critical philosophy which he called its greatest mystery. Nevertheless, as much as all these doubts might be founded on misunderstanding, and as little as they might mean in themselves, they would still have some merit if they were to help make the future elucidators and defenders of the critical philosophy aware of this point, and single it out to them as especially requiring their elucidation.

Bibliography

Adelung, Johann Christoph. (1811) *Grammatisch-kritisches Wörterbuch der hochdeutschen Mundart*. 4 vols. Vienna.
Albrecht, Michael. (2015) 'Wizenmann, Thomas,' in *Kant-Lexikon*. Edited by M. Willaschek, J. Stozlenberg, G. Mohr, and S. Bacin. Berlin/Boston: De Gruyter, pp. 2677–78.
  (2018) 'Wolff an den deutschsprachigen Universitäten,' in *Handbuch Christian Wolff*. Edited by Robert Theis and Alexander Aichele. Wiesbaden: Springer, pp. 427–66.
Allison, Henry E. (1990) *Kant's Theory of Freedom*. Cambridge: Cambridge University Press.
  (2006) 'Kant on Freedom of the Will,' in *The Cambridge Companion to Kant and Modern Philosophy*. Edited by Paul Guyer. Cambridge: Cambridge University Press, pp. 381–415.
  (2011) *Kant's Groundwork for the Metaphysics of Morals: A Commentary*. Oxford: Oxford University Press.
Anonymous. (1776) 'Kurzgefasste Lebensgeschichte Herrn Christian August Crusius,' in *Acta historico-ecclesiastica*. Vol. XVII. Weimar, pp. 970–93.
  (1799) 'Todesfall,' in *Intelligenzblatt der Neuen allgemeinen deutschen Bibliothek*. No. 31. Appendix to Vol. 45, pp. 249–53.
Baum, Manfred. (2020) 'Kant und Ciceros *De officiis*,' in *Kleine Schriften II. Arbeiten zur praktischen Philosophie Kants*. Edited by Dieter Hüning. Berlin/Boston: De Gruyter, pp. 45–56.
Baumgarten, Alexander. (2013) *Metaphysics*. Edited and translated by Courtney D. Fugate and John Hymers. London: Bloomsbury.
  (2020) *Elements of First Practical Philosophy*. Edited and translated by Courtney D. Fugate and John Hymers. London: Bloomsbury.
Beck, Lewis White. (1949) 'Introduction,' in *Critique of Practical Reason and Other Writings in Moral Philosophy by Immanuel Kant*. Edited and translated with an Introduction by Lewis White Beck. Chicago: University of Chicago Press, pp. 1–49.
  (1960) *A Commentary on Kant's Critique of Practical Reason*. Chicago: University of Chicago Press.
  (Ed.) (1966) *Eighteenth-Century Philosophy*. New York: Free Press.

Beiser, Frederick C. (1987) *The Fate of Reason: German Philosophy from Kant to Fichte*. Cambridge, MA: Harvard University Press.

(2020) 'August Wilhelm Rehberg.' *The Stanford Encyclopedia of Philosophy* (Spring 2020 Edition). Edited by Edward N. Zalta. https://plato.stanford.edu/archives/spr2020/entries/august-rehberg/

Biller, Gerhard. (2018) 'Biographie und Bibliographie,' in *Handbuch Christian Wolff*. Edited by Robert Theis and Alexander Aichele. Wiesbaden: Springer, pp. 5–32.

Birken-Bertsch, Hanno. (2015) 'Feder, Johann Georg Heinrich,' in *Kant-Lexikon*. Edited by M. Willaschek, J. Stozlenberg, G. Mohr, and S. Bacin. Berlin/Boston: De Gruyter, pp. 602–3.

Bittner, Rüdiger and Cramer, Konrad. (Eds.) (1975) *Materialien zu Kants 'Kritik der praktischen Vernunft.'* Frankfurt am Main: Suhrkamp.

Böning, Holder. (2016) 'Rehberg, August Wilhelm,' in *The Bloomsbury Dictionary of Eighteenth-Century German Philosophers*. Edited by Heiner F. Klemme and Manfred Kuehn. London: Bloomsbury, pp. 605–8.

Campe, Joachim Heinrich. (1801) *Wörterbuch zur Erklärung und Verdeutschung der unserer Sprache aufgedrungenen fremden Ausdrücke*, 2 vols. Braunschweig.

Chance, Brian A. and Pasternack, Lawrence. (2018) 'Rational Faith and the Pantheism Controversy: Kant's "Orientation Essay" and the Evolution of His Moral Argument,' in *Kant and His German Contemporaries*. Volume 2. Edited by Daniel O. Dahlstrom Cambridge: Cambridge University Press, pp. 195–214.

Chignell, Andrew. (2007) 'Belief in Kant.' *The Philosophical Review* 116(3), pp. 323–60.

Clewis, Robert R. (2018) 'The Feeling of Enthusiasm,' in *Kant and the Faculty of Feeling*. Edited by K. Sorensen and D. Williamson. Cambridge: Cambridge University Press, pp. 184–207.

Crusius, Christian August. (1744) *Anweisung vernünftig zu leben*. Leipzig.

(1745) *Entwurf der nothwendigen Vernunft-Wahrheiten*. Leipzig.

(1747) *Weg zur Gewißheit und Zuverläßigkeit der menschlichen Erkenntniß*. Leipzig.

(1749) *Anleitung über natürliche Begebenheiten ordentlich and vorsichtig nachzudenken*, 2 vols. Leipzig.

(1752) *Epistola ad perillustrem et generosissimum dominum Ioannem Ernestum L. B. ab Hardenberg [...] De summis rationis principiis*. Leipzig.

(1964ff.) *Die philosophischen Hauptwerke*, 4 vols. Edited by Giorgio Tonelli. Hildesheim: Olms.

Di Giovanni, George. (2005) *Freedom and Religion in Kant and His Immediate Successors: The Vocation of Humankind, 1774–1800*. Cambridge: Cambridge University Press.

Dyck, Corey. (forthcoming) 'Kant's Canon, Garve's Cicero, and the Stoic Doctrine of the Highest Good.'

(Ed. and Trans.) (2019) *Early Modern German Philosophy (1690–1750)*. Oxford: Oxford University Press.

Eberhard, Johann August. (1781) *Sittenlehre der Vernunft*. Berlin: Nicolai.
Epstein, Klaus. (1966) *The Genesis of German Conservatism*. Princeton: Princeton University Press.
Feder, Johann Georg Heinrich. (1765) *Homo Natura non ferus. Dissertatio philosophica sectionem secundam*. Erlangen.
  (1767) *Grundriß der Philosophischen Wissenschaften nebst der nöthigen Geschichte*. Coburg.
  (1769) *Logik und Metaphysik, nebst der Philosophischen Geschichte im Grundrisse*. Göttingen and Gotha.
  (1770) *Lehrbuch der Praktischen Philosophie*. Göttingen.
  (1779–86) *Untersuchungen über den menschlichen Willen, dessen Naturtriebe, Veränderlichkeit, Verhältniß zur Tugend und Glückseligkeit und die Grundregeln, die menschlichen Gemüther zu erkennen und zu regieren*, 4 vols. Göttingen and Lemgo.
  (1782) *Grundlehren zur Kenntniß des menschlichen Willens und der natürlichen Gesetze des Rechtverhaltens*. Göttingen.
  (1787) *Über Raum und Caussalität zur Prüfung der Kantischen Philosophie*. Göttingen.
  (1788). 'Critik der praktischen Vernunft. Von Immanuel Kant.' *Philosophische Bibliothek*. 1. Band, pp. 182–218.
  (2018). 'Immanuel Kant: Kritik der praktischen Vernunft,' in *Ausgewählte Schriften*. Edited by Hans-Peter Nowitzki, Udo Roth, and Gideon Stiening. Berlin/Boston: De Gruyter, pp. 228–41.
Feder, J.G.H. and Meiners, C. (Eds.) (1790) *Philosophische Bibliothek*. 3. Band. Göttingen.
Franz, Michael. (2005) 'Johann Friedrich Flatt als Professor der Philosophie in Tübingen (1785–1792),' in *"... im Reiche des Wissens cavalieremente"? Hölderlins, Hegels und Schellings Philosophiestudium an der Universität Tübingen*. Edited by Michael Franz. Tübingen: Hölderlin-Gesellschaft, pp. 535–54.
  (2016) 'Wizenmann, Thomas,' in *The Bloomsbury Dictionary of Eighteenth-Century German Philosophers*. Edited by Heiner F. Klemme and Manfred Kuehn. London: Bloomsbury, pp. 858–59.
Franz, Michael and Bürzele, Ralf. (2005) 'Erläuterungen zu Böks moralphilosophischen Inauguralthesen (1790–1792),' in *"... im Reiche des Wissens cavalieremente"? Hölderlins, Hegels und Schellings Philosophiestudium an der Universität Tübingen*. Edited by Michael Franz. Tübingen: Hölderlin-Gesellschaft, pp. 128–57.
Frederick the Great. (2021) *Philosophical Writings*. Edited by Avi Lifschitz, translated by Angela Scholar. Princeton: Princeton University Press.
Garve, Christian. (1766) *Dissertatio de nonnullis, quae pertinent ad Logicam probabilium*. Halle.
  (1768) *De ratione scribendi historiam Philosophiae*. Leipzig.
  (1772) *Adam Fergusons Grundsätze der Moralphilosophie*. Uebersetzt und mit einigen Anmerkungen versehen. Leipzig.

(1783) 'Critique of Pure Reason by Immanuel Kant.' *Allgemeine Deutsche Bibliothek*, Supplement to Volumes 37–52, Part II, pp. 838–62.
(1787) (Trans.) *Abhandlung über die menschlichen Pflichten in drey Büchern.* By Marcus Tullius Cicero. Breslau.
(1787–88) *Philosophische Anmerkungen und Abhandlungen zu Cicero's Büchern von den Pflichten*, 3 vols. Breslau.
(1792) *Versuche über verschiedene Gegenstände aus der Moral, der Litteratur und dem gesellschaftlichen Leben.* Breslau.
(1798) *Uebersicht der vornehmsten Principien der Sittenlehre, von dem Zeitalter des Aristoteles an bis auf unsre Zeiten.* Breslau.
(1800) 'Über die Gränzen des bürgerlichen Gehorsams, in Beziehung auf den Auffsatz von Kant über den Gemeinspruch: das mag in der Theorie richtig seyn, taugt aber nicht für die Praxis,' in *Vermischte Aufsätze*. 2. Band, pp. 389–427.

Gawlick, Günter, Kreimendahl, Lothar, and Stark, Werner. (Eds.) (2019) *Neue Reflexionen: Die frühen Notate zu Baumgartens "Metaphysica"* by Immanuel Kant. Stuttgart Bad-Canstatt: fromann-holzboog.

Gesang, Bernward. (2016). 'Pistorius, Hermann Andreas,' in *The Bloomsbury Dictionary of Eighteenth-Century German Philosophers*. Edited by Heiner F. Klemme and Manfred Kuehn. London: Bloomsbury, pp. 589–91.

(Ed.) (2007) *Kants vergessener Rezensent: Die Kritik der theoretischen und praktischen Philosophie Kants in fünf Rezensionen von Hermann Andreas Pistorius*. Hamburg: Meiner.

Gilbert, Carlos Melches. (1994) *Der Einfluß von Christian Garves Übersetzung Ciceros "De officiis" auf Kants "Grundlegung zur Metaphysik der Sitten."* Regensburg: S. Roderer.

Goy, Ina. (2015) 'Kritik der praktischen Vernunft,' in *Kant-Lexikon*. Edited by M. Willaschek, J. Stozlenberg, G. Mohr, and S. Bacin. Berlin/Boston: De Gruyter, pp. 1315–23.

Gregor, Mary J. (1996) '*Critique of Practical Reason*: Introduction,' in *Practical Philosophy by Immanuel Kant*. Edited and translated by Mary J. Gregor. Cambridge: Cambridge University Press, pp. 135–36.

Gregory, Michael L. (2021) 'A.W. Rehberg, "On the Relationship between theory and Practice."' *British Journal for the History of Philosophy* 29(6), pp. 1166–76.

(2022) 'Kant and Rehberg on Political Theory and Practice.' *British Journal for the History of Philosophy* 30(4), pp. 566–88.

Grimm, Jacob and Wilhelm. (2023) *Deutsches Wörterbuch von Jacob Grimm und Wilhelm Grimm*. Digitalisierte Fassung im *Wörterbuchnetz des Trier Center for Digital Humanities*, Version 01/23. www.woerterbuchnetz.de/DWB

Grote, Simon. (2023) 'Wolffianism and Pietism in Eighteenth-Century German Philosophy.' *Intellectual History Review* 33(4), pp. 673–701.

Grunert, Frank, Hahmann, Andree, and Stiening, Gideon. (Eds.) (2021) *Christian August Crusius (1715–1775): Philosophy between Reason and Revelation*. Berlin/Boston: De Gruyter.

Guyer, Paul. (2000) 'Editor's Introduction,' in *Critique of the Power of Judgment*. By Immanuel Kant. Edited by Paul Guyer, translated by Paul Guyer and Eric Matthews. Cambridge: Cambridge University Press, pp. xiii–lii.

(2021) 'The Original Empty Formalism Objection,' in *Practical Philosophy from Kant to Hegel*. Edited by James A. Clarke and Gabriel Gottlieb. Cambridge: Cambridge University Press, pp. 10–27.

(forthcoming) *The Impact of Kant's Moral Philosophy*. Oxford: Oxford University Press.

Häckermann, Adolf. (1888) 'Pistorius', in *Hermann Andreas' in Allgemeine Deutsche Biographie* 26, pp. 194–96. www.deutsche-biographie.de/pnd120198851.html#adbcontent

Hamann, Johann Georg. (1959) *Briefwechsel*. Vierter Band: 1778–82. Edited by Arthur Henkel. Wiesbaden: Insel.

(1965) *Briefwechsel*. Fünfter Band: 1783–85. Edited by Arthur Henkel. Wiesbaden: Insel.

(1975) *Briefwechsel*. Sechster Band: 1785–86. Edited by Arthur Henkel. Wiesbaden: Insel.

(1979) *Briefwechsel*. Siebter Band: 1786–88. Edited by Arthur Henkel. Wiesbaden: Insel.

Hanley, Ryan Patrick. (2020) *The Political Philosophy of Fénelon*. Oxford: Oxford University Press.

Hartley, David. (1772–73) *Betrachtungen über den Menschen*, 2 vols. Rostock and Leipzig: Koppe.

(1791) *Observations on Man [. . .] To which are now added Notes and Additions to the second part; translated from the German of the Rev. Herman Andrew Pistorius, Rector of the Poseritz in the Island of Rugen*. London.

Hatfield, Gary. (2002) 'Translator's Introduction [to the *Prolegomena*],' in *Theoretical Philosophy after 1781* by Immanuel Kant. Edited by Henry Allison and Peter Heath, translated by Gary Hatfield, Michael Friedman, Henry Allison, and Peter Heath. Cambridge: Cambridge University Press, pp. 31–47.

(2004) 'Introduction,' in *Prolegomena to Any Future Metaphysics That Will Be Able to Come Forward as Science*. Edited and translated by Gary Hatfield. Cambridge: Cambridge University Press, pp. ix–xxxiv.

Heinze, Max. (1898) 'Wizenmann, Thomas,' in *Allgemeine Deutsche Biographie* 43, pp. 678–80. www.deutsche-biographie.de/pnd117446122.html#adbcontent

Henrich, Dieter. (Ed.) (1967) *Kant. Gentz. Rehberg: Über Theorie und Praxis*. Frankfurt am Main: Suhrkamp.

Höffe, Otfried. (Ed.) (1993) *Grundlegung zur Metaphysik der Sitten: Ein kooperativer Kommentar*, 2nd ed. Frankfurt am Main: Klostermann.

Hogan, Des. (2013) 'Metaphysical Motives of Kant's Analytic-Synthetic Distinction.' *Journal of the History of Philosophy* 51(2), pp. 267–307.

(2016) 'Crusius, Christian August,' in *The Bloomsbury Dictionary of Eighteenth-Century German Philosophers*. Edited by Heiner F. Klemme and Manfred Kuehn. London: Bloomsbury, pp. 149–54.

Horace (2011) *Satires and Epistles*. Translated by John Davie. Oxford: Oxford University Press.

Hume, David. (1754–56) *Vermischte Schriften*, 4 vols. Hamburg and Leipzig.

Jacobi, F.H. (1785) *Ueber die Lehre des Spinoza in Briefen an den Herrn Moses Mendelssohn*. Breslau: Löwe [2nd ed. 1789].

   (1789) *Ueber die Lehre des Spinoza in Briefen an den Herrn Moses Mendelssohn*. Neue vermehrte Ausgabe. Breslau: Löwe.

Kant, Immanuel. (1786) 'Was heißt: sich im Denken orientieren?' *Berlinische Monatsschrift*. 8. Band, October, pp. 304–30.

   (1793) 'Über den Gemeinspruch: Das mag in der Theorie richtig sein, taugt aber nicht für die Praxis.' *Berlinische Monatsschrift*. Band 22, September, pp. 201–84.

   (1900ff.) *Gesammelte Schriften*. Vols. 1–22 edited by Preussische Akademie der Wissenschaften, Vol. 23 edited by Deutsche Akademie der Wissenschaften zu Berlin, Vols. 24ff. edited by Akademie der Wissenschaften zu Göttingen. Berlin.

   (1968) *Über den Gemeinspruch: Das mag in der Theorie richtig sein, taugt aber nicht für die Praxis*. Edited by Julius Ebbinghaus. Frankfurt am Main: Klostermann.

   (1992) *Über den Gemeinspruch: Das mag in der Theorie richtig sein, taugt aber nicht für die Praxis. Zum ewigen Frieden: Ein philosophischer Entwurf*. Edited with an Introduction by Heiner F. Klemme. Hamburg: Meiner.

   (1996a) *Religion and Rational Theology*. Edited and translated by Allen W. Wood and George Di Giovanni. Cambridge: Cambridge University Press.

   (1996b) *Practical Philosophy*. Edited and translated by Mary J. Gregor. Cambridge: Cambridge University Press.

   (1999) *Was ist Aufklärung? Ausgewählte kleine Schriften*. Edited by Horst D. Brandt with an Introduction by Ernst Cassirer. Hamburg: Meiner.

   (2004) *Prolegomena to Any Future Metaphysics*. Edited and translated by Gary Hatfield. Revised ed. Cambridge: Cambridge University Press.

   (2011) *Groundwork of the Metaphysics of Morals*. Edited and translated by Mary Gregor and Jens Timmermann. Cambridge: Cambridge University Press.

Kertscher, Hans Joachim. (2018) *"Er brachte Licht und Ordnung in die Welt": Christian Wolff – eine Biographie*. Halle: Mitteldeutscher Verlag.

Kertscher, Hans Joachim and Stöckmann, Ernst. (Eds.) (2012) *Ein Antipode Kants? Johann August Eberhard im Spannungsfeld von spätaufklärerischer Philosophie und Theologie*. Berlin/Boston: De Gruyter.

Klemme, Heiner F. (2000) 'Introduction,' in *The Reception of the Scottish Enlightenment in Germany*. Volume 1: *Philosophische Versuche über die menschliche Erkenntniss*. Edited by Johann Georg Sulzer. Bristol: Thoemmes Press, pp. v–xii.

   (2003) 'Einleitung,' in *Kritik der praktischen Vernunft* by Immanuel Kant. Edited by Horst D. Brandt and Heiner Klemme. Hamburg: Meiner, pp. ix–lxiii.

(2006) 'Praktische Gründe und moralische Motivation. Eine deontologische Perspektive,' in *Moralische Motivation: Kant und die Alternativen*. Edited by H. F. Klemme and M. Kuehn. Hamburg: Meiner, pp. 113–53.

(2010) 'The Origin and Aim of Kant's *Critique of Practical Reason*,' in *Kant's Critique of Practical Reason: A Critical Guide*. Edited by Andrews Reath and Jens Timmermann. Cambridge: Cambridge University Press, pp. 11–30.

(2021) 'Critique of Practical Reason,' in *The Cambridge Kant Lexicon*. Edited by Julian Wuerth. Cambridge: Cambridge University Press, pp. 640–50.

Kraus, Hans-Christof. (2003) 'Rehberg, August Wilhelm,' in *Neue Deutsche Biographie* 21, pp. 277–78. www.deutsche-biographie.de/pnd118743872.html#ndbcontent

Kuehn, Manfred. (2001) *Kant: A Biography*. Cambridge: Cambridge University Press.

(2009) 'Ethics and Anthropology in the Development of Kant's Moral Philosophy,' in *Kant's Groundwork of the Metaphysics of Morals: A Critical Guide*. Edited by Jens Timmermann. Cambridge: Cambridge University Press, pp. 7–28.

(2010) 'Kant's *Metaphysics of Morals*: The History and Significance of its Deferral,' in *Kant's Metaphysics of Morals: A Critical Guide*. Edited by Lara Denis. Cambridge: Cambridge University Press, pp. 9–27.

Kühlmann, Wilhelm. (2009) *Facetten der Aufklärung in Baden: Johann Peter Hebel und die Karlsruher Lateinische Gesellschaft*. Freiburg: Rombach.

Küttner, C.G. and Williamson, N. (1805–13) *New and Complete Dictionary of the German Language for Englishmen According to the German Dictionary of Mr. J.C. Adelung*, 3 vols. Leipzig.

Lambert, Johann Heinrich. (1764) *Neues Organon*. 1. Band. Leipzig: Wendler.

Landau, Albert. (Ed.) (1991) *Rezensionen zur Kantischen Philosophie: 1781–87*. Bebra: Albert Landau Verlag.

Liebmann, Otto. (1894) 'Tittel, Gottlieb August,' in *Allgemeine Deutsche Biographie* 38, p. 382. www.deutsche-biographie.de/pnd117727741.html#adbcontent

Locke, John. (1975) *An Essay Concerning Human Understanding*. Edited by Peter H. Nidditch. Oxford: Clarendon Press.

Mbuyi, Mukendi. (2001) *Kants Tübinger Kritiker: Die Kritik von Johann Friedrich Flatt an Kants moralischen Argument für die Annahme Gottes*. Aachen: Shaker.

Mendelssohn, Moses. (1785) *Morgenstunden oder Vorlesungen über das Daseyn Gottes*. Berlin: Voß und Sohn.

(1786) *An die Freunde Lessings. Ein Anhang zu Herrn Jacobi Briefwechsel über die Lehre des Spinoza*. Berlin: Voß und Sohn.

Morrison, James C. (Trans.) (1995) *Exposition of Kant's Critique of Pure Reason* by Johann Schultz. Ottawa: University of Ottawa Press.

Müller, Kurt. (1961) 'Feder, Georg Heinrich,' in *Neue Deutsche Biographie* 5, pp. 41–42. www.deutsche-biographie.de/pnd100796923.html#ndbcontent

Natorp, Paul. (1913) 'Kritik der praktischen Vernunft: Einleitung,' in *Kant's Gesammelte Schriften*. Edited by the Königlich Preußischen Akademie der Wissenschaften. Band V. Berlin: Reimer, pp. 489–98.

Noller, Jörg and Walsh, John. (Eds.) (2022) *Kant's Early Critics on Freedom of the Will*. Cambridge: Cambridge University Press.
Nowitzki, Hans-Peter. (2011) 'Denken – Sprechen – Handeln. Johann Georg Sulzers semiotische Fundierung der *Allgemeinen Theorie der Schönen Künste*,' in *Johann Georg Sulzer (1720–1779): Aufklärung zwischen Christian Wolff und David Hume*. Edited by Frank Grunert and Gideon Stiening. Berlin/Boston: De Gruyter, pp. 137–68.
Nowitzki, H.P., Roth, U., and Stiening, G. (Eds.) (2018) *Johann Georg Heinrich Feder (1740–1821): Empirismus und Popularphilosophie zwischen Wolff und Kant*. Berlin/Boston: De Gruyter.
Oz-Salzburger, Fania. (1995) *Translating the Enlightenment: Scottish Civic Discourse in Eighteenth-Century Germany*. Oxford: Oxford University Press.
Pältz, Eberhard H. (1961) 'Flatt, Johann Friedrich,' in *Neue Deutsche Biographie 5*, pp. 223–24. www.deutsche-biographie.de/pnd115612408.html#ndbcontent
Pistorius, Hermann Andreas. (1784) 'Prolegomena zu einer jeden künftigen Metaphysik, von Immanuel Kant.' *Allgemeine deutsche Bibliothek*. 59. Band, 2. Stück, pp. 322–56.
  (1786a) 'Erläuterungen über des Herrn Professor Kant Critik der reinen Vernunft von Joh. Schulze, Königl. Preußischen Hofprediger.' *Allgemeine deutsche Bibliothek*. 66. Band, 1. Stück, pp. 92–123.
  (1786b). 'Grundlegung zur Metaphysik der Sitten von Immanuel Kant.' *Allgemeine deutsche Bibliothek*. 66. Band, 2. Stück, pp. 447–63.
  (1788a) 'Critic der reinen Vernunft von Immanuel Kant. Zweyte Auflage.' *Allgemeine deutsche Bibliothek*. 81. Band, 2. Stück, pp. 343–54.
  (1788b) 'Prüfung der Mendelssohnschen Morgenstunden von Ludwig Heinrich Jakob. Nebst einer Abhandlung vom Herrn Professor Kant.' *Allgemeine deutsche Bibliothek*. 82. Band, 2. Stück, pp. 427–70.
  (1794) 'Kritik der praktischen Vernunft, von Immanuel Kant.' *Allgemeine Deutsche Bibliothek*. 117. Band, 1. Stück, pp. 78–105.
Raupp, Werner. (2016) 'Flatt, Johann Friedrich,' in *The Bloomsbury Dictionary of Eighteenth-Century German Philosophers*. Edited by Heiner F. Klemme and Manfred Kuehn. London: Bloomsbury, pp. 219–20.
Reath, Andrews. (2015) 'Introduction,' in *Critique of Practical Reason* by Immanuel Kant. Edited and translated by Mary Gregor. Cambridge: Cambridge University Press, pp. vii–xxxiv.
Rehberg, August Wilhelm. (1780) *Cato oder Gespräche über die Bestimmung des Menschen*. Basel.
  (1785) *Philosophische Gespräche über das Vergnügen*. Nuremberg.
  (1787) *Über das Verhältnis der Metaphysik zu der Religion*. Berlin.
  (1788a) 'Kritik der praktischen Vernunft, von Immanuel Kant.' *Allgemeine Literatur Zeitung*. 3. Band, Numbers 188a and 188b, Wednesday, August 6, columns 345–60.
  (1788b) Review of Herder: *Gott. Einige Gespräche. Allgemeine Literatur-Zeitung*. 1. Band, Number 2a, pp. 9–16.

(1788c) Review of Jacobi: *David Hume über den Glauben. Allgemeine Literatur-Zeitung.* 2. Band, Number 92, pp. 105–12.
(1791) Review of Reinhold: *Beyträge zur Berichtigung bisheriger Mißverständnisse der Philosophen. Allgemeine Literatur-Zeitung.* Band 1, Number 26–27, pp. 201–14.
(1793) *Untersuchungen über die französische Revolution nebst kritischen Nachrichten von den merkwürdigsten Schriften welche darüber in Frankreich erschienen sind*, 2 vols. Hanover and Osnabrück.
(1794) 'Über das Verhältnis der Theorie zur Praxis.' *Berlinische Monatsschrift* 23, pp. 114–43.
(1826) *Zur Geschichte des Königreichs Hannover in den ersten Jahren nach der Befreiung von der westfälischen und französischen Herrschaft*. Göttingen.
(1828–31) *Sämmtliche Schriften*. Vols. 1, 2, and 4. Hanover.
Reich, Klaus (1939) 'Kant and Greek Ethics (II).' (Translated by W. H. Walsh) *Mind* 48, pp. 337–54.
Reinhold, Karl Leonhard. (1792) *Brief über die Kantische Philosophie*. Zweyter Band. Leipzig.
Rivero, Gabriel. (2021) 'Dependence and Obedience: Crusius' Concept of Obligation and its Influence on Kant's Moral Philosophy,' in *Christian August Crusius (1715–1775): Philosophy between Reason and Revelation*. Edited by Frank Grunert, Andree Hahmann, and Gideon Stiening. Berlin/Boston: De Gruyter, pp. 301–18.
Roth, Udo and Stiening, Gideon. (Eds.) (2021) *Christian Garve (1742–1798): Philosoph und Philologe der Aufklärung*. Berlin/Boston: De Gruyter.
Rumore, Paola. (2018) 'Kant and Crusius on the Role of Immortality in Morality,' in *Kant and His German Contemporaries*. Volume 1. Edited by Corey Dyck and Falk Wunderlich. Cambridge: Cambridge University Press, pp. 213–31.
Sala, Giovanni B. (2004) *Kants "Kritik der praktischen Vernunft": Ein Kommentar*. Darmstadt: Wissenschaftliche Buchgesellschaft.
Saring, Hans. (1957) 'Crusius, Christian August,' in *Neue Deutsche Biographie* 3, pp. 432–33. www.deutsche-biographie.de/pnd118677438.html#ndbcontent
Sassen, Brigitte. (Ed. and Trans.) (2000) *Kant's Early Critics: The Empiricist Critique of the Theoretical Philosophy*. Cambridge: Cambridge University Press.
Schierbaum, Sonja, Walschots, Michael, and Walsh, John. (Eds.) (2024) *Christian Wolff's German Ethics: New Essays*. Oxford: Oxford University Press.
Schneewind, J.B. (1998) *The Invention of Autonomy*. Cambridge: Cambridge University Press.
(Ed.) (2003) *Moral Philosophy from Montaigne to Kant*. Cambridge: Cambridge University Press.
Schultz, Johann. (1771) 'Review of Kant's Inaugural Dissertation,' in *Königsbergsche Gelehrte und Politische Zeitungen*, November, pp. 22–25.
(1784) *Erläuterungen über des Herrn Professor Kant Critik der reinen Vernunft*. Königsberg: Dengel.

(1789/1792) *Prüfung der Kantischen Critik der reinen Vernunft*, 2 vols. Königsberg.
Schulz, Eberhard Günter. (1975) *Rehbergs Opposition gegen Kants Ethik*. Marburg: Symon.
Schwaiger, Clemens. (2016) 'Wolff, Christian,' in *The Bloomsbury Dictionary of Eighteenth-Century German Philosophers*. Edited by Heiner F. Klemme and Manfred Kuehn. London: Bloomsbury, pp. 862–67.
Specht, Andrew. (2014) 'F. A. Trendelenburg and the Neglected Alternative.' *British Journal for the History of Philosophy* 22(3), pp. 514–34.
Stang, Nicholas F. (2022) 'Kant's Transcendental Idealism,' in *The Stanford Encyclopedia of Philosophy* (Spring 2022 Edition), Edward N. Zalta (ed.). https://plato.stanford.edu/archives/spr2022/entries/kant-transcendental-idealism/
Stern, Albert. (1884) *Über die Beziehungen Chr. Garve's zu Kant*. Leipzig.
Thiel, Udo. (2016) 'Feder, Johann Georg Heinrich,' in *The Bloomsbury Dictionary of Eighteenth-Century German Philosophers*. Edited by Heiner F. Klemme and Manfred Kuehn. London: Bloomsbury, pp. 204–8.
Thomas, Andreas. (2016) 'Tittel, Gottlob August,' in *The Bloomsbury Dictionary of Eighteenth-Century German Philosophers*. Edited by Heiner F. Klemme and Manfred Kuehn. London: Bloomsbury, pp. 792–93.
Thomasius, Christian. (2011) *Institutes of Divine Jurisprudence, with Selections from Foundations of the Law of Nature and Nations*. Edited and translated by Thomas Ahnert. Indianapolis: Liberty Fund.
Timmermann, Jens. (2010) 'Reversal or Retreat? Kant's Deductions of Freedom and Morality,' in *Kant's Critique of Practical Reason: A Critical Guide*. Edited by Andrews Reath and Jens Timmermann. Cambridge: Cambridge University Press, pp. 73–89.
(2019) 'Emerging Autonomy: Dealing with the Inadequacies of the "Canon" of the *Critique of Pure Reason* (1781),' in *The Emergence of Autonomy in Kant's Moral Philosophy*. Edited by S. Bacin and O. Sensen. Cambridge: Cambridge University Press, pp. 102–21.
(2022) *Kant's Will at the Crossroads: An Essay on the Failings of Practical Rationality*. Oxford: Oxford University Press.
Tonelli, Giorgio. (1969) 'Einleitung,' in *Anweisung vernünftig zu leben* by Christian August Crusius. Hildesheim: Olms, pp. vii–lxiv.
Vorländer, Karl. (1951) 'Einleitung,' in *Kritik der praktischen Vernunft* by Immanuel Kant. Edited by Karl Vorländer. Leipzig: Meiner, pp. xi–xlvii.
(1965) 'Einleitung,' in *Grundlegung der Metaphysik der Sitten* by Immanuel Kant. Edited by Karl Vorländer. Hamburg: Meiner, pp. v–xxvii.
Walschots, Michael. (2020) 'Merely a New Formula? G.A. Tittel on Kant's Reform of Moral Science.' *Studi Kantiani* 33, pp. 49–64.
(2021a) 'Kant and Consequentialism in Context: The Second *Critique*'s Response to Pistorius.' *Archiv für Geschichte der Philosophie* 103(2), pp. 313–40.

(2021b) 'Crusius on Freedom of the Will,' in *Christian August Crusius (1715–1775): Philosophy Between Reason and Revelation*. Edited by Frank Grunert and Andree Hahmann. Berlin/Boston: De Gruyter, pp. 189–208.

(2021c) 'Garves Eudämonismus [Garve's Eudaimonism],' in *Christian Garve (1742–1798): Philosopher and Philologist of the Enlightenment*. Edited by F. Grunert and G. Stiening. Berlin/Boston: De Gruyter, pp. 171–82.

(2022) *'Achtung* in Kant and Smith.' Kant-Studien 133(2), pp. 238–68.

Walsh, John. (forthcoming) 'C.C.E. Schmid's Intelligible Fatalism in Context,' in *Carl Christian Erhard Schmid (1761–1812): Spätaufklärung im Spannungsfeld zwischen Leibniz und Kant*. Edited by Marion Heinz and Gideon Stiening. Berlin/Boston: De Gruyter.

Warda, Arthur. (1922) *Kants Bücher*. Berlin: Martin Breslauer.

Watkins, Eric. (2001) 'Kant on Rational Cosmology,' in *Kant and the Sciences*. Edited by Eric Watkins. Oxford: Oxford University Press, pp. 80–90.

(Ed. and Trans.) (2009) *Kant's Critique of Pure Reason: Background Source Materials*. Cambridge: Cambridge University Press.

Willaschek, Marcus. (2010) 'The Primacy of Practical Reason and the Idea of a Practical Postulate,' in *Kant's Critique of Practical Reason: A Critical Guide*. Edited by Andrews Reath and Jens Timmermann. Cambridge: Cambridge University Press, pp. 168–96.

Wizenmann, Thomas. (1782) *Göttliche Entwicklung des Satans durch das Menschengeschlecht*. Dessau: Buchhandlung der Gelehrten.

(1786) *Die Resultate der Jacobischer und Mendelsohnischer Philosophie; kritisch untersucht von einem Freywilligen*. Leipzig: Göschen.

(1787) 'To Herr Professor Kant.' *Deutsches Museum*. 1. Band, 2. Stück, February, pp. 116–56.

Wölfel, Kurt. (1964) 'Garve, Christian,' in *Neue Deutsche Biographie* 6, pp. 77–78. www.deutsche-biographie.de/pnd118537636.html#ndbcontent

Wolff, Christian. (1703) *Philosophia practica universalis, mathematica methodo conscripta*. Leipzig.

(1713) *Vernünfftige Gedanken von den Kräfften des menschlichen Verstandes und ihrem richtigen Gebrauche in Erkänntnis der Wahrheit*. Halle.

(1720a) *Vernünfftige Gedanken von Gott, der Welt und der Seele des Menschen, auch allen Dingen überhaupt*. Halle [2003 – Reprint of the 1751 edition, Hildesheim: Olms].

(1720b) *Vernünfftige Gedanken von der Menschen Thun und Lassen, zu Beförderung ihrer Glückseeligkeit, den Liebhabern der Wahrheit mitgetheilet*. Halle [2006 – Reprint of the third edition from 1728, Hildesheim: Olms].

(1739) *Philosophia practica universalis*. Part I. Verona.

(1770) *Logic, or Rational Thoughts on the Powers of the Human Understanding, with their Use and Application in the Knowledge and Search of Truth*. London: Hawes, Clarke, and Collins.

(2006) *Vernünfftige Gedanken von der Menschen Thun und Lassen, zu Beförderung ihrer Glückseeligkeit*. With an Introduction by Hans Werner

Arndt. Hildesheim: Olms [Reprint of the original fourth edition from 1733 (first edition 1720)].
Wood, Allen W. (2002) 'Preface and Introduction (3–16),' in *Immanuel Kant: Kritik der praktischen Vernunft*. Edited by Otfried Höffe. Berlin: Akademie, pp. 25–42.
  (2006) 'The Supreme Moral Principle,' in *The Cambridge Companion to Kant and Modern Philosophy*. Edited by Paul Guyer. Cambridge: Cambridge University Press, pp. 342–80.
Wunderlich, Falk. (2016) 'Garve, Christian,' in *The Bloomsbury Dictionary of Eighteenth-Century German Philosophers*. Edited by Heiner F. Klemme and Manfred Kuehn. London: Bloomsbury, pp. 246–51.
Xenophon. (1914) *Cyropaedia*. Volume 2. Translated by Walter Miller. London: Macmillan.
Zweig, Arnulf. (2002) 'Albrecht Von Haller: "Uncompleted Poem on Eternity."' *The Philosophical Forum* 33, pp. 304–11.
  (Ed. and Trans.) (1999) *Correspondence* by Immanuel Kant. Cambridge: Cambridge University Press.

Index

a posteriori, 53–54, 74–76, 78–79
a priori, 6, 53–54, 69–71, 75–76, 88–89, 129–30, 203–4, 206–7, 216–17, 259, 264
Allgemeine deutsche Bibliothek, 8, 20, 118, 149, 273
Allgemeine Literatur-Zeitung, 4–5, 7, 227–28

Baumgarten, Alexander, 15, 247
Berlinische Monatsschrift, 226, 246
Biester, Johann Erich, 94, 246

categorical imperative
  in Feder's Review of the *Groundwork*, 210–12
  in Flatt's Review of the *Groundwork*, 86, 91–92
  impossibility of in Pistorius' review of *Groundwork*, 150, 158–64
  in Pistorius' Review of the second *Critique*, 259, 267–68
  in Tittel's commentary on the *Groundwork*, 94, 99–101, 104–17
Critique of Practical Reason (Kant)
  decision to publish as a separate book, 6
  doctrine of rational belief or faith, 166
  God's existence, 166
  the *Groundwork of the Metaphysics of Morals* and, 3–4
  Kant's decision to write, 1–6
  Preface, 149
  as a response to reviews and criticism of *Critique of Pure Reason*, 6–7, 9–10, 121
Critique of Pure Reason (Kant) *see also Elucidations of Herr Professor Kant's Critique of Pure Reason* (Schultz)
  B edition, 5
  book-length commentary on, 9
  inconsistencies with *Groundwork*, 120, 127, 142–45, 147–48
  initial reception, 2
  Kant's intentions for, 1
  references to Wolff, 15–16

  revisions for the second edition, 4–5
  third antinomy, 120, 136–40
Crusius, Christian August *see also Guide to Living Rationally* (Crusius)
  critiques of Wolff, 40–41
  influence on Kant, 41

desire
  Crusius' theory of will and desire, 44–50, 54, 58–63
  in Feder's Review of the second *Critique*, 203, 205–6
  foundational (first) desires in Crusius, 57–63
  in Pistorius' Review of the second *Critique*, 258, 261–63
divine law
  Crusius' definition of, 61–62, 67–71
  in Wolff's *German Ethics*, 27–28, 30

Elucidations of Herr Professor Kant's Critique of Pure Reason (Schultz) *see also* Review of Schultz's *Elucidations* (Pistorius)
  Kant's bias towards moral ideas, 120–21, 136
  the neglected alternative objection, 120, 127–30, 134–35, 140–42
  problem of affection, 120
  space and time as subjective forms of intuition, 120, 130–34
  theory of appearance and truth, 120, 123–27, 135–36
  theory of space and time, 120, 123
  third antinomy, 120, 136–40
  writing of, 119–20
existence
  of both subject and object in Pistorius, 120
  in Feder's Review of the *Groundwork*, 222–24
  of God, 166, 172–73, 239–40
  of God in the second *Critique*, 166
  of God in Wizenmann, 166–67, 172–73, 180–82

293

existence (cont.)
    happiness and the existence of God, 233–34, 242–45
    of non-rational beings, 89
    reason and the demonstration of, 166, 170–77, 180–82
    in Rehberg's Review of the second *Critique*, 239–40

fanaticism
    and blind faith in Wizenmann, 166, 169–70, 172–74, 189
    moral fanaticism, 237–38
    natural thinking contrasted with, 145–47
    reason and the demonstration of existence, 182–83, 185, 244, 272–73
Feder, Johann Georg Heinrich *see also* Review of the *Critique of Practical Reason* (Feder); Review of the *Groundwork* (Feder)
    academic career, 199–200
    as an anti-Kantian, 85, 200–2
    involvement with Garve's review of the first *Critique*, 2
    Tittel's admiration for, 93–94
Flatt, Johann, Friedrich *see also* Review of the *Groundwork* (Flatt)
    academic career, 85
    writings on Kant's philosophy, 85–86
Friedrich Wilhelm I, 14
Friedrich II (Frederick the Great), 14, 225, 247–48

Garve, Christian *see also* 'On Patience' (Garve)
    career, 247–48
    comments on Ferguson's moral philosophy, 275
    influence on Kant, 248
    Kant's response in the 'Theory and Practice' essay, 246–47, 249
    review of the *Critique of Pure Reason*, 2–3, 200, 248
    translation of Cicero, 3
    writings on Kant's philosophy, 249
German Ethics (Wolff)
    atheism, 25–26
    bliss of human beings, 32–34, 38
    civil laws, 30
    definition of law, 25
    definition of obligation, 22
    divine law, 25, 27–28, 30
    divine obligation, 27–28, 30, 36
    divine punishments and rewards, 30–31
    free actions of human beings, 18–20, 31–32
    good and evil in human actions, 20–23, 26, 28–31
    on happiness, 34–36
    happiness and observance to the law of nature, 36–39
    the highest good, 32–34
    human law, 25
    law of nature, 25–30, 33–36, 38–39
    philosophy and the Christian religion, 37
    principle of perfection, 23–25, 27
    self-interest and the law of nature, 32
    theory of the good, 19–21
    theory of the will, 18, 21–22
    universal rule for free actions, 23–25
    virtue and vice, 37–39
good and evil
    in Crusius, 48–50, 54, 56
    definition of the concept of good, 149, 152–53
    in Feder's Review of the second *Critique*, 213–15
    in Pistorius' Review of the second *Critique*, 261, 273
    Wolff on good and evil, 20–23, 26, 28–31
    Wolff's theory of the good, 19–21, 32–34
Groundwork of the Metaphysics of Morals
    first *Critique*'s inconsistencies with, 120, 127, 142–45, 147–48
    freedom and moral capacity, 6, 229
    as a preparatory work for the second *Critique*, 3–4, 7
    as a response to Garve, 3
    reviews, 7–9
Guide to Living Rationally (Crusius)
    contingent first desires, 57
    dependence of spirits, 67–68
    desire and aversion, 47–48
    divine law, 61–62, 67–71
    drive of conscience and divine law, 60–63
    drive of perfection, 58–59
    drive of unification with perfection, 59–60
    duties of virtue and prudence, 65–66, 73
    foundational (first) desires, 57–63
    on good and evil, 48–50, 54, 56
    human perfection and happiness, 63–65
    immortality of the soul, 79–82
    imperfect freedom, 55
    innate ideas, 57–58
    intentions or ends, 48
    law of nature, definition, 72
    law of nature within natural theology, 72–73
    obligation of indebtedness, 61–63, 66, 68
    obligation of prudence, 65–66, 73
    obligation of virtue, 65–66, 71–73
    overview of, 41–42
    perfect freedom, 55
    practice of virtue, 78–79
    the soul, 46

the spirit, 45–46
theory on the end of human life, 74–79
theory of freedom, 50–56
theory of will and desire, 44–50, 54, 58–63
universal practical philosophy, 73–74
virtue, definition, 71
virtue as the main end of human life, 77–78
voluntarist theory of ethics, 63–74
the will, definition, 45
the will as distinct from understanding, 46–47
the will and divine natural laws, 63–64

Hamann, Johann Georg, 3, 86
happiness
  divine law and, 64–65
  and the existence of God, 233–34, 242–45
  in Feder's Review of the second *Critique*, 206–8, 212–13, 219–21
  in Flatt's Review of the *Groundwork*, 89–91
  guide to living rationally and, 64–65
  as the highest good in Pistorius, 258, 263–66, 273–76
  instinctual happiness vs happiness from reason, 150, 153–54
  and moral virtue, 251–54
  and the principle of perfection in Crusius, 63–65
  as the sole end for human beings, 206–8, 212–13, 219–21, 251–54
  Stoic concepts of, 104, 232–33, 237, 264–65, 273–74
  in Tittel's commentary of the *Groundwork*, 110–11, 114
Hartley, David, 118–19
Hume, David, 118, 127, 225

Jacobi, Friedrich Heinrich, 86, 165–68, 170–72
Jakob, Ludwig Heinrich, 7–8, 94
Jenisch, Daniel, 149

Lange, Joachim, 13–14
law of nature
  Crusius' definition of, 72
  happiness and observance to the law of nature, 36–39
  natural moral theology and, 72–73
  self-interest and the law of nature, 32
  in Wolff, 25–30, 33–36, 38–39
Leibniz, Gottfried Wilhelm, 13, 139–41, 225
Lessing, G. E., 165–66
Locke, John, 93–94, 101, 200

Meiners, Christoph, 85
Mendelssohn, Moses, 2, 165–66, 170–72, 174–76, 185–86

morality
  duty and morality's basis in pure reason, 101–4, 111, 115–17
  freedom and moral capacity in *Groundwork*, 6, 229
  Kant's moral philosophy in Garve's 'On Patience,' 248, 251–54
  moral fanaticism, 237–38
  the moral law, 213, 216–18
  natural moral theology, 72–73
  Pistorius on Kant's bias towards moral ideas, 120–21, 136
  principle of morality, 220–21, 223–24
  pure practical reason and morality, 234–41, 258–61, 266–67

Nicolai, Friedrich, 118
noumena, 126, 128–29, 138, 235, 239–40

obligation
  divine obligation in Crusius, 61–63
  divine obligation in Wolff, 27–28, 30, 36
  obligations of indebtedness in Crusius, 62–63, 66, 68
  of prudence in Crusius, 65–66, 73
  of virtue in Crusius, 65–66, 71–73
  Wolff's definition of obligation, 22
On Herr Kant's Reform of Moral Science (Tittel)
  the categorical imperative, 94, 99–101, 104–17
  duty and morality's basis in pure reason, 101–4, 111, 115–17
  as the first book length commentary, 9
  good will and the principle of happiness, 110–11, 114
  humanity as the end, 109–11
  the imperative of prudence, 105–6
  the imperative of skill, 105
  importance of motive of duty for duty's sake, 94, 104
  Kant's consequentialism, 94
  Kant's empirical principles, 114
  Kant's knowledge of, 94–95
  Kant's mysticism, 94, 104
  reason-inclination contradiction, 108–9
  Tittel's introduction to the reader, 96–97
  the universally legislating will, 111–13, 117
'On Patience' (Garve)
  aims of, 246–49
  causes and aids of patience, 250
  footnote on Kant's moral philosophy, 246–48, 251–54
'Orientation' essay, 9, 166–67

pantheism controversy
  and the 'Orientation' essay, 9, 166–67
  overview of, 165–66
  Rehberg's writing on, 226
  Wizenmann's *Results* and the pantheism controversy, 9, 165–67, 169–72
Pietism, 13–14, 41
Pistorius, Hermann Andreas *see also* Review of Schultz's *Elucidations* (Pistorius); Review of the *Critique of Practical Reason* (Pistorius); Review of the *Groundwork* (Pistorius)
principle of perfection
  human perfection and happiness in Crusius, 63–65
  in Rehberg's Review of the second *Critique*, 242
  Wolff's principle of perfection, 23–25, 27
Prolegomena
  critique of Crusius, 41
  on Hume's principle of reason, 127
  initial reception, 2–3, 7
  Pistorius' criticism of, 123
prudence
  in Flatt's Review of the *Groundwork*, 89–90
  the imperative of prudence, 105–6
  obligation of prudence, 65–66, 73

reason
  in Crusius' guide to living rationally, 63
  and the demonstration of existence, 166, 170–77, 180–82
  duty and morality's basis in pure reason, 101–4, 111, 115–17
  and the highest good, 180–81, 207–8, 213, 215–16, 221–22, 232–33
  instinctual happiness vs happiness from reason, 150, 153–54
  pure practical reason and morality, 234–41, 258–61, 266–67
  reason-inclination contradiction, 108–9
  Wizenmann on the nature of reason, 183–95
Rehberg, August Wilhelm *see also* Review of the *Critique of Practical Reason* (Rehberg)
  career, 118–19, 225–26
  engagement with Kant's philosophy, 226–27
  pantheism controversy, 226
Reinhold, Karl Leonhard, 226–27
Religion within the Boundaries of Mere Reason (Kant), 246
Review of the *Critique of Practical Reason* (Feder)
  a priori cognition, 203–4, 206–7
  the faculty of desire, 203, 205–6
  happiness as the highest good, 206–8, 212–13, 219–21

the moral law, 213, 216–18
natural laws, 206–7
nature of good and evil, 213–15
practical reason, 205–6
practical rules and faculty of desire, 205
practical rules and maxims, 204–5
principle of morality, 220–21, 223–24
the principle of self-love, 218–19
Review of the *Critique of Practical Reason* (Pistorius)
  categorical imperative, 259, 267–68
  the concept of causality, 261
  faculty of desire, 258, 261–63
  good and evil, 261, 273
  happiness and the highest good, 258, 263–66, 273–76
  Kant's distinction between the empirical and intelligible character of human beings, 260–61, 269–70, 277–80
  Kant's inconsistency, 275–76
  overview of Kant's theory of morality, 257–66
  principle of sufficient reason, 270–73
  pure practical reason and morality, 258–61, 266–67
  Stoicism and happiness, 264–65, 273–74
  theory of freedom, 276–77
  universalization of maxims, 258–60, 267–69
Review of the *Critique of Practical Reason* (Rehberg)
  absolute freedom, 231–32
  existence of God, 239–40
  happiness and the existence of God, 233–34, 242–45
  laws of freedom, 230–32, 241–42
  objects of pure practical reason, 230
  principle of perfection, 242
  principle of pure practical reason, 229–30
  pure practical reason and morality, 234–41
  reason and the highest good, 232–33
Review of the *Groundwork* (Feder)
  categorical imperative, 210–12
  freedom of the will, 208–10, 224
  God's existence, 222–24
  on holiness, 221
  Kant's knowledge of, 8
  reason and the highest good, 207–8, 215–16, 221–22
Review of the *Groundwork* (Flatt)
  the categorial imperative, 86, 91–92
  the derivation of natural theology from moral science, 92
  dialectical illusion, 88
  the existence of non-rational beings, 89
  Flatt's authorship of, 85–86

Kant's knowledge of, 8, 86–87
  moral motivation, 86–89, 91–92
  on the principle of happiness, 89–91
  on the principle of prudence, 89–90
Review of the *Groundwork* (Pistorius)
  aims of Kant's *Groundwork*, 151–52
  definition of the concept of good, 149, 152–53
  empty formalism objection, 149
  importance of, 149
  impossibility of the categorial imperative, 150, 158–64
  instinctual happiness vs happiness from reason, 150, 153–54
  Kant's knowledge of, 149
  overview of, 149–50
  on universalization of maxims, 150, 154–58
Review of Schultz's *Elucidations* (Pistorius)
  first *Critique*'s inconsistencies with *Groundwork*, 120, 127, 142–45, 147–48
  Kant's bias towards moral ideas, 120–21, 136
  overview of, 119–23
  space and time as both subjective and objective, 120, 127–30, 134–35, 140–42, 145–47
  space and time as subjective forms of intuition, 130–34
  theory of appearance and truth, 120, 123–27, 135–36
  third antinomy, 120, 136–40

Schiller, Friedrich, 167, 247
Schultz, Johann, 2, 9
Schütz, Christian Gottfried, 5, 227–28
Smith, Adam, 200, 247
space and time
  as both objective and subjective, 120, 127–30, 134–35, 140–42, 145–47
  the neglected alternative objection, 120
  as subjective forms of intuition, 120, 130–34
Spinoza, Baruch, 225
Spinozism, 165–66, 173–74
Stoicism, 99, 104, 162, 208, 232–33, 237, 242, 264–65, 273–74

Tetens, Johann Nicolaus, 2
thelematology, 41, 44–45, 63, 66, 82, 236
theory of freedom
  Crusius' theory of freedom, 50–56
  free actions of human beings in Wolff, 18–20
  freedom and moral capacity in *Groundwork*, 6, 229
  freedom of the will, 208–10, 224
  Pistorius' criticism of, 120, 276–77

  in Rehberg's Review of the second *Critique*, 230–32, 241–42
  Wolff's universal rule for free actions, 23–25
'Theory and Practice' essay (Kant), 246–47, 249
theory of the will
  Crusius' freedom of human will, 50–56
  Crusius' theory of will and desire, 44–50, 54, 58–63
  in Rehberg's Review of the second *Critique*, 236
  in Wolff, 18, 21–22
Thomasius, Christian, 13
Tittel, Gottlob August *see also On Herr Kant's Reform of Moral Science* (Tittel)
  academic career, 93
  admiration for Feder's philosophy, 93–94
  criticism of Kant, 94

understanding
  things in themselves, 142–45, 147
  the will as distinct from understanding, 46–47
universal practical philosophy, 73–74

virtue
  Crusius' definition of, 71
  duties of virtue and prudence in Crusius, 65–66, 71–73
  in Flatt's Review of the *Groundwork*, 89
  as the main end of human life, 77–78
  practice of, 78–79
  virtue and vice in Wolff, 37–39
voluntarist theory of ethics, 63–74

Wizenmann, Thomas
  career and life, 167–68
  experience and knowledge of existence, 166
  on fanaticism and blind faith, 166, 169–70, 172–74, 189
  on God's existence, 166–67, 172–73, 180–82
  Kant's response to in the second *Critique*, 167–68
  on the nature of reason, 183–95
  open letter to Kant, 166–67
  orientation of self/subjective assent, 167, 177–83
  origin of the concept of God, 183–95
  reason and the demonstration of existence, 166, 170–77, 180–82
  reciprocal love, 167
  response to Kant's 'Orientation' essay, 9, 172–77
  the *Results* and the pantheism controversy, 165–67, 169–72
  on the Spinozistic concept of God, 173–74

Wolff, Christian *see also German Ethics* (Wolff)
   academic career, 40
   Crusius' critique of, 40
   early career, 13
   influence on Kant, 15–16
   philosophy (Wolffianism), 15
   Pietist critics of, 13–15, 41
   time at Martin Luther University Halle-Wittenberg, 13–14
   writings, 14–15, 40–41